ACCA

STUDY TEXT

PAPER F6

TAXATION (UK)

FA 2009

In this edition approved by ACCA

- We **discuss** the **best strategies** for studying for ACCA exams

- We **highlight** the **most important elements** in the syllabus and the **key skills** you will need

- We **signpost** how each chapter links to the syllabus and the study guide

- We **provide** lots of **exam focus points** demonstrating what the examiner will want you to do

- We **emphasise key points** in regular **fast forward summaries**

- We **test your knowledge** of what you've studied in **quick quizzes**

- We **examine your understanding** in our **exam question bank**

- We **reference all the important topics** in our **full index**

BPP's **i-Learn** and **i-Pass** products also support this paper.

FOR EXAMS IN JUNE AND DECEMBER 2010

LEARNING MEDIA

First edition March 2007
Fourth edition August 2009

Printed text ISBN 9780 7517 6368 3
(Previous ISBN 9780 7517 4727 0)
e text ISBN 9780 7517 7590 7

British Library Cataloguing-in-Publication Data
A catalogue record for this book
is available from the British Library

Published by

BPP Learning Media Ltd
BPP House, Aldine Place
London W12 8AA

www.bpp.com/learningmedia

Printed in the United Kingdom

We are grateful to the Association of Chartered Certified Accountants for permission to reproduce past examination questions. The suggested solutions in the exam answer bank have been prepared by BPP Learning Media Ltd, unless otherwise stated.

Your learning materials, published by BPP Learning Media Ltd, are printed on paper sourced from sustainable, managed forests.

Contents

A note about copyright

How the BPP ACCA-approved Study Text can help you pass your exams – AND help you with your Practical Experience Requirement!

Before you can qualify as an ACCA member, you do not only have to pass all your exams but also fulfil a three year **practical experience requirement** (PER). To help you to recognise areas of the syllabus that you might be able to apply in the workplace to achieve different performance objectives, we have introduced the 'PER alert' feature. You will find this feature throughout the Study Text to remind you that what you are **learning to pass** your ACCA exams is **equally useful to the fulfilment of the PER requirement**.

Tackling studying

Studying can be a daunting prospect, particularly when you have lots of other commitments. The **different features** of the text, the **purposes** of which are explained fully on the **Chapter features** page, will help you whilst studying and improve your chances of **exam success**.

Developing exam awareness

Our Texts are completely **focused** on helping you pass your exam.

Our advice on **Studying F6** outlines the **content** of the paper and the **necessary skills** the examiner expects you to demonstrate.

Exam focus points are included within the chapters to highlight when and how specific topics were examined, or how they might be examined in the future.

Using the Syllabus and Study Guide

You can find the syllabus, Study Guide and other useful resources for F6 on the ACCA web site:

www.accaglobal.com/students/acca/exams/f6/

The Study Text covers **all aspects** of the syllabus to ensure you are as fully prepared for the exam as possible.

Testing what you can do

Testing yourself helps you develop the skills you need to pass the exam and also confirms that you can recall what you have learnt.

We include **Questions** – lots of them – both within chapters and in the **Exam Question Bank**, as well as **Quick Quizzes** at the end of each chapter to test your knowledge of the chapter content.

Chapter features

Each chapter contains a number of helpful features to guide you through each topic.

Topic list

Topic list	Syllabus reference

Tells you what you will be studying in this chapter and the relevant section numbers, together the ACCA syllabus references.

Introduction

Puts the chapter content in the context of the syllabus as a whole.

Study Guide

Links the chapter content with ACCA guidance.

Exam Guide

Highlights how examinable the chapter content is likely to be and the ways in which it could be examined.

FAST FORWARD

Summarises the content of main chapter headings, allowing you to preview and review each section easily.

Examples

Demonstrate how to apply key knowledge and techniques.

Key terms

Definitions of important concepts that can often earn you easy marks in exams.

Exam focus points

Tell you when and how specific topics were examined, or how they may be examined in the future.

This is a new feature that gives you a useful indication of syllabus areas that closely relate to performance objectives in your Practical Experience Requirement (PER).

Question

Give you essential practice of techniques covered in the chapter.

Chapter Roundup

A full list of the Fast Forwards included in the chapter, providing an easy source of review.

Quick Quiz

A quick test of your knowledge of the main topics in the chapter.

Exam Question Bank

Found at the back of the Study Text with more comprehensive chapter questions. Cross referenced for easy navigation.

Studying F6

As the name suggests, this paper examines the basic principles of taxation. This is a very important area for certified accountants as many areas of practice involve a consideration of taxation issues. It also provides a foundation for P6: Advanced Taxation which will be chosen by those who work in a tax environment.

1 What F6 is about

The UK tax system

The syllabus introduces the rationale behind – and the functions of – the tax system.

The taxes

It then covers the **main UK taxes** which apply to individuals and businesses.

Income tax and corporation tax cover the widest areas of the syllabus, forming the basis for questions 1 and 2 totalling 55% of the marks. Value added tax is likely to be covered in one of these questions, in which case at least 10 of the 55 marks will be awarded for VAT, although it is possible that a separate question on VAT will be included instead. Capital gains will be covered in Question 3, for which 20 marks will be available. National insurance may be examined in any question on income tax or corporation tax.

You will be expected to have a detailed knowledge of these taxes, but **no previous knowledge is assumed**. You should study the basics carefully and **learn the proforma computations**. It then becomes straightforward to complete these by slotting in figures from your detailed workings.

As well as being able to calculate tax liabilities you will be expected to explain the basis of the calculations and how a taxpayer can minimise or defer tax liabilities

Compliance

The final part of the syllabus covers the **compliance obligations** of the taxpayer. Although not a major part of the syllabus it is likely to form an element in one or more questions in the exam. A knowledge of tax is incomplete without an understanding of how the tax is collected.

2 What skills are required?

- Be able to **integrate** knowledge and understanding from across the syllabus to enable you to complete detailed computations of tax liabilities.

- Be able to **explain** the underlying principles of taxation by providing a simple summary of the rules and how they apply to the particular situation.

- Be able to **apply** tax planning techniques by identifying available options and testing them to see which has the greater effect on tax liabilities.

3 How to improve your chances of passing

Study the **entire** syllabus – all the questions in the exam are **compulsory**. This gives the examiner the opportunity to test all major areas of the syllabus on every paper.

Practise as many questions as you can under **timed conditions** – this is the best way of developing good exam technique. Make use of the **Question Bank** at the back of this Text. **BPP's Practice and Revision Kit** contains numerous exam standard questions (many of them taken from past exam papers) as well as three mock exams for you to try.

Answer selectively – the examiner will expect you to consider carefully what is relevant and significant enough to include in your answer. Don't include unnecessary information.

Present your answers in a **professional** manner – use subheadings and leave spaces between paragraphs, make sure that your numerical workings are clearly set out. Even if you make a mistake in your calculations, you will still gain marks if you show that you understand the principles involved.

Answer all parts of the question – leaving out a five mark part may be the difference between a pass and a fail.

The exam paper

The syllabus is assessed by a three-hour paper-based examination.

The paper will be predominantly computational and will have five questions, all of which will be compulsory.

- Question one will focus on income tax and question two will focus on corporation tax. The two questions will be for a total of 55 marks, with one of the questions being for 30 marks and the other being for 25 marks.

- Question three will focus on chargeable gains (either personal or corporate) and will be for 20 marks.

- Questions four and five will be on any area of the syllabus and will respectively be for 15 marks and 10 marks.

There will always be at a minimum of 10 marks on value added tax. These marks will normally be included within question one or question two, although there might be a separate question on value added tax.

National insurance contributions will not be examined as a separate question, but may be examined in any question involving income tax or corporation tax.

Groups and overseas aspects of corporation tax will only be examined in question two, and will account for no more than one third of the marks available for that question.

Questions one or two might include a small element of chargeable gains.

Any of the five questions might include the consideration of issues relating to the minimisation or deferral of tax liabilities.

Analysis of past papers

The table below provides details of when each element of the syllabus has been examined and the question number and section in which each element appeared. Further details can be found in the Exam Focus Points in the relevant chapters.

Covered in Text chapter		Dec 2008	June 2008	Dec 2007	Pilot Paper
	UK TAX SYSTEM				
1	Introduction to the UK tax system				
	INCOME TAX AND AND NATIONAL INSURANCE CONTRIBUTIONS				
2	The computation of taxable income and the income tax liability	1a	1b, 1c	1a	1a
3	Employment income	1a	1a	1a	1a
4	Taxable and exempt benefits. The PAYE system	1a	1a	1a	1a
5	Pensions	5		1a	
6	Property income	1a		4	1a
7	Computing trading income		1a		
8	Capital allowances			1a	1a
9	Assessable trading income			1a	1a, 4
10	Trading losses			5	
11	Partnerships and limited liability partnerships	4			
12	National insurance contributions	1b		1a	
	CHARGEABLE GAINS FOR INDIVIDUALS				
13	Computing chargeable gains		3	3	3
14	Chattels and the principal private residence exemption			3	3
15	Business reliefs		3		
16	Shares and securities			3	3
	TAX ADMINISTRATION FOR INDIVIDUALS				
17	Self assessment and payment of tax for individuals		4	1a	1b
	CORPORATION TAX				
18	Computing profits chargeable to corporation tax	2a	2a, 5	2a	2a
19	Computing the corporation tax liability	3a	5		2a
20	Chargeable gains for companies	3a, 3b			
21	Losses	2a			5
22	Groups			2b	
23	Overseas matters for companies		2a		
24	Self assessment and payment of tax by companies	2a			
	VALUE ADDED TAX				
25	An introduction to VAT	2b	2b	1b	
26	Further aspects of VAT	2b		1b	2b

UK tax system

Introduction to the UK tax system

Topic list	Syllabus reference
1 The overall function and purpose of taxation in a modern economy	A1(a)
2 Different types of taxes	A2(a), (b)
3 Principal sources of revenue law and practice	A3(a)-(c)
4 Tax avoidance and tax evasion	A4(a), (b)

Introduction

We start our study of tax with an introduction to the UK tax system.

First we consider briefly the purpose of raising taxes, both economic and social. We next consider the specific UK taxes, both revenue and capital, and also direct and indirect.

We see how the collection of tax is administered in the UK, and where the UK tax system interacts with overseas tax jurisdictions.

Finally we highlight the difference between tax avoidance and tax evasion.

When you have finished this chapter you should be able to discuss the broad features of the tax system. In the following chapters we will consider specific UK taxes, starting with income tax.

Study guide

		Intellectual level
A1	**The overall function and purpose of taxation in a modern economy**	
(a)	Describe the purpose (economic, social etc) of taxation in a modern economy.	2
A2	**Different types of taxes**	
(a)	Identify the different types of capital and revenue tax.	1
(b)	Explain the difference between direct and indirect taxation.	2
A3	**Principal sources of revenue law and practice**	
(a)	Describe the overall structure of the UK tax system.	1
(b)	State the different sources of revenue law.	1
(c)	Appreciate the interaction of the UK tax system with that of other tax jurisdictions.	2
A4	**Tax avoidance and tax evasion**	
(a)	Explain the difference between tax avoidance and tax evasion.	1
(b)	Explain the need for an ethical and professional approach.	2

Exam guide

You are unlikely to be asked a whole question on this part of the syllabus. You may, however, be asked to comment on one aspect, such as the difference between tax avoidance and tax evasion, as part of a question.

1 The overall function and purpose of taxation in a modern economy

FAST FORWARD

Economic, social and environmental factors may affect the government's tax policies.

1.1 Economic factors

In terms of economic analysis, government **taxation represents a withdrawal from the UK economy** while its expenditure acts as an injection into it. So the government's net position in terms of taxation and expenditure, together with its public sector borrowing policies, has an effect on the level of economic activity within the UK.

The government favours longer-term planning, currently publishing and then sticking to three year plans for expenditure. These show the proportion of the economy's overall resources which will be allocated by the government and how much will be left for the private sector.

This can have an effect on demand for particular types of goods, eg health and education on the one hand, which are predominately the result of public spending, and consumer goods on the other, which results from private spending. Changing demand levels will have an impact on employment levels within the different sectors, as well as on the profitability of different private sector suppliers.

Within that overall proportion left in the private sector, **the government uses tax policies to encourage and discourage certain types of activity**.

It **encourages**:

(a) **saving** on the part of the individual, by offering tax incentives such as tax-free Individual Savings Accounts and tax relief on pension contributions

(b) **donations to charities**, through the Gift Aid scheme

(c) **entrepreneurs** who build their own business, through reliefs from capital gains tax

(d) **investment in industrial buildings and plant and machinery** through capital allowances;

while it **discourages**:

(a) **smoking** and **alcoholic drinks**, through the duties placed on each type of product;

(b) **motoring**, through fuel duties.

Governments can and do argue that these latter taxes and duties to some extent mirror the extra costs to the country as a whole of such behaviours, such as the cost of coping with smoking related illnesses. However, the Government needs to raise money for spending in areas where there are no consumers on whom the necessary taxes can be levied, such as defence, law and order, overseas aid and the cost of running the government and Parliament.

1.2 Social factors

Social justice lies at the heart of politics, since what some think of as just is regarded by others as completely unjust. Attitudes to the redistribution of wealth are a clear example.

In a free market some individuals generate greater amounts of income and capital than others and once wealth has been acquired, it tends to grow through the reinvestment of investment income received. This can lead to the rich getting richer and the poor poorer, with economic power becoming concentrated in relatively few hands.

Some electors make the value judgement that these trends should be countered by **taxation policies which redistribute income and wealth** away from the rich towards the poor. This is one of the key arguments in favour of some sort of capital gains tax and inheritance tax, taxes which, relative to the revenue raised, cost a very great deal to collect.

Different taxes have different social effects:

(a) **Direct taxes** based on income and profits (income tax), gains (capital gains tax) or wealth (inheritance tax) **tax only those who have these resources**.

(b) **Indirect taxes** paid by the consumer (VAT) **discourage spending** and encourage saving. Lower or nil rates of tax can be levied on essentials, such as food.

(c) **Progressive taxes** such as income tax, where the proportion of the income or gains paid over in tax increases as income/gains rise, **target those who can afford to pay**. Personal allowances and the rates of taxation can be adjusted so as to ensure that those on very low incomes pay little or no tax.

(d) Taxes on capital or wealth ensure that that people cannot avoid taxation by having an income of zero and just living off the sale of capital assets.

Almost everyone would argue that taxation should be **equitable** or 'fair', but there are many different views as to what is equitable.

An **efficient tax** is one where the costs of collection are low relative to the tax paid over to the government. The government publishes figures for the administrative costs incurred by government departments in operating the taxation systems, but there are also compliance costs to be taken into account. Compliance costs are those incurred by the taxpayer, whether they be the individual preparing tax returns under the self assessment system or the employer operating the PAYE system to collect income tax or the business collecting value added tax. Some of the more equitable taxes may be less efficient to collect.

1.3 Environmental factors

The taxation system is moving slowly to accommodate the environmental concerns which have come to the fore over the last twenty years or so, especially the concerns about renewable and non-renewable sources of energy and global warming.

Examples of tax changes which have been introduced for environmental reasons are:

(a)   the **climate change levy**, raised on businesses in proportion to their consumption of energy. Its claimed purpose is to encourage reduced consumption;

(b)   the **landfill tax** levied on the operators of landfill sites on each tonne of rubbish/waste processed at the site. Its claimed purpose is to encourage recycling by taxing waste which has to be stored;

(c)   the changes to rules on the lease or purchase of cars, and taxation of **cars and private fuel provided for employees** to be dependent on CO_2 emissions. Its claimed purpose is to encourage the manufacture and purchase of low CO_2 emission cars to reduce emissions into the atmosphere caused by driving.

Only the last of these will be directly felt by individuals, even if the other taxes are passed on by being factored into a business's overheads.

2 Different types of taxes

 Central government raises revenue through a wide range of taxes. Tax law is made by statute.

2.1 Taxes in the UK

Central government raises revenue through a wide range of taxes. Tax law is made by **statute.**

The main taxes, their incidence and their sources, are set out in the table below.

Tax	Suffered by	Source
Income tax	**Individuals** **Partnerships**	Capital Allowances Act 2001 (CAA 2001); Income Tax (Earnings and Pensions) Act 2003 (ITEPA 2003); Income Tax (Trading and Other Income) Act 2005 (ITTOIA 2005); Income Tax Act 2007 (ITA 2007)
Corporation tax	**Companies**	Income and Corporation Taxes Act 1988 (ICTA 1988), CAA 2001 as above, Corporation Tax Act 2009 (CTA 2009)
Capital gains tax	**Individuals** **Partnerships** **Companies** (which pay tax on capital gains in the form of corporation tax)	Taxation of Chargeable Gains Act 1992 (TCGA 1992)
Value added tax	**Businesses**, both incorporated and unincorporated	Value Added Tax Act 1994 (VATA 1994)

You will also meet National Insurance. **National insurance is payable by employers, employees and the self employed.** Further details of all these taxes are found later in this Text.

The other taxes referred to in the previous section, such as inheritance tax and landfill tax, are not examinable at F6.

Finance Acts are passed each year, incorporating proposals set out in the **Budget**. They make changes which apply mainly to the tax year ahead. **This Study Text includes the provisions of the Finance Act 2009**. This is examinable in June and December 2010.

2.2 Revenue and capital taxes

Revenue taxes are those charged on income. In this Text this covers:

(a)   **income tax**,
(b)   **corporation tax**, and
(c)   **national insurance**.

Capital taxes are those charged on capital gains or on wealth. In this Text this covers **capital gains tax (CGT)**.

2.3 Direct and indirect taxes

Direct taxes are those charged on **income, gains and wealth**, whilst **indirect taxes** are those **paid by the consumer to the supplier**, and thence to the Government. **VAT** is an indirect tax, whilst income tax, national insurance, corporation tax and CGT are direct taxes.

3 Principal sources of revenue law and practice

FAST FORWARD   Tax is administered by HM Revenue and Customs (HMRC).

3.1 The overall structure of the UK tax system

The **Treasury** formally imposes and collects taxation. The management of the Treasury is the responsibility of the Chancellor of the Exchequer. **The administrative function for the collection of tax is undertaken by Her Majesty's Revenue and Customs (HMRC).**

The HMRC staff are referred to in the tax legislation as **'Officers of the Revenue and Customs'**. They are responsible for supervising the self-assessment system and agreeing tax liabilities. Officers who collect tax may be referred to as **receivable management officers**. These officers are local officers who are responsible for following up amounts of unpaid tax referred to them by the **HMRC Accounts Office.**

The **Revenue and Customs Prosecutions Office (R&CPO)** has been established to provide legal advice and institute and conduct criminal prosecutions in England and Wales where there has been an investigation by HMRC.

Tax appeals are heard by the **Tax Tribunal** which is made up of **two tiers:**

(a)   **First-tier Tribunal**, and
(b)   **Upper Tribunal**

The **First Tier Tribunal deals with most cases** other than complex cases. The **Upper Tribunal deals with complex cases** which either involve an important issue of tax law or a large financial sum. The Upper Tribunal **also hears appeals** against decisions of the First Tier Tribunal. We look at the appeals system in more detail later in this Study Text.

Many taxpayers arrange for their accountants to prepare and submit their tax returns. **The taxpayer is still the person responsible for submitting the return and for paying whatever tax becomes due**: the accountant is only acting as the taxpayer's agent.

3.2 Different sources of revenue law

As stated above, taxes are imposed by statute. This comprises not only **Acts of Parliament** but also regulations laid down by **Statutory Instruments**. Statute is interpreted and amplified by **case law**.

HM Revenue and Customs also issue:

(a)   **Statements of practice**, setting out how they intend to apply the law

(b)   **Extra-statutory concessions**, setting out circumstances in which they will not apply the strict letter of the law where it would be unfair

(c) A wide range of **explanatory leaflets**

(d) **Business economic notes**. These are notes on particular types of business, which are used as background information by HMRC and are also published

(e) The **Tax Bulletin**. This is a newsletter giving HMRC's view on specific points

(f) The **Internal Guidance**, a series of manuals used by HMRC staff

(g) **Working Together**, for tax practitioners

A great deal of information and HMRC publications can be found on the HM Revenue and Customs Internet site (www.hmrc.gov.uk).

Although the HMRC publications do not generally have the force of law, some of the VAT notices do where power has been delegated under regulations. This applies, for example, to certain administrative aspects of the cash accounting scheme.

3.3 The interaction of the UK tax system with that of other tax jurisdictions

3.3.1 The European Union

Membership of the European Union has a significant effect on UK taxes although there is not yet a general requirement imposed on the EU member states to move to a common system of taxation or to harmonise their individual tax systems. The states may, however, agree jointly to enact specific laws, known as '**Directives**', which provide for a common code of taxation within particular areas of their taxation systems.

The most important example to date is **VAT**, where the UK is obliged to pass its laws in conformity with the rules laid down in the European legislation. The VAT Directives still allow for a certain amount of flexibility between member states, eg in setting rates of taxation. There are only limited examples of Directives in the area of Direct Taxes, generally concerned with cross-border dividend and interest payments and corporate reorganisations.

However, under the EU treaties, member states are also obliged to permit freedom of movement of workers, freedom of movement of capital and freedom to establish business operations within the EU. These treaty provisions have '**direct effect**', ie a taxpayer is entitled to claim that a UK tax provision is ineffective because it **breaches one or more of the freedoms** guaranteed under European Law.

The European Court of Justice has repeatedly held that taxation provisions which discriminate against non-residents (ie treat a non-resident less favourably than a resident in a similar situation) are contrary to European Law, unless there is a very strong public interest justification.

There are provisions regarding the **exchange of information** between European Union Revenue authorities.

3.3.2 Other countries

The UK has entered into **double tax treaties** with various countries, such as the USA. These contain rules which prevent income and gains being taxed twice, but often include non-discrimination provisions, preventing a foreign national from being treated more harshly than a national. There are also usually rules for the **exchange of information** between the different Revenue authorities.

Even where there is no double tax relief, the UK tax system gives some relief for foreign taxes paid.

4 Tax avoidance and tax evasion

Tax avoidance is the legal minimisation of tax liabilities, tax evasion is illegal.

4.1 Tax evasion

Tax evasion consists of seeking to pay too little tax by deliberately misleading HMRC by either:

(a) **suppressing information to which they are entitled** (eg failing to notify HMRC that you are liable to tax, understating income or gains or omitting to disclose a relevant fact, eg that business expenditure had a dual motive), or

(b) **providing them with deliberately false information** (eg deducting expenses which have not been incurred or claiming capital allowances on plant that has not been purchased).

Tax evasion is illegal. Minor cases of tax evasion have generally been settled out of court on the payment of penalties. However, there is now a **statutory offence of evading income tax,** which enables such matters as deliberate failure to operate PAYE to be dealt with in magistrates' courts.

Serious cases of tax evasion, particularly those involving fraud, will continue to be the subject of **criminal prosecutions** which may lead to **fines and/or imprisonment on conviction.**

4.2 Tax avoidance

Tax avoidance is more difficult to define.

In a very broad sense, it could include **any legal method of reducing your tax burden,** eg taking advantage of tax shelter opportunities explicitly offered by tax legislation such as ISAs. However, the term is more commonly used in a more narrow sense, to denote ingenious arrangements designed to produce unintended tax advantages for the taxpayer.

The effectiveness of tax avoidance schemes has often been examined in the courts. Traditionally the tax rules were applied to the legal form of transactions, although this principle was qualified in later cases. It was held that the Courts could disregard transactions which were preordained and solely designed to avoid tax.

Traditionally, the response of HMRC has been to seek to mend the **loopholes** in the law as they come to their attention. In general, there is a presumption that the effect of such changes should not be backdated.

The Finance Act 2004 introduced new **disclosure obligations** on promoters of certain tax **avoidance schemes**, and on taxpayers, to provide details to HMRC of any such schemes used by the taxpayer. This enables HMRC to introduce anti avoidance measures at the earliest opportunity.

4.3 The distinction between avoidance and evasion

The distinction between tax evasion and tax avoidance is generally clear cut, since tax avoidance is an entirely legal activity and does not entail misleading HMRC.

However, care should be taken in giving advice in some circumstances. For example, a taxpayer who does not return income or gains because he wrongly believes that he has successfully avoided having to pay tax on them may, as a result, be guilty of tax evasion.

4.4 The need for an ethical and professional approach

Under self assessment, all taxpayers (whether individuals or companies) are responsible for disclosing their taxable income and gains and the deductions and reliefs they are claiming against them.

The practising accountant often acts for taxpayers in their dealings with HMRC and situations can arise where the accountant has concerns as to whether the taxpayer is being honest in providing information to the accountant for onward transmission.

How the accountant deals with such situations is a matter of **professional judgement**, but in deciding what to do, the accountant will be expected to uphold the standards of the Association of Chartered Certified Accountants. He must act **honestly** and **objectively**, with **due care and diligence**, and showing the highest standards of **integrity**.

Chapter Roundup

- Economic, social and environmental factors may affect the government's tax policies.
- Central government raises revenue through a wide range of taxes. Tax law is made by statute.
- Tax is administered by HM Revenue and Customs (HMRC).
- Tax avoidance is the legal minimisation of tax liabilities, tax evasion is illegal.

Quick Quiz

1   What is the difference between a direct and an indirect tax?

2   What is an Extra Statutory Concession?

3   Tax avoidance is legal. TRUE /FALSE?

Answers to Quick Quiz

1   A direct tax is one charged on income or gains; an indirect tax is paid by a consumer to the supplier, who then passes it to HMRC.

2   In Extra Statutory Concession is a relaxation by HMRC of the strict rules where their imposition would be unfair.

3   True. Tax avoidance is legal; tax evasion is illegal.

Income tax and national insurance contributions

The computation of taxable income and the income tax liability

Topic list	Syllabus reference
1 The scope of income tax	B1(a)
2 Computing taxable income	B5(a)
3 Various types of income	B4(f), (g), B5(a)
4 Tax exempt income	B4(h)
5 Deductible interest	B5(d)
6 Personal allowance	B5(b)
7 Computing tax payable	B5(c)
8 Gift Aid	B5(e)
9 Jointly held property	B5(f) B6(c)

Introduction

In the previous chapter we considered the UK tax system generally. Now we look at income tax, which is a tax on what individuals make from their jobs, their businesses and their savings and investments. We consider the scope of income tax and see how to collect together all of an individual's income in a personal tax computation, and we also see which income can be excluded as being exempt from tax.

Next we look at the circumstances in which interest paid can be deducted in the income tax computation.

Each individual is entitled to a personal allowance, and only if that is exceeded will any tax be due. Older taxpayers are entitled to a higher allowance, the age allowance, although this is restricted if the taxpayer's income is too high.

We then learn how to work out the tax on the individual's taxable income, and we see how donations to charity under the gift aid scheme can save tax.

Finally we consider how income from property held jointly by married couples or civil partners is allocated for tax purposes.

In later chapters, we look at particular types of income in more detail.

Study guide

		Intellectual level
B1	**The scope of income tax**	
(a)	Explain how the residence of an individual is determined.	1
B4	**Property and investment income**	
(f)	Compute the tax payable on savings income.	2
(g)	Compute the tax payable on dividend income.	2
(h)	Explain the treatment of individual savings accounts (ISAs) and other tax exempt investments.	1
B5	**The comprehensive computation of taxable income and income tax liability**	
(a)	Prepare a basic income tax computation involving different types of income.	2
(b)	Calculate the amount of personal allowance available to people aged 65 and above.	2
(c)	Compute the amount of income tax payable.	2
(d)	Explain the treatment of interest paid.	2
(e)	Explain the treatment of gift aid donations.	1
(f)	Explain the treatment of property owned jointly by a married couple, or by a couple in a civil partnership.	1
B6	**The use of exemptions and reliefs in deferring and minimising income tax liabilities**	
(c)	Explain how a married couple or couple in a civil partnership can minimise their tax liabilities.	2

Exam guide

It is very likely that you will have to prepare an income tax computation in your exam. You should familiarise yourself with the layout of the computation, and the three types of income: non-savings, savings and dividends. It is then a simple matter of slotting the final figures into the computation from supporting workings for the different types of income.

Gift aid donations are likely to feature regularly, and you will come across the technique of extending the basic rate band again when you deal with pensions later in this Text.

1 The scope of income tax

FAST FORWARD An individual may be resident and/or ordinarily in the UK, and his liability to UK income tax will be determined accordingly.

1.1 Introduction

A taxpayer's **residence and ordinary residence** have important consequences in establishing the tax treatment of his UK and overseas income and capital gains.

1.2 Residence

An individual is resident in the UK for a given tax year if, in that tax year, he satisfies either of the following criteria.

(a) **He is present in the UK for 183 days or more**.

(b) He makes substantial annual visits to the UK. **Visits averaging 91 days or more a year for each of four or more consecutive years** will make the person resident for each of these tax years (for someone emigrating from the UK, the four years are reduced to three).

If days are spent in the UK because of exceptional circumstances beyond the individual's control (such as illness), those days are ignored for the purposes of the 91 day rule (but not for the 183 day rule above).

Generally, an individual is present in the UK on a particular day if he is in the UK at midnight.

1.3 Ordinary residence

A person who is resident in the UK will be ordinarily resident in the UK where his residence in the UK is of a habitual nature. Ordinary residence implies a greater degree of permanence than residence.

A person who is resident in the UK and who goes abroad for a period which does not include a complete tax year is regarded as remaining resident and ordinarily resident in the UK throughout the period of absence.

1.4 Tax consequences

Generally, a UK resident is liable to UK income tax on his UK and overseas income whereas a non-resident is liable to UK income tax only on income arising in the UK.

Exam focus point

> The taxation of the overseas income of a UK resident and the taxation of non-residents is outside the scope of your syllabus.

2 Computing taxable income

FAST FORWARD In a personal income tax computation, we bring together income from all sources, splitting the sources into non-savings, savings and dividend income.

PER alert

> This section relates to your PER requirement:
> 19 Evaluate and compute taxes payable

An individual's income from all sources is brought together (aggregated) in a personal tax computation. Three columns are needed to distinguish between non-savings income, savings income and dividend income. Here is an example. All items are explained later in this Text.

RICHARD: INCOME TAX COMPUTATION 2009/10

	Non-savings income £	Savings income £	Dividend income £	Total £
Income from employment	48,000			
Building society interest		1,000		
National Savings & Investments interest		400		
UK dividends			1,000	
Total income	48,000	1,400	1,000	
Less interest paid	(2,000)			
Net income	46,000	1,400	1,000	48,400
Less personal allowance	(6,475)			
Taxable income	39,525	1,400	1,000	41,925

	£	£
Income tax		
Non savings income		
£37,400 × 20%		7,480
£2,125 × 40%		850
		8,330
Savings income		
£1,400 × 40% ?		560
Dividend income		
£1,000 × 32.5%		325
Tax liability		9,215
Less tax suffered		
Tax credit on dividend income	100	
PAYE tax on salary (say)	8,000	
Tax on building society interest	200	
		(8,300)
Tax payable		915

Income tax is charged on **'taxable income'**. Non-savings income is dealt with first, then savings income and then dividend income.

For non-savings income, the first £37,400 (the basic rate band) is taxed at the basic rate (20%) and the rest at the higher rate (40%). We will look at the taxation of the other types of income later in this chapter.

The remainder of this chapter gives more details of the income tax computation.

3 Various types of income

3.1 Classification of income

All income received must be **classified** according to the nature of the income. This is because different computational rules apply to different types of income. The main types of income are:

(a)   **Income from employment and pensions**
(b)   **Profits of trades, professions and vocations**
(c)   **Income from property letting**
(d)   **Savings and investment income, including interest and dividends**.

The rules for computing employment income, profits from trades, professions and vocations and property letting income will be covered in later chapters. These types of income are **non-savings income**. Pension income is also non-savings income.

An individual may receive interest net of 20% tax suffered at source. The amount received must be grossed up by multiplying by 100/80 and must be included gross in the income tax computation. Dividends are received net of a 10% tax credit and must be grossed up for inclusion in the tax computation.

3.2 Savings income

3.2.1 What is savings income?

Savings income is interest. Interest is paid on bank and building society accounts, on Government securities, such as Treasury Stock, and on company debentures and loan stock.

Interest may be paid net of 20% tax or it may be paid gross.

3.2.2 Savings income received net of 20% tax

The following savings income is received net of 20% tax. **This is called income taxed at source.**

(a) Bank and building society interest paid to individuals
(b) Interest paid to individuals by unlisted UK companies on debentures and loan stocks

The amount received is grossed up by multiplying by 100/80 and is included gross in the income tax computation. The tax deducted at source is deducted in computing tax payable and may be repaid.

Exam focus point

In examinations you may be given either the net or the gross amount of such income: read the question carefully. If you are given the net amount (the amount received or credited), you should gross up the figure at the rate of 20%. For example, net building society interest of £160 is equivalent to gross income of £160 × 100/80 = £200 on which tax of £40 (20% of £200) has been suffered.

3.2.3 Savings income received gross

Some savings income is received gross, ie without tax having been deducted. Examples are:

(a) National Savings & Investments interest including interest from Easy Access Savings Accounts (EASAs), Investment Accounts, Income Bonds
(b) Interest on government securities (these are also called 'gilts')
(c) Interest from quoted company debentures and loan stock.

3.3 Dividend income

Dividends on UK shares are received net of a 10% tax credit. This means a dividend of £90 has a £10 tax credit, giving gross income of £100 to include in the income tax computation. The tax credit can be deducted in computing tax payable **but it cannot be repaid**.

4 Tax exempt income

4.1 Types of tax exempt investments

This section relates to your PER requirement:
20   Assist with tax planning

Income from certain investments is exempt from income tax. They are therefore useful for tax planning to minimise tax from investments.

In the examination you may be given details of exempt income. You should state in your answer that the income is exempt to show that you have considered it and have not just overlooked it.

4.2 Individual savings accounts

An individual savings account (ISA) is a special tax exempt way of saving. In 2009/10 an individual aged 50 or under can invest £7,200 in ISAs, of which up to £3,600 can be held as cash. Individuals who are aged 50 or over in 2009/10 can invest £10,200 in ISAs, of which up to £5,100 can be held as cash.

Funds invested in ISAs can be used to buy stock market investments, such as shares in quoted companies or OEICs, units in unit trusts, fixed interest investments, or insurance policies.

Dividend income and interest received from ISAs is exempt from income tax, whether it is paid out to the investor or retained and reinvested within the ISA.

4.3 Savings certificates

Savings certificates are issued by National Savings and Investments (NS&I). They may be fixed rate certificates or index linked, and are for fixed terms of between two and five years. On maturity the profit is tax exempt. This profit is often called interest.

4.4 Premium bonds

Prizes received from premium bonds are exempt from tax.

5 Deductible interest

FAST FORWARD

Deductible interest is deducted from total income to compute net income.

5.1 Interest payments

An individual who pays interest on a loan in a tax year is entitled to relief in that tax year if the loan is for one of the following purposes:

(a) **Loan to buy plant or machinery for partnership use**. Interest is allowed for three years from the end of the tax year in which the loan was taken out. If the plant is used partly for private use, the allowable interest is apportioned.

(b) **Loan to buy plant or machinery for employment use.** Interest is allowed for three years from the end of the tax year in which the loan was taken out. If the plant is used partly for private use, the allowable interest is apportioned.

(c) **Loan to buy interest in employee-controlled company.** The company must be an unquoted trading company resident in the UK with at least 50% of the voting shares held by employees.

(d) **Loan to invest in a partnership.** The investment may be a share in the partnership or a contribution to the partnership of capital or a loan to the partnership. The individual must be a partner (other than a limited partner) and relief ceases when he ceases to be a partner.

(e) **Loan to invest in a co-operative.** The investment may be shares or a loan. The individual must spend the greater part of his time working for the co-operative.

Tax relief is given by deducting the interest from total income to calculate net income for the tax year in which the interest is paid. It is deducted from **non-savings income first, then from savings income and lastly from dividend income.**

5.2 Example

Frederick has taxable trading income for 2009/10 of £45,000, savings income of £1,320 (gross) and dividend income of £1,000 (gross).

Frederick pays interest of £1,370 in 2009/10 on a loan to invest in a partnership.

Frederick's taxable income is:

	Non-savings income £	Savings income £	Dividend income £	Total £
Total income	45,000	1,320	1,000	
Less: interest paid	(1,370)			
Net income	43,630	1,320	1,000	45,950
Less: personal allowance	(6,475)			
Taxable income	37,155	1,320	1,000	39,475

6 Personal allowance

FAST FORWARD

All persons are entitled to a personal allowance. It is deducted from net income, first against non savings income, then against savings income and lastly against dividend income. Taxpayers aged 65-74 are entitled to an age allowance, and taxpayers aged 75 and over to a higher age allowance.

6.1 Basic personal allowance

Once taxable income from all sources has been aggregated and any deductible interest deducted, the remainder is the taxpayer's net income. An allowance, the **personal allowance, is deducted from net income**. Like deductible interest, it reduces non **savings income first, then savings income and lastly dividend income**.

All persons **under the age of 65** (including children) are entitled to the personal allowance of **£6,475**.

6.2 Age allowance

An individual **aged 65-74 receives an age allowance of £9,490** instead of the personal allowance of £6,475.

An individual **aged 75** or over receives a higher age allowance of **£9,640** instead of the personal allowance of £6,475.

If the individual's net income exceeds £22,900 the age allowance is reduced by £1 for each £2 by which net income exceeds £22,900. The age allowance **cannot be reduced below £6,475**.

An individual is entitled to the age allowance, or higher age allowance, provided he attains the age of 65 or 75 respectively **before the end of the tax year**, or would have had he not died before his birthday.

Question   Age allowance

Three taxpayers have the following net income for 2009/10.   *Age Allowance*

A   £23,800 *(23800 − 22900) = (900 ÷ 2) = (9490 − 450) = 9040*
B   £32,350 *cannot be less than 6475, so answer is 6475*
C   £27,700 *(27,700 − 22900) = (4800 ÷ 2) = (9640 − 2400) = 7240*

Calculate their taxable income assuming taxpayers A and B are aged 68 and taxpayer C is aged 78.

	A	B	C
Taxable income is:			
	£	£	£
Net income	23,800	32,350	27,700
Less age allowance (Working)	(9,040)	(6,475)	(7,240)
Taxable income	14,760	25,875	20,460

Working

	A	B	C
Net income	23,800	32,350	27,700
Less income limit	(22,900)	(22,900)	(22,900)
Excess	900	9,450	4,800
Age allowance	9,490	9,490	9,640
Less half the excess £900/9,450/4,800 × 1/2	(450)	(4,725)	(2,400)
	9,040	4,765	7,240
Minimum		6,475	

7 Computing tax payable

FAST FORWARD

Work out income tax on the taxable income. Deduct the tax credit on dividend income and any income tax suffered at source to arrive at tax payable. The tax credit on dividend income cannot be repaid if it exceeds the tax liability calculated so far. Other tax suffered at source can be repaid.

This section relates to your PER requirement:
19   Evaluate and compute taxes payable

7.1 Taxable income

Income tax payable is computed on an individual's taxable income, which comprises the net income less the personal or age allowance. The **rate of income tax payable depends on the nature of the income**: non-savings, savings income, or dividend income.

7.2 Savings income starting rate

There is a **tax rate of 10% for savings income between £0 and £2,440 (the starting rate band)**. This rate is called the **savings income starting rate**.

The savings income starting rate only applies where the savings income falls wholly or partly in the starting rate band. Remember that income tax is charged first on non-savings income. So, in most cases, an individual's non-savings income will exceed the starting rate limit and the savings income starting rate will not be available on savings income. In this case, the individual's savings income will be charged to tax at the 20% basic rate up to the basic rate limit of £37,400 and 40% thereafter.

However, **if an individual's non-savings income is less than the starting rate limit**, then **savings income will be taxable at the 10% savings income starting rate up to the starting rate limit, at 20% up to the basic rate limit of £37,400 and 40% thereafter**.

Question   Savings income starting rate

Joe is aged 55. In 2009/10, he earns a salary of £7,500 from a part-time job and receives bank interest of £4,000.
Calculate Joe's tax liability for 2009/10.

	Non-savings income £	Savings income £	Total £
Employment income	7,500		
Bank interest £4,000 × 100/80		5,000	
Net income	7,500	5,000	12,500
Less: personal allowance	(6,475)		
Taxable income	1,025	5,000	6,025
Income tax			
Non-savings income			
£1,025 × 20 %			205
Savings income			
£1,415 × 10%			141
£3,585 × 20%			717
Tax liability			1,063

Handwritten annotation: $(6025 - 2440) = 3585 = (5000 - 3585) = 1415$

7.3 Steps in the income tax computation

Step 1   **The first step in preparing a personal tax computation is to set up three columns**
One column for non-savings income, one for savings income and one for dividend income. Add up income from different sources. The sum of these is known as 'total income'.

Step 2   **Deal with non-savings income first**
Any income in the basic rate band is taxed at 20% and income above the basic rate threshold is taxed at 40%.

Step 3   **Now deal with savings income**
If non-savings income is below the starting rate limit, savings income can be taxed at the savings income starting rate of 10% up to starting rate limit. If savings income falls within the basic rate band it is taxed at 20%. Once income is above the higher rate threshold, it is taxed at 40%. In most cases, non-savings income and savings income can be added together and tax calculated on the total, provided that the savings income starting rate does not apply.

Step 4   **Lastly, tax dividend income**
If dividend income falls within the starting or basic rate bands, it is taxed at 10% (never 20%). If, however, the dividend income exceeds the basic rate threshold, it is taxable at 32.5%.

Step 5   Add the amounts of tax together. The resulting figure is the income tax liability.

Step 6   Next, deduct the tax credit on dividends. Although deductible this tax credit cannot be repaid if it exceeds the tax liability calculated so far.

Step 7   Finally deduct the tax deducted at source from savings income and any PAYE. These amounts can be repaid to the extent that they exceed the income tax liability.

7.4 Examples: personal tax computations

(a) Kathe has a salary of £15,000 and receives dividends of £4,500.

	Non-savings income £	Dividend income £	Total £
Earnings	15,000		
Dividends £4,500 × 100/90		5,000	
Net income	15,000	5,000	20,000
Less personal allowance	(6,475)		
Taxable income	8,525	5,000	13,525

	£
Income tax	
Non savings income	
£8,525 × 20%	1,705
Dividend income	
£5,000 × 10%	500
Tax liability	2,205
Less tax credit on dividend	(500)
Tax payable	1,705

The dividend income falls within the basic rate band so it is taxed at 10% (*not* 20%).

Some of the tax payable has probably already been paid on the salary under PAYE.

(b) Jules has a salary of £20,000, business profits of £33,000, net dividends of £6,750 and building society interest of £3,000 net. He is entitled to relief on interest paid of £2,000.

	Non-savings income £	Savings income £	Dividend income £	Total £
Business profits	33,000			
Employment income	20,000			
Dividends £6,750 × 100/90			7,500	
Building society interest £3,000 × 100/80	–	3,750	-	
Total income	53,000	3,750	7,500	
Less interest paid	(2,000)			
Net income	51,000	3,750	7,500	62,250
Less personal allowance	(6,475)			
Taxable income	44,525	3,750	7,500	55,775

	£
Income tax	
Non savings income	
£37,400 × 20%	7,480
£7,125 × 40%	2,850
Savings income	
£3,750 × 40%	1,500
Dividend income	
£7,500 × 32.5%	2,438
Tax liability	14,268
Less tax credit on dividend income	(750)
Less tax suffered on building society interest	(750)
Tax payable	12,768

Savings income and dividend income fall above the basic rate threshold so they are taxed at 40% and 32.5% respectively.

(c) Jim does not work. He receives net bank interest of £40,000. He is entitled to relief on interest paid of £2,000.

	Savings income £	Total £
Bank interest £40,000 × 100/80/Total income	50,000	
Less interest paid	(2,000)	
Net income	48,000	48,000
Less personal allowance	(6,475)	
Taxable income	41,525	41,525

	£
Savings income	
£2,440 × 10%	244
£34,960 × 20%	6,992
£4,125 × 40%	1,650
Tax liability	8,886
Less tax suffered	(10,000)
Tax repayable	(1,114)

The savings income starting rate applies to the first £2,440 of savings income. The balance of the basic rate band £(37,400 − 2,440) = £34,960 then applies.

7.5 The complete proforma

Here is a complete proforma computation of taxable income. It is probably too much for you to absorb at this stage, but refer back to it as you come to the chapters dealing with the types of income shown. You will also see how trading losses fit into the proforma later in this study text.

	Non-savings income £	Savings income £	Dividend income £	Total £
Trading income	X			
Employment income	X			
Property business income	X			
Bank/building society interest (gross)		X		
Other interest (gross)		X		
(as many lines as necessary)				
Dividends (gross)			X	
Total income	X	X	X	
Less interest paid	(X)	(X)	(X)	
Net income	X	X	X	X
Less personal allowance	(X)	(X)	(X)	
Taxable income	X	X	X	X

8 Gift Aid

FAST FORWARD

Extend the basic rate band by the gross amount of any gift aid payment.

8.1 Gift aid donations

Key term

One-off and regular charitable gifts of money qualify for tax relief under the **gift aid scheme** provided the donor gives the charity a gift aid declaration.

Gift aid declarations can be made in writing, electronically through the internet or orally over the phone. A declaration can cover a one-off gift or any number of gifts made after a specified date (which may be in the past).

The gift must not be repayable, and must not confer any more than a minimal benefit on the donor. Gift aid may be used for entrance fees (for example to National Trust properties or historic houses) provided the right of admission applies for at least one year or the visitor pays at least 10% more than the normal admission charge.

8.2 Tax relief for gift aid donations

A gift aid donation is treated as though it is paid net of basic rate tax (20%). Additional tax relief for higher rate taxpayers is given in the personal tax computation by increasing the donor's basic rate band by the gross amount of the gift. To arrive at the gross amount of the gift you must multiply the amount paid by 100/80.

No additional relief is due for basic rate taxpayers. Extending the basic rate band is irrelevant as taxable income is below the basic rate threshold.

Question	Gift Aid

James earns a salary of £65,180 but has no other income. In 2009/10 he paid £8,000 (net) under the gift aid scheme.

Compute James' income tax liability for 2009/10.

Answer	

		Non-savings income
		£
Salary/Net income		65,180
Less: personal allowance		(6,475)
Taxable income		58,705
Income tax	£	£
Basic rate band	37,400 × 20%	7,480
Basic rate band (extended)	10,000 × 20%	2,000
Higher rate band	11,305 × 40%	4,522
	58,705	14,002

The basic rate band is extended by the gross amount of the gift (£8,000 × 100/80).

9 Jointly held property

FAST FORWARD

Income on property held jointly by married couples and members of a civil partnership is treated as if it were shared equally unless the couple make a joint declaration of the actual shares of ownership.

PER alert

This section relates to your PER requirement:
20   Assist with tax planning

9.1 Allocation of joint income

If property is held jointly by a married couple or civil partners the income arising from that property is taxed as if it was shared equally between the members of the couple.

Civil partners are members of a same sex couple which has registered as a civil partnership under the Civil Partnerships Act 2004.

This 50:50 split of income from jointly held property applies even if the property is not owned in equal shares, **unless the members of the couple make a joint declaration to HMRC specifying the actual proportion to which each is entitled**.

9.2 Example: joint income

Janet owns 40% of a holiday cottage and John, her husband, owns the other 60%.

If no declaration is made each will be taxed on one half of the income arising when he property is let out.

If a declaration is made, Janet will be taxed on her 40% of the income and John will be taxed on his 60%.

9.3 Tax planning for married couples/civil partners

Where one member of a married couple/civil partnership is a basic rate taxpayer and the other a higher rate taxpayer, income tax liabilities can be minimised by transferring income producing assets from the higher rate taxpayer to the other spouse or civil partner.

If assets are owned jointly but in unequal proportions, then:

(a)   if the higher rate taxpayer owns more than 50% of the asset, no declaration of beneficial interest should be made so that the income is shared equally, or

(b)   if the higher rate taxpayer owns less than 50% of the asset, a declaration of beneficial interest should be made so that the other spouse or civil partner is taxed on their full amount of income.

Thus in the above example a declaration is beneficial if Janet is a higher rate taxpayer whilst John is a basic rate taxpayer,

Chapter Roundup

- An individual may be resident and/or ordinarily in the UK, and his liability to UK income tax will be determined accordingly.

- In a personal income tax computation, we bring together income from all sources, splitting the sources into non-savings, savings and dividend income.

- An individual may receive interest net of 20% tax suffered at source. The amount received must be grossed up by multiplying by 100/80 and must be included gross in the income tax computation. Dividends are received net of a 10% tax credit and must be grossed up for inclusion in the tax computation.

- Deductible interest is deducted from total income to compute net income.

- All persons are entitled to a personal allowance. It is deducted from net income, first against non savings income, then against savings income and lastly against dividend income. Taxpayers aged 65-74 are entitled to an age allowance, and taxpayers aged 75 and over to a higher personal allowance.

- Work out income tax on the taxable income. Deduct the tax credit on dividend income and any income tax suffered at source to arrive at tax payable. The tax credit on dividend income cannot be repaid if it exceeds the tax liability calculated so far. Other tax suffered at source can be repaid.

- Extend the basic rate band by the gross amount of any gift aid payment.

- Income on property held jointly by married couples and members of a civil partnership is treated as if it were shared equally unless the couple make a joint declaration of the actual shares of ownership.

Quick Quiz

1   When will an individual be resident in the UK?

2   Income tax on non-savings income is charged at ___ % in the basic rate band and at ___% in the higher rate band. Fill in the blanks.

3   Give one type of savings income that is received by individuals net of 20% tax.

4   How is dividend income taxed?

5   If Dennis has taxable income of £38,100 and makes gift aid payments of £400, on how much of his income will he pay higher rate tax?

    A   £200
    B   £300
    C   £400
    D   £500

6   Mike and Matt have registered a civil partnership. Mike owns 25% of an investment property and Matt owns 75%. How will the income be taxed?

Answers to Quick Quiz

1   An individual is resident in the UK if he is here for 183 days or more, or he makes visits to the UK averaging 91 days or more a year for each of four consecutive years.

2   Income tax on non-savings income is charged at 20% in the basic rate band and at 40% in the higher rate band.

3   Bank (or building society) interest.

4   Dividend income in the basic rate band is taxed at 10%. Dividend income in excess of the higher rate threshold is taxed at 32.5%

                                                                 (37400 + 500)

5   A. The basic rate band is extended by £400 × 100/80 = £500 to £37,900. Dennis will be liable to higher rate tax on £38,100 − £37,900 = £200.

6   Mike and Matt will each be taxed on 50% of the income from the investment property unless they make a joint declaration in which case Mike will be taxed on 25% of the income and Matt on 75%.

Number	Level	Marks	Time
Q1	Introductory	12	22 mins
Q2	Introductory	7	13 mins
Q3	Examination	15	27 mins

Now try the questions below from the Exam Question Bank

Employment income

Topic list	Syllabus reference
1 Employment and self employment	B2(a)
2 Basis of assessment for employment income	B2(c) B2(b)
3 Allowable deductions	B2(c) B2(d)
4 Statutory mileage allowances	B2(c) B2(e)
5 Charitable donations under the payroll deduction scheme	B2(c) B2(k)

Introduction

In the previous chapter we saw how to construct the income tax computation. Now we start to look in greater detail at the different types of income that people may receive so that the income can be slotted into the computation.

Many people earn money by working. We look at the important distinction between employment and self employment, so that we can consider the way in which people are taxed on the wages or salaries from their jobs.

Sometimes the employee may incur expenses when carrying out his job. We look at the rules determining when these can be deducted from employment income for tax purposes. We also look at the rules covering mileage payments made by employers to employees who use their own cars for business journeys. Finally employees can make tax efficient contributions to charity under the payroll giving scheme.

In the next chapter we look at how benefits received as a result of employment are taxed and at how tax is deducted from employment income under the PAYE system.

Study guide

Exam guide

You are very likely to be asked a question concerning at least one aspect of employment taxation in your exam. This could range from a discussion of the distinction between employment and self employment to a full computation of employment income, including benefits.

1 Employment and self employment

FAST FORWARD

Employment involves a contract of service whereas self employment involves a contract for services. The distinction between employment and self employment is decided by looking at all the facts of the engagement.

1.1 Employment income

Employment income includes income arising from an employment under a **contract of service**.

Some people, however, set themselves up in business and carry out work for customers under a **contract for services**.

Before we can calculate employment income, we must be sure that the individual is employed rather than self employed. This can only be decided by looking at all the facts of the engagement.

1.2 Employment and self employment

Exam focus point

> Many of the tax rules have come about as a result of legal cases. In the exam you are not required to know the relevant cases. However we have included the case names in the Text for your information.

The distinction between employment (receipts taxable as earnings) and self employment (receipts taxable as trading income) is a fine one. Employment involves a contract of service, whereas self employment involves a contract for services. Taxpayers tend to prefer self employment, because the rules on deductions for expenses are more generous.

Factors which may be of importance include:

- The degree of control exercised over the person doing the work
- Whether he must accept further work
- Whether the other party must provide further work
- Whether he provides his own equipment
- Whether he hires his own helpers
- What degree of financial risk he takes
- What degree of responsibility for investment and management he has
- Whether he can profit from sound management
- Whether he can work when he chooses
- The wording used in any agreement between the parties.

Relevant cases include:

(a) *Edwards v Clinch 1981*

A civil engineer acted occasionally as an inspector on temporary ad hoc appointments.

Held: there was no ongoing office which could be vacated by one person and held by another so the fees received were from self employment not employment.

(b) *Hall v Lorimer 1994*

A vision mixer was engaged under a series of short-term contracts.

Held: the vision mixer was self employed, not because of any one detail of the case but because the overall picture was one of self-employment.

(c) *Carmichael and Anor v National Power plc 1999*

Individuals engaged as visitor guides on a casual 'as required' basis were not employees. An exchange of correspondence between the company and the individuals was not a contract of employment as there was no provision as to the frequency of work and there was flexibility to accept work or turn it down as it arose. Sickness, holiday and pension arrangements did not apply and neither did grievance and disciplinary procedures.

A worker's status also affects national insurance contributions (NIC). The self-employed generally pay less than employees. NIC is covered later in this Text.

2 Basis of assessment for employment income

FAST FORWARD

General earnings are taxed in the year of receipt. Money earnings are generally received on the earlier of the time payment is made and the time entitlement to payment arises.

2.1 Outline of the charge

Employment income includes income arising from an employment under a contract of service and the income of office holders, such as directors. The term 'employee' is used in this Text to mean anyone who receives employment income (ie both employees and directors).

General earnings are an employee's earnings (see key term below) plus the 'cash equivalent' of any taxable non-monetary benefits.

Key term

'Earnings' means any salary, wage or fee, any gratuity or other profit or incidental benefit obtained by the employee if it is money or money's worth (something of direct monetary value or convertible into direct monetary value) or anything else which constitutes a reward of the employment.

Taxable earnings from an employment in a tax year are the general earnings received in that tax year.

2.2 When are earnings received?

General earnings consisting of money are treated as received at the earlier of:

- **The time when payment is made**
- **The time when a person becomes entitled to payment of the earnings.**

If the employee is a director of a company, earnings from the company are received on the earliest of:

- The earlier of the two alternatives given in the general rule (above)
- The time when the amount is credited in the company's accounting records
- The end of the company's period of account (if the amount was determined by then)
- The time the amount is determined (if after the end of the company's period of account).

Taxable benefits (see next chapter) **are generally treated as received when they are provided to the employee.**

The receipts basis does not apply to pension income. Pensions are taxed on the amount accruing in the tax year, whether or not it has actually been received in that year.

2.3 Net taxable earnings

Total taxable earnings less total allowable deductions (see below) **are net taxable earnings of a tax year.** Deductions cannot usually create a loss: they can only reduce the net taxable earnings to nil. If there is more than one employment in the tax year, separate calculations are required for each employment.

3 Allowable deductions

FAST FORWARD

> Deductions for expenses are extremely limited. Relief is available for the costs that an employee is obliged to incur in travelling in the performance of his duties or in travelling to the place he has to attend in performance of his duties. Relief is **not** available for normal commuting costs.

3.1 The general rules

Deductions for expenses are extremely limited and are notoriously hard to obtain. Although there are some specific deductions, which are covered below, the general rule is that relief is limited to:

- **Qualifying travel expenses**
- **Other expenses the employee is obliged to incur and pay as holder of the employment which are incurred wholly, exclusively and necessarily in the performance of the duties of the employment.**

3.2 Travel expenses

3.2.1 Qualifying travel expenses

Tax relief is not available for an employee's normal commuting costs. This means relief is not available for any costs an employee incurs in getting from home to his normal place of work. However **employees are entitled to relief for travel expenses that they are obliged to incur and pay in travelling in the performance of their duties or travelling to or from a place which they have to attend in the performance of their duties (other than a permanent workplace).**

3.2.2 Example: travel in the performance of duties

Judi is an accountant. She often travels to meetings at the firm's offices in the North of England returning to her office in Leeds after the meetings. Relief is available for the full cost of these journeys as the travel is undertaken in the performance of her duties.

Question   Relief for travelling costs

Zoe lives in Wycombe and normally works in Chiswick. Occasionally she visits a client in Wimbledon and travels direct from home. Distances are shown in the diagram below:

What tax relief is available for Zoe's travel costs?

Answer

Zoe is not entitled to tax relief for the costs incurred in travelling between Wycombe and Chiswick since these are normal commuting costs. However, relief is available for all costs that Zoe incurs when she travels from Wycombe to Wimbledon to visit her client.

To prevent manipulation of the basic rule normal commuting will not become a business journey just because the employee stops en-route to perform a business task (eg make a 'phone call). Nor will relief be available if the journey is essentially the same as the employee's normal journey to work.

3.2.3 Example: normal commuting

Judi is based at her office in Leeds City Centre. One day she is required to attend a 9.00 am meeting with a client whose premises are around the corner from her Leeds office. Judi travels from home directly to the meeting. As the journey is substantially the same as her ordinary journey to work relief is not available.

Site based employees (eg construction workers, management consultants etc) **who do not have a permanent workplace, are entitled to relief for the costs of all journeys made from home to wherever they are working**. This is because these employees do not have an ordinary commuting journey or any normal commuting costs.

3.2.4 Temporary workplace

If an employee is seconded to work at another location for some considerable time, then the question arises as to whether the journey from home to that workplace can become normal commuting. There is a 24 month rule.

Tax relief is available for travel, accommodation and subsistence expenses incurred by an employee who is working at a temporary workplace on a secondment expected to last up to 24 months. If a secondment is initially expected not to exceed 24 months, but it is extended, relief ceases to be due from the date the employee becomes aware of the change.

When looking at how long a secondment is expected to last, HMRC will consider not only the terms of the written contract but also any verbal agreement by the employer and other factors such as whether the employee buys a house etc.

Philip works for Vastbank at its Newcastle City Centre branch. Philip is sent to work full-time at another branch in Morpeth for 20 months at the end of which he will return to the Newcastle branch. Morpeth is about 20 miles north of Newcastle.

What travel costs is Philip entitled to claim as a deduction?

Answer

Although Philip is spending all of his time at the Morpeth branch it will not be treated as his normal work place because his period of attendance will be less than 24 months. Thus Philip can claim relief in full for the costs of travel from his home to the Morpeth branch.

3.3 Other expenses

Relief is given for other expenses incurred **wholly, exclusively and necessarily in the performance of the duties** of the employment. The word 'exclusively' strictly implies that the expenditure must **give no private benefit at all**. If it does, none of it is deductible. In practice HMRC may ignore a small element of private benefit or make an apportionment between business and private use.

Whether an expense is 'necessary' is not determined by what the employer requires. The test is **whether the duties of the employment could not be performed without the outlay.**

The following cases illustrate how the requirements are interpreted. Remember you are not expected to know the case names, they are given for information only.

- *Sanderson v Durbridge 1955*

  The cost of evening meals taken when attending late meetings was not deductible because it was not incurred in the performance of the duties.

- *Blackwell v Mills 1945*

  As a condition of his employment, an employee was required to attend evening classes. The cost of his text books and travel was not deductible because it was not incurred in the performance of the duties.

- *Lupton v Potts 1969*

  Examination fees incurred by a solicitor's articled clerk were not deductible because they were incurred neither wholly nor exclusively in the performance of the duties, but in furthering the clerk's ambition to become a solicitor.

- *Brown v Bullock 1961*

  The expense of joining a club that was virtually a requisite of an employment was not deductible because it would have been possible to carry on the employment without the club membership, so the expense was not necessary.

- *Elwood v Utitz 1965*

  A managing director's subscriptions to two residential London clubs were claimed by him as an expense on the grounds that they were cheaper than hotels.

  The expenditure was deductible as it was necessary in that it would be impossible for the employee to carry out his London duties without being provided with first class accommodation. The residential facilities (which were cheaper than hotel accommodation) were given to club members only.

- *Lucas v Cattell 1972*

  The cost of business telephone calls on a private telephone is deductible, but **no part of the line or telephone rental charges is deductible**.

- *Fitzpatrick v IRC 1994; Smith v Abbott 1994*

  Journalists cannot claim a deduction for the cost of buying newspapers which they read to keep themselves informed, since they are merely preparing themselves to perform their duties.

The cost of clothes for work is not deductible, except for certain trades requiring protective clothing where there are annual deductions on a set scale.

An employee required to work at home may be able to claim a deduction for the marginal costs of working from home, such as an appropriate proportion of his or her expenditure on lighting and heating. Employers can pay up to £3 per week without the need for supporting evidence of the costs incurred by the employee. Payments above the £3 limit require evidence of the employee's actual costs.

3.4 Other deductions

Certain expenditure is specifically deductible in computing net taxable earnings:

(a) **Contributions to registered occupational pension schemes**

(b) **Subscriptions to professional bodies** on the list of bodies issued by the HMRC (which includes most UK professional bodies), if relevant to the duties of the employment

(c) Payments for certain liabilities relating to the employment and for insurance against them (see below).

Employees may also claim capital allowances on plant and machinery (other than cars or other vehicles) necessarily provided for use in the performance of those duties. The computation of capital allowances is discussed later in this Text.

3.5 Liabilities and insurance

If a director or employee incurs a liability related to his employment or pays for insurance against such a liability, the cost is a deductible expense. If the employer pays such amounts, there is no taxable benefit.

A liability relating to employment is one which is imposed in respect of the employee's acts or omissions as employee. Thus, for example, liability for negligence would be covered. Related costs, for example the costs of legal proceedings, are included.

For insurance premiums to qualify, the insurance policy must:

(a) Cover only liabilities relating to employment, vicarious liability in respect of liabilities of another person's employment, related costs and payments to the employee's own employees in respect of their employment liabilities relating to employment and related costs, and

(b) It must not last for more than two years (although it may be renewed for up to two years at a time), and the insured person must not be not required to renew it.

4 Statutory mileage allowances

FAST FORWARD

Employers may pay a mileage allowance to employees who use their own car on business journeys. Payments up to the statutory limits are tax free, any excess is taxable, and a deduction can be claimed if the payment is lower.

A single authorised mileage allowance for business journeys in an employee's own vehicle applies to all cars and vans. There is no income tax on payments up to this allowance and employers do not have to report mileage allowances up to this amount. The allowance for 2009/10 is **40p per mile on the first 10,000 miles** in the tax year with **each additional mile over 10,000 miles at 25p per mile**.

The authorised mileage allowance for **employees using their own motor cycle is 24p per mile**. For **employees using their own pedal cycle it is 20p per mile**.

If employers pay less than the statutory mileage allowance, employees can claim tax relief up to that level.

The statutory mileage allowance does not prevent employers from paying higher rates, but any excess will be subject to income tax. There is a similar (but slightly different) system for NICs, covered later in this Text.

Employers can make income tax and NIC free payments of up to 5p per mile for each fellow employee making the same business trip who is carried as a passenger. If the employer does not pay the employee for carrying business passengers, the employee cannot claim any tax relief.

Question	Mileage allowance

Sophie uses her own car for business travel. During 2009/10, Sophie drove 15,400 miles in the performance of her duties. Sophie's employer paid her a mileage allowance. How is the mileage allowance treated for tax purposes assuming that the rate paid is:

(a)   35p a mile, or
(b)   25p a mile?

Answer

(a)

	£
Mileage allowance received (15,400 × 35p)	5,390
Less: tax free [(10,000 × 40p) + (5,400 × 25p)]	(5,350)
Taxable benefit	40

£5,350 is tax free and the excess amount received of £40 is a taxable benefit.

(b)

	£
Tax free amount [(10,000 × 40p) + (5,400 × 25p)]	5,350
Less: mileage allowance received (15,400 × 25p)	(3,850)
Shortfall	1,500

There is no taxable benefit and Sophie can claim a deduction from her employment income for the shortfall of £1,500.

5 Charitable donations under the payroll deduction scheme

FAST FORWARD

Employees can make tax deductible donations to charity under the payroll deduction scheme. The amount paid is deducted from gross pay.

Employees can make charitable donations under the payroll deduction scheme by asking their employer to make deductions from their gross earnings. The deductions are then passed to a charitable agency which will either distribute the funds to the employees' chosen charities on receipt of their instructions, or provide the employee with vouchers that can be encashed by the recipient charities.

The donation is an allowable deduction from the employee's earnings for tax purposes. Tax relief is given at source as the employer must deduct the donation from gross pay before calculating PAYE due thereon.

Chapter Roundup

- Employment involves a contract of service whereas self employment involves a contract for services. The distinction between employment and self employment is decided by looking at all the facts of the engagement.

- General earnings are taxed in the year of receipt. Money earnings are generally received on the earlier of the time payment is made and the time entitlement to payment arises.

- Deductions for expenses are extremely limited. Relief is available for the costs that an employee is obliged to incur in travelling in the performance of his duties or in travelling to the place he has to attend in performance of his duties. Relief is not available for normal commuting costs.

- Employers may pay a mileage allowance to employees who use their own car on business journeys. Payments up to the statutory limits are tax free, any excess is taxable, and a deduction can be claimed if the payment is lower.

- Employees can make tax deductible donations to charity under the payroll deduction scheme. The amount paid is deducted from gross pay.

Quick Quiz

1   On what basis are earnings taxed?

2   In order for general expenses of employment to be deductible, they must be incurred _____, _____, and _____, in the performance of the duties of the employment. Fill in the blanks.

3   What relief can Karen claim if she is paid 35p for each mile that she drives her own car on company business and she drives 5,000 miles in 2009/10?

    A   £250
    B   £1,750
    C   £2,000
    D   £2,250

4   Could Karen claim any extra relief if she was accompanied by a work colleague for 1,000 of those miles?

Answers to Quick Quiz

1   Earnings are taxed on a receipts basis.

2   In order for general expenses of employment to be deductible, they must be incurred wholly, exclusively and necessarily in the performance of the duties of the employment.

3   A. Karen could claim relief of 5,000 x (40 – 35)p = £250. The 35p per mile received would not be taxable.

4   Karen could not claim any extra relief if she was accompanied by a work colleague for 1,000 of those miles. If her employer had made extra payments of up to 5p per mile for those journeys the extra payment would have been tax free.

Now try the question below from the Exam Question Bank

Number	Level	Marks	Time
Q4	Examination	15	27 mins

Taxable and exempt benefits. The PAYE system

4

Topic list	Syllabus reference
1 P11D employees	B2(g)
2 Benefits taxable on all employees	B2(h)
3 Benefits taxable on P11D employees	B2(h)
4 Exempt benefits	B2(h)
5 P11D dispensations	B2(i)
6 The PAYE system	B2(f)

Introduction

In the previous chapter we discussed when a worker was an employee and when he was self employed. We then considered the taxation of salaries and wages and the deduction of expenses and charitable donations.

In this chapter we look at benefits provided to employees. Benefits are an integral part of many remuneration packages, but the tax cost of receiving a benefit must not be overlooked. Special rules apply to fix the taxable value of certain benefits.

Finally we look at how tax is deducted from employment income under the PAYE system. Tax is deducted from cash payments, and benefits are dealt with through the PAYE code.

In the next chapter we look at how employees can save for their retirement through pension provision and the tax reliefs available.

Study guide

		Intellectual level
B2	**Income from employment**	
(f)	Explain the PAYE system.	1
(g)	Identify P11D employees.	1
(h)	Compute the amount of benefits assessable.	2
(i)	Explain the purpose of a dispensation from HM Revenue & Customs.	2

Exam guide

Benefits are a very important part of employment income and you are likely to come across them in your exam. Most employees these days are P11D employees, but you may need to know which benefits apply to excluded employees. If you come across exempt benefits in a question, note this in your answer to show that you have considered each item.

The PAYE system is a very sophisticated system of deduction of tax at source and you should be able to explain how it can cope with collecting the correct amount of tax. The construction of the PAYE code is important.

1 P11D employees

FAST FORWARD

Most employees are taxed on benefits under the benefits code. 'Excluded employees' (lower paid/non-directors) are only subject to part of the provisions of the code.

1.1 Excluded employees

There is comprehensive legislation which covers the taxation of benefits.

The legislation generally applies to all employees. However, only certain parts of it apply to 'excluded employees'.

An excluded employee is an employee in lower paid employment who is either not a director of a company or is a director but has no material interest in the company ('material' means control of more than 5% of the ordinary share capital) and either:

(a)   He is full time working director, or

(b)   The company is non-profit-making or is established for charitable purposes only.

The term 'director' refers to any person who acts as a director or any person in accordance with whose instructions the directors are accustomed to act (other than a professional adviser).

1.2 Lower paid employment

A lower paid employment is one where earnings for the tax year are less than £8,500. To decide whether this applies, add together the total earnings and benefits that would be taxable if the employee were **not** an excluded employee.

A number of specific deductions must be taken into account to determine lower paid employment. These include contributions to registered pension schemes and payroll charitable deductions. However, general deductions from employment income (see earlier in this Text) are not taken into account.

1.3 P11D employees

Employees, including directors, who are not excluded employees may be referred to as 'P11D employees'; the P11D is the form that the employer completes for each such employee with details of expenses and benefits.

Question	Excluded employee

Tim earns £6,500 per annum working full time as a sales representative at Chap Co Ltd. The company provides the following staff benefits to Tim:

Private health insurance	£300
Company car	£1,500
Expense allowance	£2,000

Tim used £1,900 of the expense allowance on business mileage petrol and on entertaining clients.

Is Tim an excluded employee?

Answer

No. Although Tim's taxable income is less than £8,500 this is only after his expense claim. The figure to consider and compare to £8,500 is the £10,300 as shown below.

		£
Salary		6,500
Benefits:	health insurance	300
	car	1,500
	expense allowance	2,000
Earnings to consider if Tim is an 'excluded employee'		10,300
Less claim for expenses paid out		(1,900)
Taxable income		8,400

2 Benefits taxable on all employees

2.1 Introduction

All employees, including excluded employees, are taxable on the provision of:

- vouchers
- living accommodation.

For excluded employees, other benefits are taxed on their "second-hand value", which is usually nil. The special rules for P11D employees are covered in the next Section.

2.2 Vouchers

If any employee (including an excluded employee):

(a) receives cash vouchers (vouchers exchangeable for cash)
(b) uses a credit token (such as a credit card) to obtain money, goods or services, or
(c) receives exchangeable vouchers (such as book tokens), also called non-cash vouchers

he is taxed on the cost for the employer of providing the benefit, less any amount made good.

The first 15p per working day of meal vouchers (eg luncheon vouchers) is not taxed.

2.3 Accommodation

FAST FORWARD

The benefit in respect of accommodation is its annual value. There is an additional benefit if the property cost over £75,000.

2.3.1 Annual value charge

The taxable value of accommodation provided to an employee (including an excluded employee) is the rent that would have been payable if the premises had been let at their annual value (sometimes called 'rateable value'). If the premises are rented rather than owned by the employer, then the taxable benefit is the higher of the rent actually paid and the annual value. If property does not have a rateable value HMRC estimate a value.

2.3.2 Additional benefit charge

If a property was bought by the employer for a cost of more than £75,000, an additional amount is chargeable as follows:

(Cost of providing the living accommodation − £75,000) × the official rate of interest at the start of the tax year.

Thus with an official rate of 4.75%, the total benefit for accommodation costing £95,000 and with an annual value of £2,000 would be £2,000 + £(95,000 − 75,000) × 4.75% = £2,950.

The 'cost of providing' the living accommodation is the aggregate of the cost of purchase and the cost of any improvements made before the start of the tax year for which the benefit is being computed. It is therefore not possible to avoid the charge by buying an inexpensive property requiring substantial repairs and improving it.

Where the property was acquired more than six years before first being provided to the employee, the market value when first so provided plus the cost of subsequent improvements is used as the cost of providing the living accommodation. However, unless the actual cost plus improvements up to the start of the tax year in question exceeds £75,000, the additional charge cannot be imposed, however high the market value.

Exam focus point

The 'official rate' of interest will be given to you in the exam.

2.3.3 Job related accommodation

There is no taxable benefit in respect of job related accommodation. Accommodation is job related if:

(a) Residence in the accommodation **is necessary for the proper performance of the employee's duties** (as with a caretaker), or

(b) The accommodation is provided **for the better performance of the employee's duties** and the employment is of a kind in which it is **customary for accommodation to be provided** (as with a policeman), or

(c) The **accommodation is provided as part of arrangements in force because of a special threat to the employee's security**.

Directors can only claim exemptions (a) or (b) if:

(i) They have no **material interest** ('material' means over 5%) in the company, and

(ii) Either they are **full time working directors** or the company is **non-profit making or is a charity**.

2.3.4 Other points

Any contribution paid by the employee is deducted from the annual value of the property and then from the additional benefit.

If the employee is given a cash alternative to living accommodation, the benefits code still applies in priority to treating the cash alternative as earnings. If the cash alternative is greater than the taxable benefit, the excess is treated as earnings.

Question	Accommodation

Mr Quinton was provided with a company flat in Birmingham in January 2009. The rateable value of the flat is £1,200. The property cost his employer £125,000, but was valued at £150,000 in January 2009. Mr Quinton paid rent of £500 pa.

What is the taxable benefit for 2009/10 assuming:

(a)   His employer purchased the property in 2007, or

(b)   His employer purchased the property in 2001, or

(c)   Mr Quinton was required to live in the flat as he was employed as the caretaker for the company premises (of which the flat was part).

Answer

(a)

	£
Annual value	1,200
Less: rent paid	(500)
	700
Additional amount £(125,000 – 75,000) × 4.75%	2,375
Taxable benefit	3,075

(b)

	£
Annual value	1,200
Less: rent paid	(500)
	700
Additional amount £(150,000 – 75,000) × 4.75%	3,562
Taxable benefit	4,262

As Mr Quinton first moved in more than six years after the company bought the flat, the value at the date he moved in is used.

(c)   Job related accommodation: taxable benefit   £ nil

3 Benefits taxable on P11D employees

3.1 Introduction

Special rules apply to determine the taxable value of expenses and benefits paid to or provided for P11D employees.

3.2 Expenses

3.2.1 General business expenses

If business expenses on such items as travel or hotel stays are reimbursed by an employer, the reimbursed amount is a taxable benefit for P11D employees. To avoid being taxed on this amount, **an employee must then make a claim to deduct it as an expense** under the rules set out below.

A P11D dispensation may be obtained from HMRC to avoid the need to report expenses and claim a deduction (see earlier in this Text).

3.2.2 Private incidental expenses

When an individual has to spend one or more nights away from home, his employer may reimburse expenses on items incidental to his absence (for example laundry and private telephone calls). **Such incidental expenses are exempt** if:

(a) The expenses of travelling to each place where the individual stays overnight, throughout the trip, are incurred necessarily in the performance of the duties of the employment (or would have been, if there had been any expenses).

(b) The total (for the whole trip) of incidental expenses not deductible under the usual rules is no more than £5 for each night spent wholly in the UK and £10 for each other night. If this limit is exceeded, all of the expenses are taxable, not just the excess. The expenses include any VAT.

This incidental expenses exemption applies to expenses reimbursed, and to benefits obtained using credit tokens and non-cash vouchers.

3.2.3 Expenses related to living accommodation

In addition to the benefit of living accommodation itself, P11D **employees are taxed on related expenses paid by the employer**, such as:

(a) **Heating, lighting or cleaning the premises**
(b) **Repairing, maintaining or decorating the premises**
(c) **The provision of furniture (the annual value is 20% of the cost).**

If the accommodation is 'job related', however, the **taxable amount is restricted to a maximum of 10% of the employee's 'net earnings'**. For this purpose, net earnings comprises the total employment income, net of expenses and pension contributions, but excluding these related expenses.

Council tax and water or sewage charges paid by the employer are taxable in full as a benefit unless the accommodation is 'job-related'.

3.3 Cars

FAST FORWARD

Employees who have a company car are taxed on a % of the car's list price which depends on the level of the car's CO_2 emissions. The same % multiplied by £16,900 determines the benefit where private fuel is also provided.

3.3.1 Cars provided for private use

A car provided by reason of the employment to a P11D employee or member of his family or household for private use gives rise to a taxable benefit. 'Private use' includes home to work travel.

A tax charge arises whether the car is provided by the employer or by some other person. The benefit is computed as shown below, even if the car is taken as an alternative to another benefit of a different value.

The starting point for calculating a car benefit is the list price of the car (plus accessories). **The percentage of the list price that is taxable depends on the car's CO_2 emissions.**

3.3.2 Taxable benefit

For cars that emit CO_2 between 121-135/km (2009/10), the taxable benefit is 15% of the car's list price. This percentage increases by 1% for every 5g/km (rounded down to the nearest multiple of 5) by which CO_2 emissions exceed the baseline figure of 135g/km up to a maximum of 35%. For cars that emit CO_2 of exactly 120g/km or less, the taxable benefit is 10% of the car's list price.

Exam focus point

The CO_2 baseline figure will be given to you in the tax rates and allowances section of the exam paper.

Diesel cars have a supplement of 3% of the car's list price added to the taxable benefit. The maximum percentage, however, remains 35% of the list price.

3.3.3 List price

The price of the car is the sum of the following items:

(a) **The list price of the car** for a single retail sale at the time of first registration, inclu delivery and standard accessories. The manufacturer's, importer's or distributor's be used, even if the retailer offered a discount. A notional list price is estimated if published.

(b) **The price (including fitting) of all optional accessories provided when the car was first provided** to the employee, excluding mobile telephones and equipment needed by a disabled employee. The extra cost of adapting or manufacturing a car to run on road fuel gases is not included.

(c) **The price (including fitting) of all optional accessories fitted later** and costing at least £100 each, excluding mobile telephones and equipment needed by a disabled employee. Such accessories affect the taxable benefit from and including the tax year in which they are fitted. However, accessories which are merely replacing existing accessories and are not superior to the ones replaced are ignored. Replacement accessories which *are* superior are taken into account, but the cost of the old accessory is then deducted.

There is a special rule for **classic cars**. If the car is at least 15 years old (from the time of first registration) at the end of the tax year, and its market value at the end of the year (or, if earlier, when it ceased to be available to the employee) is over £15,000 and greater than the price found under the above rules, that market value is used instead of the price. The market value takes account of all accessories (except mobile telephones and equipment needed by a disabled employee).

Capital contributions made by the employee in that and previous tax years up to a maximum of £5,000 are deducted from the list price. Capital contributions are payments by the employee in respect of the price of the car or accessories for the same car. Contributions beyond the maximum are ignored.

If the price or value exceeds £80,000, then £80,000 is used instead. This £80,000 is after capital contributions have been taken into account.

Question	Car benefit (1)

Nigel Issan is provided with a diesel car which had a list price of £22,000 when it was first registered. The car has CO_2 emissions of 198g/km.

You are required to calculate Nigel's car benefit for 2009/10.

Answer

Car benefit £22,000 × 30% (15% + (195 – 135) × 1/5 + 3%) = £6,600

Note that 198 is rounded down to 195 to be exactly divisible by 5.

Question	Car benefit (2)

Robyn is provided with a petrol car which had a list price of £12,000 when it was first registered. The car has CO_2 emissions of 123 g/km.

You are required to calculate Robyn's car benefit for 2009/10.

Answer

Car benefit £12,000 x 15% = £1,800

Note that the 10% car benefit rate only applies if the CO_2 emissions are exactly 120g/km or less. In this case there is no rounding down to be exactly divisible by 5.

3.3.4 Reductions in the benefit

The benefit is reduced on a time basis where a car is first made available or ceases to be made available during the tax year or is incapable of being used for a continuous period of not less than 30 days (for example because it is being repaired).

The benefit is reduced by any payment the user must make for the private use of the car (as distinct from a capital contribution to the cost of the car). The benefit cannot become negative to create a deduction from the employee's income.

| Question | Time apportioning benefits |

Vicky Olvo starts her employment on 6 January 2010 and is immediately provided with a new petrol car with a list price of £25,000. The car was more expensive than her employer would have provided and she therefore made a capital contribution of £6,200. The employer was able to buy the car at a discount and paid only £23,000. Vicky contributed £100 a month for being able to use the car privately. CO_2 emissions are 262g/km.

You are required to calculate her car benefit for 2009/10.

Answer

	£
List price *	25,000
Less capital contribution (maximum)	(5,000)
	20,000

	£
£20,000 × 35%** × 3/12 ***	1,750
Less contribution to running costs (£100 × 3)	(300)
Car benefit	1,450

*   The discounted price is not relevant
**   15% + (260 – 135) × 1/5 = 40% restricted to 35% max
***   Only available for 3 months in 2009/10.

3.3.5 Pool cars

Pool cars are exempt. A car is a pool car if all the following conditions are satisfied:

(a)   It is used by more than one employee and is not ordinarily used by any one of them to the exclusion of the others

(b)   Any private use is merely incidental to business use

(c)   It is not normally kept overnight at or near the residence of an employee.

3.3.6 Ancillary benefits

There are many ancillary benefits associated with the provision of cars, such as insurance, repairs, vehicle licences and a parking space at or near work. No extra taxable benefit arises as a result of these, with the exception of the cost of providing a driver.

3.4 Fuel for cars

3.4.1 Introduction

Where fuel is provided there is a further benefit in addition to the car benefit.

No taxable benefit arises where either

(a) **All the fuel provided was made available only for business travel**, or

(b) **The employee is required to make good, and has made good, the whole of the cost of any fuel provided for his private use**.

Unlike most benefits, a reimbursement of only part of the cost of the fuel available for private use does not reduce the benefit.

3.4.2 Taxable benefit

The taxable benefit is a percentage of a base figure. The base figure for 2009/10 is £16,900. The percentage is the same percentage as is used to calculate the car benefit (see above).

Exam focus point

> The fuel base figure will be given to you in the tax rates and allowances section of the exam paper.

3.4.3 Reductions in the benefit

The fuel benefit is reduced in the same way as the car benefit **if the car is not available for 30 days or more**.

The fuel benefit is also reduced if private fuel is not available for part of a tax year. However, if private fuel later becomes available in the same tax year, the reduction is not made. If, for example, fuel is provided from 6 April 2009 to 30 June 2009, then the fuel benefit for 2009/10 will be restricted to just three months. This is because the provision of fuel has permanently ceased. However, if fuel is provided from 6 April 2009 to 30 June 2009, and then again from 1 September 2009 to 5 April 2010, then the fuel benefit will not be reduced since the cessation was only temporary.

Question   Car and fuel benefit

An employee was provided with a new car costing £15,000 on 6 April 2009. The car emits 186g/km of CO_2. During 2009/10 the employer spent £900 on insurance, repairs and a vehicle licence. The firm paid for all petrol, costing £1,500, without reimbursement. The employee paid the firm £270 for the private use of the car. Calculate the taxable benefit.

Answer

Round CO_2 emissions figure down to the nearest 5, ie 185g/km.

Amount by which CO_2 emissions exceed the baseline:

(185 – 135) = 50 g/km

Divide by 5 = 10

Taxable percentage = 15% + 10% = 25%

	£
Car benefit £15,000 × 25%	3,750
Fuel benefit £16,900 × 25%	4,225
	7,975
Less contribution towards use of car	(270)
	7,705

If the contribution of £270 had been towards the petrol the benefit would have been £7,975.

3.5 Vans and heavier commercial vehicles

If a van (of normal maximum laden weight up to 3,500 kg) **is made available for an employee's private use, there is an annual scale charge of £3,000**. The scale charge covers ancillary benefits such as insurance and servicing. The benefit is scaled down if the van is not available for the full year (as for cars) and is reduced by any payment made by the employee for private use.

There is, however, **no taxable benefit where an employee takes a van home** (ie uses the van for home to work travel) but is not allowed any other private use.

Where private fuel is provided, there is an additional charge of £500. If the van is unavailable for part of the year, or fuel for private use is only provided for part of the year, the benefit is scaled down.

If a commercial vehicle of normal maximum laden weight over 3,500 kg is made available for an employee's private use, but the employee's use of the vehicle is not wholly or mainly private, no taxable benefit arises except in respect of the provision of a driver.

3.6 Beneficial loans

FAST FORWARD

Cheap loans are charged to tax on the difference between the official rate of interest and any interest paid by the employee.

3.6.1 Taxable benefit

Employment related loans to P11D employees and their relatives give rise to a benefit equal to:

(a) **Any amounts written off** (unless the employee has died), and

(b) The excess of the interest based on an official rate prescribed by the Treasury, over any interest actually charged ('taxable cheap loan'). Interest payable during the tax year but paid after the end of the tax year is taken into account.

The following loans are normally not treated as taxable cheap loans for calculation of the interest benefits (but not for the purposes of the charge on loans written off).

(a) A loan on normal commercial terms made in the ordinary course of the employer's money-lending business.

(b) A loan made by an individual in the ordinary course of the lender's domestic, family or personal arrangements.

3.6.2 Calculating the interest benefit

There are two alternative methods of calculating the taxable benefit. The simpler **'average' method** automatically applies unless the taxpayer or HMRC elect for the alternative **'strict' method**. (HMRC normally only make the election where it appears that the 'average' method is being deliberately exploited.) In both methods, the benefit is the interest at the official rate minus the interest payable.

The 'average' method averages the balances at the beginning and end of the tax year (or the dates on which the loan was made and discharged if it was not in existence throughout the tax year) and applies the official rate of interest to this average. If the loan was not in existence throughout the tax year only the number of complete tax months (from the 6th of the month) for which it existed are taken into account.

The 'strict' method is to compute interest at the official rate on the actual amount outstanding on a daily basis. However, for exam purposes, it is acceptable to work on a monthly basis.

Question

Loan benefit

At 6 April 2009 a taxable cheap loan of £30,000 was outstanding to an employee earning £12,000 a year, who repaid £20,000 on 6 December 2009. The remaining balance of £10,000 was outstanding at 5 April 2010. Interest paid during the year was £250. What was the benefit under both methods for 2009/10, if the official rate of interest is 4.75%?

Average method

$$4.75\% \times \frac{30,000+10,000}{2}$$

	£
	950
Less interest paid	(250)
Benefit	700

Alternative method (strict method)

	£
£30,000 $\times \frac{8}{12}$ (6 April – 5 December) $\times$ 4.75%	950
£10,000 $\times \frac{4}{12}$ (6 December – 5 April) $\times$ 4.75%	158
	1,108
Less interest paid	(250)
Benefit	858

HMRC might opt for the alternative method.

Note. You must always show the workings for the average method. If it appears likely that the taxpayer should or HMRC might opt for the alternative method you will need to show those workings as well.

3.6.3 The de minimis test

The interest benefit is not taxable if the total of all non-qualifying loans to the employee did not exceed £5,000 at any time in the tax year.

A qualifying loan is one on which all or part of any interest paid would qualify for tax relief (see further below).

When the £5,000 threshold is exceeded, a benefit arises on interest on the whole loan, not just on the excess of the loan over £5,000.

3.6.4 Qualifying loans

If the whole of the interest payable on a qualifying loan is eligible for tax relief as deductible interest, then no taxable benefit arises. If the interest is only partly eligible for tax relief, then the employee is treated as receiving earnings because the actual rate of interest is below the official rate. He is also treated as paying interest equal to those earnings. This **deemed interest paid may qualify as a business expense or as deductible interest in addition to any interest actually paid.**

Question

Beneficial loans

Anna, who is single, has an annual salary of £30,000, and two loans from her employer.

(a) A season ticket loan of £2,300 at no interest
(b) A loan, 90% of which was used to buy a partnership interest, of £54,000 at 1.5% interest

The official rate of interest is 4.75%.

What is Anna's tax liability for 2009/10?

	£
Salary	30,000
Season ticket loan (non-qualifying): not over £5,000	0
Loan to buy shares (qualifying): £54,000 × (4.75 – 1.5 = 3.25%)	1,755
Earnings/Total income	31,755
Less deductible interest paid (£54,000 × 4.75% × 90%)	(2,308)
Net income	29,447
Less personal allowance	(6,475)
Taxable income	22,972
Income tax	
Tax liability £22,972 × 20%	4,594

3.7 Private use of other assets

20% of the value of assets made available for private use is taxable.

When assets are made available to employees or members of their family or household, the taxable benefit is the higher of 20% of the market value when first provided as a benefit to any employee, or on the rent paid by the employer if higher. The 20% charge is time-apportioned when the asset is provided for only part of the year. The charge after any time apportionment is reduced by any contribution made by the employee.

Certain assets, such as bicycles provided for journeys to work, are exempt. These are described later in this chapter.

If an asset made available is subsequently acquired by the employee, **the taxable benefit on the acquisition is the** *greater* **of:**

- The **current market value minus the price paid by the employee.**
- The **market value when first provided minus any amounts already taxed (ignoring contributions by the employee) minus the price paid by the employee.**

This rule prevents tax free benefits arising on rapidly depreciating items through the employee purchasing them at their low secondhand value.

There is an exception to this rule for bicycles which have previously been provided as exempt benefits. The taxable benefit on acquisition is restricted to current market value, minus the price paid by the employee.

3.8 Example: assets made available for private use

A suit costing £400 is purchased by an employer for use by an employee on 6 April 2008. On 6 April 2009 the suit is purchased by the employee for £30, its market value then being £50.

The benefit in 2008/09 is £400 × 20% = £80

The benefit in 2009/10 is £290, being the *greater* of:

		£
(a)	Market value at acquisition by employee	50
	Less price paid	(30)
		20
(b)	Original market value	400
	Less taxed in respect of use	(80)
		320
	Less price paid	(30)
		290

Question

Rupert is provided with a new bicycle by his employer on 6 April 2009. The bicycle is available for private use as well as commuting to work. It cost the employer £1,500 when new. On 6 October 2009 the employer transfers ownership of the bicycle to Rupert when it is worth £800. Rupert does not pay anything for the bicycle.

What is the total taxable benefit on Rupert for 2009/10 in respect of the bicycle?

Answer

Use benefit	Exempt
Transfer benefit (use MV at acquisition by employee only)	
MV at transfer	£800

3.9 Scholarships

If scholarships are given to members an employee's family, the **employee is taxable on the cost** unless the scholarship fund's or scheme's payments by reason of people's employments are not more than 25% of its total payments.

3.10 Other benefits

FAST FORWARD

There is a residual charge for other benefits, usually equal to the cost to the employer of the benefits.

We have seen above how certain specific benefits are taxed. **There is a sweeping up charge for all other benefits. Under this rule the taxable value of a benefit is the cost of the benefit less any part of that cost made good by the employee to the persons providing the benefit.**

The residual charge applies to any benefit provided for a P11D employee or a member of his family or household, by reason of the employment. There is an exception where the employer is an individual and the provision of the benefit is made in the normal course of the employer's domestic, family or personal relationships.

3.11 Example: other benefits

A private school offers free places to the children of its staff. The marginal cost to the school of providing the place is £2,000 pa, although the fees charged to other pupils is £5,000 pa.

The taxable value of the benefit to the staff is the actual cost of £2,000 per pupil, not the full £5,000 charged to other pupils.

4 Exempt benefits

FAST FORWARD

There are a number of exempt benefits including removal expenses, childcare, meal vouchers and workplace parking.

Various benefits are exempt from tax. These include:

(a) **Entertainment provided to employees by genuine third parties** (eg seats at sporting/cultural events), even if it is provided by giving the employee a voucher.

(b) **Gifts of goods** (or vouchers exchangeable for goods) from third parties (ie not provided by the employer or a person connected to the employer) if the total cost (incl. VAT) of all gifts by the same donor to the same employee in the tax year is £250 or less. If the £250 limit is exceeded, the full amount is taxable, not just the excess.

(c) **Non-cash awards for long service** if the period of service was at least 20 years, no similar award was made to the employee in the past 10 years and the cost is not more than £50 per year of service.

(d) **Awards under staff suggestion schemes if:**

    (i)   There is a formal scheme, open to all employees on equal terms.

    (ii)   The suggestion is outside the scope of the employee's normal duties.

    (iii)   Either the award is not more than £25, or the award is only made after a decision is taken to implement the suggestion.

    (iv)   Awards over £25 reflect the financial importance of the suggestion to the business, and either do not exceed 50% of the expected net financial benefit during the first year of implementation or do not exceed 10% of the expected net financial benefit over a period of up to five years.

    (v)   Awards of over £25 are shared on a reasonable basis between two or more employees putting forward the same suggestion.

    If an award exceeds £5,000, the excess is always taxable.

(e) **The first £8,000 of removal expenses if:**

    (i)   The employee does not already live within a reasonable daily travelling distance of his new place of employment, but will do so after moving.

    (ii)   The expenses are incurred or the benefits provided by the end of the tax year following the tax year of the start of employment at the new location.

(f) The cost of running a **workplace nursery or playscheme (without limit). Otherwise up to £55 a week of childcare is tax free** if the employer contracts with an approved childcarer or provides childcare vouchers to pay an approved childcarer. The childcare must be available to all employees and the childcare must either be registered or approved home-childcare.

(g) **Sporting or recreational facilities available to employees generally and not to the general public**, unless they are provided on domestic premises, or they consist of an interest in or the use of any mechanically propelled vehicle or any overnight accommodation. Vouchers only exchangeable for such facilities are also exempt, but membership fees for sports clubs are taxable.

(h) **Assets or services used in performing the duties of employment** provided any private use of the item concerned is insignificant. This exempts, for example, the benefit arising on the private use of employer-provided tools.

(i) **Welfare counselling** and similar minor benefits if the benefit concerned is available to employees generally.

(j) **Bicycles or cycling safety equipment provided to enable employees to get to and from work or to travel between one workplace and another**. The equipment must be available to the employer's employees generally. Also, it must be used mainly for the aforementioned journeys.

(k) **Workplace parking**

(l) **Up to £15,000 a year paid to an employee who is on a full-time course lasting at least a year**, with average full-time attendance of at least 20 weeks a year. If the £15,000 limit is exceeded, the whole amount is taxable.

(m) **Work related training and related costs. This includes the costs of** training material and assets either made during training or incorporated into something so made.

(n) **Air miles or car fuel coupons** obtained as a result of business expenditure but used for private purposes.

(o) **The cost of work buses and minibuses or subsidies to public bus services**.

A works bus must have a seating capacity of 12 or more and a works minibus a seating capacity of 9 or more but not more than 12 and be available generally to employees of the employer concerned. The bus or minibus must mainly be used by employees for journeys to and from work and for journeys between workplaces.

(p) **Transport/overnight costs where public transport is disrupted by industrial action,** late night taxis and travel costs incurred where car sharing arrangements unavoidably breakdown.

(q) The private use of one **mobile phone**. Top up vouchers for exempt mobile phones are also tax free. If more than one mobile phone is provided to an employee for private use only the second or subsequent phone is a taxable benefit valued using 'cost of provision to the employer'.

(r) **Employer provided uniforms** which employees must wear as part of their duties.

(s) The cost of **staff parties** which are open to staff generally provided that the **cost per head per year (including VAT) is £150 or less**. The £150 limit may be split between several parties. If exceeded, the full amount is taxable, not just the excess over £150.

(t) **Private medical insurance premiums paid to cover treatment when the employee is outside the UK in the performance of his duties**. Other medical insurance premiums are taxable as is the cost of medical diagnosis and treatment except for routine check ups. Eye tests and glasses for employees using VDUs are exempt.

(u) **The first 15p per day of meal vouchers (eg luncheon vouchers).**

(v) **Cheap loans that do not exceed £5,000** at any time in the tax year (see above).

(w) **Job related accommodation** (see above).

(x) **Employer contributions towards additional household costs incurred by an employee who works wholly or partly at home**. Payments up to £3 pw (£156 pa) may be made without supporting evidence (see earlier in this Text).

(y) **Meals or refreshments for cyclists** provided as part of official 'cycle to work' days.

(z) **Personal incidental expenses** (see earlier in this Text).

Where a voucher is provided for a benefit which is exempt from income tax the provision of the voucher itself is also exempt.

5 P11D dispensations

As we have seen expense payments to P11D employees should be reported to HMRC. They form part of the employee's employment income and a claim must be made to deduct the expenses in computing net employment income.

To avoid this cumbersome procedure **the employer and HMRC can agree for a dispensation to apply to avoid the need to report expenses covered by the dispensation, and the employee then need not make a formal claim for a deduction.**

Dispensations can only apply to genuine business expenses. Some employers only reimburse business expenses, so that a dispensation may be agreed to cover all payments. Other employers may agree to cover a particular category of expenses, such as travel expenses.

A dispensation cannot be given for mileage allowances paid to employees using their own cars for business journeys as these payments are governed by a statutory exemption (see earlier in this Text).

6 The PAYE system

Most tax in respect of employment income is deducted under the PAYE system. The objective of the PAYE system is to collect the correct amount of tax over the year. An employee's PAYE code is designed to ensure that allowances etc are given evenly over the year.

6.1 Introduction

6.1.1 Cash payments

The objective of the PAYE system is to deduct the correct amount of tax over the year. Its scope is very wide. It applies to most cash payments, other than reimbursed business expenses, and to certain non cash payments.

In addition to wages and salaries, PAYE applies to round sum expense allowances and payments instead of benefits. It also applies to any readily convertible asset.

A readily convertible asset is any asset which can effectively be exchanged for cash. The amount subject to PAYE is the amount that would be taxed as employment income. This is usually the cost to the employer of providing the asset.

Tips paid direct to an employee are normally outside the PAYE system (although still assessable as employment income). An exception may apply in the catering trades where tips are often pooled. Here the PAYE position depends on whether a 'tronc', administered other than by the employer, exists.

It is the employer's duty to deduct income tax from the pay of his employees, whether or not he has been directed to do so by HMRC. **If he fails to do this he** (or sometimes the employee) **must pay over the tax which he should have deducted and the employer may be subject to penalties**. Interest will also run from 14 days after the end of the tax year concerned on any underpaid PAYE. Officers of HMRC can inspect employer's records in order to satisfy themselves that the correct amounts of tax are being deducted and paid over to HMRC.

6.1.2 Benefits

PAYE is not normally operated on benefits; instead the employee's PAYE code is restricted (see below).

However, PAYE must be applied to remuneration in the form of a taxable non-cash voucher if at the time it is provided:

(a)   the voucher is capable of being exchanged for readily convertible assets; or
(b)   the voucher can itself be sold, realised or traded.

PAYE must normally be operated on cash vouchers and on each occasion when a director/employee uses a credit-token (eg a credit card) to obtain money or goods which are readily convertible assets. However, a cash voucher or credit token which is used to defray expenses is not subject to PAYE.

6.2 How PAYE works

6.2.1 Operation of PAYE

To operate PAYE the employer needs:

(a)   deductions working sheets
(b)   codes for employees that reflect the tax allowances to which the employees are entitled
(c)   tax tables.

The employer works out the amount of PAYE tax to deduct on any particular pay day by using the employee's code number (see below) in conjunction with the PAYE tables. The tables are designed so that tax is normally worked out on a cumulative basis. This means that with each payment of earnings the running total of tax paid is compared with tax due on total earnings to that date. The difference between the tax due and the tax paid is the tax to be deducted on that particular payday.

National insurance tables are used to work out the national insurance due on any payday.

6.2.2 Records

The employer must keep records of each employee's pay and tax at each pay day. The records must also contain details of National Insurance. The employer has a choice of three ways of recording and returning these figures:

(a)   he may use the official deductions working sheet (P11)
(b)   he may incorporate the figures in his own pay records using a substitute document
(c)   he may retain the figures on a computer.

These records will be used to make a return at the end of the tax year.

6.3 Payment under the PAYE system

Under PAYE income tax and national insurance is normally paid over to HMRC monthly, 14 days after the end of each tax month.

If an employer's average monthly payments under the PAYE system are less than £1,500, the employer may choose to pay quarterly, within 14 days of the end of each tax quarter. Tax quarters end on 5 July, 5 October, 5 January and 5 April. Payments can continue to be made quarterly during a tax year even if the monthly average reaches or exceeds £1,500, but a new estimate must be made and a new decision taken to pay quarterly at the start of each tax year. Average monthly payments are the average net monthly payments due to HMRC for income tax and NICs.

6.4 PAYE codes

An employee is normally entitled to various allowances. Under the PAYE system an amount reflecting the effect of a proportion of these allowances is set against his pay each pay day. To determine the amount to set against his pay the allowances are expressed in the form of a code which is used in conjunction with the Pay Adjustment Table (Table A).

An employee's code may be any one of the following:

L   tax code with basic personal allowance
P   tax code with age 65-74 age allowance
Y   tax code with age 75+ age allowance

The codes BR, DO and OT are generally used where there is a second source of income and all allowances have been used in a tax code which is applied to the main source of income.

Generally, a tax code number is arrived at by deleting the last digit in the sum representing the employee's tax free allowances. Every individual is entitled to a personal tax free allowance of £6,475. The code number for an individual who is entitled to this but no other allowance is 647L.

The code number may also reflect other items. For example, **it will be restricted to reflect benefits, small amounts of untaxed income** and **unpaid tax on income from earlier years**. If an amount of tax is in point, it is necessary to gross up the tax in the code using the taxpayer's estimated marginal rate of income tax.

Question		PAYE codes

Adrian is a 40 year old single man (suffix letter L) who earns £15,000 pa. He has benefits of £560 and his unpaid tax for 2007/08 was £58. Adrian is entitled to a tax free personal allowance of £6,475 in 2009/10.

Adrian is a basic rate taxpayer.

What is Adrian's PAYE code for 2009/10?

	£
Personal allowance	6,475
Benefits	(560)
Unpaid tax £58 × 100/20	(290)
Available allowances	5,625

Adrian's PAYE code is 562L

Codes are determined and amended by HMRC. They are normally notified to the employer on a code list. The employer must act on the code notified to him until amended instructions are received from HMRC, even if the employee has appealed against the code.

By using the code number in conjunction with the tax tables, an employee is generally given 1/52nd or 1/12th of his tax free allowances against each week's/month's pay. However because of the cumulative nature of PAYE, if an employee is first paid in, say, September, that month he will receive six months' allowances against his gross pay. In cases where the employee's previous PAYE history is not known, this could lead to under-deduction of tax. To avoid this, codes for the employees concerned have to be operated on a 'week 1/month1' basis, so that only 1/52nd or 1/12th of the employee's allowances are available each week/month.

6.5 PAYE forms

FAST FORWARD

Employers must complete forms P60, P14, P35, P9D, P11D and P45 as appropriate. A P45 is needed when an employee leaves. Forms P9D and P11D record details of benefits. Forms P60, P14 and P35 are year end returns.

At the end of each tax year, the employer must provide each employee with a form P60. This shows total taxable earnings for the year, tax deducted, code number, NI number and the employer's name and address. **The P60 must be provided by 31 May following the year of assessment.**

Following the end of each tax year, the employer must submit to HMRC:

(a) **by 19 May**:

   (i) **End of year Returns P14** (showing the same details as the P60)
   (ii) **Form P35** (summary of total tax and NI deducted from all employees)

(b) **by 6 July**:

   (i) **Forms P11D** (benefits etc for directors and employees paid £8,500+ pa)
   (ii) **Forms P11D(b)** (return of Class 1A NICs (see later in this Text))
   (iii) **Forms P9D** (benefits etc for other employees)

A copy of the form P11D (or P9D) must also be provided to the employee by 6 July. The details shown on the P11D include the full cash equivalent of all benefits, so that the employee may enter the details on his self-assessment tax return. Specific reference numbers for the entries on the P11D are given to assist with the preparation of the employee's self assessment tax return.

When an employee leaves, a form P45 (particulars of Employee Leaving) must be prepared. This form shows the employee's code and details of his income and tax paid to date and is a four part form. One part is sent to HMRC, and three parts handed to the employee. One of the parts (part 1A) is the employee's personal copy.

If the employee takes up a new employment, he must hand the other two parts of the form P45 to the new employer. The new employer will fill in details of the new employment and send one part to HMRC, retaining the other. The details on the form are used by the new employer to calculate the PAYE due on the next payday. If the employee dies a P45 should be completed, and the whole form sent to HMRC.

If an employee joins with a form P45, the new employer can operate PAYE. If there is no P45 the employer still needs to operate PAYE. **The employee is required to complete a form P46**.

If he declares that the employment is his first job since the start of the tax year and he has not received a taxable state benefit, or that it is now his only job but he previously had another job or received a taxable state benefit, the emergency code (647L for 2009/10) applies, on a cumulative basis or week 1/month 1 basis respectively. If the employee declares that he has another job or receives a pension the employer must use code BR.

The P46 is sent to HMRC, unless the pay is below the PAYE and NIC thresholds, and the emergency code applies. In this case no PAYE is deductible until the pay exceeds the threshold.

6.6 Penalties

A form P35 is due on 19 May after the end of the tax year. In practice, a 7 day extension to the due date of 19 May is allowed.

Where a form P35 is late, a penalty of £100 per month per 50 employees may be imposed. This penalty cannot be mitigated. **This penalty ceases 12 months after the due date and a further penalty of up to 100% of the tax (and NIC) for the year which remains unpaid** at 19 April may be imposed. This penalty can be mitigated. HMRC automatically reduce the penalty by concession to the greater of £100 and the total PAYE/NIC which should be reported on the return.

Where a person has fraudulently or negligently submitted an incorrect form P35 the penalty is 100% of the tax (and NIC) attributable to the error. This penalty can be mitigated.

6.7 PAYE settlement agreements

PAYE settlement agreements (PSAs) are arrangements under which employers can make single payments to settle their employees' income tax liabilities on expense payments and benefits which are minor, irregular or where it would be impractical to operate PAYE.

Chapter Roundup

- Most employees are taxed on benefits under the benefits code. 'Excluded employees' (lower paid/non-directors) are only subject to part of the provisions of the code.

- The benefit in respect of accommodation is its annual value. There is an additional benefit if the property cost over £75,000.

- Employees who have a company car are taxed on a % of the car's list price which depends on the level of the car's CO_2 emissions. The same % multiplied by £16,900 determines the benefit where private fuel is also provided.

- Cheap loans are charged to tax on the difference between the official rate of interest and any interest paid by the employee.

- 20% of the value of assets made available for private use is taxable.

- There is a residual charge for other benefits, usually equal to the cost to the employer of the benefits.

- There are a number of exempt benefits including removal expenses, childcare, meal vouchers and workplace parking.

- Most tax in respect of employment income is deducted under the PAYE system. The objective of the PAYE system is to collect the correct amount of tax over the year. An employee's PAYE code is designed to ensure that allowances etc are given evenly over the year.

- Employers must complete forms P60, P14, P35, P9D, P11D and P45 as appropriate. A P45 is needed when an employee leaves. Forms P9D and P11D record details of benefits. Forms P60, P14 and P35 are year end returns.

Quick Quiz

1   What accommodation does not give rise to a taxable benefit?

2   Mike is provided with a petrol-engined car by his employer throughout 2009/10. The car has a list price of £15,000 (although the employer actually paid £13,500 for it) and has CO_2 emissions of 150g/km. Mike's taxable car benefit is:

    A   £2,430
    B   £2,700
    C   £4,050
    D   £4,500

3   When may an employee who is provided with a fuel by his employer avoid a fuel scale charge?

4   To what extent are removal expenses paid for by an employer taxable?

5   Give an example of a PAYE code.

Answers to Quick Quiz

1   Job related accommodation

2   B. Amount by which CO_2 emissions exceed the baseline is $(150 - 135)$ $= 15 \div 5 = 3 + 15\%$
                                                                                 $= 18\% \times £15,000$
                                                                                 $= £2,700$

3   There is no fuel scale charge if:

    (a)   All the fuel provided was made available only for business travel, or
    (b)   The full cost of any fuel provided for private use was completely reimbursed by the employee.

4   The first £8,000 of removal expenses are exempt. Any excess is taxable.

5   647L.

<table>
<tr><td colspan="4">Now try the question below from the Exam Question Bank</td></tr>
<tr><th>Number</th><th>Level</th><th>Marks</th><th>Time</th></tr>
<tr><td>Q5</td><td>Examination</td><td>15</td><td>27 mins</td></tr>
</table>

Pensions

Topic list	Syllabus reference
1 Types of pension scheme and membership	B6(a), (b)
2 Contributing to a pension scheme	B6(a), (b)
3 Receiving benefits from pension arrangements	B6(a), (b)

Introduction

In the previous two chapters we have discussed the taxation of employment income. Many employers offer their employees the option of joining an occupational pension scheme, and they may choose instead or in addition to take out a personal pension scheme run by a financial institution such as a bank or building society.

Self-employed or non-working individuals can only make provision for a pension using a personal pension scheme.

Whichever type of scheme is chosen the amount of tax relief available is calculated in the same way, and this is covered in this chapter. Note however that contributions to occupational schemes are usually deducted from gross pay before PAYE is calculated whilst contributions to personal pensions are paid net of basic rate tax.

Study guide

		Intellectual level
B6	**The use of exemptions and reliefs in deferring and minimising income tax liabilities**	
(a)	Explain and compute the relief given for contributions to personal pension schemes, using the rules applicable from 6 April 2006.	2
(b)	Describe the relief given for contributions to occupational pension schemes, using the rules applicable from 6 April 2006.	1

Exam guide

Pension contributions can be paid by all individuals and you may come across them as part of an income tax question. You may be required to discuss the types of pension schemes available and the limits on the tax relief due, or you may have to deal with them in an income tax computation. You must be sure that you know how to deal with the two ways of giving relief – contributions to occupational schemes are deducted from earnings whilst contributions to personal pensions are paid net of basic rate tax and higher rate tax relief is given by extending the basic rate band.

1 Types of pension scheme and membership

FAST FORWARD

> An employee may be a member of his employer's occupational pension scheme. Any individual whether a member of an occupational pension scheme or not, can take out a 'personal pension' plan with a financial institution such as an insurance company, bank or building society.

1.1 Introduction

An individual is encouraged by the Government to make financial provision to cover his needs when he reaches a certain age. There are state pension arrangements which provide some financial support, but the Government would prefer an individual to make his own pension provision.

Therefore tax relief is given for private pension provision. This includes relief for contributions to pension schemes and an exemption from tax on income and gains arising in a pension fund.

1.2 Pension arrangements

An individual may make pension provision in a number of ways.

1.2.1 Occupational pension scheme

Key term

> Employers may set up an **occupational pension scheme**. Such schemes may either require contributions from employees or be non-contributory. The employer may use the services of an insurance company (an insured scheme) or may set up a totally self administered pension fund.

There are two kinds of occupational pension scheme – earnings-related (**defined benefits arrangements**) and investment-related (**money purchase arrangements**). In a **defined benefits arrangements** – also known as a **final salary scheme** – the pension is generally based on employees' earnings at retirement and linked to the number of years they have worked for the firm.

A **money purchase pension** – also known as a **defined contribution scheme** – does not provide any guarantee regarding the level of pension which will be available. The individual invests in the pension scheme and the amount invested is used to build up a pension.

1.2.2 Personal pensions

Personal pensions are money purchase schemes, which are provided by banks, insurance companies and other financial institutions.

Stakeholder pensions are a particular type of personal pension scheme. They must satisfy certain rules, such as a maximum level of charges, ease of transfer etc.

Any individual (whether employed or not) may join a personal pension scheme.

1.2.3 More than one pension arrangement

An individual may make a number of different pension arrangements depending on his circumstances. For example, he may be a member of an occupational pension scheme and also make pension arrangements independently with a financial provider. If the individual has more than one pension arrangement, the rules we will be looking at in detail later apply to all the pension arrangements he makes. For example, **there is a limit on the amount of contributions that the individual can make in a tax year. This limit applies to all the pension arrangements that he makes, not *each* of them**.

The rules below apply to registered pension schemes, ie those registered with HMRC.

2 Contributing to a pension scheme

FAST FORWARD

Anyone can contribute to a personal pension scheme, even if they are not earning, subject to the contributions threshold of £3,600 (gross).

2.1 Contributions by a scheme member

Any individual **under the age of 75 can make tax relievable pension contributions** in a tax year.

The maximum amount of contributions attracting tax relief made by an individual in a tax year is the higher of:

(a)   **the individual's relevant UK earnings chargeable to income tax in the year; and**
(b)   **the basic amount (set at £3,600 for 2009/10).**

Relevant UK earnings are broadly employment income, trading income and income from furnished holiday lettings (see later in this Text).

If the individual does not have any UK earnings in a tax year, the maximum pension contribution he can obtain tax relief on is £3,600.

Where an individual contributes to more than one pension scheme, the aggregate of his contributions will be used to give the total amount of tax relief.

There is an interaction between this provision and the annual allowance, which will be discussed later.

2.2 Methods of giving tax relief

FAST FORWARD

Contributions to personal pension plans are paid net of basic rate tax. Higher rate relief is given through the personal tax computation. Contributions to occupational pension schemes are usually paid under the net pay scheme.

2.2.1 Pension tax relief given at source

This method will be used where an individual makes a contribution to a pension scheme run by a personal pension provider such as an insurance company.

Relief is given at source by the contributions being deemed to be made net of basic rate tax. This applies whether the individual is an employee, self-employed or not employed at all and whether or not he has taxable income. HMRC then pay an amount of basic rate tax to the pension provider.

Further tax relief is given if the individual is a higher rate taxpayer. The relief is given by increasing the basic rate band for the year by the gross amount of contributions for which he is entitled to relief. (You will recognise this as the same way in which relief is given for gift aid donations.)

Exam focus point

> Make sure your workings show clearly how you have extended the basic rate tax band. Note the difference between this method and that used for net pay arrangements (see below).

Question
Higher rate relief

Joe has earnings of £60,000 in 2009/10. He pays a personal pension contribution of £7,200 (net). He has no other taxable income.

Show Joe's tax liability for 2009/10.

Answer

	Non savings income £
Earnings/Net income	60,000
Less PA	(6,475)
Taxable income	53,525

Tax

	£
£37,400 × 20%	7,480
£9,000 (7,200 × 100/80) × 20%	1,800
£7,125 × 40%	2,850
53,525	12,130

2.2.2 Net pay arrangements

An occupational scheme will normally operate net pay arrangements.

In this case, the employer will deduct gross pension contributions from the individual's earnings before operating PAYE. The individual therefore obtains tax relief at his marginal rate of tax automatically.

Question
Net pay arrangements

Maxine has taxable earnings of £60,000 in 2009/10. Her employer deducts a pension contribution of £9,000 from these earnings before operating PAYE. She has no other taxable income.

Show Maxine's tax liability for 2009/10.

	Non-savings income £
Earnings/Total income	60,000
Less pension contribution	(9,000)
Net income	51,000
Less PA	(6,475)
Taxable income	44,525

Tax

	£
£37,400 × 20%	7,480
£7,125 × 40%	2,850
44,525	10,330

This is the same result as Joe in the previous example. Joe had received basic rate tax relief of £(9,000 – 7,200) = £1,800 at source, so his overall tax position was £(12,130 – 1,800) = £10,330.

2.3 Contributions not attracting tax relief

An individual can also make contributions to his pension arrangements which do not attract tax relief, for example out of capital. The member must notify the scheme administrator if he makes contributions in excess of the higher of his UK relevant earnings and the basic amount.

Such contributions do not count towards the annual allowance limit (discussed below) but will affect the value of the pension fund for the lifetime allowance.

2.4 Employer pension contributions

Where the individual is an employee, his **employer may make contributions to his pension scheme** as part of his employment benefits package. Such contributions are **exempt benefits** for the employee.

There is **no limit** on the amount of the contributions that may be made by an employer but **they always count towards the annual allowance** and will also affect the value of the pension fund for the lifetime allowance (see further below).

All contributions made by an employer are made gross and the employer will usually obtain tax relief for the contribution by deducting it as an expense in calculating trading profits for the period of account in which the payment is made.

2.5 Annual allowance

 FAST FORWARD

There is an overriding limit on the amount that can be paid into an individual's pension schemes for each tax year. This is called the annual allowance.

The **annual allowance** restricts the amount of tax relievable contributions that can be paid into an individual's pension scheme each year. The amount of the annual allowance for 2009/10 is **£245,000**.

If pension contributions exceed the annual allowance there is a charge to income tax on the individual on the excess at the rate of 40%.

BPP
LEARNING MEDIA

Question

For 2009/10 Freda has trading profits of £400,000 and made gross personal pension contributions of £280,000.

Calculate Freda's income tax liability for the year and state how she will obtain relief for the pension contributions she makes.

Answer

Freda has earnings of £400,000 for the tax year 2009/10. The contributions of £280,000 qualify for tax relief, and she will have paid £224,000 (£280,000 less 20%) to the pension company. Higher rate tax relief will be given by extending Freda's basic rate tax band for 2009/10 by £280,000. However, there will be a tax charge at the rate of 40% on the excess of contributions above the annual allowance of £245,000. Freda's income tax liability for the tax year 2009/10 is as follows:

	£
Trading profit	400,000
Personal allowance	(6,475)
Taxable income	393,525

		£
Income tax:	£37,400 × 20%	7,480
	£280,000 × 20% (extended band)	56,000
	£76,125 × 40%	30,450
		93,930
Excess contribution charge £35,000 (280,000 – 245,000) at 40%		14,000
Tax liability		107,930

2.6 Changes to tax relief for pension contributions from 2011/12

From 6 April 2011, income tax relief on pension contributions will be restricted for individuals with high incomes.

Between 22 April 2009 and 5 April 2011, individuals cannot take advantage of pension tax relief by making large additional pension contributions before the new rules take effect because of anti-forestalling rules which restrict tax relief on such contributions.

Exam focus point

> The examiner has stated that the anti-forestalling rules are not examinable and that students should therefore assume that in any examination question involving pension contributions that the contributions are not excessive and so will not fall under these rules.

3 Receiving benefits from pension arrangements

3.1 Pension benefits

Normally an individual may take one quarter of his pension fund as a tax free lump sum, and the balance as a pension. The benefits need not all be taken at one time, but may be phased over several years, but not beyond age 75.

3.2 The lifetime allowance

An individual is not allowed to build up an indefinitely large pension fund. There is a maximum value for a pension fund called the lifetime allowance.

The amount of the **lifetime allowance for 2009/10 is £1,750,000**.

If the pension fund exceeds the lifetime allowance at the time the benefit starts to be taken ('vested') this will give rise to an income tax charge on the excess value of the fund. The rate of the charge is 55% if the excess value is taken as a lump sum, or 25% if the funds are left in the scheme to provide a pension.

Chapter Roundup

- An employee may be a member of his employer's occupational pension scheme. Any individual whether a member of an occupational pension scheme or not, can take out a 'personal pension' plan with a financial institution such as an insurance company, bank or building society.

- Anyone can contribute to a personal pension scheme, even if they are not earning, subject to the contributions threshold of £3,600 (gross).

- Contributions to personal pension plans are paid net of basic rate tax. Higher rate relief is given through the personal tax computation. Contributions to occupational pension schemes are usually paid under the net pay scheme.

- There is an overriding limit on the amount that can be paid into an individual's pension schemes for each tax year. This is called the annual allowance.

- An individual is not allowed to build up an indefinitely large pension fund. There is a maximum value for a pension fund called the lifetime allowance.

Quick Quiz

1   Martha has UK earnings of £3,000 in 2009/10. What is the maximum actual amount of pension contribution she can pay in 2009/10 to a personal pension?

    A   £2,400
    B   £2,880
    C   £3,000
    D   £3,600

2   What are the consequences of the total of employee and employer pension contributions exceeding the annual allowance?

3   What are the consequences of exceeding the lifetime allowance?

Answers to Quick Quiz

1   B. The maximum gross contribution that Martha can pay is the higher of her relevant earnings (£3,000) and the basic amount (£3,600). She will actually pay £3,600 × 80% = £2,880 to the pension provider.

2   The excess is subject to the annual allowance charge on the employee at 40%.

3   If the lifetime allowance is exceeded the excess is charged at 55% (if taken as a lump sum) or 25% (if taken as a pension).

Now try the question below from the Exam Question Bank

Number	Level	Marks	Time
Q6	Introductory	7	13 mins
Q7	Examination	15	27 mins

Property income

Topic list	Syllabus reference
1 Property business income	B4(a)
2 Furnished holiday lettings	B4(b)
3 Rent a room relief	B4(c)
4 Premiums on leases	B4(d)
5 Property business losses	B4(e)

Introduction

We have finished looking at an individual's employment income and can turn our attention to other income to be slotted into the tax computation.

We are now going to look at the computation and taxation of the profits of a property letting business. First we see how to work out the profit (you may like to return to this section once you have studied chapters 7 and 8).

Next we look at the special conditions which must be satisfied if a letting is to be treated as a furnished holiday lettings and at the extra tax reliefs available if it is.

We then consider the special relief available to taxpayers who let out rooms in their own homes, rent a room relief.

Finally we see how part of a premium for granting a short lease is taxed as income.

In the following chapters we shall turn our attention to the profits of an actual trade, profession or vocation.

Study guide

		Intellectual level
B4	**The use of exemptions and reliefs in deferring and minimising income tax liabilities**	
(a)	Compute property business profits.	2
(b)	Explain the treatment of furnished holiday lettings.	1
(c)	Describe rent-a-room relief.	1
(d)	Compute the amount assessable when a premium is received for the grant of a short lease.	2
(e)	Understand how relief for a property business loss is given.	2

Exam guide

You are very likely to have to compute property income as part of question. You may find it in the context of income tax or corporation tax – the basic computational rules are the same (apart from interest paid which is not included as an expense for corporation tax purposes). Rent a room relief is an important relief for individuals (it does not apply to companies), and the special rules for furnished holiday lettings will only be examined in an income tax context. Remember that property income is non-savings income even though a property portfolio is usually regarded as an investment.

1 Property business income

FAST FORWARD
> Property business profits are calculated on an accruals basis.

1.1 Profits of a property business

Income from land and buildings in the UK is taxed as non-savings income.

The profits of the UK property business are computed for tax years. Each tax year's profit is taxed in that year.

1.2 Computation of profits

A taxpayer with UK rental income is treated as running a business, his 'UK property business'. All the rents and expenses for all properties are pooled, to give a single profit or loss. Profits and losses are computed in the same way as trading profits are computed for tax purposes, on an **accruals basis**.

Expenses will often include rent payable where a landlord is himself renting the land which he in turn lets to others. For individuals, interest on loans to buy or improve properties is treated as an expense (on an accruals basis).

Relief is available for irrecoverable rent as an impaired debt.

1.3 Capital allowances

FAST FORWARD
> If property is let furnished a wear and tear allowance may be claimed in respect of the furniture. Capital allowances are not available.

Capital allowances are given on plant and machinery used in the UK property business and on industrial buildings, in the same way as they are given for a trading business with an accounting date of 5 April. **Capital allowances are not normally available on plant or machinery used in a dwelling but someone who lets property furnished can instead claim the wear and tear allowance.**

Under the wear and tear basis, the actual cost of furniture is ignored. Instead, an annual allowance is given of **10% of rents**. The rents are first reduced by amounts which are paid by the landlord but are normally a tenant's burden. These amounts include any **water rates** and **council tax** paid by the landlord.

Question   Property business income

Over the last few years Pete has purchased several properties in Manchester as 'buy to let' investments.

5 Whitby Ave is let out furnished at £500 per month. A tenant moved in on 1 March 2009 but left unexpectedly on 1 May 2010 having paid rent only up to 31 December 2009. The tenant left no forwarding address.

17 Bolton Rd has been let furnished to the same tenant for a number of years at £800 per month.

A recent purchase, 27 Turner Close, has been let unfurnished since 1 August 2009 at £750 per month. Before then, it had been empty whilst Pete redecorated it after its purchase in March 2009.

Pete's expenses during 2009/10 are:

	No 5 £	No 17 £	No 27 £
Insurance	250	250	200
Letting agency fees	–	–	100
Repairs	300	40	–
Redecoration	–	–	500

No 27 was in a fit state to let when Pete bought it but he wanted to redecorate the property as he felt this would allow him to achieve a better rental income.

Water rates and council tax are paid by the tenants.

What is Pete's property business income for 2009/10?

Answer

	No 5 £	No 17 £	No 27 £
Accrued income			
12 × £500	6,000		
12 × £800		9,600	
8 × £750			6,000
Less:			
Insurance	(250)	(250)	(200)
Letting agency fees			(100)
Repairs	(300)	(40)	(500)
Impairment (irrecoverable rent) 3 × £500	(1,500)		
Wear and Tear Allowance			
£(6,000 – 1,500) × 10%	(450)		
£9,600 × 10%		(960)	
Property business income	3,500	8,350	5,200
Taxable property income for 2009/10			£17,050

2 Furnished holiday lettings

FAST FORWARD

Special rules apply to income from furnished holiday lettings. Whilst the income is taxed as normal as property business income, relief for losses is available as if they were trading losses. Capital allowances are available on the furniture, and the income is relevant earnings for pension purposes.

2.1 Introduction

There are special rules for furnished holiday lettings (FHLs). The letting is treated as if it were a trade. This means that, although the income is taxed as income from a property business, the provisions which apply to actual trades also apply to furnished holiday lettings, as follows:

(a)   Relief for losses is available as if they were trading losses, including the facility to set losses against other income. The usual property business loss reliefs do not apply (see below).

(b)   Capital allowances are available on furniture.

(c)   The income qualifies as relevant earnings for pension relief (see earlier in this Text).

(d)   Capital gains tax rollover relief, entrepreneurs' relief and relief for gifts of business assets are available (see later in this Text).

Note, however, that the basis period rules for trades do not apply, and the profits or losses must be computed for tax years.

2.2 Conditions

The letting must be of furnished accommodation made on a **commercial basis with a view to the realisation of profit**. The property must also satisfy the following three conditions.

(a)   **The availability condition** – the accommodation is available for commercial let as holiday accommodation to the public generally, for **at least 140 days during the year**.

(b)   **The letting condition** – the accommodation is commercially let as holiday accommodation to members of the public for **at least 70 days during the year**.

(c)   **The pattern of occupation condition** – **not more than 155 days in the year** fall during periods of longer term occupation. Longer term occupation is defined as **a continuous period of more than 31 days during which the accommodation is in the same occupation** unless there are abnormal circumstances.

If someone has furnished holiday lettings and other lettings, **draw up two profit and loss accounts as if they had two separate property businesses.** This is so that the profits and losses treated as trade profits and losses can be identified.

3 Rent a room relief

FAST FORWARD

Rents received from letting a room in the taxpayer's home may be tax free under the rent a room scheme.

3.1 The exemption

If an individual lets a room or rooms, furnished, in his or her main residence as living accommodation, then a special exemption may apply.

The limit on the exemption is gross rents (before any expenses or capital allowances) of £4,250 a year. This limit is halved if any other person (eg spouse/civil partner) also received income from renting accommodation in the property.

If gross rents are not more than the limit, the rents are wholly exempt from income tax and expenses are ignored. However, the taxpayer may claim to ignore the exemption, for example to generate a loss by taking into account both rent and expenses.

3.2 Alternative basis

If gross rents exceed the limit, the taxpayer will be taxed in the ordinary way, ignoring the rent a room scheme, unless he elects for the 'alternative basis'. If he so elects, he will be taxable on gross receipts less £4,250 (or £2,125 if the limit is halved), with no deductions for expenses.

An election to ignore the exemption or an election for the alternative basis must be made by the 31 January which is 22 months from the end of the tax year concerned. An election to ignore the exemption applies only for the tax year for which it is made, but an election for the alternative basis remains in force until it is withdrawn or until a year in which gross rents do not exceed the limit.

Question
Rent a room relief

Sylvia owns a house near the sea in Norfolk. She has a spare bedroom and during 2009/10 this was let to a chef working at a nearby restaurant for £85 per week which includes the cost of heating, lighting etc.

Sylvia estimates that her lodger costs her an extra:

£50 on gas
£25 on electricity
£50 on insurance

each year.

How much property income must Sylvia pay tax on?

Answer

Sylvia has a choice:

(1)   Total rental income of £85 × 52 = £4,420 exceeds £4,250 limit so taxable income is £170 (ie 4,420 − 4,250) if rent a room relief claimed.

(2)   Alternatively she can be taxed on her actual profit:

	£
Rental income	4,420
Less expenses (50 + 25 + 50)	(125)
	4,295

Sylvia would be advised to claim rent a room relief.

4 Premiums on leases

FAST FORWARD

A premium paid on the grant of a lease may be partly taxable as rent. If the premium is paid by a trader, a deduction can be made in computing taxable trading profits.

When a premium or similar consideration is received on the grant (that is, by a landlord to a tenant) **of a short lease (50 years or less), part of the premium is treated as rent received in the year of grant.**

The premium taxed as rent is the whole premium, less 2% of the premium for each complete year of the lease, except the first year.

This rule does not apply on the **assignment** of a lease (one tenant selling his entire interest in the property to another).

4.1 Example: income element of premium

Janet granted a lease to Jack on 1 March 2010 for a period of 40 years. Jack paid a premium of £16,000. How much of the premium received by Janet is taxed as rent received?

	£
Premium received	16,000
Less 2% × (40 −1) × £16,000	(12,480)
Taxable as rent received	3,520

Note that if Janet had **assigned** the lease, no part of the amount received would be taxed as rent received.

4.2 Premiums paid by traders

Where a trader pays a premium for a lease he may deduct an amount when computing his taxable trading profits in each year of the lease. The amount deductible is the figure treated as rent received by the landlord divided by the number of years of the lease. For example, suppose that B, a trader, pays A a premium of £30,000 for a ten year lease. A is treated as receiving £30,000 − (£30,000 × (10 − 1) × 2%) = £24,600. B can therefore deduct £24,600/10 = £2,460 in each of the ten years. He starts with the accounts year in which the lease starts and apportions the relief to the nearest month.

4.3 Premiums for granting subleases

A tenant may decide to sublet property and to charge a premium on the grant of a lease to the subtenant. This premium is treated as rent received in the normal way (because this is a grant and not an assignment, the original tenant retaining an interest in the property). **Where the tenant originally paid a premium for his own head lease, this deemed rent is reduced by:**

$$\text{Rent part of premium for head lease} \times \frac{\text{duration of sublease}}{\text{duration of head lease}}$$

If the relief exceeds the part of the premium for the sub-lease treated as rent (including cases where there is a sub-lease with no premium), the balance of the relief is treated as rent payable by the head tenant, spread evenly over the period of the sub-lease. This rent payable is an expense, reducing the overall property business profit.

Question   **Taxable premium received**

Charles granted a lease to David on 1 March 1999 for a period of 40 years. David paid a premium of £16,000. On 1 June 2009 David granted a sublease to Edward for a period of ten years. Edward paid a premium of £30,000. Calculate the amount treated as rent out of the premium received by David.

Answer

	£
Premium received by David	30,000
Less £30,000 × 2% × (10-1)	(5,400)
	24,600
Less allowance for premium paid	
(£16,000 − (£16,000 × 39 × 2%)) × 10/40	(880)
Premium treated as rent	23,720

You may wish to return to this section once you have covered trade profits in the next chapter.

5 Property business losses

A loss on a property letting business is carried forward to set against future property business profits.

A loss from a UK property business is carried forward to set against the **first future profits from the UK property business**. It may be carried forward until the UK property business ends, but it must be used as soon as possible.

As explained above, however, FHL losses are dealt with under the special rules that apply to trading losses (see later in this Text). Only if these are not claimed would a FHL loss be available to carry forward.

Chapter Roundup

- Property business profits are calculated on an accruals basis.

- If property is let furnished a wear and tear allowance may be claimed in respect of the furniture. Capital allowances are not available.

- Special rules apply to income from furnished holiday lettings. Whilst the income is taxed as normal as property business income, relief for losses is available as if they were trading losses. Capital allowances are available on the furniture, and the income is relevant earnings for pension purposes.

- Rents received from letting a room in the taxpayer's home may be tax free under the rent-a-room scheme.

- A premium paid on the grant of a lease may be partly taxable as rent. If the premium is paid by a trader, a deduction can be made in computing taxable trading profits.

- A loss on a property letting business is carried forward to set against future property business profits.

Quick Quiz

1   How is capital expenditure relieved for furnished lettings?

2   In order for property to be a furnished holiday letting it must be:

  (a)   available for letting for at least _____ days during the year; and

  (b)   actually let for at least _____ days during the year

  (c)   not let as longer term accommodation for more than _____ days in the year (longer term occupation is a continuous period of more than _____ days in the same occupation). Fill in the blanks.

3   How much income per annum is tax free under the rent a room scheme?

  A   £2,125
  B   £4,250
  C   £4,500
  D   £6,475

Answers to Quick Quiz

1   Except for furnished holiday lettings where capital allowances are available for the cost of furniture, capital expenditure on furnishings is relieved through the wear and tear allowance. The allowance is equal to 10% of rents less council tax and water rates.

2   In order for property to be a furnished holiday letting it must be:

   (a)   available for letting for at least 140 days during the year; and

   (b)   actually let for at least 70 days during the year

   (c)   not let as longer term accommodation for more than 155 days in the year (longer term occupation is a continuous period of more than 31 days in the same occupation).

3   B. £4,250

| Now try the questions below from the Exam Question Bank | | | |
Number	Level	Marks	Time
Q8	Examination	15	27 mins

7

Computing trading income

Topic list	Syllabus reference
1 The badges of trade	B3(b)
2 The adjustment of profits	B3(c)
3 Pre-trading expenditure	B3(d)

Introduction

The final figure to slot into the income tax computation is income from self employment.

We are therefore going to look at the computation of profits of unincorporated businesses. We work out a business's profit as if it were a separate entity (the separate entity concept familiar to you from basic bookkeeping) but, as an unincorporated business has no legal existence apart from its trader, we cannot tax it separately. We have to feed its profit into the proprietor's personal tax computation.

Later chapters will consider capital allowances, which are allowed as an expense in the computation of profits, the taxation of business profit, and how trading losses can be relieved. We will then extend our study to partnerships, ie to groups of two or more individuals trading together.

Study guide

		Intellectual level
B3	**Income from self-employment**	
(b)	Describe and apply the badges of trade.	2
(c)	Recognise the expenditure that is allowable in calculating the tax-adjusted trading profit.	2
(d)	Recognise the relief that can be obtained for pre-trading expenditure.	2

Exam guide

You are likely to have to compute trading profits at some point in the exam. The computation may be for an individual, a partnership or a company. In each case the same principles are applied. You must however watch out for the adjustments which only apply to individuals, such as private use expenses.

1 The badges of trade

FAST FORWARD

The badges of trade are used to decide whether or not a trade exists. If one does exist, the accounts profits need to be adjusted in order to establish the taxable profits.

Key term

A trade is defined in the legislation only in an unhelpful manner as including every trade, manufacture, adventure or concern in the nature of a trade. It has therefore been left to the courts to provide guidance. This guidance is summarised in a collection of principles known as the **'badges of trade'**. These are set out below. They apply to both corporate and unincorporated businesses.

Exam focus point

You are not expected to know case names – we have included these below for your information only. The rules relating to trades apply equally to all professions and vocations.

1.1 The subject matter

Whether a person is trading or not may sometimes be decided by examining the subject matter of the transaction. Some assets are commonly held as investments for their intrinsic value: an individual buying some shares or a painting may do so in order to enjoy the income from the shares or to enjoy the work of art. A subsequent disposal may produce a gain of a capital nature rather than a trading profit. But **where the subject matter of a transaction is such as would not be held as an investment** (for example 34,000,000 yards of aircraft linen (*Martin v Lowry 1927*) or 1,000,000 rolls of toilet paper (*Rutledge v CIR 1929*)), **it is presumed that any profit on resale is a trading profit.**

1.2 The frequency of transactions

Transactions which may, in isolation, be of a capital nature will be interpreted as trading transactions where their **frequency indicates the carrying on of a trade**. It was decided that whereas normally the purchase of a mill-owning company and the subsequent stripping of its assets might be a capital transaction, where the taxpayer was embarking on the same exercise for the fourth time he must be carrying on a trade (*Pickford v Quirke 1927*).

1.3 The length of ownership

The courts may infer adventures in the nature of trade where **items purchased are sold soon afterwards**.

1.4 Supplementary work and marketing

When work is done to make an asset more marketable, or steps are taken to find purchasers, the courts will be more ready to ascribe a trading motive. When a group of accountants bought, blended and recasked a quantity of brandy they were held to be taxable on a trading profit when the brandy was later sold (*Cape Brandy Syndicate v CIR 1921*).

1.5 A profit motive

The absence of a profit motive will not necessarily preclude a tax charge as trading income, but its presence is a strong indication that a person is trading. The purchase and resale of £20,000 worth of silver bullion by the comedian Norman Wisdom, as a hedge against devaluation, was held to be a trading transaction (*Wisdom v Chamberlain 1969*).

1.6 The way in which the asset sold was acquired

If goods are acquired deliberately, trading may be indicated. If goods are acquired unintentionally, for example by gift or inheritance, their later sale is unlikely to be trading.

1.7 The taxpayer's intentions

Where a transaction is clearly trading on objective criteria, **the taxpayer's intentions are irrelevant**. If, however, a transaction has (objectively) a dual purpose, the taxpayer's intentions may be taken into account. An example of a transaction with a dual purpose is the acquisition of a site partly as premises from which to conduct another trade, and partly with a view to the possible development and resale of the site.

This test is not one of the traditional badges of trade, but it may be just as important.

2 The adjustment of profits

FAST FORWARD

The net profit in the profit and loss account must be adjusted to find the taxable trading profit.

2.1 Illustrative adjustment

Although the **net profit before taxation** shown in the accounts is the starting point in computing the taxable trade profits, many adjustments may be required to calculate the taxable amount.

Here is an illustrative adjustment.

		£	£
Net profit per accounts			140,000
Add:	expenditure charged in the accounts which is not deductible from trading profits	50,000	
	income taxable as trading profits which has not been included in the accounts	30,000	
			80,000
			220,000
Less:	profits included in the accounts but which are not taxable trading profits	40,000	
	expenditure which is deductible from trading profits but has not been charged in the accounts	20,000	
			(60,000)
Profit adjusted for tax purposes			160,000

You may refer to deductible and non-deductible expenditure as allowable and disallowable expenditure respectively. The two sets of terms are interchangeable.

An examination question requiring adjustment to profit will direct you to start the adjustment with the net profit per accounts of £XXXX and deal with all the items listed indicating with a zero (0) any items which do not require adjustment. Marks will not be given for relevant items unless this approach is used. Therefore students who attempt to rewrite the profit and loss account will be penalised.

2.2 Accounting policies

The fundamental concept is that the profits of the business must be calculated in accordance with generally accepted accounting practice. These profits are subject to any adjustment specifically required for income tax purposes.

2.3 Deductible and non-deductible expenditure

FAST FORWARD

Disallowable (ie non-deductible) expenditure must be added back to the accounts profit in the computation of the taxable trading profit. Any item not deducted wholly and exclusively for trade purposes is disallowable expenditure. Certain other items, such as depreciation, are specifically disallowable.

2.3.1 Introduction

Certain expenses are specifically disallowed by the legislation. These are covered below. If however a deduction is specifically permitted this overrides the disallowance.

2.3.2 Payments contrary to public policy and illegal payments

Fines and penalties are not deductible. However, **HMRC usually allow employees' parking fines incurred in parking their employer's cars while on their employer's business. Fines relating to traders, however, are never allowed.**

A payment is not deductible if making it constitutes an offence by the payer. This covers protection money paid to terrorists, and also bribes. Statute also prevents any deduction for payments made in response to blackmail or extortion.

2.3.3 Capital expenditure

Capital expenditure is not deductible. This denies a deduction for depreciation or amortisation. The most contentious items of expenditure will often be repairs (revenue expenditure) **and improvements** (capital expenditure).

- The cost of restoration of an asset by, for instance, replacing a subsidiary part of the asset is revenue expenditure. Expenditure on a new factory chimney replacement was allowable since the chimney was a subsidiary part of the factory (*Samuel Jones & Co (Devondale) Ltd v CIR 1951*). However, in another case a football club demolished a spectators' stand and replaced it with a modern equivalent. This was held not to be repair, since repair is the restoration by renewal or replacement of subsidiary parts of a larger entity, and the stand formed a distinct and *separate* part of the club (*Brown v Burnley Football and Athletic Co Ltd 1980*).

- The cost of initial repairs to improve an asset recently acquired to make it fit to earn profits is disallowable capital expenditure. In *Law Shipping Co Ltd v CIR 1923* the taxpayer failed to obtain relief for expenditure on making a newly bought ship seaworthy prior to using it.

- The cost of initial repairs to remedy normal wear and tear of recently acquired assets is allowable. *Odeon Associated Theatres Ltd v Jones 1971* can be contrasted with the *Law Shipping* judgement. Odeon were allowed to charge expenditure incurred on improving the state of recently acquired cinemas.

Capital allowances may, however, be available as a deduction for capital expenditure from trading profits (see later in this Text).

Two exceptions to the 'capital' rule are worth noting.

(a)   The costs of **registering patents and trade marks** are deductible.

(b)   **Incidental costs of obtaining loan finance**, or of attempting to obtain or redeeming it, are deductible other than a discount on issue or a premium on redemption (which are really alternatives to paying interest).

2.3.4 Expenditure not wholly and exclusively for the purposes of the trade

Expenditure is not deductible if it is not for trade purposes (the remoteness test), or if it reflects more than one purpose (the duality test). The private proportion of payments for motoring expenses, rent, heat and light and telephone expenses of a trader is not deductible. If an exact apportionment is possible relief is given on the business element. Where the payments are to or on behalf of employees, the full amounts are deductible but the employees are taxed under the benefits code (see earlier in this Text).

The remoteness test is illustrated by the following cases.

*   *Strong & Co of Romsey Ltd v Woodifield 1906*
    A customer injured by a falling chimney when sleeping in an inn owned by a brewery claimed compensation from the company. The compensation was not deductible: 'the loss sustained by the appellant was not really incidental to their trade as innkeepers and fell upon them in their character not of innkeepers but of householders'.

*   *Bamford v ATA Advertising Ltd 1972*
    A director misappropriated £15,000. The loss was not allowable: 'the loss is not, as in the case of a dishonest shop assistant, an incident of the company's trading activities. It arises altogether outside such activities'.

*   Expenditure which is wholly and exclusively to benefit the trades of several companies (for example in a group) but is not wholly and exclusively to benefit the trade of one specific company is not deductible *(Vodafone Cellular Ltd and others v Shaw 1995)*.

*   *McKnight (HMIT) v Sheppard (1999)* concerned expenses incurred by a stockbroker in defending allegations of infringements of Stock Exchange regulations. It was found that the expenditure was incurred to prevent the destruction of the taxpayer's business and that as the expenditure was incurred for business purposes it was deductible. It was also found that although the expenditure had the effect of preserving the taxpayer's reputation, that was not its purpose, so there was no duality of purpose.

The **duality test** is illustrated by the following cases.

*   *Caillebotte v Quinn 1975*
    A self-employed carpenter spent an average of 40p per day when obliged to buy lunch away from home but just 10p when he lunched at home. He claimed the excess 30p. It was decided that the payment had a dual purpose and was not deductible: a taxpayer 'must eat to live not eat to work'.

*   *Mallalieu v Drummond 1983*
    Expenditure by a lady barrister on black clothing to be worn in court (and on its cleaning and repair) was not deductible. The expenditure was for the dual purpose of enabling the barrister to be warmly and properly clad as well as meeting her professional requirements.

*   *McLaren v Mumford 1996*
    A publican traded from a public house which had residential accommodation above it. He was obliged to live at the public house but he also had another house which he visited regularly. It was held that the private element of the expenditure incurred at the public house on electricity, rent, gas, etc was not incurred for the purpose of earning profits, but for serving the non-business purpose of satisfying the publican's ordinary human needs. The expenditure, therefore had a dual purpose and was disallowed.

However, the cost of overnight accommodation when on a business trip may be deductible and reasonable expenditure on an evening meal and breakfast in conjunction with such accommodation is then also deductible.

2.3.5 Impaired trade receivables (bad debts)

Only impairment debts incurred wholly and exclusively for the purposes of the trade are deductible for taxation purposes. Thus loans to employees written off are not deductible unless the business is that of making loans, or it can be shown that the writing-off of the loan was earnings paid out for the benefit of the trade. If a trade debt is released as part of a voluntary arrangement under the Insolvency Act 1986, or a compromise or arrangement under s 425 Companies Act 1985, the amount released is deductible as an impaired debt.

Under FRS 26 Financial Instruments: measurement, a review of all trade receivables should be carried out to assess their fair value at the balance sheet date, and any impairment debts written off. As a specific provision, no adjustment to the accounts profit is needed for impairment review.

2.3.6 Unpaid remuneration and employee benefit contributions

If earnings for employees are charged in the accounts but are not paid within nine months of the end of the period of account, the cost is only deductible for the period of account in which the earnings are paid. When a tax computation is made within the nine month period, it is initially assumed that unpaid earnings will not be paid within that period. The computation is adjusted if they are so paid.

Earnings are treated as paid at the same time as they are treated as received for employment income purposes.

Similar rules apply to employee benefit contributions.

2.3.7 Entertaining and gifts

The general rule is that expenditure on entertaining and gifts is non-deductible. This applies to amounts reimbursed to employees for specific entertaining expenses and gifts, and to round sum allowances which are exclusively for meeting such expenses.

There are specific exceptions to the general rule:

- **Entertaining for and gifts to employees are normally deductible** although where gifts are made, or the entertainment is excessive, a charge to tax may arise on the employee under the benefits legislation.
- **Gifts to customers not costing more than £50 per donee per year are allowed if they carry a conspicuous advertisement for the business and are not food, drink, tobacco or vouchers exchangeable for goods.**
- **Gifts to charities may also be allowed** although many will fall foul of the 'wholly and exclusively' rule above. If a gift aid declaration is made in respect of a gift, tax relief will be given under the gift aid scheme, not as a trading expense.

2.3.8 Lease charges for cars with CO_2 emissions exceeding 160g/km

There is a restriction on the leasing costs of a car with CO_2 emissions exceeding 160 g/km. 15% of the leasing costs will be disallowed in the calculation of taxable profits.

2.3.9 Patent royalties and copyright royalties

Patent royalties and copyright royalties paid in connection with an individual's trade are deductible as trading expenses.

2.3.10 National insurance contributions

No deduction is allowed for any national insurance contributions **except for employer's contributions**. For your exam, these are Class 1 secondary contributions and Class 1A contributions (see later in this Text).

2.3.11 Penalties and interest on tax

Penalties and interest on late paid tax are not allowed as a trading expense. For the purpose of your exam, tax includes income tax, capital gains tax and VAT.

2.3.12 Appropriations

Salary or interest on capital paid to a trader are not deductible. A salary paid to a member of the trader's family is allowed as long as it is not excessive in respect of the work performed by that family member.

The private proportion of payments for motoring expenses, rent, heat and light and telephone expenses of a trader is not deductible. Where the payments are to or on behalf of employees, the full amounts are deductible but are taxed on the employees as benefits for income tax.

Payments of the trader's income tax and national insurance contributions are not deductible.

Question	Adjusted taxable trade profits

Here is the profit and loss account of John Dodd, a trader.

PROFIT AND LOSS ACCOUNT FOR THE YEAR ENDED 31 MAY 2009

	£	£
GROSS OPERATING PROFIT		30,000
Less: wages and salaries	7,000	
rent and rates	2,000	
depreciation	1,500	
motor expenses – cars owned by business	5,000	
motor expenses – cost of leased car CO_2 emissions 170g/km	2,000	
entertainment expenses – customers	750	
office expenses	1,350	
		(19,600)
NET PROFIT		10,400

You ascertain the following:

(a)   Salaries include £1,000 paid to John Dodd's wife who works part time in the business.

(b)   Motor expenses on cars owned by the business are £3,000 for John Dodd's car used 20% privately and £2,000 for his part-time salesman's car used 40% privately. There is no private use on the leased car.

(c)   There are also capital allowances of £860.

Compute the adjusted taxable trade profit for the year ended 31 May 2009. You should start with the net profit figure of £10,400 and indicate by the use of zero (0) any items which do not require adjustment.

ADJUSTED PROFIT COMPUTATION: John Dodd
YEAR TO 31 MAY 2009

		£	£
Net profit			10,400
Add:	wages and salaries	0	
	rents and rates	0	
	depreciation	1,500	
	trader private motor expenses (£3,000 × 20%)	600	
	leased car cost disallowed (£2,000 × 15%)	300	
	entertainment expenses - customers	750	
	office expenses	0	
			3,150
			13,550
Deduct:	capital allowances		(860)
Adjusted trading profit			12,690

Note. The employee's private motor expenses are allowable for the trader but the provision of the car will be taxed on the employee as an income tax benefit. The salary paid to John Dodd's wife is allowed as it is reasonable remuneration for the work actually done.

2.3.13 Subscriptions and donations

The general 'wholly and exclusively' rule determines the deductibility of expenses. Subscriptions and donations are not deductible unless the expenditure is for the benefit of the trade. The following are the main types of subscriptions and donations you may meet and their correct treatments.

- Trade subscriptions (such as to a professional or trade association) are generally deductible.
- Charitable donations are deductible only if they are small and to local charities.
- Political subscriptions and donations are generally not deductible.
- When a business makes a gift of equipment manufactured, sold or used in the course of its trade to an educational establishment or for a charitable purpose, nothing need be brought into account as a trading receipt.

2.3.14 Legal and professional charges

Legal and professional charges relating to capital or non-trading items are not deductible. These include charges incurred in acquiring new capital assets or legal rights, issuing shares, drawing up partnership agreements and litigating disputes over the terms of a partnership agreement.

Professional charges are deductible if they relate directly to trading. Deductible items include:

- Legal and professional charges incurred defending the taxpayer's title to fixed assets
- Charges connected with an action for breach of contract
- Expenses of the **renewal** (not the original grant) of a lease for less than 50 years
- Charges for trade debt collection
- Normal charges for preparing accounts/assisting with the self assessment of tax liabilities

Accountancy expenses arising out of an enquiry into the accounts information in a particular year's return are not allowed where the enquiry reveals discrepancies and additional liabilities for the year of enquiry, or any earlier year, which arise as a result of negligent or fraudulent conduct.

Where, however, the enquiry results in no addition to profits, or an adjustment to the profits for the year of enquiry only and that assessment does not arise as a result of negligent or fraudulent conduct, the additional accountancy expenses are allowable.

2.3.15 Interest

Interest paid by an individual on borrowings for trade purposes is deductible as a trading expense on an accruals basis, so no adjustment to the accounts figure is needed.

Individuals cannot deduct interest on overdue tax.

2.3.16 Miscellaneous deductions

Here is a list of various other items that you may meet.

Item	Treatment	Comment
Educational courses for staff	Allow	
Educational courses for trader	Allow	If to update existing knowledge or skills, not if to acquire new knowledge or skills
Removal expenses (to new business premises)	Allow	Only if not an expansionary move
Travelling expenses to the trader's place of business	Disallow	*Ricketts v Colquhoun 1925*: unless an itinerant trader (*Horton v Young 1971*)
Counselling services for employees leaving employment	Allow	If qualify for exemption from employment income charge on employees
Pension contributions (to schemes for employees and company directors)	Allow	If paid, not if only provided for; special contributions may be spread over the year of payment and future years
Premiums for insurance: • against an employee's death or illness • to cover locum costs or fixed overheads whilst the policyholder is ill	Allow	Receipts are taxable
Damages paid	Allow	If not too remote from trade: *Strong and Co v Woodifield 1906*
Improving an individual's personal security	Allow	Provision of a car, ship or dwelling is excluded

2.4 Income taxable as trading income but excluded from the accounts

The usual example is when a trader takes goods for his own use. In such circumstances the selling price of the goods if sold in the open market is added to the accounting profit. If the trader pays anything for the goods, this is left out of the account. In other words, the trader is treated for tax purposes as having made a sale to himself. This rule does not apply to supplies of services, which are treated as sold for the amount (if any) actually paid (but the cost of services to the trader or his household is not deductible).

2.5 Accounting profits not taxable as trading income

FAST FORWARD

Receipts not taxable as trading profit must be deducted from the accounts profit. For example, rental income and interest received are not taxable as trading profit. The rental income is taxed instead as property business income, whilst the interest is taxed as savings income.

There are three types of receipts which may be found in the accounting profits but which must be excluded from the taxable trading profit computation. These are:

(a) **Capital receipts**
(b) **Income taxed in another way** (at source or as another type of income)
(c) **Income specifically exempt from tax**

However, compensation received in one lump sum for the loss of income is likely to be treated as income (*Donald Fisher (Ealing) Ltd v Spencer 1989*).

Income taxed as another type of income, for example rental income, is excluded from the computation of taxable trading profits but it is brought in again further down in the computation as property business income. Similarly capital receipts are excluded from the computation of taxable trading profits but they may be included in the computation of chargeable gains (see later in this Text).

2.6 Deductible expenditure not charged in the accounts

FAST FORWARD

Amounts not charged in the accounts that are deductible from trading profits must be deducted when computing the taxable trading income. An example is capital allowances.

Capital allowances (see the next chapter) are an example of deductible expenditure not charged in the accounts.

A second example is **an annual sum which can be deducted by a trader that has paid a lease premium to a landlord who is taxable on the premium as property business income** (see earlier in this Text).

Normally, the amortisation of the lease will have been deducted in the accounts and must be added back as an appropriation of profit.

Question		Adjustment of profits

Here is the profit and loss account of S Pring, a trader.

	£	£
Gross operating profit		30,000
Taxed interest received		860
		30,860
Wages and salaries	7,000	
Rent and rates	2,000	
Depreciation	1,500	
Impairment of trade receivables	150	
Entertainment expenses for customers	750	
Patent royalties paid (gross)	1,200	
Bank interest paid (gross)	300	
Legal expenses on acquisition of new factory	250	
		(13,150)
Net profit		17,710

Salaries include £500 paid to Mrs Pring who works full time in the business.

Compute the taxable trade profits. You should start with the net profit figure of £17,710 and indicate by the use of zero (0) any items which do not require adjustment.

	£	£
Profit per accounts		17,710
Add: wages and salaries	0	
rent and rates	0	
depreciation	1,500	
impairment of trade receivables	0	
entertainment expenses for customers	750	
patent royalties	0	
bank interest paid	0	
legal expenses (capital)	250	
		2,500
		20,210
Less interest received (to tax as taxed income)		(860)
Taxable trading profit		19,350

3 Pre-trading expenditure

Pre-trading expenditure incurred within the seven years prior to the commencement of trade is allowable if it would have been allowable had the trade already started.

Expenditure incurred before the commencement of trade is deductible, if it is incurred within seven years of the start of trade and it is of a type that would have been deductible had the trade already started. **It is treated as a trading expense incurred on the first day of trading**.

Chapter Roundup

- The badges of trade are used to decide whether or not a trade exists. If one does exist, the accounts profits need to be adjusted in order to establish the taxable profits.

- The net profit in the profit and loss account must be adjusted to find the taxable trading profit.

- Disallowable (ie non-deductible) expenditure must be added back to the accounts profit in the computation of the taxable trading profit. Any item not deducted wholly and exclusively for trade purposes is disallowable expenditure. Certain other items, such as depreciation, are specifically disallowable.

- Receipts not taxable as trading profit must be deducted from the accounts profit. For example, rental income and interest received are not taxable as trading profit. The rental income is taxed instead as property business income, whilst the interest is taxed as savings income.

- Amounts not charged in the accounts that are deductible from trading profits must be deducted when computing the taxable trading income. An example is capital allowances.

- Pre-trading expenditure incurred within the seven years prior to the commencement of trade is allowable if it would have been allowable had the trade already started.

Quick Quiz

1   List the traditional badges of trade.

2   What are the remoteness test and the duality test?

3   No adjustment for taxation is required to the accounts for deduction of a trader's salary. TRUE/FALSE?

4   Pre-trading expenditure is deductible if it is incurred within _____ years of the start of trade and is of a type that would have been deductible if the trade had already started. Fill in the blank.

Answers to Quick Quiz

1   The subject matter
    The frequency of transactions
    The length of ownership
    Supplementary work and marketing
    A profit motive
    The way in which the goods were acquired

2   Expenditure is not deductible if it is not for trade purposes (the remoteness test), or if it reflects more than one purpose (the duality test).

3   False. The trader's salary must be added back as it is an appropriation of profits.

4   Pre-trading expenditure is deductible if it is incurred within seven years of the start of the trade and is of a type that would have been deductible if the trade had already started.

Now try the questions below from the Exam Question Bank

Number	Level	Marks	Time
Q9	Examination	15	27 mins

Capital allowances

Topic list	Syllabus reference
1 Capital allowances in general	B3(g)
2 Plant and machinery – qualifying expenditure	B3(g)(i)
3 Main pool	B3(g)(ii), (iii), (iv)
4 Special rate pool	B3(g)(iii), (vi)
5 Private use assets	B3(g)(ii), (iv)
6 Motor cars	B3(g)(iii)
7 Short life assets	B3(g)(v)
8 Industrial buildings allowance	B3(g)(vii), (viii)

Introduction

We saw in the last chapter that depreciation cannot be deducted in computing taxable trade profits and that capital allowances are given instead. In this chapter, we look at the rules for calculating capital allowances, starting with plant and machinery.

Our study of plant and machinery falls into three parts. Firstly, we look at what qualifies for allowances: many business assets obtain no allowances at all. Secondly, we see how to compute the allowances and lastly, we look at special rules for assets with short and long lives and features integral to a building such as heating systems.

We then look at industrial buildings. Again, we start off by looking at what qualifies for the allowances and then how to compute the allowances.

You may wish to return to this chapter while you are studying Chapter 18 on companies.

Study guide

		Intellectual level
B3	**Income from self-employment**	
(g)	Capital allowances	
(i)	Define plant and machinery for capital allowances purposes.	1
(ii)	Compute writing down allowances and the annual investment allowance.	2
(iii)	Compute capital allowances for motor cars.	2
(iv)	Compute balancing allowances and balancing charges.	2
(v)	Recognise the treatment of short life assets.	2
(vi)	Explain the treatment of assets included in the special rate pool.	2
(vii)	Define an industrial building for industrial buildings allowance purposes.	1
(viii)	Compute industrial buildings allowance for new buildings.	2

Exam guide

You may have to answer a whole question on capital allowances or a capital allowances computation may be included as a working in a computation of taxable trading profits. The computation may be for either income tax or corporation tax purposes; the principle is basically the same. Look out for private use assets; only restrict the capital allowances if there is private use by **proprietors**, never restrict capital allowances for private use by **employees**. Also watch out for the length of the period of account; you may need to scale WDAs up (income tax only) or down (income tax or corporation tax).

1 Capital allowances in general

FAST FORWARD

Capital allowances are available to give tax relief for certain capital expenditure.

Capital expenditure may not be deducted in computing taxable trade profits, but it *may* attract capital allowances. Capital allowances are treated as a trading expense and are deducted in arriving at taxable trade profits. Balancing charges, effectively negative allowances, are added in arriving at those profits.

Capital expenditure on plant and machinery qualifies for capital allowances. Expenditure on industrial buildings may also qualify for allowances.

Both in incorporated businesses and companies are entitled to capital allowances. For completeness, in this chapter we will look at the rules for companies alongside those for unincorporated businesses. We will look at companies in more detail later in this Text.

For unincorporated businesses, capital allowances are calculated for periods of account. These are simply the periods for which the trader chooses to make up accounts. For companies, capital allowances are calculated for accounting periods (see later in this Text).

For capital allowances purposes, expenditure is generally deemed to be incurred when the obligation to pay becomes unconditional. This will often be the date of a contract, but if for example payment is due a month after delivery of a machine, it would be the date of delivery. However, amounts due more than four months after the obligation becomes unconditional are deemed to be incurred when they fall due.

2 Plant and machinery – qualifying expenditure

FAST FORWARD There are various statutory rules on what does or does not qualify as plant.

2.1 Definition of plant and machinery

Capital expenditure on plant and machinery qualifies for capital allowances if the plant or machinery is used for a qualifying activity, such as a trade. 'Plant' is not fully defined by the legislation, although some specific exclusions and inclusions are given. The word 'machinery' may be taken to have its normal everyday meaning.

2.2 The statutory exclusions

2.2.1 Buildings

Expenditure on a building and on any asset which is incorporated in a building or is of a kind normally incorporated into buildings does not qualify as expenditure on plant, but see below for exceptions.

In addition to complete buildings, **the following assets count as 'buildings', and are therefore not plant**.

- Walls, floors, ceilings, doors, gates, shutters, windows and stairs
- Mains services, and systems, of water, electricity and gas
- Waste disposal, sewerage and drainage systems
- Shafts or other structures for lifts etc

2.2.2 Structures

Expenditure on structures and on works involving the alteration of land **does not qualify as expenditure on plant**, but see below for exceptions.

A 'structure' is a fixed structure of any kind, other than a building.

2.2.3 Exceptions

Over the years a large body of case law has been built up under which plant and machinery allowances have been given on certain types of expenditure which might be thought to be expenditure on a building or structure. Statute therefore gives a list of various assets which *may* still be plant. These include:

- Any machinery not within any other item in this list
- Electrical (including lighting), cold water, gas and sewerage systems:
    - Provided mainly to meet the particular requirements of the trade, or
    - Provided mainly to serve particular machinery or plant used for the purposes of the trade
- Space or water heating systems and powered systems of ventilation
- Manufacturing and display equipment
- Cookers, washing machines, refrigeration or cooling equipment, sanitary ware and furniture and furnishings
- Lifts etc
- Sound insulation provided mainly to meet the particular requirements of the trade
- Computer, telecommunication and surveillance systems
- Sprinkler equipment, fire alarm and burglar alarm systems
- Partition walls, where movable and intended to be moved
- Decorative assets provided for the enjoyment of the public in the hotel, restaurant or similar trades; advertising hoardings
- Movable buildings intended to be moved in the course of the trade
- Expenditure on altering land for the purpose only of installing machinery or plant

Items falling within the above list of exclusions will only qualify as plant if they fall within the meaning of plant as established by case law. This is discussed below.

2.2.4 Land

Land or an interest in land does not qualify as plant and machinery. For this purpose 'land' excludes buildings, structures and assets which are installed or fixed to land in such a way as to become part of the land for general legal purposes.

2.2.5 Computer software

Capital expenditure on computer software (both programs and data) **normally qualifies as expenditure on plant and machinery.**

2.3 Case law

FAST FORWARD

> There are also cases on the definition of plant. To help you to absorb them, try to see the function/setting theme running through them.

Exam focus point

> In this chapter we mention the names of cases where it was decided what was or wasn't 'plant'. You are **not** expected to know the names of cases for your examination. We have included them for your information only.

The original case law **definition of plant** (applied in this case to a horse) is **'whatever apparatus is used by a businessman for carrying on his business: not his stock in trade which he buys or makes for sale; but all goods and chattels, fixed or movable, live or dead, which he keeps for permanent employment in the business'** (*Yarmouth v France 1887*).

Subsequent cases have refined the original definition and have largely been concerned with the **distinction between plant actively used in the business (qualifying) and the setting in which the business is carried on (non-qualifying). This is the 'functional' test.** Some of the decisions have now been enacted as part of statute law, but they are still relevant as examples of the principles involved.

A barrister succeeded in his claim for his law library: 'Plant includes a man's tools of his trade. It extends to what he uses day by day in the course of his profession. It is not confined to physical things like the dentist's chair or the architect's table' (*Munby v Furlong 1977*).

Office partitioning was allowed. Because it was movable it was not regarded as part of the setting in which the business was carried on (*Jarrold v John Good and Sons Ltd 1963*) (actual item now covered by statute).

At a motorway service station, false ceilings contained conduits, ducts and lighting apparatus. **They did not qualify because they did not perform a function in the business. They were merely part of the setting in which the business was conducted** (*Hampton v Fortes Autogrill Ltd 1979*).

Similarly, it has been held that when an attractive floor is provided in a restaurant, the fact that the floor performs the function of making the restaurant attractive to customers is not enough to make it plant. It functions as premises, and the cost therefore does not qualify for capital allowances (*Wimpy International Ltd v Warland 1988*).

Conversely, light fittings, decor and murals can be plant. A company carried on business as hoteliers and operators of licensed premises. The function of the items was the creation of an atmosphere conducive to the comfort and well being of its customers (*CIR v Scottish and Newcastle Breweries Ltd 1982*) (decorative assets used in hotels etc, now covered by statute).

General lighting in a department store is not plant, as it is merely setting. Special display lighting, however, can be plant (*Cole Brothers Ltd v Phillips 1982*).

3 The main pool

FAST FORWARD

With capital allowances computations, the main thing is to get the layout right. Having done that, you will find that the figures tend to drop into place.

3.1 Main pool expenditure

Most expenditure on plant and machinery is put into a pool of expenditure (the main pool) on which capital allowances may be claimed, including cars with CO_2 emissions of 160g/km or less acquired on or after 6 April 2009 (1 April 2009 for companies). An addition increases the pool whilst a disposal decreases it.

Exceptionally the following items are not put into the main pool:
(a)   assets dealt with in the special rate pool
(b)   assets with private use by the trader
(c)   short life assets where an election has been made.

These exceptions are dealt with later in this Chapter.

Expenditure on plant and machinery by a person about to begin a trade is treated as incurred on the first day of trading. Assets previously owned by a trader and then brought into the trade (at the start of trading or later) are treated as bought for their market values at the times when they are brought in.

3.2 Annual investment allowance

FAST FORWARD

Businesses are entitled to an Annual Investment Allowance (AIA) of £50,000 for a 12 month period of account.

Businesses can claim an **Annual Investment Allowance (AIA) on the first £50,000 spent on plant or machinery**, including assets in the main pool, but not including motor cars. Expenditure on motorcycles does qualify for the AIA.

Where the period of account is more or less than a year, the maximum allowance is proportionately increased or reduced.

Main pool expenditure which qualifies for the AIA but is in excess of £50,000 will qualify for a first year allowance if the expenditure is made between 6 April 2009 and 5 April 2010 (1 April 2009 and 31 March 2010 for companies) (see further below).

If there is no first year allowance available on the excess expenditure, for example if the expenditure is made in March 2009 or in May 2011, the balance of expenditure after the AIA is transferred to the main pool immediately and will be eligible for writing down allowances in the same period.

3.3 First year allowances

FAST FORWARD

A first year allowance (FYA) at the rate of 40% is available on the balance of expenditure on plant and machinery (excluding cars and special rate pool expenditure) not covered by the Annual Investment Allowance. A FYA at the rate of 100% is available on low emission cars. FYAs are never pro-rated in short periods of account.

3.3.1 FYA on plant and machinery

There is a temporary first year allowance (FYA) of 40% available on expenditure on most plant and machinery between 6 April 2009 and 5 April 2010 (between 1 April 2009 and 31 March 2010 for companies). Expenditure on motor cars and assets in the special rate pool (see further below) does not qualify for this FYA.

The FYA is applied after the AIA. Any remaining balance will be added to the main pool.

It is important to note that the remaining balance after applying the FYA is transferred to the main pool AFTER writing down allowances have been calculated. This is because the temporary FYA is given instead of writing down allowances.

3.3.2 FYA on low emission cars

A low emission car is one which has **CO_2 emissions of 110g/km or less**.

A 100% FYA is available for expenditure incurred on low emission motor cars registered between 17 April 2002 and 31 March 2013.

If the FYA is not claimed in full, the balance of expenditure is transferred to the main pool.

In the exam you will be given a car's CO_2 emissions. You will not be told whether it is low emission.

3.3.3 Short periods of account

FYAs are not reduced pro-rata in a short period of account, unlike the AIA and writing down allowances.

3.4 Writing down allowances

Expenditure on plant and machinery in the main pool qualifies for a WDA at 20% every 12 months.

A **writing down allowance (WDA)** is given on main pool expenditure **at the rate of 20% a year** (on a reducing balance basis). The WDA is calculated on the tax written down value (TWDV) of pooled plant, after adding the current period's additions and taking out the current period's disposals.

When plant is sold, **proceeds, limited to a maximum of the original cost,** are taken out of the pool. Provided that the trade is still being carried on, the pool balance remaining is written down in the future by WDAs, even if there are no assets left.

3.5 Example

Elizabeth has tax written down value on her main pool of plant and machinery of £16,000 on 6 April 2009. In the year to 5 April 2010 she bought a car with CO_2 emissions of 130g/km for £8,000 (no non-business use) and she disposed of plant which originally cost £4,000 for £6,000.

Calculate the maximum capital allowances claim for the year.

	Main pool £	Allowances £
TWDV b/f	16,000	
Addition (not qualifying for AIA or FYA)	8,000	
Less disposal (limited to cost)	(4,000)	
	20,000	
WDA @ 20%	(4,000)	4,000
TWDV c/f	16,000	
Maximum capital allowances claim		4,000

Question

Julia is a sole trader making up accounts to 5 April each year. At 5 April 2009, the tax written down value on her main pool is £20,000.

In the year to 5 April 2010, Julia bought the following assets:

1 June 2009	Machine	£40,000
12 November 2009	Van	£17,500
10 February 2009	Car for salesman (CO_2 emissions 150g/km)	£9,000

She disposed of plant on 15 December 2009 for £12,000 (original cost £16,000).

Calculate the maximum capital allowances claim that Julia can make for the year ended 5 April 2010.

Answer

	AIA/FYA £	Main pool £	Allowances £
y/e 5 April 2010			
TWDV b/f		20,000	
Additions qualifying for AIA/FYA			
1.6.09 Machine	40,000		
12.11.09 Van	17,500		
	57,500		
AIA	(50,000)		50,000
	7,500		
FYA @ 40%	(3,000)		3,000
Additions not qualifying for AIA/FYA			
10.2.10 Car		9,000	
Disposal			
15.12.09 Plant		(12,000)	
		17,000	
WDA @ 20%		(3,400)	3,400
		13,600	
Transfer balance to pool	(4,500)	4,500	
TWDV c/f		18,100	
Maximum capital allowances			56,400

Question

Marcus is a sole trader making up accounts to 31 December each year. At 1 January 2009, the tax written down value on his main pool is £30,000.

In the year to 31 December 2009, Marcus bought the following assets:

1 February 2009	Plant	£60,000
15 September 2009	Machinery	£22,500

He made no disposals in the year to 31 December 2009.

Calculate the maximum capital allowances claim that Marcus can make for the year ended 31 December 2009.

	AIA/FYA £	Main pool £	Allowances £
y/e 31 December 2009			
TWDV b/f		30,000	
Additions qualifying for AIA only (N1)			
1.2.09 Machinery	60,000		
AIA	(50,000)		50,000
	10,000		
Transfer balance to pool	(10,000)	10,000	
		40,000	
Additions qualifying for AIA/FYA (N2)			
15.9.09 Plant	22,500		
FYA @ 40%	(9,000)		9,000
	13,500		
WDA @ 20%		(8,000)	8,000
		32,000	
Transfer balance to pool	(13,500)	13,500	
TWDV c/f		45,500	
Maximum capital allowances			67,000

Notes

1. The best use of the AIA is to set it against expenditure which only qualifies for this allowance and not for the FYA, thus leaving excess expenditure eligible for the FYA @ 40% instead of the WDA @ 20%.

2. Technically this expenditure is eligible for both these allowances, although in this case the AIA has already been used as explained in note 1. You may have a situation where there not all of the AIA has been used up against expenditure only qualifying for the AIA. You would deal with the remaining AIA in the same way as in the previous example by setting it off against expenditure qualifying for both the AIA and FYA before applying the FYA.

3.6 Short and long periods of account

WDAs are 20% × number of months/12:

(a) For unincorporated businesses where the period of account is longer or shorter than 12 months

(b) For companies where the accounting period is shorter than 12 months (a company's accounting period for tax purposes is never longer than 12 months), or where the trade concerned started in the accounting period and was therefore carried on for fewer than 12 months. Remember that we will be studying companies in detail later in this Text.

Venus is a sole trader and has made up accounts to 30 April each year. At 30 April 2009, the tax written down value of her main pool was £80,000. She decides to make up her next set of accounts to 31 December 2009.

In the period to 31 December 2009, the following acquisitions were made:

1 May 2009	Plant	£60,000
10 July 2009	Car (CO_2 emissions 130 g/km)	£9,000
3 August 2009	Car (CO_2 emissions 105 g/km)	£11,000

Venus disposed of plant on 1 November 2009 for £20,000 (original cost £28,000).

Calculate the maximum capital allowances that Venus can claim for the period ending 31 December 2009.

Answer

	AIA/FYA @ 40%	FYA @ 100%	Main pool	Allowances
	£	£	£	£
p/e 31 December 2009				
TWDV b/f			80,000	
Additions qualifying for AIA and FYA				
1.5.09 Plant	60,000			
AIA £50,000 × 8/12	(33,333)			33,333
	26,667			
FYA on balance @ 40%	(10,667)			10,667
Additions qualifying for FYA only				
3.8.09 Car (low emission)		11,000		
Less: 100% FYA		(11,000)		11,000
Additions not qualifying for AIA or FYA				
10.7.09 Car			9,000	
Disposals				
1.11.09 Plant			(20,000)	
			69,000	
WDA @ 20% × 8/12			(9,200)	9,200
			59,800	
Transfer balance to pool	(16,000)		16,000	
Transfer balance to pool		0	0	
TWDVs c/f			75,800	
Maximum allowances claim				64,200

Note that the annual investment allowance and the writing down allowance are reduced for the short period of account, but the first year allowance is given in full.

Oscar started trading on 1 July 2009 and made up his first set of accounts to 31 December 2010. He bought the following assets:

10 July 2009	Plant	£60,000
10 October 2009	Car for business use only (CO_2 emissions 140g/km)	£11,000
12 February 2010	Plant	£80,000

Calculate the maximum capital allowances claim that Oscar can make for the period ended 31 December 2010.

	AIA/FYA £	Main pool £	Allowances £
p/e 31 December 2010			
Additions qualifying for AIA/FYA			
10.7.09 Plant	60,000		
12.2.10 Plant	80,000		
	140,000		
AIA £50,000 × 18/12	(75,000)		75,000
	65,000		
FYA @ 40%	(26,000)		26,000
Additions not qualifying for AIA/FYA			
1.10.09 Car		11,000	
WDA @ 20% × 18/12		(3,300)	3,300
		7,700	
Transfer balance to main pool	(39,000)	39,000	
TWDV c/f		46,700	
Maximum capital allowances			104,300

Note that the annual investment allowance and the writing down allowance are increased for the long period of account, but the first year allowance is not increased.

3.7 Small balance on main pool

A writing down allowance equal to unrelieved expenditure in the main pool can be claimed where this is **£1,000 or less**. If the maximum WDA is claimed, the main pool will then have a nil balance carried forward.

Question   **Small balance on main pool**

Alan has traded for many years, making up accounts to 30 April each year. At 1 May 2009, the tax written down value of his main pool was £15,000. On 1 October 2009, he sold some plant and machinery for £14,200 (original cost £16,000).

Calculate the maximum capital allowances claim that Alan can make for the period ending 30 April 2010.

Answer

	Main pool £	Allowances £
y/e 30 April 2010		
TWDV b/f	15,000	
Disposal	(14,200)	
	800	
WDA (small pool)	(800)	800
TWDV c/f	nil	
Maximum capital allowances		800

Note the tax planning opportunities available. If plant is bought just before an accounting date, allowances become available as soon as possible. Alternatively, it may be desirable to claim less than the maximum allowances to even out annual taxable profits and avoid a higher rate of tax in later years.

3.8 Balancing charges and allowances

Balancing charges occur when the disposal value deducted exceeds the balance remaining in the pool. The charge equals the excess and is effectively a negative capital allowance, increasing profits. Most commonly this happens when the trade ceases and the remaining assets are sold. It may also occur, however, whilst the trade is still in progress.

Balancing allowances on the main and special pools of expenditure arise only when the trade ceases. The balancing allowance is equal to the remaining unrelieved expenditure after deducting the disposal value of all the assets. Balancing allowances may also arise on single pool items (see below) whenever those items are disposed of.

4 Special rate pool

The special rate pool contains expenditure on thermal insulation, long life assets, features integral to a building and cars with CO_2 emissions over 160g/km. The AIA can be used against such expenditure except cars. The WDA is 10%.

4.1 Operation of the special rate pool

Expenditure on thermal insulation, long life assets, features integral to a building, and cars with CO_2 emissions over 160g/km acquired on or after 6 April 2009 (1 April 2009 for companies), is not dealt with in the main pool but in a special rate pool.

The Annual Investment Allowance can apply to expenditure on such assets except on cars. The taxpayer can decide how to allocate the AIA. It will be more tax efficient to set the allowance against special rate pool expenditure in priority to main pool expenditure where there is expenditure on assets in both pools in the period. Expenditure in excess of the AIA is added to the special rate pool and will be eligible for writing down allowance in the same period in which the expenditure is incurred.

The writing down allowance for the special rate pool is 10% for a twelve month period. As with the writing down allowance on the main pool, this is adjusted for short and long periods of account.

Where the tax written down balance of the special rate pool is £1,000 or less, a writing down allowance can be claimed of up to £1,000. This is in addition to any similar claim in relation to the main pool.

4.2 Long life assets

Key term

Long life assets are assets with an expected working life of 25 years or more.

The **long life asset rules only apply to businesses whose total expenditure on assets with an expected working life of 25 years or more in a chargeable period is more than £100,000**. If the expenditure exceeds £100,000, the whole of the expenditure enters the special rate pool. For this purpose all expenditure incurred under a contract is treated as incurred in the first chargeable period to which that contract relates.

The £100,000 limit is reduced or increased proportionately in the case of a chargeable period of less or more than 12 months.

The following are **not** treated as long life assets:

(a) **Plant and machinery in dwelling houses, retail shops, showrooms, hotels and offices**
(b) **Cars**

4.3 Integral features

Features which are integral to a building include the following:

- **electrical and lighting systems**
- **cold water systems**
- **space or water heating systems**
- **powered systems of ventilation, cooling or air conditioning**
- **lifts and escalators**

When a building is sold, the vendor and purchaser can make a joint election to determine how the sale proceeds are apportioned between the building and its integral features.

4.4 Example

Lucy has been trading for many years, making up accounts to 5 April each year. The tax written down value of her main pool at 5 April 2009 was £110,000. In the year to 5 April 2010, Lucy had the following expenditure:

10 June 2009	General plant costing £45,000
12 December 2009	Lighting system in shop £40,000
15 January 2010	Car for business use only (CO_2 emissions 175 g/km) £25,000
26 January 2010	Delivery van £15,000
4 March 2010	Lifts £20,000

The maximum capital allowances claim that Lucy can make for the year to 5 April 2010 is:

		AIA/FYA £	Main pool £	Special rate pool £	Allowances £
y/e 5 April 2010					
TWDV b/f			110,000		
Additions qualifying for AIA only					
12.12.09	Lighting	40,000			
4.3.10	Lifts	20,000			
		60,000			
AIA		(50,000)			50,000
Transfer balance to special rate pool		10,000		10,000	
c/f				10,000	50,000
Additions qualifying for FYA (AIA already used)					
10.6.09	Plant	45,000			
26.1.10	Van	15,000			
		60,000			
FYA @ 40%		(24,000)			24,000
Additions not qualifying for AIA/FYA					
15.1.10	Car			25,000	
				35,000	
WDA @ 20%			(22,000)		22,000
WDA @ 10%				(3,500)	3,500
			88,000		
Transfer balance to main pool		36,000	36,000		
TWDVs c/f			124,000	31,500	
Allowances					99,500

5 Private use assets

An asset which is used privately by a trader is dealt with in a single asset pool and the capital allowances are restricted.

An asset which is used partly for private purposes by a sole trader or a partner is put into its own pool (single asset pool).

Capital allowances are calculated on the full cost. However, only the business use proportion of the allowances is allowed as a deduction from trading profits. This restriction applies to the AIA, FYAs, WDAs, balancing allowances and balancing charges.

An asset with some private use by an employee (not the owner of the business) suffers no such restriction. The employee may be taxed under the benefits code (see earlier in this Text) so the business receives capital allowances on the full cost of the asset.

Exam focus point

Capital allowances on assets with some private use is a common exam topic. Check carefully whether the private use is by the owner of the business or by an employee.

Question — Capital allowances on private use asset

Jacinth has been in business as a sole trader for many years, making up accounts to 31 March. On 1 November 2009 she bought computer equipment for £2,700 which she uses 75% in her business and 25% privately. She has already used the AIA against other expenditure in the year to 31 December 2009.

Calculate the maximum capital allowance that Jacinth can claim in respect to the computer equipment in the year to 31 March 2010 and the year to 31 March 2011.

Answer

	Computer equipment £	Allowances @ 75% £
y/e 31 March 2010		
Acquisition	2,700	
FYA @ 40%	(1,080)	810
TWDV c/f	1,620	
Maximum capital allowance on computer equipment		810
y/e 31 March 2011		
WDA @ 20%	(324)	243
TWDV c/f	1,296	
Maximum capital allowance on computer equipment		243

6 Motor cars

6.1 Motor cars acquired before April 2009

Motor cars acquired before 6 April 2009 (1 April 2009 for companies) which cost more than £12,000 are dealt with in a single asset pool. The maximum WDA on such cars is £3,000 for a 12 month period.

Each motor car acquired before 6 April 2009 (1 April 2009 for companies) which cost more than £12,000 (sometimes called 'expensive' cars) is dealt with in a single asset pool. This means that a separate record of allowances and WDV is kept for each such car and when it is sold a balancing allowance or charge arises.

Expensive cars are eligible for writing down allowances at 20% regardless of their CO_2 emissions. However, the maximum WDA is £3,000 a year. The limit is £3,000 × months/12 in periods of account which are not 12 months long.

Motor cars acquired before 6 April 2009 which cost £12,000 or less were pooled in the main pool, unless there was private use by a sole trader or partner.

Question

Cars acquired before April 2009

Niall is a sole trader making up accounts to 5 April each year. His business already owns four cars, used only for business purposes:

Car 1: This car was acquired for £24,000 and had a tax written down value at 6 April 2009 of £18,000. The car has CO_2 emissions of 150g/km.

Car 2: This car cost £19,000 and had a tax written down value at 6 April 2009 of £13,000. The car has CO_2 emissions of 180g/km.

Car 3: This car cost £15,000 and had a tax written down value at 6 April 2009 of £9,000. The car has CO_2 emissions of 140g/km. It was sold on 10 December 2009 for £7,500.

Car 4: This car cost £9,000. It is included in the main pool which had a total tax written down value at 6 April 2009 of £33,000. The car has CO_2 emissions of 120g/km. It was sold on 10 March 2010 for £6,600.

There were no acquisition and no other disposals of assets in the year ended 5 April 2010.

Calculate the maximum capital allowances that Niall can claim for the year ended 5 April 2010.

Answer

	Main pool	Car 1	Car 2	Car 3	Allowances
	£	£	£	£	£
y/e 5 April 2010					
TWDVs b/f	33,000	18,000	13,000	9,000	
Disposals					
10.12.09 Car 3				(7,500)	
Balancing allowance				1,500	1,500
10.3.10 Car 4	(6,600)				
	26,400				
WDA @ 20%	(5,280)				5,280
WDA @ 20% (max)		(3,000)			3,000
WDA @ 20%			(2,600)		2,600
TWDVs c/f	21,120	15,000	10,400		
Maximum allowances claim					12,380

Notes

1. The writing down allowance for Car 3 is 20% even though it has CO_2 emissions of 180g/km. This is because it was acquired before 6 April 2009. If it had been acquired on or after 6 April 2009, it would only have been eligible for a writing down allowance of 10% (see further below).

2. The disposal of Car 4 does not result in a balancing event because it is part of the main pool. Contrast this treatment with the disposal of Car 3 which does lead to a balancing allowance.

A motor car with private use by a sole trader or partner is always dealt with in a single asset pool, regardless of cost. Such cars acquired before 6 April 2009 will be eligible for writing down allowances at 20%, subject to a maximum of £3,000 per year. Only the business use proportion of the allowances is allowed as a deduction from trading profit, but the full allowance is deducted in calculating the car's tax written down value carried forward.

6.2 Motor cars acquired from April 2009

FAST FORWARD

Motor cars acquired from 6 April 2009 (1 April 2009 for companies) are generally dealt with in the special rate pool (cars emitting over 160g/km) or the main pool, unless there is private use by the trader.

As we have already seen, motor cars acquired from 6 April 2009 (1 April 2009 for companies) are categorised in accordance with their CO_2 emissions:

(a) **Cars emitting over 160g/km**: expenditure is added to the special rate pool,

(b) **Cars emitting between 111 and 160 g/km**: expenditure is added to the main pool,

(c) **Cars emitting 110 g/km or less**: expenditure eligible for 100% first year allowance, if allowance not claimed in full, excess added to main pool.

Cars with an element of private use continue to be kept separate from the main and special pools and are dealt with in single asset pools. They are entitled to a WDA of 20% (car with CO_2 emissions between 111 and 160 g/km) or 10% (car with CO_2 emissions over 160 g/km). There is no maximum WDA for such cars.

Question   Capital allowances on private use car

Quodos started to trade on 1 July 2009, making up accounts to 31 December 2009 and each 31 December thereafter. On 1 August 2009 he bought a car for £17,000 with CO_2 emissions of 130 g/km. The private use proportion is 10%. The car was sold in July 2012 for £4,000. Calculate the capital allowances, assuming:

(a) The car was used by an employee, or
(b) The car was used by Quodos.

Answer

(a)

	Car £	Allowances £
1.7.09 – 31.12.09		
Purchase price	17,000	
WDA 20% × 6/12 x £17,000	(1,700)	1,700
	15,300	
1.1.10 – 31.12.10		
WDA 20% x £15,300	(3,060)	3,060
	12,240	
1.1.11 – 31.12.11		
WDA 20% x £12,240	(2,448)	2,448
	9,792	
1.1.12 – 31.12.12		
Proceeds	(4,000)	
Balancing allowance	5,792	5,792

The private use of the car by the employee has no effect on the capital allowances due to Quodos.

(b)

	Car	Allowances 90%
	£	£
1.7.09 – 31.12.09		
Purchase price	17,000	
WDA 20% × 6/12 x £17,000	(1,700)	1,530
	15,300	
1.1.10 – 31.12.10		
WDA 20% x £15,300	(3,060)	2,754
	12,240	
1.1.11 – 31.12.11		
WDA 20% x £12,240	(2,448)	2,203
	9,792	
1.1.12 – 31.12.12		
Proceeds	(4,000)	
Balancing allowance	5,792	5,213

As the private use is by the proprietor, Quodos, only 90% of the WDAs and balancing allowance are available.

6.3 Motor cars: summary table

	Main pool WDA @ 20%	Special rate pool WDA @ 10%	Single asset pool WDA @ 20%	Single asset pool WDA @ 10%
Car acquired before 6.4.09 (1.4.09 for companies)				
Cost less than £12,000, no private use	•			
Cost £12,000 or more, no private use			• max £3,000	
Cost less than £12,000, private use (sole trader or partner only)			•	
Cost £12,000 or more, private use (sole trader or partner only)			• max £3,000	
Car acquired on or after 6.4.09 (1.4.09 for companies)				
CO_2 emissions 111g/km – 160g/km, no private use	•			
CO_2 emissions over 160g/km, no private use		•		
CO_2 emissions 111g/km – 160g/km, private use (sole trader or partner only)			•	
CO_2 emissions over 160g/km, private use (sole trader or partner only)				•

7 Short life assets

FAST FORWARD

Short life asset elections can bring forward the allowances due on an asset.

A trader can elect that specific items of plant be kept separately from the main pool. The election is irrevocable. For an unincorporated business, the time limit for electing is the 31 January which is 22 months after the end of the tax year in which the period of account of the expenditure ends. (For a company, it is two years after the end of the accounting period of the expenditure.) **Any asset subject to this election is known as a 'short life asset', and the election is known as a 'de-pooling election'.**

Key term

Provided that the asset is disposed of within four years of the end of the accounting period in which it was bought, it is a short life asset and a balancing charge or allowance arises on its disposal.

If the asset is not disposed of within this time period, its tax written down value is added to the main pool at the end of that time. Short life asset treatment cannot be claimed for any motor cars, or plant used partly for non-trade purposes.

The election should be made for assets likely to be sold for less than their tax written down values within four years. It should not usually be made for assets likely to be sold within four years for more than their tax written down values.

The Annual Investment Allowance can be set against short life assets. The taxpayer can decide how to allocate the AIA. It will be more tax efficient to set the allowance against main pool expenditure in priority to short life asset expenditure. The FYA is also available for short life assets where relevant.

Question

Short life assets

Caithlin bought a machine for business use on 1 May 2009 for £12,000 and elected for de-pooling. She did not claim the AIA in respect of this asset. Her accounting year end is 30 April. Calculate the capital allowances due if:

(a) The asset is scrapped for £300 in August 2013.
(b) The asset is scrapped for £200 in August 2014.

Answer

		£
(a)	*Year to 30.4.10*	
	Cost	12,000
	FYA 40%	(4,800)
		7,200
	Year to 30.4.11	
	WDA 20%	(1,440)
		5,760
	Year to 30.4.12	
	WDA 20%	(1,152)
		4,608
	Year to 30.4.13	
	WDA 20%	(922)
		3,686
	Year to 30.4.14	
	Disposal proceeds	(300)
	Balancing allowance	3,386

(b)   If the asset is still in use at 30 April 2014, WDAs up to 30.4.13 will be as above. In the year to 30.4.14, a WDA can be claimed of 20% × £3,686 = £737. The tax written down value of £3,686 – £737 = £2,949 will be added to the main pool at the beginning of the next period of account. The disposal proceeds of £200 will be deducted from the main pool in that period's capital allowances computation. No balancing allowance will arise and the main pool will continue.

8 Industrial buildings allowance

FAST FORWARD

Industrial buildings allowance can be claimed in respect of expenditure on buildings in industrial use such as factories.

Exam focus point

Remember, you do not need to know the case names below. They are included for information only.

8.1 General definition

A special type of capital allowance (an **industrial buildings allowance** or IBA) is available in respect of **expenditure on industrial buildings**. It is being phased out and will be abolished from 2010/11.

The allowance is available to traders and to landlords who let qualifying buildings to traders.

Key term

Industrial buildings include:

(a)   All factories and ancillary premises used in:

(i)   A manufacturing business
(ii)   A trade in which goods and materials are subject to any process
(iii)   A trade in which goods or raw materials are stored

(b)   Staff welfare buildings (such as workplace nurseries and canteens, but not directors' restaurants) where the trade is qualifying

(c)   Sports pavilions in any trade

(d)   Buildings in use for a transport undertaking, agricultural contracting, mining or fishing

(e)   Roads operated under highway concessions. The operation of such roads is treated as a trade for capital allowances purposes. The operator is treated as occupying the roads.

The key term in (a) (ii) above is 'the subjection of goods to any process'.

- The unpacking, repacking and relabelling of goods in a wholesale cash and carry supermarket did not amount to a 'process' but was a mere preliminary to sale (*Bestway Holdings Ltd v Luff 1998*).

- The mechanical processing of cheques and other banking documents was a process but pieces of paper carrying information were not 'goods' and thus the building housing the machinery did not qualify (*Girobank plc v Clarke 1998*).

Estate roads on industrial estates qualify, provided that the estate buildings are used wholly or mainly for a qualifying purpose.

Dwelling houses, retail shops, showrooms and general offices are not industrial buildings. Drawing offices (is those used for technical product and manufacturing planning) which serve an industrial building are regarded as industrial buildings themselves (*CIR v Lambhill Ironworks Ltd 1950*).

Warehouses used for storage often cause problems in practice. A warehouse used for storage which is merely a transitory and necessary incident of the conduct of the business is not an industrial building. Storage is only a qualifying purpose if it is an end in itself.

Any building is an industrial building if it is constructed for the welfare of employees of a trader whose trade is a qualifying one (that is, the premises in which the trade is carried on are industrial buildings). Sports pavilions provided for the welfare of employees qualify as industrial buildings. In this case, it does not matter whether the taxpayer is carrying on a trade in a qualifying building or not. Thus a retailer's sports pavilion would qualify for IBAs.

8.2 Hotels

Allowances on hotels are given as though they were industrial buildings.

For a building to qualify as a '**hotel**' for industrial buildings allowance purposes:

(a)   It must have at least ten letting bedrooms

(b)   It must have letting bedrooms as the whole or main part of the sleeping accommodation

(c)   It must offer ancillary services including at least:

     (i)   Breakfast
     (ii)   Evening meals
     (iii)   The cleaning of rooms
     (iv)   The making of beds

(d)   It must be open for at least four months during the April to October season.

8.3 Eligible expenditure

Allowances are computed on the amount of eligible expenditure incurred on qualifying buildings. The eligible expenditure is:

- The original cost of a building if built by the trader, or
- The purchase price if the building was acquired from a person trading as a builder.

If the building was acquired other than from a person trading as a builder, the eligible expenditure is the lower of the purchase price and the original cost incurred by the person incurring the construction expenditure.

If a building is sold more than once before being brought into use, the last buyer before the building is brought into use obtains the allowances. If, in such cases, the building was first sold by someone trading as a builder, the eligible expenditure is the lower of the price paid by the first buyer and the price paid by the last buyer.

Where part of a building qualifies as an industrial building and part does not, the whole cost qualifies for IBAs, provided that the cost of the non-qualifying part is not more than 25% of the total expenditure. If the non-qualifying part of the building does cost more than 25% of the total, its cost must be excluded from the capital allowances computation.

The cost of land is disallowed but expenditure incurred in preparing land for building does qualify. The cost of items which would not be included in a normal commercial lease (such as rental guarantees) also does not qualify.

Professional fees, for example architects' fees, incurred in connection with the construction of an industrial building qualify. The cost of repairs to industrial buildings also qualifies, provided that the expenditure is not deductible as a trading expense.

Question	IBAs: eligible expenditure

Sue purchased an industrial building for £2,500,000. This cost was made up of:

	£
Factory	2,100,000
Land	400,000
	2,500,000

The costs attributable to showrooms and offices within the factory were £400,000 and £200,000 respectively.

What is the expenditure qualifying for industrial buildings allowances?

The showrooms and offices are non-qualifying parts of the building. As the cost of the non qualifying parts, £600,000, is more than 25% of the total expenditure on the building (£2,100,000), industrial buildings allowances are not available on it. The cost of the land is not qualifying expenditure.

The qualifying expenditure for industrial buildings allowance purposes is therefore £1,500,000 (£2,100,000 – £600,000).

8.4 Writing down allowances

Industrial buildings allowance at the rate of 2% a year is given if a building is in industrial use on the last day of the period of account concerned.

Exam focus point

In preparation for the abolition of Industrial building allowance, WDAs are being reduced. The examiner has said that he will not set a question which has a period of account which falls partly before and partly after 6 April 2009 (accounting periods before/after 1 April 2009 for companies) which would require apportionment.

A writing down allowance (WDA) is given to the person holding the 'relevant interest'. Broadly, the relevant interest is the interest of the first acquirer of the industrial building and may be a freehold or leasehold interest.

Where a long lease (more than 50 years) has been granted on an industrial building, the grant may be treated as a sale so that allowances may be claimed by the lessee rather than the lessor. A claim must be made by the lessor and lessee jointly, within four years of the start of the lease. The election allows allowances to be claimed on industrial buildings where the lessor is not subject to tax (as with local authorities).

The WDA is given for a period provided that the industrial building was in use as such on the last day of the period concerned. The WDA is 2% (2009/10) of the eligible expenditure incurred by the taxpayer. **The allowance is calculated on a straight line basis** (in contrast to WDAs on plant and machinery which are calculated on the reducing balance), starting when the building is brought into use. **The WDA is 2% × months/12 if the period concerned is not 12 months long.** Buildings always have a **separate computation for each building.** They are never pooled.

Question   Industrial buildings allowance

Mark has been a sole trader for many years, making up accounts to 5 April each year.

On 12 September 2009, he bought a new industrial building from a builder at a cost of £800,000 which he brought into use immediately.

The total cost can be analysed as follows:

	£
Land	200,000
Preparing land	50,000
Architect's fees	40,000
Factory	150,000
Storage warehouse	100,000
Staff canteen	90,000
Offices	170,000
Total expenditure	800,000

Calculate the industrial buildings allowance available to Mark for the year ended 5 April 2010.

Answer

Eligible expenditure

	£
Preparing land	50,000
Architect's fees	40,000
Factory	150,000
Storage warehouse	100,000
Staff canteen	90,000
Eligible expenditure	430,000

The cost of land is never eligible expenditure.

The cost of the offices is not eligible expenditure because it exceeds 25% of the total cost (excluding land) as £(800,000 – 200,000) x 25% = £150,000.

Industrial buildings allowance y/e 5 April 2010

£430,000 x 2%	£8,600

8.5 Sales of industrial buildings

Until 21 March 2007, the disposal of an industrial building gave rise to a balancing adjustment (ie a balancing change or a balancing allowance). In preparation for the eventual abolition of industrial buildings allowance, **no balancing adjustments apply for disposals from 21 March 2007 onwards**.

Exam focus point

> The examiner has stated that questions will not be set involving a balancing adjustment on the sale of an industrial building.

Chapter Roundup

- Capital allowances are available to give tax relief for certain capital expenditure.

- There are various statutory rules on what does or does not qualify as plant.

- There are also cases on the definition of plant. To help you to absorb them, try to see the function/setting theme running through them.

- With capital allowances computations, the main thing is to get the layout right. Having done that, you will find that the figures tend to drop into place.

- Businesses are entitled to an Annual Investment Allowance (AIA) of £50,000 for a 12 month period of account.

- A first year allowance (FYA) at the rate of 40% is available on the balance of expenditure on plant and machinery (excluding cars and special rate pool expenditure) not covered by the Annual Investment Allowance. A FYA at the rate of 100% is available on low emission cars. FYAs are never pro-rated in short periods of account.

- Expenditure on plant and machinery in the main pool qualifies for a WDA at 20% every 12 months.

- The special rate pool contains expenditure on thermal insulation, long life assets, features integral to a building and cars with CO_2 emissions over 160g/km. The AIA can be used against such expenditure except cars. The WDA is 10%.

- An asset which is used privately by a trader is dealt with in a single asset pool and the capital allowances are restricted.

- Motor cars acquired before 6 April 2009 (1 April 2009 for companies) which cost more than £12,000 are dealt with in a single asset pool. The maximum WDA on such cars is £3,000 for a 12 month period.

- Motor cars acquired from 6 April 2009 (1 April 2009 for companies) are generally dealt with in the special rate pool (cars emitting over 160g/km) or the main pool, unless there is private use by the trader.

- Short life asset elections can bring forward the allowances due on an asset.

- Industrial buildings allowance can be claimed in respect of expenditure on buildings in industrial use such as factories.

- Industrial buildings allowance at the rate of 2% a year is given if a building is in industrial use on the last day of the period of account concerned.

Quick Quiz

1   Writing down allowances are pro-rated in a six month period of account. TRUE/FALSE.

2   Lucas makes up accounts for a 15 month period to 30 June 2010. What Annual Investment Allowance is he entitled to?

    A   £12,500
    B   £37,500
    C   £50,000
    D   £62,500

3   Are first year allowances pro-rated in a six month period of account?

4   When may balancing allowances arise?

5   An asset must be disposed of within ____ years of the end of the accounting period (or period of account) in which it was acquired in order for it to be advantageous to treat it as a short life asset. FILL IN THE BLANK.

6   Paula makes up accounts to 5 April each year. She buys a car in August 2009 costing £20,000 for use in her business. Her private use of the car is 30%. The CO_2 emissions of the car are 170g/km.

    What WDA is available on the car for the year ended 5 April 2010?

    A   £1,400
    B   £2,000
    C   £2,800
    D   £4,000

7   What is the writing down allowance on industrial buildings?

1   True. In a six month period, writing down allowance are pro-rated by multiplying by 6/12.

2   D. £50,000 × 15/12 = £62,500.

3   No. First year allowances are given in full in a short period of account.

4   Balancing allowances may arise in respect of main or special pooled expenditure only when the trade ceases. Balancing allowances may arise on single pool assets whenever those assets are disposed of.

5   An asset must be disposed of within 4 years of the end of the accounting period (or period of account) in which it was acquired in order for it to be advantageous to treat it as a short life asset.

6   A. £20,000 x 10% (CO_2 emissions of the car exceed 160g/km) = £2,000. WDA is £2,000 x 70% = £1,400.

7   2%

Now try the questions below from the Exam Question Bank

Number	Level	Marks	Time
Q10	Examination	15	27 mins
Q11	Examination	10	18 mins

Assessable trading income

Topic list	Syllabus reference
1 Recognise the basis of assessment	B3(a)
2 Commencement and cessation	B3(e)
3 Change of accounting date	B3(f)(i)-(iii)

Introduction

In the previous two chapters we have seen how to calculate the taxable trading profits after capital allowances. We are now going to look at how these are taxed in the owner's hands.

Businesses do not normally prepare accounts for tax years so we look at the basis of assessment which is the method by which the taxable trading profits of periods of account are allocated to tax years. As well as the normal rules for a continuing business we need special rules for the opening years of a trade, and again in the closing years.

Special rules are also needed if the business changes its accounting date.

In the next chapter we will look at the tax reliefs available should the business make a loss.

Study guide

		Intellectual level
B3	**Income from self-employment**	
(a)	Recognise the basis of assessment for self employment income.	2
(e)	Compute the assessable profits on commencement and on cessation.	2
(f)	Change of accounting date	
(i)	Recognise the factors that will influence the choice of accounting date.	2
(ii)	State the conditions that must be met for a change of accounting date to be valid.	1
(iii)	Compute the assessable profits on a change of accounting date.	2

Exam guide

You are likely to have to deal with a tax computation for an unincorporated business at some point in the exam. It may be a simple computation for a continuing business, or you may have to deal with a business in its opening or closing years, including computing taxable trading profits and allocating them to tax years. You must be totally familiar with the rules and be able to apply them in the exam.

1 Recognise the basis of assessment

FAST FORWARD

> Basis periods are used to link periods of account to tax years. Broadly, the profits of a period of account ending in a tax year are taxed in that year.

1.1 Basis periods and tax years

A tax year runs from 6 April to 5 April, but most businesses do not have periods of account ending on 5 April. **Thus there must be a link between a period of account of a business and a tax year.** The procedure is to **find a period to act as the basis period for a tax year. The profits for a basis period are taxed in the corresponding tax year**. If a basis period is not identical to a period of account, the profits of periods of account are time-apportioned as required on the assumption that profits accrue evenly over a period of account. We will apportion to the nearest month for exam purposes.

The general rule is that **the basis period is the year of account ending in the tax year**. This is known as the **current year basis of assessment**.

This general rule does not apply in the opening or closing years of a business. This is because in the first few years the business has not normally established a pattern of annual accounts, and very few businesses cease trading on the annual accounting date.

Special rules are also needed when the trader changes his accounting date.

We will look at these rules in the next sections.

2 Commencement and cessation

FAST FORWARD

In the first tax year of trade actual profits of the tax year are taxed. In the second tax year, the basis period is either the first 12 months, the 12 months to the accounting date ending in year two or the actual profits from April to April. Profits of the twelve months to the accounting date are taxed in year three.

2.1 The first tax year

The first tax year is the year during which the trade commences. For example, if a trade commences on 1 June 2009 the first tax year is 2009/10.

The **basis period for the first tax year runs from the date the trade starts to the next 5 April** (or to the date of cessation if the trade does not last until the end of the tax year).

So continuing the above example a trader commencing in business on 1 June 2009 will be taxed on profits arising form 1 June 2009 to 5 April 2010 in 2009/10, the first tax year.

2.2 The second tax year

(a)   **If the accounting date falling in the second tax year is at least 12 months after the start of trading, the basis period is the 12 months to that accounting date**.

(b)   **If the accounting date falling in the second tax year is less than 12 months after the start of trading, the basis period is the first 12 months of trading**.

(c)   **If there is no accounting date falling in the second tax year**, because the first period of account is a very long one which does not end until a date in the third tax year, **the basis period for the second tax year is the year itself (from 6 April to 5 April)**.

The following flowchart may help you determine the basis period for the second tax year.

2.3 Example: period of twelve months or more ending in second year

John starts to trade on 1 January 2010 making up accounts to 31 December 2010.

1st tax year: 2009/10 – tax profits 1 January 2010 to 5 April 2010, ie 3/12 × year ended 31 December 2010

2nd tax year: 2010/11

- Is there a period of account ending in 2010/11?
  Yes – Year ended 31 December 2010 ends in 2010/11.
- How long is the period of account?
  12 months or more, ie 12 months (exactly) to 31 December 2010.
- So in 2010/11 tax profits of 12 months to 31 December 2010.

2.4 Example: short period ending in second year

Janet starts to trade on 1 January 2010 making up accounts as follows:

- 6 months to 30 June 2010
- 12 months to 30 June 2011.

1st tax year: 2009/10 – tax profits 1 January 2010 to 5 April 2010, ie 3/6 × 6 months ended 30 June 2010

2nd tax year: 20010/11.

- Is there a period of account ending in 2010/11?
  Yes – period ended 30 June 2010 ends in 2010/11.
- How long is the period of account?
  Less than 12 months.
- So in 2010/11 tax profits of first 12 months of trade ie 1 January 2010 to 31 December 2010, ie period ended 30 June 2010 profits plus 6/12 of year ended 30 June 2011 profits

2.5 Example: No period ending in second year

Jodie starts to trade on 1 March 2010 making up a 14 month set of accounts to 30 April 2011.

1st tax year: 2009/10 – tax profits 1 March 2010 to 5 April 2010, ie 1/14 × 14 months ended 30 April 2011

2nd tax year: 2010/11

- Is there a period of account ending in 2010/11?
  No (period ended 30 April 2011 ends in 2011/12)
- So in 2010/11 tax profits of 6 April 2010 to 5 April 2011, ie 12/14 × 14 months ended 30 April 2011

2.6 The third tax year

(a) **If there is an accounting date falling in the second tax year, the basis period for the third tax year is the period of account ending in the third tax year.**

(b) If there is no accounting date falling in the second tax year, the basis period for the third tax year is the 12 months to the accounting date falling in the third tax year.

2.7 Example: Accounting date in second year

Wilma starts to trade on 1 October 2009. She made taxable profits of £9,000 for the first 9 months to 30 June 2010 and £30,000 for the year to 30 June 2011.

The taxable profits for the first three tax years are as follows:

Year	Basis period	Working	Taxable profits £
2009/10	1.10.09 – 5.4.10	£9,000 × 6/9	6,000
2010/11	1.10.09 – 30.9.10	£9,000 + £30,000 × 3/12	16,500
2011/12	1.7.10 – 30.6.11		30,000
	(period of account ending in 3rd year)		

2.8 Example: No accounting date in the second year

Thelma starts to trade on 1 March 2010. Her first accounts, covering the 16 months to 30 June 2011, show a profit of £36,000. The taxable profits for the first three tax years are as follows.

Year	Basis period	Working	Taxable profits £
2009/10	1.3.10 – 5.4.10	£36,000 × 1/16	2,250
2010/11	6.4.10 – 5.4.11	£36,000 × 12/16	27,000
2011/12	1.7.10 – 30.6.11	£36,000 × 12/16	27,000

2.9 Later tax years

For later tax years, except the year in which the trade ceases, the normal current year basis of assessment applies, ie the basis period is the period of account ending in the tax year (see above).

Question	Basis periods

Peter commenced trading on 1 September 2005 preparing accounts to 30 April each year with the following results.

Period	Profit £
1.9.05 – 30.4.06	8,000
1.5.06 – 30.4.07	15,000
1.5.07 – 30.4.08	9,000
1.5.08 – 30.4.09	10,500

Show the profits to be taxed in each year from 2005/06 to 2009/10.

Answer

Year	Basis period	Working	Taxable profits £
2005/06	1.9.05 – 5.4.06	£8,000 × 7/8	7,000
2006/07	1.9.05 – 31.8.06	£8,000 + (£15,000 × 4/12)	13,000
2007/08	1.5.06 – 30.4.07		15,000
2008/09	1.5.07 – 30.4.08		9,000
2009/10	1.5.08 – 30.4.09		10,500

2.10 The choice of an accounting date

A new trader should consider which accounting date would be best. There are **three factors to consider** from the point of view of taxation.

- **If profits are expected to rise, a date early in the tax year** (such as 30 April) will delay the time when rising accounts profits feed through into rising taxable profits, whereas a date late in the tax year (such as 31 March) will accelerate the taxation of rising profits. This is because with an accounting date of 30 April, the taxable profits for each tax year are mainly the profits earned in the previous tax year. With an accounting date of 31 March the taxable profits are almost entirely profits earned in the current year.

- If the accounting date in the second tax year is less than 12 months after the start of trading, the taxable profits for that year will be the profits earned in the first 12 months. If the accounting date is at least 12 months from the start of trading, they will be the profits earned in the 12 months to that date. **Different profits may thus be taxed twice**, and if profits are fluctuating this can make a considerable difference to the taxable profits in the first few years. (See below for the relief given where profits are taxed twice – 'overlap relief'.)

- **The choice of an accounting date affects the profits shown in each set of accounts**, and this may affect the taxable profits.

Christine starts to trade on 1 December 2007. Her monthly profits are £1,000 for the first seven months, and £2,000 thereafter. Show the taxable profits for the first three tax years with each of the following accounting dates (in all cases starting with a period of account of less than 12 months).

(a)   31 March
(b)   30 April
(c)   31 December

Answer

(a)   *31 March*

Period of account	Working	Profits £
1.12.07 – 31.3.08	£1,000 × 4	4,000
1.4.08 – 31.3.09	£1,000 × 3 + £2,000 × 9	21,000
1.4.09 – 31.3.10	£2,000 × 12	24,000

Year	Basis period	Taxable profits £
2007/08	1.12.07 – 5.4.08	4,000
2008/09	1.4.08 – 31.3.09	21,000
2009/10	1.4.09 – 31.3.10	24,000

(b)   *30 April*

Period of account	Working	Profits £
1.12.07 – 30.4.08	£1,000 × 5	5,000
1.5.08 – 30.4.09	£1,000 × 2 + £2,000 ×10	22,000

Year	Basis period	Working	Taxable profits £
2007/08	1.12.07 – 5.4.08	£5,000 × 4/5	4,000
2008/09	1.12.07 – 30.11.08	£5,000 + £22,000 × 7/12	17,833
2009/10	1.5.08 – 30.4.09		22,000

(c)   *31 December*

Period of account	Working	Profits £
1.12.07 – 31.12.07	£1,000 × 1	1,000
1.1.08 – 31.12.08	£1,000 × 6 + £2,000 × 6	18,000
1.1.09 – 31.12.09	£2,000 × 12	24,000

Year	Basis period	Working	Taxable profits £
2007/08	1.12.07 – 5.4.08	£1,000 + £18,000 × 3/12	5,500
2008/09	1.1.08 – 31.12.08		18,000
2009/10	1.1.09 – 31.12.09		24,000

2.11 The final year

FAST FORWARD

On a cessation the basis period runs from the end of the basis period for the previous tax year.

(a) If a trade starts and ceases in the same tax year, the basis period for that year is the whole lifespan of the trade.

(b) If the final year is the second year, the basis period runs from 6 April at the start of the second year to the date of cessation. This rule overrides the rules that normally apply for the second year.

(c) If the final year is the third year or a later year, **the basis period runs from the end of the basis period for the previous year to the date of cessation**. This rule overrides the rules that normally apply in the third and later years.

Question — Ceasing to trade

Harriet, who has been trading since 1997, ceases her trade on 31 March 2010.

Her results for recent years were:

Year ended 31 December	£
2007	10,000
2008	14,000
2009	21,000
Period ended 31 March 2010	4,000

Show the taxable trade profits for the last three tax years of trading.

Answer

Trade ceases in 2009/10.

Year	Basis period	Working	Assessment £
2007/08	Y/e 31.12.07		10,000
2008/09	Y/e 31.12.08		14,000
2009/10	1.1.09 – 31.3.10	Y/e 31.12.09 plus p/e 31.3.10	25,000

2.12 Overlap profits

Key term

Profits which have been taxed more than once are called **overlap profits**.

When a business starts, some profits may be taxed twice because the basis period for the second year includes some or all of the period of trading in the first year or because the basis period for the third year overlaps with that for the second year, or both.

Overlap profits may be deducted on a change of accounting date (see below). Any overlap profits unrelieved when the trade ceases are deducted from the final year's taxable profits. Any deduction of overlap profits may create or increase a loss. The usual loss reliefs (covered later in this Text) are then available.

Exam focus point

A business with a 31 March year end will have no overlap profits as its accounting year coincides with the tax year. A business with a 31 December year end, for example, will have 3 months of overlap profit as its accounting year ends three months before the end of the tax year. Use this rule of thumb to check your calculation of overlap profits.

2.13 Examples: overlap profits

(a) John starts to trade on 1 January 2010 making up accounts to 31 December 2010. Show the overlap period.

Tax year	Basis period
2009/10	1.1.10 – 5.4.10
2010/11	1.1.10 – 31.12.10
2011/12	1.1.11 – 31.12.11

Overlap period: 1.1.10 – 5.4.10 (3 months)

(b) Janet starts to trade on 1 January 2010 making up accounts as follows:

6m to 30 June 2010
12m to 30 June 2011

Show the overlap period.

Tax year	Basis period
2009/10	1.1.10 – 5.4.10
2010/11	1.1.10 – 31.12.10
2011/12	1.7.10 – 30.6.11

Overlap period: 1.1.10 – 5.4.10 plus 1.7.10 – 31.12.10 (9 months)

(c) Jodie starts to trade on 1 March 2010 making up a 14 month set of accounts to 30 April 2011. Show the overlap period.

Tax year	Basis period
2009/10	1.3.10 – 5.4.10
2010/11	6.4.10 – 5.4.11
2011/12	1.5.10 – 30.4.11

Overlap period: 1.5.10 – 5.4.11 (11 months)

 Question   **Ceasing to trade and overlap profits**

Jenny trades from 1 July 2004 to 31 December 2009, with the following results.

Period	Profit £
1.7.04 – 31.8.05	7,000
1.9.05 – 31.8.06	12,000
1.9.06 – 31.8.07	15,000
1.9.07 – 31.8.08	21,000
1.9.08 – 31.8.09	18,000
1.9.09 – 31.12.09	5,600
	78,600

Calculate the taxable trade profits to be taxed from 2004/05 to 2009/10, the overlap profits and state when these overlap profits can be relieved.

The profits to be taxed in each tax year from 2004/05 to 2009/10. and the total of these taxable profits are calculated as follows.

Year	Basis period	Working	Taxable profit £
2004/05	1.7.04 – 5.4.05	£7,000 × 9/14	4,500
2005/06	1.9.04 – 31.8.05	£7,000 × 12/14	6,000
2006/07	1.9.05 – 31.8.06		12,000
2007/08	1.9.06 – 31.8.07		15,000
2008/09	1.9.07 – 31.8.08		21,000
2009/10	1.9.08 – 31.12.09	£(18,000 + 5,600 – 3,500)	20,100
			78,600

The overlap profits are those in the period 1 September 2004 to 5 April 2005, a period of seven months. They are £7,000 × 7/14 = £3,500. Overlap profits are either relieved on a change of accounting date (see below) or are deducted from the final year's taxable profit when the business ceases. In this case the overlap profits are deducted when the business ceases.

Exam focus point

Over the life of the business, the total taxable profits equal the total actual profits.

3 Change of accounting date

FAST FORWARD

On a change of accounting date, special rules may apply for fixing basis periods. Overlap profits may either be created or relieved on a change of accounting date. Overlap profits may be relieved if more than 12 months worth of profits would otherwise be taxed in a year following a change of accounting date. On cessation any remaining overlap profits are relieved.

3.1 Need for special rules

A trader may change the date to which he prepares his annual accounts for a variety of reasons. For example, he may wish to move to a calendar year end or to fit in with seasonal variations of his trade. Special rules normally apply for fixing basis periods when a trader changes his accounting date.

On a change of accounting date there may be

- One set of accounts covering a period of less than twelve months, or
- One set of accounts covering a period of more than twelve months,

ending in a tax year. In each case, the basis period for the year relates to the new accounting date. We will look at each of the cases in turn.

3.2 One short period of account

When a change of accounting date results in one short period of account ending in a tax year, the basis period for that year is always the 12 months to the new accounting date.

3.3 Example: change of accounting date – short period

Sue prepares accounts to 31 December each year until she changes her accounting date to 30 June by preparing accounts for the six months to 30 June 2009.

There is one short period of account ending during 2009/10. This means the basis period for 2009/10 is the twelve months to 30 June 2009.

Sue's basis period for 2008/09 was the twelve months to 31 December 2008. This means the profits of the six months to 31 December 2008 are overlap profits that have been taxed twice. These overlap profits must be added to any overlap profits that arose when the business began. The total is either relieved when the business ceases or is relieved on a subsequent change of accounting date.

3.4 One long period of account

When a change of accounting date results in one long period of account ending in a tax year, the basis period for that year ends on the new accounting date. It begins immediately after the basis period for the previous year ends. This means the basis period will exceed 12 months.

No overlap profits arise in this situation. However, more than twelve months worth of profits are taxed in one income tax year and to compensate for this, relief is available for brought forward overlap profits. The overlap relief cannot reduce the number of months worth of profits taxed in the year to below twelve. So, if you have a fourteen month basis period you can give relief for up to two months worth of overlap profits.

3.5 Example: change of accounting date – long period

Zoe started trading on 1 October 2006 and prepared accounts to 30 September until she changed her accounting date by preparing accounts for the fifteen months to 31 December 2009. Her results were as follows

	£
Year to 30 September 2007	24,000
Year to 30 September 2008	48,000
Fifteen months to 31 December 2009	75,000

Profits for the first three tax years of the business are:

	£
2006/07 (1.10.06 – 5.4.07) 6/12 × £24,000	12,000
2007/08 (1.10.06 – 30.9.07)	24,000
2008/09 (1.10.07 – 30.9.08)	48,000

Overlap profits are £12,000. These arose in the six months to 5.4.07.

The change in accounting date results in one long period of account ending during 2009/10 which means the basis period for 2009/10 is the fifteen months to 31 December 2009. Three months worth of the brought forward overlap profits can be relieved.

	£
2009/10 (1.10.08 – 31.12.09)	75,000
Less overlap profits 3/6 × £12,000	(6,000)
	69,000

The unrelieved overlap profits of £6,000 (£12,000 – £6,000) are carried forward for relief either when the business ceases or on a further change of accounting date.

3.6 Conditions

The above changes in basis period automatically occur if the trader changes his accounting date during the first three tax years of his business.

In other cases **the following conditions must be met before a change in basis periods can occur**:

- The trader must notify HMRC of the change by the 31 January, following the tax year in which the change is made (by 31 January 2011 for a change made during 2009/10.)
- The period of account resulting from the change must not exceed 18 months.
- In general, there must have been no previous change of accounting date in the last 5 tax years. However, a second change can be made within this period if the later change is for genuine commercial reasons. If HMRC do not respond to a notification of a change of accounting date within 60 days of receiving it, the trader can assume that they are satisfied that the reasons for making the change are genuine commercial ones.

If the above conditions are not satisfied because the first period of account ending on the new date exceeds 18 months or the change of accounting date was not notified in time, but the 'five year gap or commercial reasons' condition is satisfied, then the basis period for the year of change is the 12 months to the *old* accounting date in the year of change. The basis period for the next year is then found using rules above as if it were the year of change.

If the 'five year gap or commercial reasons' test is not satisfied, the old accounting date remains in force for tax purposes (with the profits of accounts made up to the new date being time-apportioned as necessary) until there have been five consecutive tax years which were not years of change. The sixth tax year is then treated as the year of change to the new accounting date, and the rules above apply.

Chapter Roundup

- Basis periods are used to link periods of account to tax years. Broadly, the profits of a period of account ending in a tax year are taxed in that year.

- In the first tax year of trade actual profits of the tax year are taxed. In the second tax year, the basis period is either the first 12 months, the 12 months to the accounting date ending in year two or the actual profits from April to April. Profits of the twelve months to the accounting date are taxed in year three.

- On a cessation the basis period runs from the end of the basis period for the previous tax year.

- On a change of accounting date, special rules may apply for fixing basis periods. Overlap profits may either be created or relieved on a change of accounting date. Overlap profits may be relieved if more than 12 months worth of profits would otherwise be taxed in a year following a change of accounting date. On cessation any remaining overlap profits are relieved.

Quick Quiz

1   What is the normal basis of assessment?

2   Isabella started trading on 1 September 2009. She made up her first set of accounts to 31 December 2010. The basis period for the year of commencement is:

 A   1 September 2009 to 31 December 2009

 B   1 September 2009 to 5 April 2010

 C   1 September 2009 to 31 August 2010

 D   1 September 2009 to 31 December 2010

3   On what two occasions can overlap profits potentially be relieved?

Answers to Quick Quiz

1   The normal basis of assessment is that the profits for a tax year are those of the 12 month accounting period ending in the tax year.

2   B. 1 September 2009 to 5 April 2010 ie the actual tax year.

3   On a change of accounting date where a basis period resulting from the change exceeds 12 months or on the cessation of a business.

Now try the questions below from the Exam Question Bank

Number	Level	Marks	Time
Q12	Examination	15	27 mins
Q13	Examination	15	27 mins
Q14	Examination	15	27 mins

Trading losses

Topic list	Syllabus reference
1 Losses	B3(h)
2 Carry forward trade loss relief	B3h(i)
3 Trade transferred to company	B3h(ii)
4 Trade loss relief against general income	B3h(iii)
5 Losses in the early years of a trade	B3h(iv)
6 Terminal trade loss relief	B3h(v)

Introduction

We have seen how to calculate taxable trading profits and how to allocate them to tax years so that they can be slotted into the income tax computation.

Traders sometimes make losses rather than profits. In this chapter we consider the reliefs available for losses. A loss does not in itself lead to getting tax back from HMRC. Relief is obtained by setting a loss against trading profits, against general income or against capital gains (which are covered later in this Text), so that tax need not be paid on them. An important consideration is the choice between different reliefs. The aim is to use a loss to save as much tax as possible, as quickly as possible.

In the next chapter we will see how the rules for sole traders are extended to those trading in partnership.

Study guide

Exam guide

Losses are likely to be included to some degree in the exam. The focus may, however, be on corporation tax losses, and you may not have to deal with trading losses for income tax purposes at all. Alternatively you could have a detailed computational question involving the carry back and carry forward of losses. Ensure you know the rules for ongoing trades and the additional relief in the early years of trading. On a cessation carry forward is only possible if the business is incorporated, but terminal loss relief may be due instead. Once you have established the reliefs available look to see which is most beneficial.

1 Losses

FAST FORWARD

Trading losses may be relieved against future profits of the same trade, against general income and against capital gains.

1.1 Introduction

When computing taxable trade profits, profits may turn out to be negative, meaning a loss has been made in the basis period. **A loss is computed in exactly the same way as a profit**, making the same adjustments to the accounts profit or loss.

If there is a loss in a basis period, the taxable trade profits for the tax year based on that basis period are nil.

This chapter considers how losses are calculated and how a loss-suffering taxpayer can use a loss to reduce his tax liability.

The rules in this chapter apply only to individuals, trading alone or in partnership. Loss reliefs for companies are completely different and are covered later in this Text.

1.2 The computation of the loss

The trade loss for a tax year is the trade loss in the basis period for that tax year.

1.3 Example: computation of trade loss

Here is an example of a trader with a 31 December year end who has been trading for many years.

Period of account	Loss £
Y/e 31.12.2009	9,000
Y/e 31.12.2010	24,000

Tax year	Basis period	Trade loss for the tax year £
2009/10	Y/e 31.12.09	9,000
2010/11	Y/e 31.12.10	24,000

1.4 How loss relief is given

Loss relief is given by deducting the loss from total income to calculate net income. Carry forward loss relief, extended carry back loss relief and terminal loss relief can only be set against the trading profits of the same trade. Other loss reliefs may be set against general income (ie any component of total income).

2 Carry forward trade loss relief

Trading losses may be relieved against future profits of the same trade. The relief is against the first available profits of the same trade.

2.1 The relief

A trade loss not relieved in any other way will be **carried forward to set against the first available trade profits of the same trade** in the calculation of net trading income. Losses may be carried forward for any number of years.

2.2 Example: carrying forward losses

Brian has the following results.

Year ending	£
31 December 2007	(6,000)
31 December 2008	5,000
31 December 2009	11,000

Brian's net trading income, assuming that he claims carry forward loss relief only are:

	2007/08 £		2008/09 £		2009/10 £
Trade profits	0		5,000		11,000
Less carry forward loss relief	(0)	(i)	(5,000)	(ii)	(1,000)
Net trading income	0		0		10,000

Loss memorandum		£
Trading loss, y/e 31.12.07		6,000
Less: claim in y/e 31.12.08 (08/09)	(i)	(5,000)
claim in y/e 31.12.09 (balance of loss) (09/10)	(ii)	(1,000)
		0

3 Trade transferred to company

Where a business is transferred to a company, loss relief is available for any remaining unrelieved losses of the unincorporated business against income received from the company.

Although carry forward loss relief is restricted to future profits of the same business, this is extended to cover income received from a company to which the business is transferred.

The amount carried forward is the total unrelieved trading losses of the business.

The set off is against income derived from the company including dividends, interest and salary. Set-off the loss against non-savings income or savings income and then against dividend income.

The consideration for the transfer of the business must be wholly or mainly in the form of shares (at least 80%) which must be retained by the vendor throughout any tax year in which the loss is relieved .

4 Trade loss relief against general income

A trading loss may be set against general income in the year of the loss and/or the preceding year. Personal allowances may be lost as a result of a claim. Once a claim has been made in any year, the remaining loss can be set against net chargeable gains.

4.1 The relief

Instead of carrying a trade loss forward against future trade profits, a claim may be made to relieve it against general income.

4.2 Relieving the loss

Relief is against the income of the tax year in which the loss arose. In addition or instead, relief may be claimed against the income of the preceding year.

If there are losses in two successive years, and relief is claimed against the first year's income both for the first year's loss and for the second year's loss, relief is given for the first year's loss before the second year's loss.

A claim for a loss must be made by the 31 January which is 22 months after the end of the tax year of the loss: thus by 31 January 2012 for a loss in 2009/10.

The taxpayer cannot choose the amount of loss to relieve: thus the loss may have to be set against income part of which would have been covered by the personal allowance. However, the taxpayer can choose whether to claim full relief in the current year and then relief in the preceding year for any remaining loss, or the other way round.

Question   Loss relief against general income

Janet has a loss in her period of account ending 31 December 2009 of £25,000. Her other income is £18,000 part time employment income a year, and she wishes to claim loss relief against general income for the year of loss and then for the preceding year. Her trading income in the previous year was £nil. Show her taxable income for each year, and comment on the effectiveness of the loss relief. Assume that tax rates and allowances for 2009/10 have always applied.

The loss-making period ends in 2009/10, so the year of the loss is 2009/10.

	2008/09 £	2009/10 £
Total income	18,000	18,000
Less loss relief against general income	(7,000)	(18,000)
Net income	11,000	0
Less personal allowance	(6,475)	(6,475)
Taxable income	4,525	0

In 2009/10, £6,475 of the loss has been wasted because that amount of income would have been covered by the personal allowance. If Janet just claims loss relief against general income, there is nothing she can do about this waste of loss relief.

4.3 Capital allowances

The trader may adjust the size of the loss relief claim by not claiming all the capital allowances he is entitled to: a reduced claim will increase the balance carried forward to the next year's capital allowances computation. This may be a useful **tax planning point where the effective rate of relief for capital allowances in future periods will be greater than the rate of tax relief for the loss relief.**

4.4 Trading losses relieved against capital gains

Where relief is claimed against general income of a given year, the taxpayer may include **a further claim to set the loss against his chargeable gains for the year** less any allowable capital losses for the same year or for previous years. This amount of net gains is computed ignoring the annual exempt amount (see later in this Text).

The trading loss is first set against general income of the year of the claim, and only any excess loss is set against capital gains. The taxpayer cannot specify the amount to be set against capital gains, so the annual exemption may be wasted. We include an example here for completeness. You will study chargeable gains later in this Text and we suggest that you come back to this example at that point.

Question   Loss relief against income and gains

Sibyl had the following results for 2009/10.

	£
Loss available for relief against general income	27,000
Income	19,500
Capital gains less current year capital losses	11,000
Annual exemption for capital gains tax purposes	10,100
Capital losses brought forward	5,000

Show how the loss would be relieved against income and gains.

	£
Income	19,500
Less loss relief against general income	(19,500)
Net income	0
Capital gains	11,000
Less loss relief: lower of £(27,000 – 19,500) = £7,500 (note 1) and	
£(11,000 – 5,000) = £6,000 (note 2)	(6,000)
	5,000
Less annual exemption (restricted)	(5,000)
	0

Notes

1   This equals the loss left after the loss relief claim against general income
2   This equals the gains left after losses b/fwd but ignoring the annual exemption.

A trading loss of £(7,500 – 6,000) = £1,500 is carried forward. Sibyl's personal allowance and £(10,100 – 5,000) = £5,100 of her capital gains tax annual exemption are wasted. Her capital losses brought forward of £5,000 are carried forward to 2010/11. Although we deducted this £5,000 in working out how much trading loss we were allowed to use in the claim, we do not actually need to use any of the £5,000.

4.5 Restrictions on trade loss relief against general income

Relief cannot be claimed against general income unless a business is conducted on a commercial basis with a view to the realisation of profits throughout the basis period for the tax year; this condition applies to all types of business.

There is also a limit on the amount of loss relief that a trader can claim against general income if he is a non-active trader. A non-active trader is one who spends less than 10 hours a week personally engaged in trade activities. The limit is £25,000 per tax year.

This restriction applies also to early years trading loss relief (see later in this chapter).

4.6 Temporary extension to carry back loss relief

FAST FORWARD

It is possible to carry back losses for three years against trading income where a trading loss arises in 2009/10.

There is a temporary extension to carry back loss relief where a loss arises in 2008/09 or 2009/10. In order to make a claim for the extended relief, **the taxpayer must make a claim for trade loss relief either in the year of the loss and/or the preceding year, or be unable to make any claim because he does not have any other income in both years.**

Exam focus point

The examiner has stated that any question involving extended loss relief will be confined to a loss arising in 2009/10 and where there is other income in that year.

Any remaining losses are carried back three years before the year of the loss against trading income only, later years being relieved first. The extended claim is for a maximum of £50,000 in total of losses from 2009/10 against trading income in 2007/08 and 2006/07. There is no restriction against trading income in 2008/09 where the claim against general income is only made for 2009/10.

Nicola's trading results are as follows.

Year ended 5 April	Trading profit/(loss) £
2007	25,000
2008	33,000
2009	5,000
2010	(74,000)

Her other income (all non-savings income) is as follows.

	£
2006/07	3,000
2007/08	7,000
2008/09	4,000
2009/10	12,000

Nicola claims loss relief against general income in 2009/10 and 2008/09 and then extended carry back loss relief as far as possible.

Show Nicola's taxable income for 2006/07 to 2009/10 inclusive.

Answer

	2006/07 £	2007/08 £	2008/09 £	2009/10 £
Trading income	25,000	33,000	5,000	0
Less carry back loss relief	(17,000)	(33,000)	(0)	(0)
	8,000	0	5,000	0
Other income	3,000	7,000	4,000	12,000
	11,000	7,000	9,000	12,000
Less loss relief against general income	(0)	(0)	(9,000)	(12,000)
Net income	11,000	7,000	0	0
Less personal allowance	(6,475)	(6,475)	(6,475)	(6,475)
Taxable income	4,525	525	0	0

Note that the total loss relief available in 2007/08 and 2006/07 from the loss in 2009/10 is £50,000. Therefore the loss relief for 2006/07 is £(50,000 – 33,000) = £17,000.

The remaining loss of £(74,000– 12,000 – 9,000 – 33,000 – 17,000) = £3,000 is carried forward to be set against the first available trading profits from 2010/11 onwards.

4.7 The choice between loss reliefs

 It is important for a trader to choose the right loss relief, so as to save tax at the highest possible rate and so as to obtain relief reasonably quickly.

When a trader has a choice between loss reliefs, he should aim to obtain relief both quickly and at the highest possible tax rate. However, do consider that losses relieved against income which would otherwise be covered by the personal allowance are wasted.

If the extended loss relief against trading income is available, consider whether it would be better in the year preceding the loss to make a claim against general income or only against trading income.

Another consideration is that a trading loss cannot be set against the capital gains of a year unless relief is first claimed against general income of the same year. It may be worth making the claim against income and wasting the personal allowance in order to avoid a CGT liability.

Felicity's trading results are as follows.

Year ended 30 September	Trading profit/(loss) £
2007	1,900
2008	(21,000)
2009	13,000

Her other income (all non-savings income) is as follows.

	£
2007/08	2,200
2008/09	28,500
2009/10	15,000

Show the most efficient use of Felicity's trading loss. Assume that the personal allowance has been £6,475 throughout.

Answer

Relief could be claimed against general income for 2007/08 and/or 2008/09, with any unused loss being carried forward. Relief in 2007/08 would be against general income of £(1,900 + 2,200) = £4,100, all of which would be covered by the personal allowance anyway, so this claim should not be made and neither should a claim be made for extended carry back loss relief for the same reason. A claim against general income should be made for 2008/09 as this saves tax quicker than a carry forward claim in 2009/10 would. The final results will be as follows:

	2007/08 £	2008/09 £	2009/10 £
Trading income	1,900	0	13,000
Less carry forward loss relief	(0)	(0)	(0)
	1,900	0	13,000
Other income	2,200	28,500	15,000
	4,100	28,500	28,000
Less loss relief against general income	(0)	(21,000)	(0)
Net income	4,100	7,500	28,000
Less personal allowance	(6,475)	(6,475)	(6,475)
Taxable income	0	1,025	21,525

Exam focus point

> Before recommending loss relief against general income consider whether it will result in the waste of the personal allowance. Such waste is to be avoided if at all possible.

5 Losses in the early years of a trade

5.1 The computation of the loss

Under the rules determining the basis period for the first three tax years of trading, there may be periods where the basis periods overlap. If profits arise in these periods, they are taxed twice but are relieved later (on cessation or on a change of accounting date). However, a loss in an overlap period can only be relieved once. It must not be double counted.

If basis periods overlap, **a loss in the overlap period is treated as a loss for the earlier tax year only.**

5.2 Example: losses in early years

Here is an example of a trader who starts to trade on 1 July 2009 and makes losses in opening periods.

Period of account	Loss £
P/e 31.12.2009	9,000
Y/e 31.12.2010	24,000

Tax year	Basis period	Working	Trade loss for the tax year £
2009/10	1.7.09 – 5.4.10	£9,000 + (£24,000 × 3/12)	15,000
2010/11	1.1.10 – 31.12.10	£24,000 – (£24,000 × 3/12)	18,000

5.3 Example: losses and profits in early years

The rule against using losses twice also applies when losses are netted off against profits in the same basis period. Here is an example, with a commencement on 1 July 2009.

Period of account	(Loss)/profit £
1.7.09 – 30.4.10	(10,000)
1.5.09 – 30.4.10	24,000

Tax year	Basis period	Working	Trade (Loss)/Profit £
2009/10	1.7.09 – 5.4.10	£(10,000) × 9/10	(9,000)
2010/11	1.7.09 – 30.6.10	£24,000 × 2/12 + £(10,000) × 1/10	3,000

5.4 Early trade losses relief

In opening years, a special relief involving the carry back of losses against general income is available. Losses arising in the first four tax years of a trade may be set against general income in the three years preceding the loss making year, taking the earliest year first.

Early trade losses relief is available for **trading losses incurred in the first four tax years of a trade**.

Relief is obtained by **setting the allowable loss against general income in the three years preceding the year of loss**, applying the loss to the earliest year first. Thus a loss arising in 2009/10 may be set off against income in 2006/07, 2007/08 and 2008/09 in that order.

A claim for early trade losses relief applies to all three years automatically, provided that the loss is large enough. The taxpayer cannot choose to relieve the loss against just one or two of the years, or to relieve only part of the loss. However, the taxpayer could reduce the size of the loss by not claiming the full capital allowances available to him. This will result in higher capital allowances in future years.

Claims for the relief must be made by the 31 January which is 22 months after the end of the tax year in which the loss is incurred.

Question	Early trade losses relief

Mr A is employed as a dustman until 1 January 2008. On that date he starts up his own business as a scrap metal merchant, making up his accounts to 30 June each year. His earnings as a dustman are:

	£
2004/05	5,000
2005/06	6,000
2006/07	7,000
2007/08 (nine months)	6,000

His trading results as a scrap metal merchant are:

	Profit/(Loss) £
Six months to 30 June 2008	(3,000)
Year to 30 June 2009	(1,500)
Year to 30 June 2010	(1,200)

Assuming that loss relief is claimed as early as possible, show the net income for each of the years 2004/05 to 2010/11 inclusive.

Answer

Since reliefs are to be claimed as early as possible, early trade loss relief is applied. The losses available for relief are as follows.

	£	£	Years against which relief is available
2007/08 (basis period 1.1.08 – 5.4.08)			
3 months to 5.4.08 £(3,000) × 3/6		(1,500)	2004/05 to 2006/07
2008/09 (basis period 1.1.08 – 31.12.08)			
3 months to 30.6.08			
(omit 1.1.08 – 5.4.08: overlap) £(3,000) × 3/6	(1,500)		
6 months to 31.12.08 £(1,500) × 6/12	(750)		
		(2,250)	2005/06 to 2007/08
2009/10 (basis period 1.7.08 – 30.6.09)			
6 months to 30.6.09			
(omit 1.7.08 – 31.12.08: overlap) £(1,500) × 6/12		(750)	2006/07 to 2008/09
2010/11 (basis period 1.7.09 – 30.6.10)			
12 months to 30.6.10		(1,200)	2007/08 to 2009/10

The net income is as follows.

	£	£
2004/05		
Original	5,000	
Less 2007/08 loss	(1,500)	
		3,500
2005/06		
Original	6,000	
Less 2008/09 loss	(2,250)	
		3,750
2006/07		
Original	7,000	
Less 2009/10 loss	(750)	
		6,250
2007/08		
Original	6,000	
Less 2010/11 loss	(1,200)	
		4,800

The taxable trade profits for 2007/08 to 2010/11 are zero because there were losses in the basis periods.

6 Terminal trade loss relief

> On the cessation of trade, a loss arising in the last 12 months of trading may be set against trade profits of the tax year of cessation and the previous 3 years, taking the latest year first.

6.1 The relief

Trade loss relief against general income will often be insufficient on its own to deal with a loss incurred in the last months of trading. For this reason there is a special relief, **terminal trade loss relief, which allows a loss on cessation to be carried back for relief against taxable trading profits in previous years.**

6.2 Computing the terminal loss

A terminal loss is **the loss of the last 12 months of trading**.

It is built up as follows.

		£
(a)	The actual trade loss for the tax year of cessation (calculated from 6 April to the date of cessation)	X
(b)	The actual trade loss for the period from 12 months before cessation until the end of the penultimate tax year	X
	Total terminal trade loss	X

If the result of either (a) or (b) is a profit rather than a loss, it is treated as zero.

Any unrelieved overlap profits are included within (a) above.

If any loss cannot be included in the terminal loss (eg because it is matched with a profit) it can be relieved instead against general income.

6.3 Relieving the terminal loss

The loss is relieved against trade profits only.

Relief is given in the tax year of cessation and the three preceding years, later years first.

Question	Terminal loss relief

Set out below are the results of a business up to its cessation on 30 September 2009.

	Profit/(loss) £
Year to 31 December 2006	2,000
Year to 31 December 2007	400
Year to 31 December 2008	300
Nine months to 30 September 2009	(1,950)

Overlap profits on commencement were £450. These were all unrelieved on cessation.

Show the available terminal loss relief, and suggest an alternative claim if the trader had had other non-savings income of £10,000 in each of 2008/09 and 2009/10. Assume that 2009/10 tax rates and allowances apply to all years.

The terminal loss comes in the last 12 months, the period 1 October 2008 to 30 September 2009. This period is split as follows.

2008/09   Six months to 5 April 2009
2009/10   Six months to 30 September 2009

The terminal loss is made up as follows.

		£	£
Unrelieved trading losses			
2009/10			
6 months to 30.9.09	£(1,950) × 6/9		(1,300)
Overlap relief	£(450)		(450)
2008/09			
3 months to 31.12.08	£300 × 3/12	75	
3 months to 5.4.09	£(1,950) × 3/9	(650)	
			(575)
			(2,325)

Taxable trade profits will be as follows.

Year	Basis period	Profits	Terminal loss relief	Final taxable profits
		£	£	£
2006/07	Y/e 31.12.06	2,000	1,625	375
2007/08	Y/e 31.12.07	400	400	0
2008/09	Y/e 31.12.08	300	300	0
2009/10	1.10.08 – 30.9.09	0	0	0
			2,325	

If the trader had had £10,000 of other income in 2008/09 and 2009/10, we could consider loss relief claims against general income for these two years, using the loss of £(1,950 + 450) = £2,400 for 2009/10.

The final results would be as follows. (We could alternatively claim loss relief in 2008/09.)

	2006/07	2007/08	2008/09	2009/10
	£	£	£	£
Trade profits	2,000	400	300	0
Other income	0	0	10,000	10,000
	2,000	400	10,300	10,000
Less loss relief against general income	0	0	0	(2,400)
Net income	2,000	400	10,300	7,600

Another option would be to make a claim against general income for the balance of the loss not relieved as a terminal loss £(2,400 – 2,325) = £75 in either 2008/09 or 2009/10.

However, as there is only taxable income in 2008/09 and 2009/10 the full claim against general income is more tax efficient.

Chapter Roundup

- Trading losses may be relieved against future profits of the same trade, against general income and against capital gains.

- Trading losses may be relieved against future profits of the same trade. The relief is against the first available profits of the same trade.

- Where a business is transferred to a company, loss relief is available for any remaining unrelieved losses of the unincorporated business against income received from the company.

- A trading loss may be set against general income in the year of the loss and/or the preceding year. Personal allowances may be lost as a result of the claim. Once a claim has been made in any year, the remaining loss can be set against net chargeable gains.

- It is possible to carry back losses for three years against trading income where a trading loss arises in 2009/10.

- It is important for a trader to choose the right loss relief, so as to save tax at the highest possible rate and so as to obtain relief reasonably quickly.

- In opening years, a special relief involving the carry back of losses against general income is available. Losses arising in the first four tax years of a trade may be set against general income in the three years preceding the loss making year, taking the earliest year first.

- On the cessation of trade, a loss arising in the last 12 months of trading may be set against trade profits of the tax year of cessation and the previous 3 years, taking the latest year first.

Quick Quiz

1   Against what income can trade losses carried forward be set off?

    A   General income
    B   Non-savings income
    C   Any trading income
    D   Trading income from the same trade

2   When a loss is to be relieved against general income, how are losses linked to particular tax years?

3   Against which years' general income may a loss be relieved, for a continuing business which has traded for many years?

4   Maggie has been in business for many years and has always made profits of £10,000 each year. She has no other income apart from savings income of £2,000 in 2009/10 only. Maggie makes a loss of £(28,000) in 2009/10 and expects to make either a loss or smaller profits in the foreseeable future. How can Maggie obtain loss relief?

5   Joe starts trading on 6 April 2009, having previously been employed for many years. He makes a loss in his first year of trading. Against income of which years can he set the loss under early trade loss relief?

6   Terminal loss relief can be given in the year of _____ and then in the _____ preceding years, _____ years first. Fill in the blanks.

Answers to Quick Quiz

1   D. Against trading income from the same trade.

2   The loss for a tax year is the loss in the basis period for that tax year. However, if basis periods overlap, a loss in the overlap period is a loss of the earlier tax year only.

3   The year in which the loss arose and/or the preceding year.

4   Maggie can make a claim to set the loss against general income of £2,000 in 2009/10. She can then claim extended loss relief against trading profits of £10,000 in 2008/09, £10,000 in 2007/08 and £6,000 in 2006/07.

5   Loss incurred 2009/10: set against general income of 2006/07, 2007/08 and 2008/09 in that order.

6   Terminal loss relief can be given in the year of cessation and then in the three preceding years, later years first.

Now try the question below from the Exam Question Bank

Number	Level	Marks	Time
Q15	Examination	15	27 mins

11

Partnerships and limited liability partnerships

Topic list	Syllabus reference
1 Partnerships	B3(i)(i)-(iii)
2 Loss reliefs	B3(i)(iv)
3 Limited liability partnerships	B3(i)(v)

Introduction

We have covered sole traders, learning how to calculate taxable trading profits after capital allowances and allocate them to tax years and how to deal with losses.

We now see how the income tax rules for traders are adapted to deal with business partnerships. On the one hand, a partnership is a single trading entity, making profits as a whole. On the other hand, each partner has a personal tax computation, so the profits must be apportioned to the partners. The general approach is to work out the profits of the partnership, then tax each partner as if he were a sole trader running a business equal to his slice of the partnership (for example 25% of the partnership).

This chapter concludes our study of the income tax computation. In the next chapter we will turn our attention to national insurance.

Study guide

		Intellectual level
B3	**Income from self-employment**	
(i)	Partnerships and limited liability partnerships	
(i)(i)	Explain how a partnership is assessed to tax.	2
(i)(ii)	Compute the assessable profits for each partner following a change in the profit sharing ratio.	2
(i)(iii)	Compute the assessable profits for each partner following a change in the membership of the partnership.	2
(i)(iv)	Describe the alternative loss relief claims that are available to partners.	1
(i)(v)	Explain the loss relief restriction that applies to the partners of a limited liability partnership.	1

Exam guide

Although partnerships are an important topic you are not guaranteed to get a question on them in your exam. This does not mean that you can ignore them. As long as you remember to allocate the profits between the partners according to their profit sharing arrangements for the period of account you should be able to cope with any aspect of partnership tax. Remember that each partner is taxed as a sole trader, and you should apply the opening and closing year rules and loss reliefs as appropriate to that partner.

1 Partnerships

FAST FORWARD

A partnership is simply treated as a source of profits and losses for trades being carried on by the individual partners. Divide profits or losses between the partners according to the profit sharing arrangements in the period of account concerned. If any of the partners are entitled to a salary or interest on capital, apportion this first, not forgetting to pro-rate in periods of less than 12 months.

1.1 Introduction

A partnership is a group of individuals who are trading together. They will agree amongst themselves how the business should be run and how profits and losses should be shared. It is not treated as a separate entity for tax purposes (in contrast to a company).

1.2 Basis of assessment

A business partnership is treated like a sole trader for the purposes of computing its profits. Partners' salaries and interest on capital are not deductible expenses and must be added back in computing profits, because they are a form of drawings.

Once the partnership's profits for a period of account have been computed, they are shared between the partners according to the profit sharing arrangements for that period of account.

Question

Allocating profits

Steve and Tanya have been in partnership for many years. For the year ended 31 October 2009, taxable trading profits were £70,000.

Steve is allocated an annual salary of £12,000 and Tanya's salary is £28,000.

The profit sharing ratio is 2:1.

Allocate the trade profit to each partner for the year ended 31 October 2009.

Allocate the profits for the year ended 31 October 2009.

	Total £	Steve £	Tanya £
Profit	70,000		
Salaries	40,000	12,000	28,000
Balance (2:1)	30,000	20,000	10,000
Total	70,000	32,000	38,000

1.3 Change in profit sharing arrangements

If the profit sharing arrangements change part way through the period of account, the profits, salaries and interest for the period of account must be pro-rated accordingly.

Question   Change in profit sharing arrangements

Sue and Tim have been in partnership for many years. For the year ended 31 December 2009, taxable trading profits were £50,000.

Sue is allocated an annual salary of £10,000 and Tim's salary is £15,000.

The profit sharing ratio was 1:1 until 31 August 2009 when it changed to 1:2 with no provision for salaries.

Allocate the trade profit to each partner for the year ended 31 December 2009.

Answer

Allocate the profits for the year ended 31 December 2009.

	Total £	Sue £	Tim £
Profit	50,000		
1 January – 31 August (8 months)	33,333		
Salaries (8/12 × £10,000/£15,000)	16,667	6,667	10,000
Balance (1:1)	16,666	8,333	8,333
	33,333		
1 September – 31 December (4 months)	16,667		
Salaries	Nil	–	–
Balance (1:2)	16,667	5,556	11,111
	16,667		
Total	50,000	20,556	29,444

Note. Since the profit sharing arrangements changed part way through the period of account, the profits and salaries for the period of account must be pro-rated accordingly.

1.4 The tax positions of individual partners

Each partner is taxed like a sole trader who runs a business which:

- Starts when he joins the partnership
- Finishes when he leaves the partnership
- Has the same periods of account as the partnership (except that a partner who joins or leaves during a period will have a period which starts and/or ends part way through the partnership's period)
- Makes profits or losses equal to the partner's share of the partnership's profits or losses

1.5 Assets owned individually

Where the partners own assets (such as their cars) individually, a capital allowances computation must be prepared for each partner in respect of the assets he owns (not forgetting any adjustment for private use). **The capital allowances must go into the partnership's tax computation.**

1.6 Changes in membership

FAST FORWARD

Commencement and cessation rules apply to partners individually when they join or leave.

When a trade continues but partners join or leave (including cases when a sole trader takes in partners or a partnership breaks up leaving only one partner as a sole trader), **the special rules for basis periods in opening and closing years do not apply to the people who were carrying on the trade both before and after the change. They carry on using the period of account ending in each tax year as the basis period for the tax year (ie the current year basis). The commencement rules only affect joiners, and the cessation rules only affect leavers.**

However, when no-one carries on the trade both before and after the change, as when a partnership transfers its trade to a completely new owner or set of owners, the cessation rules apply to the old owners and the commencement rules apply to the new owners.

1.7 Example: a comprehensive partnership example

Alice and Bertrand start a partnership on 1 July 2006, making up accounts to 31 December each year. On 1 May 2008, Charles joins the partnership. On 1 November 2009, Charles leaves. On 1 January 2010, Deborah joins. The profit sharing arrangements are as follows.

	Alice	Bertrand	Charles	Deborah
1.7.06 – 31.1.07				
Salaries (per annum)	£3,000	£4,500		
Balance	3/5	2/5		
1.2.07 – 30.4.08				
Salaries (per annum)	£3,000	£6,000		
Balance	4/5	1/5		
1.5.08 – 31.10.09				
Salaries (per annum)	£2,400	£3,600	£1,800	
Balance	2/5	2/5	1/5	
1.11.09 – 31.12.10				
Salaries (per annum)	£1,500	£2,700		
Balance	3/5	2/5		
1.1.10 onwards				
Salaries (per annum)	£1,500	£2,700		£600
Balance	3/5	1/5		1/5

Profits as adjusted for tax purposes are as follows.

Period	Profit
	£
1.7.06 – 31.12.06	22,000
1.1.07 – 31.12.07	51,000
1.1.08 – 31.12.08	39,000
1.1.09 – 31.12.09	15,000
1.1.10 – 31.12.10	18,000

When approaching the question, we must first share the trade profits for the periods of account between the partners, remembering to adjust the salaries for periods of less than a year.

	Total £	Alice £	Bertrand £	Charles £	Deborah £
1.7.06 – 31.12.06					
Salaries	3,750	1,500	2,250		
Balance	18,250	10,950	7,300		
Total (P/e 31.12.06)	22,000	12,450	9,550		
1.1.07 – 31.12.07					
January					
Salaries	625	250	375		
Balance	3,625	2,175	1,450		
Total	4,250	2,425	1,825		
February to December					
Salaries	8,250	2,750	5,500		
Balance	38,500	30,800	7,700		
Total	46,750	33,550	13,200		
Total for y/e 31.12.07	51,000	35,975	15,025		
1.1.08 – 31.12.08					
January to April					
Salaries	3,000	1,000	2,000		
Balance	10,000	8,000	2,000		
Total	13,000	9,000	4,000		
May to December					
Salaries	5,200	1,600	2,400	1,200	
Balance	20,800	8,320	8,320	4,160	
Total	26,000	9,920	10,720	5,360	
Total for y/e 31.12.08	39,000	18,920	14,720	5,360	
1.1.09 – 31.12.09					
January to October					
Salaries	6,500	2,000	3,000	1,500	
Balance	6,000	2,400	2,400	1,200	
Total	12,500	4,400	5,400	2,700	
November and December					
Salaries	700	250	450		
Balance	1,800	1,080	720		
Total	2,500	1,330	1,170		
Total for y/e 31.12.09	15,000	5,730	6,570	2,700	
1.1.10 – 31.12.10					
Salaries	4,800	1,500	2,700		600
Balance	13,200	7,920	2,640		2,640
Total for y/e 31.12.10	18,000	9,420	5,340		3,240

The next stage is to work out the basis periods and hence the taxable trade profits for the partners. All of them are treated as making up accounts to 31 December, but Alice and Bertrand are treated as starting to trade on 1 July 2006, Charles as trading only from 1 May 2008 to 31 October 2009 and Deborah as starting to trade on 1 January 2010. Applying the usual rules gives the following basis periods and taxable profits.

Alice

Year	Basis period	Working	Taxable profits £
2006/07	1.7.06 – 5.4.07	£12,450 + (£35,975 × 3/12)	21,444
2007/08	1.1.07 – 31.12.07		35,975
2008/09	1.1.08 – 31.12.08		18,920
2009/10	1.1.09 – 31.12.09		5,730

Note that for 2006/07 we take Alice's total for the year ended 2007 and apportion that, because the partnership's period of account runs from 1 January to 31 December 2007. Alice's profits for 2006/07 are *not* £12,450 + £2,425 + (£33,550 × 2/11) = £20,975.

Alice will have overlap profits for the period 1 January to 5 April 2007 (£35,975 × 3/12 = £8,994) to deduct when she ceases to trade.

Bertrand

Year	Basis period	Working	Taxable profits £
2006/07	1.7.06 – 5.4.07	£9,550 + (£15,025 × 3/12)	13,306
2007/08	1.1.07 – 31.12.07		15,025
2008/09	1.1.08 – 31.12.08		14,720
2009/10	1.1.09 – 31.12.09		6,570

Bertrand's overlap profits are £15,025 × 3/12 = £3,756.

Charles

Year	Basis period	Working	Taxable profits £
2008/09	1.5.08 – 5.4.09	£5,360 + (£2,700 × 3/10)	6,170
2009/10	6.4.09 – 31.10.09	£2,700 × 7/10	1,890

Because Charles ceased to trade in his second tax year of trading, his basis period for the second year starts on 6 April and he has no overlap profits.

Deborah

Year	Basis period	Working	Taxable profits £
2009/10	1.1.10– 5.4.10	£3,240 × 3/12	810

Exam focus point

Partners are effectively taxed in the same way as sole traders with just one difference. Before you tax the partner you need to take each set of accounts (as adjusted for tax purposes) and divide the trade profit (or loss) between each partner.

Then carry on as normal for a sole trader – each partner is that sole trader in respect of his trade profits for each accounting period.

2 Loss reliefs

FAST FORWARD

Partners are individually entitled to loss relief in the same way as sole traders.

2.1 Entitlement to loss relief

Partners are entitled to the same loss reliefs as sole traders. The reliefs are:

(a) **Carry forward against future trading profits**. If the business is transferred to a company this is extended to carry forward against future income from the company.

(b) **Set off against general income of the same and/or preceding year**. This claim can be extended to set off against capital gains and in 2009/10 against trading profits in the preceding three years.

(c) **For a new partner, losses in the first four tax years of trade can be set off against general income of the three preceding years**. This is so even if the actual trade commenced many years before the partner joined.

(d) **For a ceasing partner, terminal loss relief is available** when he is treated as ceasing to trade. This is so even if the partnership continues to trades after he leaves.

Different partners may claim loss reliefs in different ways.

Mary and Natalie have been trading for many years sharing profits equally. On 1 January 2010 Mary retired and Oliver joined the partnership. Natalie and Oliver share profits in the ratio of 2:1. Although the partnership had previously been profitable it made a loss of £24,000 for the year to 31 March 2010. The partnership is expected to be profitable in the future.

Calculate the loss accruing to each partner for 2009/10 and explain what reliefs are available.

Answer

We must first share the loss for the period of account between the partners, remembering to adjust the salaries for periods of less than a year.

	Total £	Mary £	Natalie £	Oliver £
y/e 31.3.10				
1.4.09 – 31.12.09				
Total £24,000 × 9/12	(18,000)	(9,000)	(9,000)	
1.1.10 – 31.3.10				
Total £24,000 × 3/12	(6,000)		(4,000)	(2,000)
Total for y/e 31.03.10	(24,000)	(9,000)	(13,000)	(2,000)

Mary

For 2009/10, Mary has a loss of £9,000. She may claim relief against general income of 2009/10 and/or 2008/09, and may extend the claim to capital gains and against trading profits of 2008/09 (if she does not claim against general income in that year), 2007/08 and 2006/07.

Mary has ceased trading, and may instead claim terminal loss relief. The terminal loss will be £9,000 (a profit arose in the period 1.1.09 – 31.3.09 which would be treated as zero) and this may be set against her taxable trade profits for 2009/10 (£nil), 2008/09, 2007/08 and 2006/07.

Natalie

For 2009/10, Natalie has a loss of £13,000. She may claim relief against general income of 2009/10 and/or 2008/09, and may extend the claim to capital gains and against trading profits of 2008/09 (if she does not claim against general income in that year), 2007/08 and 2006/07 . Any loss remaining unrelieved may be carried forward against future income from the same trade.

Oliver

Oliver's loss for 2009/10 is £2,000. He may claim relief for the loss against general income (and gains) of 2009/10 and/or 2008/09. As he has just started to trade he may claim relief for the loss against general income of 2006/07, 2007/08 and 2008/09. Any loss remaining unrelieved may be carried forward against future income from the same trade.

3 Limited liability partnerships

FAST FORWARD

Limited liability partnerships are taxed on virtually the same basis as normal partnerships except that loss relief is restricted for all partners.

It is possible to form a limited liability partnership. The difference between a limited liability partnership (LLP) and a normal partnership is that **in a LLP the liability of the partners is limited to the capital they contributed.**

The partners of a LLP are taxed on virtually the same basis as the partners of a normal partnership (see above). However, the amount of loss relief that a partner can claim against general income when the claim is against non-partnership income is restricted to the capital he contributed plus his undrawn profit subject to an overall cap of £25,000.

Chapter Roundup

- A partnership is simply treated as a source of profits and losses for trades being carried on by the individual partners. Divide profits or losses between the partners according to the profit sharing arrangements in the period of account concerned. If any of the partners are entitled to a salary or interest on capital, apportion this first, not forgetting to pro-rate in periods of less than 12 months.

- Commencement and cessation rules apply to partners individually when they join or leave.

- Partners are individually entitled to loss relief in the same way as sole traders.

- Limited liability partnerships are taxed on virtually the same basis as normal partnerships except that loss relief is restricted for all partners.

1   How are partnership trading profits divided between the individual partners?

2   What loss reliefs are partners entitled to?

3   Janet and John are partners sharing profits 60:40. For the years ended 30 June 2009 and 2010 the partnership made profits of £100,000 and £150,000 respectively. John's taxable trading profits in 2009/10 are:

    A   £30,000
    B   £40,000
    C   £50,000
    D   £60,000

4   Yolanda and Yan are in partnership sharing profits 80:20. For the year ended 31 December 2009 the business makes a loss of £40,000. If Yan decides to use his share of the loss against general income what loss relief(s) can Yolanda claim?

5   Pete and Doug have been partners for many years, sharing profits equally. On 1 January 2009 Dave joins the partnership and it is agreed to share profits 40:40:20. For the year ended 30 June 2009 profits are £100,000.

Doug's share of these profits is:

    A   £42,500
    B   £45,000
    C   £47,500
    D   £50,000

Answers to Quick Quiz

1   Profits are divided in accordance with the profit sharing arrangements that existed during the period of account in which the profits arose.

2   Partners are entitled to the same loss reliefs as sole traders as appropriate.

3   B. £40,000.

     2009/10: ye 30 June 2009

     £100,000 × 40% = £40,000.

4   Yolanda has a choice of loss reliefs:

     Loss relief against general income or carry forward loss relief.

     Her loss relief claim is unaffected by Yan's.

5   B. £45,000

	Pete £	Doug £	Dave £
Y/e 30 June 2009			
1.7.08 – 31.12.09			
6m × £100,000			
£50,000 50:50	25,000	25,000	
1.1.09 – 30.6.09			
6m × £100,000			
£50,000 40:40:20	20,000	20,000	10,000
	45,000	45,000	10,000

Now try the questions below from the Exam Question Bank

Number	Level	Marks	Time
Q16	Examination	15	27 mins
Q17	Examination	15	27 mins

12

National insurance contributions

Topic list	Syllabus reference
1 Scope of national insurance contributions (NICs)	E1(a)
2 Class 1 and Class 1A NICs for employed persons	E2(a), (b)
3 Class 2 and class 4 NICs for self-employed persons	E3(a), (b)

Introduction

In the previous chapters we have covered income tax for employees and for the self employed.

We look at the national insurance contributions payable under Classes 1 and 1A in respect of employment and under Classes 2 and 4 in respect of self employment.

In the next chapter we will turn our attention to the taxation of chargeable gains.

Study guide

		Intellectual level
E1	**The scope of national insurance**	
(a)	Describe the scope of national insurance.	1
E2	**Class 1 and Class 1A contributions for employed persons**	
(a)	Compute Class 1 NIC.	2
(b)	Compute Class 1A NIC.	2
E3	**Class 2 and Class 4 contributions for self employed persons**	
(a)	Compute Class 2 NIC.	2
(b)	Compute Class 4 NIC.	2

Exam guide

You will not find a complete question on national insurance but it is likely to form part of a larger question on the taxation of employees or the self employed. You must be absolutely clear who is liable for which class of contributions; only employers, for example, pay Class 1A.

1 Scope of national insurance contributions (NICs)

Four classes of national insurance contribution (NIC) exist, as set out below.

(a)   **Class 1**. This is divided into:

   (i)   **Primary**, paid by employees
   (ii)   **Secondary**, **Class 1A and Class 1B** paid by employers

(b)   **Class 2**. Paid by the self-employed

(c)   **Class 3**. Voluntary contributions (paid to maintain rights to certain state benefits)

(d)   **Class 4**. Paid by the self-employed

Exam focus point

Class 1B and Class 3 contributions are outside the scope of your syllabus.

The National Insurance Contributions Office (NICO), which is part of HM Revenue and Customs, examines employers' records and procedures to ensure that the correct amounts of NICs are collected.

2 Class 1 and Class 1A NICs for employed persons

2.1 Class 1 NICs

FAST FORWARD

Class 1 NICs are payable by employees and employers on earnings.

Both **employees** and **employers pay NICs** related to the employee's earnings. NICs are not deductible from an employee's gross salary for income tax purposes. However, employers' contributions are deductible trade expenses.

2.1.1 Earnings

'Earnings' broadly comprise gross pay, excluding benefits which cannot be turned into cash by surrender (eg holidays). Earnings also include payments for use of the employee's own car on business over the approved amount of 40p per mile (irrespective of total mileage.) Therefore, where an employer reimburses an employee using his own car for business mileage, the earnings element is the excess of the mileage rate paid over 40 per mile. This applies even where business mileage exceeds 10,000 pa.

Certain payments are exempt. In general the income tax and NIC exemptions mirror one another. For example, payment of personal incidental expenses covered by the £5/£10 a night income tax de minimis exemption are excluded from NIC earnings. Relocation expenses of a type exempt from income tax are also excluded from NIC earnings but without the income tax £8,000 upper limit (although expenses exceeding £8,000 are subject to Class 1A NICs as described below).

An expense with a business purpose is not treated as earnings. For example, if an employee is reimbursed for business travel or for staying in a hotel on the employer's business this is not normally 'earnings'. Again the NIC rules for travel expenses follow the income tax rules.

One commonly met expenses payment is telephone calls. If an employee is reimbursed for his own telephone charges the reimbursed cost of private calls (and all reimbursed rental) is earnings.

In general, non cash vouchers are subject to Class 1 NICs. However, the following are exempt.

- Childcare vouchers up to £55 per week
- Any other voucher which is exempt from income tax

An employer's contribution to an employee's occupational or private registered pension scheme is excluded from the definition of 'earnings'.

2.1.2 Rates of Class 1 NICs

The rates of contribution for 2009/10, and the income bands to which they apply, are set out in the Rates and Allowance Tables in this Text.

Employees pay main primary contributions of 11% of earnings between the earnings threshold of £5,715 and the upper earnings limit of £43,875 or the equivalent monthly or weekly limit (see below). They also pay additional primary contributions of 1% on earnings above the upper earnings limit.

Employers pay secondary contributions of 12.8% on earnings above the earnings threshold of £5,715 or the equivalent monthly or weekly limit. There is no upper limit.

If an individual has more than one job then NIC is calculated on the earnings from each job separately and independently. However there is an overall annual maximum amount of Class 1 NIC any individual will be due to pay. If the total NIC paid from those different jobs exceeds the maximum that individual can claim a refund of the excess.

2.1.3 Earnings period

NICs are calculated in relation to an earnings period. This is the period to which earnings paid to an employee are deemed to relate. Where earnings are paid at regular intervals, the earnings period will generally be equated with the payment interval, for example a week or a month. An earnings period cannot usually be less than seven days long.

Exam focus point

In the exam NICs will generally be calculated on an annual basis.

Question   Class 1 contributions

Sally works for Red plc. She is paid £4,000 per month.

Show Sally's primary contributions and the secondary contributions paid by Red plc for 2009/10.

Answer

Earnings threshold £5,715
Upper earnings limit £43,875
Annual salary £4,000 × 12 = £48,000

Sally

	£
Primary contributions	
£(43,875 − 5,715) = £38,160 × 11% (main)	4,198
£(48,000 − 43,875) = £4,125 × 1% (additional)	41
Total primary contributions	4,239

	£
Red plc	
Secondary contributions	
£(48,000 − 5,715) = £42,285 × 12.8%	5,412

Special rules apply to company directors, regardless of whether they are paid at regular intervals or not. Where a person is a director at the beginning of the tax year, his earnings period is the tax year, even if he ceases to be director during the year. **The annual limits as shown in the Tax Tables apply.**

Question   Employees and directors

Bill and Ben work for Weed Ltd. Bill is a monthly paid employee. Ben who is a director of Weed Ltd, is also paid monthly. Each is paid an annual salary of £42,000 in 2009/10 and each also received a bonus of £3,000 in December 2009.

Show the primary and secondary contributions for both Bill and Ben, using a monthly earnings period for Bill.

Answer

Bill

Earnings threshold £5,715/12 = £476
Upper earnings limit £43,875/12 = £3,656
Regular monthly earnings £42,000/12 = £3,500

Primary contributions

	£
11 months	
£(3,500 − 476) = £3,024 × 11% × 11 (main only)	3,659
1 month (December)	
£(3,656 − 476) = £3,180 × 11% (main)	350
£(6,500 − 3,656) = £2,844 × 1% (additional)	28
Total primary contributions	4,037

Secondary contributions

	£
11 months	
£(3,500 − 476) = £3,024 × 12.8% × 11	4,258
1 month (December)	
£(3,500 + £3,000 − 476) = £6,024 × 12.8%	771
Total secondary contributions	5,029

Ben
Total earnings £(42,000 + 3,000) = £45,000

Primary contributions

	£
Total earnings exceed UEL	
£(43,875 − 5,715) = £38,160 × 11% (main)	4,198
£(45,000 − 43,875) = £1,125 × 1% (additional)	11
Total primary	4,209

Secondary contributions

£(45,000 − 5,715) = £39,285 × 12.8%	5,028

Because Ben is a director an annual earnings period applies. The effect of this is that increased primary contributions are due.

2.2 Class 1A NICs

FAST FORWARD

Class 1A NICs are payable by employers on benefits provided for employees.

Employers must pay Class 1A NIC at 12.8% in respect of most taxable benefits. Taxable benefits are calculated in accordance with income tax rules. There is no Class 1A in respect of any benefits already treated as earnings for Class 1 purposes (eg non cash vouchers). Tax exempt benefits are not liable to Class 1A NIC.

No contributions are levied when an employee is earning less than £8,500 a year.

Question

Class IA NIC

James has the following benefits for income tax purposes

	£
Company car	5,200
Living accommodation	10,000
Medical insurance	800

Calculate the Class 1A NICs that the employer will have to pay.

Answer

Total benefits are £16,000 (£10,000 + £5,200 + £800)

Class 1A NICs:

12.8% × £16,000 = £2,048

2.3 Miscellaneous points

Class 1 contributions are collected under the PAYE system described earlier in this Text. Class 1A contributions are collected annually in arrears, and are due by 19 July following the tax year.

Class 1 and 1A contributions broadly apply to amounts which are taxable as employment income. They do not apply to dividends paid to directors and employees who are also shareholders in the company.

3 Class 2 and Class 4 NICs for self-employed persons

The self employed pay Class 2 and Class 4 NICs. Class 2 NICs are paid at a flat weekly rate. Class 4 NICs are based on the level of the individual's profits.

3.1 Class 2 contributions

The self employed (sole traders and partners) pay NICs in two ways.

Class 2 contributions are payable at a flat rate. The Class 2 rate for 2009/10 is £2.40 a week.

Self employed people must register with HMRC for Class 2 contributions within three months of the end of the month in which they start self employment. People who fail to register may incur a £100 penalty.

3.2 Class 4 contributions

Additionally, **the self employed pay Class 4 NICs,** based on the level of the individual's taxable business profits.

Main rate Class 4 NICs are calculated by applying a fixed percentage (8% for 2009/10) to the individual's profits between the lower limit (£5,715 for 2009/10) and the upper limit (£43,875 for 2009/10). Additional rate contributions are 1% (for 2009/10) on profits above that limit.

3.3 Example: Class 4 contributions

If a sole trader had profits of £14,570 for 2009/10 his Class 4 NIC liability would be as follows.

	£
Profits	14,570
Less lower limit	(5,715)
	8,855

Class 4 NICs = 8% × £8,855 = <u>£708</u> (main only)

3.4 Example: additional Class 4 contributions

If an individual's profits are £46,000, additional Class 4 NICs are due on the excess over the upper limit. Thus the amount payable in 2009/10 is as follows.

	£
Profits (upper limit)	43,875
Less lower limit	(5,715)
	38,160

	£
Main rate Class 4 NICs 8% × £38,160	3,053
Additional rate Class 4 NICs £(46,000 − 43,875) = £2,125 × 1%	21
	3,074

For Class 4 NIC purposes, profits are the trade profits taxable for income tax purposes, less trading losses.

There is no deduction for personal pension premiums.

Class 4 NICs are collected by HMRC. They are paid at the same time as the associated income tax liability. Interest is charged on overdue contributions. The administration of tax is covered later in this Text.

Chapter Roundup

- Class 1 NICs are payable by employees and employers on earnings.

- Class 1A NICs are payable by employers on benefits provided for employees.

- The self employed pay Class 2 and Class 4 NICs. Class 2 NICs are paid at a flat weekly rate. Class 4 NICs are based on the level of the individual's profits.

Quick Quiz

1   What national insurance contributions are payable by employers and employees?

2   On what are Class 1A NICs based?

3   Class 2 NICs are paid by an employer. TRUE/FALSE?

4   How are Class 4 NICs calculated?

Answers to Quick Quiz

1   Employees – Class 1 primary contributions

Employers – Class 1 secondary contributions
Class 1A contributions

2   Class 1A NICs are based on taxable benefits paid to P11D employees.

3   False. Class 2 contributions are paid by the self-employed.

4   The main rate is a fixed percentage (8% in 2009/10) of an individual's tax profits between an upper limit and lower limit. The additional rate (1%) applies above the upper limit.

Now try the questions below from the Exam Question Bank

Number	Level	Marks	Time
Q18	Examination	10	18 mins
Q19	Examination	15	27 mins

Chargeable gains for individuals

13

Computing chargeable gains

Topic list	Syllabus reference
1 Chargeable persons, disposals and assets	D1 (a)-(c)
2 Computing a gain or loss	D2 (a)
3 The annual exemption	D5 (a)
4 Capital losses	D2 (c)
5 CGT payable by individuals	D5 (a)
6 Transfers between spouses/civil partners	D2 (d)
7 Part disposals	D2 (e)
8 The damage, loss or destruction of an asset	D2 (f)

Introduction

Now that we have completed our study of the income tax and national insurance liabilities we turn our attention to the capital gains tax computation. We deal with individuals in this chapter. Chargeable gains for companies are dealt with later in this Study Text.

We look at the circumstances in which a chargeable gain or allowable loss may arise. Then we look at the detailed calculation of the gain or loss on a disposal of an asset.

Then we consider the annual exemption and then we look at the relief for capital losses, including the interaction between capital losses brought forward and the annual exemption. This enables us to compute CGT payable by individuals.

We then look at part disposals. If only part of an asset has been disposed of we need to know how to allocate the cost between the part disposed of and the part retained.

Finally, we consider the damage or destruction of an asset and the receipt of compensation or insurance proceeds, and look at the reliefs available where the proceeds are applied in restoring or replacing the asset.

In the following chapters we look at further rules, including those for disposals of shares, and various CGT reliefs that may be available.

Study guide

		Intellectual level
D1	**The scope of the taxation of capital gains**	
(a)	Describe the scope of capital gains tax.	2
(b)	Explain how the residence and ordinary residence of an individual is determined.	2
(c)	List those assets which are exempt.	1
D2	**The basic principles of computing gains and losses**	
(a)	Compute capital gains for both individuals and companies.	2
(c)	Explain the treatment of capital losses for both individuals and companies.	1
(d)	Explain the treatment of transfers between a husband and wife or between a couple in a civil partnership.	2
(e)	Compute the amount of allowable expenditure for a part disposal.	2
(f)	Explain the treatment where an asset is damaged, lost or destroyed, and the implications of receiving insurance proceeds and reinvesting such proceeds.	2
D5	**The computation of capital gains tax payable by individuals**	
(a)	Compute the amount of capital gains tax payable.	2

Exam guide

Question 3 of the exam will always be a 20 mark question on capital gains, and there may also be an element of capital gains in questions 1 and/or 2. You are almost certain to have to prepare a detailed capital gains computation, whether for an individual or company. Learn the basic layout, so that slotting in the figures becomes automatic. Then in the exam you will be able to turn your attention to the particular points raised in the question. The A/(A+B) formula for part disposals must be learnt. The rules for damage or destruction of an asset are less likely to be examined in detail, but try to remember the objective of the reliefs available where the proceeds are used for restoration or replacement and they will seem more straightforward.

1 Chargeable persons, disposals and assets

FAST FORWARD
> A gain is chargeable if there is a chargeable disposal of a chargeable asset by a chargeable person.

Key term
> For a chargeable gain to arise there must be:
>
> • A **chargeable person**; and
> • A **chargeable disposal**; and
> • A **chargeable asset**
>
> otherwise no charge to tax occurs.

1.1 Chargeable persons

FAST FORWARD
> Capital gains are chargeable on individuals and companies.

The following are chargeable persons.

• **Individuals**
• **Companies**

We will look at the taxation of chargeable gains on companies later in this Text.

1.2 Chargeable disposals

The following are chargeable disposals.

- **Sales of assets or parts of assets**
- **Gifts of assets or parts of assets**
- **The loss or destruction of assets**

A chargeable disposal occurs on the date of the contract (where there is one, whether written or oral), or the date of a conditional contract becoming unconditional. This may differ from the date of transfer of the asset. However, when a capital sum is received for example on the loss or destruction of an asset, the disposal takes place on the day the sum is received.

Where a disposal involves an acquisition by someone else, the date of acquisition for that person is the same as the date of disposal.

Transfers of assets on death are exempt disposals.

1.3 Chargeable assets

All forms of property, wherever in the world they are situated, are chargeable assets unless they are specifically designated as exempt.

1.4 Overseas aspects of CGT

FAST FORWARD

CGT applies primarily to persons resident or ordinarily resident in the UK.

Individuals are liable to CGT on the disposal of assets situated anywhere in the world if for any part of the tax year in which the disposal occurs they are resident or ordinarily resident in the UK. By concession, when a person first becomes resident in the UK, he is normally charged to CGT only on those gains which arise after his arrival provided he has not been resident or ordinarily resident in the UK for four out of the last seven years.

Residence and ordinary residence are defined for CGT in the same way as for income tax (see Sections 1.2 and 1.3 in Chapter 2).

Exam focus point

The computation of capital gains arising on overseas assets is outside the scope of your syllabus.

1.5 Exempt assets

The following are exempt assets.

- **Motor vehicles** suitable for private use
- **National Savings and Investments certificates** and **premium bonds**
- Foreign currency for private use
- Decorations for bravery where awarded, not purchased
- Damages for personal or professional injury
- **Gilt-edged securities (treasury stock)**
- **Qualifying corporate bonds (QCBs)**
- **Certain chattels**
- Debts (except debts on a security)
- Investments held in individual savings accounts

If an asset is an exempt asset any gain is not chargeable and any loss is not allowable.

2 Computing a gain or loss

A gain or loss is computed by taking the proceeds and deducting the cost. Incidental costs of acquisition and disposal are deducted together with any enhancement expenditure reflected in the state and nature of the asset at the date of disposal.

2.1 Basic calculation

A gain (or an allowable loss) is generally calculated as follows.

	£
	£
Disposal consideration	45,000
Less incidental costs of disposal	(400)
Net proceeds	44,600
Less allowable costs	(21,000)
Gain	23,600

Usually the disposal consideration is the proceeds of sale of the asset, but a disposal is deemed to take place at market value:

- Where the disposal is **not a bargain at arm's length**
- Where the disposal is made for a **consideration which cannot be valued**
- Where the disposal is by way of a **gift**.

Special valuation rules apply for shares (see later in this Text).

Incidental costs of disposal may include:

- Valuation fees
- Estate agency fees
- Advertising costs
- Legal costs.

Allowable costs include:

- The original cost of acquisition
- Incidental costs of acquisition
- Capital expenditure incurred in enhancing the asset.

Enhancement expenditure is capital expenditure which enhances the value of the asset and is reflected in the state or nature of the asset at the time of disposal, or expenditure incurred in establishing, preserving or defending title to, or a right over, the asset. Excluded from this category are:

- Costs of repairs and maintenance
- Costs of insurance
- Any expenditure deductible from trading profits
- Any expenditure met by public funds (for example council grants).

Question

Calculating the gain

Joanne bought a piece of land as an investment for £20,000. The legal costs of purchase were £250.

Joanne sold the land on 12 December 2009 for £35,000. She incurred estate agency fees of £700 and legal costs of £500 on the sale.

Calculate Joanne's gain on sale.

	£
Proceeds of sale	35,000
Less costs of disposal £(700 + 500)	(1,200)
	33,800
Less costs of acquisition £(20,000 + 250)	(20,250)
Gain	13,550

3 The annual exemption

An individual is entitled to an annual exemption for each tax year.

There is an annual exemption for each tax year. For each individual for 2009/10 it is £10,100. The annual exemption is deducted from the chargeable gains for the year after the deductions of losses and other reliefs.

Thus if Susie has chargeable gains for 2009/10 of £15,500 her taxable gains are £15,500 – £10,100 = £5,400.

4 Capital losses

Losses are set off against gains of the same year and any excess carried forward. Brought forward losses are only set off to reduce net gains down to the amount of the annual exemption.

4.1 Allowable losses of the same year

Allowable capital losses arising in a tax year are deducted from gains arising in the same tax year.

Any loss which cannot be set off is carried forward to set against future gains. Losses must be used as soon as possible (but see below).

4.2 Allowable losses brought forward

Allowable losses brought forward are only set off to reduce current year gains less current year allowable losses to the annual exempt amount. No set-off is made if net chargeable gains for the current year do not exceed the annual exempt amount.

4.3 Example: the use of losses

(a)   George has gains for 2009/10 of £11,000 and allowable losses of £6,000. As the losses are *current year losses* they must be fully relieved against the £11,000 of gains to produce net gains of £5,000 despite the fact that net gains are below the annual exemption.

(b)   Bob has gains of £14,000 for 2009/10 and allowable losses brought forward of £6,000. Bob restricts his loss relief to £3,900 so as to leave net gains of £(14,000 – 3,900) = £10,100, which will be exactly covered by his annual exemption for 2009/10. The remaining £2,100 of losses will be carried forward to 2010/11.

(c)   Tom has gains of £10,000 for 2009/10 and losses brought forward from 2008/09 of £4,000. He will leapfrog 2009/10 and carry forward all of his losses to 2010/11. His gains of £10,000 are covered by his annual exemption for 2009/10.

5 CGT payable by individuals

FAST FORWARD

Individuals pay CGT on gains arising in a tax year at 18%.

Taxable gains are chargeable to capital gains tax at the rate of 18%.

Question

CGT payable by individual

Lucinda sold the following assets in 2009/10:

	Proceeds £	Cost £
Plot of land	100,000	80,000
Painting	40,000	15,000
Shares in XYZ plc	50,000	68,000

Calculate the CGT payable by Lucinda.

Answer

	£	£
Land		
Proceeds	100,000	
Less: cost	(80,000)	
Gain		20,000
Painting		
Proceeds	40,000	
Less: cost	(15,000)	
Gain		25,000
Shares		
Proceeds	50,000	
Less: cost	(68,000)	
Loss		(18,000)
Net gains		27,000
Less: annual exemption		(10,100)
Taxable gains		16,900
CGT @ 18% on £16,900		3,042

6 Transfers between spouses/civil partners

FAST FORWARD

Disposals between spouses or members of a civil partnership are made on a no gain no loss basis and do not give rise to a chargeable gain or allowable loss.

Spouses and civil partners are taxed as separate individuals. Each has his own annual exemption, and losses of one spouse or civil partner cannot be set against gains of the other spouse or civil partner.

Disposals between spouses or civil partners living together give rise to no gain no loss, whatever actual price (if any) was charged by the transferor. This means that there is no chargeable gain or allowable loss, and the transferee takes over the transferor's cost.

Question

Harry bought an asset for £150,000. He gave it to his wife Margaret when it was worth £350,000 on 10 May 2009. Margaret sold it on 27 August 2009 for £400,000.

Calculate any chargeable gains arising to Harry and Margaret.

Answer

The disposal from Harry to Margaret is a no gain no loss disposal. Harry has no chargeable gain, and the cost for Margaret is Harry's original cost.

The gain on the sale by Margaret is:

	£
Proceeds of sale	400,000
Less cost	(150,000)
Gain	250,000

7 Part disposals

FAST FORWARD

On a part disposal, the cost must be apportioned between the part disposed of and the part retained.

The disposal of part of a chargeable asset is a chargeable event. The chargeable gain (or allowable loss) is computed by deducting a fraction of the original cost of the whole asset from the disposal value. The balance of the cost is carried forward until the eventual disposal of the asset.

Exam formula

The fraction is:

$$\text{Cost} \times \frac{A}{A+B} = \frac{\text{value of the part disposed of}}{\text{value of the part disposed of} + \text{market value of the remainder}}$$

In this fraction, A is the proceeds *before* deducting incidental costs of disposal.

The part disposal fraction should not be applied indiscriminately. Any expenditure incurred wholly in respect of a particular part of an asset should be treated as an allowable deduction in full for that part and not apportioned. An example of this is incidental selling expenses, which are wholly attributable to the part disposed of.

Question

Mr Heal owns a 4 hectare plot of land which originally cost him £150,000. He sold one hectare in July 2009 for £60,000. The incidental costs of sales were £3,000. The market value of the 3 hectares remaining is estimated to be £180,000. What is the gain on the sale of the one hectare?

The amount of the indexed cost attributable to the part sold is

$$\frac{60,000}{60,000 + 180,000} \times £150,000 = £37,500$$

	£
Proceeds	60,000
Less: disposal cost	(3,000)
Net proceed of sale	57,000
Less cost (see above)	(37,500)
Gain	19,500

8 The damage, loss or destruction of an asset

FAST FORWARD

The gain which would otherwise arise on the receipt of insurance proceeds may, subject to certain conditions, be deferred.

8.1 Destruction or loss of an asset

If an asset is destroyed any compensation or insurance monies received will normally be brought into an ordinary CGT disposal computation as proceeds.

If all the proceeds are applied for the replacement of the asset within 12 months, any gain can be deducted from the cost of the replacement asset.

If only part of the proceeds are used, the gain immediately chargeable can be limited to the amount not used. The rest of the gain is then deducted from the cost of the replacement.

Question   **Asset destroyed**

Fiona bought an asset for £25,000. It was destroyed in July 2009. Insurance proceeds were £34,000, and Fiona spent £30,500 on a replacement asset in January 2010. Compute the gain immediately chargeable and the base cost of the new asset.

Answer

	£
Proceeds	34,000
Less cost	(25,000)
Gain	9,000
Gain immediately chargeable £(34,000 − 30,500)	(3,500)
Deduction from base cost	5,500

The base cost of the new asset is £(30,500 − 5,500) = £25,000.

8.2 Damage to an asset

If an asset is damaged then the receipt of any compensation or insurance monies received will normally be treated as a part disposal.

If all the proceeds are applied in restoring the asset the taxpayer can elect to disregard the part disposal. The proceeds will instead be deducted from the cost of the asset.

Question

Asset damaged

Frank bought an investment property for £100,000 in May 2009. It was damaged two and a half months later. Insurance proceeds of £20,000 were received in November 2009, and Frank spent a total of £25,000 on restoring the property. Prior to restoration the property was worth £120,000. Compute the chargeable gain immediately chargeable, if any, and the base cost of the restored property assuming Frank elects for there to be no part disposal.

How would your answer differ if no election were made?

Answer

As the proceeds have been applied in restoring the property Frank has elected to disregard the part disposal.

The base cost of the restored property is £(100,000 − 20,000 + 25,000) = £105,000.

If no election were made, the receipt of the proceeds would be a part disposal in November 2009:

	£
Proceeds	20,000
Less cost £100,000 × 20,000/(20,000 + 120,000)	(14,286)
Gain	5,714

The base cost of the restored asset is £(100,000 − 14,286 + 25,000) = £110,714.

Assuming this is Frank's only disposal in the tax year, the gain is covered by the annual exemption. It may therefore be preferable not to make the election.

Chapter Roundup

- A gain is chargeable if there is a chargeable disposal of a chargeable asset by a chargeable person.

- Capital gains are chargeable on individuals and companies.

- CGT applies primarily to persons resident or ordinarily resident in the UK.

- A gain or loss is computed by taking the proceeds and deducting the cost. Incidental costs of acquisition and disposal may be deducted together with any enhancement expenditure reflected in the state and nature of the asset at the date of disposal.

- An individual is entitled to an annual exemption for each tax year.

- Losses are set off against gains of the same year and any excess carried forward. Brought forward losses are only set off to reduce net gains down to the amount of the annual exemption.

- Individuals pay CGT on gains arising in a tax year at 18%.

- Disposals between spouses or members of a civil partnership are made on a no gain no loss basis and do not give rise to a chargeable gain or allowable loss.

- On a part disposal, the cost must be apportioned between the part disposed of and the part retained.

- The gain which would otherwise arise on the receipt of insurance proceeds may, subject to certain conditions, be deferred.

Quick Quiz

1   Give some examples of chargeable disposals.

2   On what assets does a UK resident pay CGT?

3   What is enhancement expenditure?

4   To what extent must allowable losses be set against chargeable gains?

5   At what rate or rates do individuals pay CGT?

6   10 acres of land are sold for £15,000 out of 25 acres. Original cost was £9,000. Costs of sale are £2,000. Rest of land valued at £30,000. What is the total amount deductible from proceeds?

         A   £2,000
         B   £2,872
         C   £5,000
         D   £5,600

7   Emma drops and destroys a vase. She receives compensation for £2,000 from her insurance company. How can she avoid a charge to CGT arising?

Answers to Quick Quiz

1   The following are chargeable disposals

- Sales of assets or parts of assets
- Gifts of assets or parts of assets
- Receipts of capital sums following the loss or destruction of an asset

2   All assets, whether situated in the UK or abroad, unless specifically exempt.

3   Enhancement expenditure is capital expenditure enhancing the value of the asset and reflected in the state/nature of the asset at disposal, or expenditure incurred in establishing, preserving or defending title to asset.

4   Current year losses must be set off against gains in full, even if this reduces net gains below the annual exemption. Losses brought forward are set off to bring down gains to the level of the annual exemption

5   Individuals pay CGT at the rate of 18%.

6   C. $\dfrac{15,000}{15,000 + 30,000} \times £9,000 = £3,000 + £2,000$ (costs of disposal) $= £5,000$

7   Emma can avoid a charge to CGT on receipt of the compensation by investing at least £2,000 in a replacement asset within 12 months.

Now try the questions below from the Exam Question Bank

Number	Level	Marks	Time
Q20	Introductory	7	13 mins

14

Chattels and the principal private residence exemption

Topic list	Syllabus reference
1 Chattels	D3(a), (b)
2 Wasting assets	D3(a), (c)
3 Private residences	D3(d)-(f)

Introduction

In the previous chapter we have considered the basic rules for the capital gains computation and the calculation of CGT payable by an individual, together with the rules for part disposals.

We now turn our attention to specific assets, starting with chattels. Where there is a disposal of low value assets, the chattels rules may apply to restrict the gain or allowable loss. The gain may even be exempt in certain circumstances. We look at the detailed rules.

The highest value item that an individual is likely to sell is his home. We look at the rules to see when the gain may be wholly or partly exempt.

In the next chapter we will consider the reliefs specifically available on business assets, and later we will turn our attention to the special rules for shares.

Study guide

		Intellectual level
D3	**Gains and losses on the disposal of movable and immovable property**	
(a)	Identify when chattels and wasting assets are exempt.	1
(b)	Compute the chargeable gain when a chattel is disposed of.	2
(c)	Calculate the chargeable gain when a wasting asset is disposed of.	2
(d)	Compute the exemption when a principal private residence is disposed of.	2
(e)	Calculate the chargeable gain when a principal private residence has been used for business purposes.	2
(f)	Identify the amount of letting relief available when a principal private residence has been let out.	2

Exam guide

As at least 20% of the marks for the exam will be for capital gains, you are quite likely to come across a question on either chattels or the reliefs available on the disposal of a principal private residence.

With chattels always look for the exemption for wasting chattels, a restriction of the gain if proceeds exceed £6,000, or a restriction of loss relief if proceeds are less than £6,000. The rules for chattels apply to companies as well as individuals, but watch out for assets on which capital allowances have been given.

On the disposal of a principal private residence if there has been any non-occupation or business use schedule out the relevant dates before you start to calculate the gain in case it turns out to be wholly exempt.

1 Chattels

1.1 What is a chattel?

Key term

A **chattel** is tangible moveable property.

A **wasting asset** is an asset with an estimated remaining useful life of 50 years or less.

Plant and machinery, whose predictable useful life is always deemed to be less than 50 years, is an example of a wasting chattel (unless it is immoveable, in which case it will be wasting but not a chattel). Machinery includes, in addition to its ordinary meaning, motor vehicles (unless exempt as cars), railway and traction engines, engine-powered boats and clocks.

1.2 Wasting chattels

FAST FORWARD

Gains on most wasting chattels are exempt and losses are not allowable.

Wasting chattels are exempt (so that there are no chargeable gains and no allowable losses).

There is one exception to this: assets used for the purpose of a trade, profession or vocation in respect of which capital allowances have been or could have been claimed. This means that items of plant and machinery used in a trade are not exempt merely on the ground that they are wasting. (However, cars are always exempt.)

1.3 Gains on non-wasting chattels

When a non-wasting chattel is sold for less than £6,000, any gain is exempt. There is marginal relief for gains where sale proceeds exceed £6,000.

If a chattel is not exempt under the wasting chattels rule, any gain arising on its disposal will still be exempt if the asset is sold for gross proceeds of £6,000 or less, even if capital allowances were claimed on it.

If sale proceeds exceed £6,000, any gain is limited to a maximum of 5/3 × (gross proceeds − £6,000).

Question   Chattels: gains

Adam purchased a Chippendale chair for £1,800. On 10 October 2009 he sold the chair at auction for £6,300 (which was net of the auctioneer's 10% commission). What is the gain?

Answer

	£
Proceeds (£6,300 × 100/90)	7,000
Less incidental costs of sale	(700)
Net proceeds	6,300
Less cost	(1,800)
Gain	4,500

The maximum gain is 5/3 × £(7,000 − 6,000) = £1,667

The chargeable gain is the lower of £4,500 and £1,667, so it is £1,667.

1.4 Losses on non-wasting chattels

A loss on the sale of a non-wasting chattel is restricted where proceeds are less than £6,000.

Where a chattel which is not exempt under the wasting chattels rule is sold for less than £6,000 and a loss arises, the allowable loss is restricted by assuming that the chattel was sold for £6,000. This rule cannot turn a loss into a gain, only reduce the loss, perhaps to zero.

Question   Chattels: losses

Eve purchased a rare first edition for £8,000 which she sold in October 2009 at auction for £2,700 (which was net of 10% commission). Compute the gain or loss.

Answer

	£
Proceeds (assumed)	6,000
Less incidental costs of disposal (£2,700 × 10/90)	(300)
	5,700
Less cost	(8,000)
Allowable loss	(2,300)

1.5 Chattels and capital allowances

FAST FORWARD The CGT rules are modified for assets eligible for capital allowances.

The wasting chattels exemption does not apply to chattels on which capital allowances have been claimed or could have been claimed. The chattels rules based on £6,000 do apply.

Where a chattel on which capital allowances have been obtained is sold at a loss, the allowable cost for chargeable gains purposes is reduced by the lower of the loss and the net amount of allowances given (taking into account any balancing allowances or charges). The result is no gain and no loss. This is because relief for the loss has already been given through the capital allowances computation.

If the chattel is sold at a gain the cost is not adjusted for capital allowances.

2 Wasting assets

FAST FORWARD When a wasting asset is disposed of its cost must be depreciated over its estimated useful life.

2.1 Introduction

A wasting asset is one which has an estimated remaining useful life of 50 years or less and whose original value will depreciate over time. Examples of such assets are copyrights and registered designs.

2.2 The computation

The normal capital gains computation is amended to reflect the anticipated depreciation over the life of the asset.

The cost is written down on a straight line basis, and it is this depreciated cost which is deducted in the computation.

Thus if a taxpayer acquires a wasting asset with a remaining life of 40 years and disposes of it after 15 years, so that 25 years of useful life remain, only 25/40 of the cost is deducted in the computation.

Any enhancement expenditure must be separately depreciated.

2.3 Example: wasting asset

Harry bought a copyright on 1 May 2005 for £20,000. The copyright is due to expire in May 2025. He sold it on 1 May 2009 for £22,000.

Harry's gain is:

	£
Proceeds of sale	22,000
Less depreciated cost £20,000 × 16/20	(16,000)
Gain	6,000

2.4 Capital allowances

If capital allowances have been given on a wasting asset its cost is not depreciated over time.

3 Private residences

There is an exemption for gains on principal private residences, but the exemption may be restricted because of periods of non-occupation or because of business use.

3.1 General principles

A gain arising on the sale of an individual's only or main private residence (his principal private residence or PPR) is exempt from CGT. The exemption covers total grounds, including the house, of up to half a hectare. The total grounds can exceed half a hectare if the house is large enough to warrant it, but if not, the gain on the excess grounds is taxable.

For the exemption to be available the taxpayer must have occupied the property as a residence rather than just as temporary accommodation.

3.2 Occupation

The gain is wholly exempt where the owner has occupied the whole of the residence throughout his period of ownership. Where occupation has been for only part of the period, the proportion of the gain exempted is

$$\text{Total gain} \times \frac{\text{Period of occupation}}{\text{Total period of ownership}}$$

The **last 36 months of ownership are always** treated as **a period of occupation**, if at some time the residence has been the taxpayer's main residence, even if within those last 36 months the taxpayer also has another house which is his principal private residence.

Where a loss arises and all, or a proportion of, any gain would have been exempt, all or the same proportion of the loss is not allowable.

3.3 Deemed occupation

The **period of occupation is also deemed to include certain periods of absence, provided the individual had no other exempt residence at the time and the period of absence was at some time both preceded and followed by a period of actual occupation.** The last 36 months rule (see above) takes precedence over this rule.

These periods of **deemed occupation** are:

(a) **Any period** (or periods taken together) of absence, **for any reason**, **up to three years**, and

(b) **Any periods** during which the owner was **required by his employment (ie employed taxpayer) to live abroad**, and

(c) **Any period** (or periods taken together) **up to four years** during which the owner was **required to live elsewhere due to his work** (ie both employed and self employed taxpayer) so that he could not occupy his private residence.

It does not matter if the residence is let during the absence.

Exempt periods of absence must normally be preceded and followed by periods of actual occupation. An extra-statutory concession relaxes this where an individual who has been required to work abroad or elsewhere (ie (b) and (c) above) is unable to resume residence in his home because the terms of his employment require him to work elsewhere.

Mr A purchased a house on 1 April 1984 for £88,200. He lived in the house until 30 June 1984. He then worked abroad for two years before returning to the UK to live in the house again on 1 July 1986. He stayed in the house until 31 December 2002 before retiring and moving out to live with friends in Spain until the house was sold on 31 December 2009 for £150,000.

Calculate the gain arising.

Answer

	£
Proceeds	150,000
Less cost	(88,200)
Gain before PPR exemption	61,800
Less PPR exemption (working)	
$\frac{261}{309} \times £61,800$	(52,200)
Gain	9,600

Working

Exempt and chargeable periods

Period		Total months	Exempt months	Chargeable months
(ii)	April 1984 – June 1984 (occupied)	3	3	0
(iii)	July 1984 – June 1986 (working abroad)	24	24	0
(iv)	July 1986 – December 2002 (occupied)	198	198	0
(v)	January 2003 – December 2006 (see below)	48	0	48
(vi)	January 2007 – December 2009 (last 36 months)	36	36	0
		309	261	48

No part of the period from January 2003 to December 2006 can be covered by the exemption for three years of absence for any reason because it is not followed at any time by actual occupation.

Exam focus point

To help you to answer questions such as that above it is useful to draw up a table showing the period of ownership, exempt months (real/deemed occupation) and chargeable months (non-occupation) similar to that in the working.

3.4 Business use

Where part of a residence is used exclusively for business purposes throughout the period of ownership, the gain attributable to use of that part is taxable. The 'last 36 months always exempt' rule does not apply to that part.

 Question
Business use of PPR

Mr Smail purchased a property for £35,000 on 31 May 2003 and began operating a dental practice from that date in one quarter of the house. He closed the dental practice on 31 December 2009, selling the house on that date for £130,000.

Compute the gain.

	£
Proceeds	130,000
Less: cost	(35,000)
Gain before PPR exemption	95,000
Less PPR exemption 0.75 × £95,000	(71,250)
Gain	23,750

Exemption is lost on one quarter throughout the period of ownership (including the last 36 months) because of the use of that fraction for business purposes.

If part of a residence was used for business purposes for only part of the period of ownership, the gain is apportioned between chargeable and exempt parts. If the business part was *at some time* used as part of the residence, the gain apportioned to that part *will* qualify for the last 36 months exemption.

3.5 Letting relief

The principal private residence exemption is extended to any gain accruing while the property is let, up to a certain limit. The two main circumstances in which the letting exemption applies are:

(a) When the owner is absent and lets the property, where the absence is not a deemed period of occupation.

(b) When the owner lets part of the property while still occupying the rest of it. The absence from the let part cannot be a deemed period of occupation, because the owner has another residence (the rest of the property). However, the let part will qualify for the last 36 months exemption *if* the let part has *at some time* been part of the only or main residence.

In both cases the letting must be for residential use. **The extra exemption is restricted to the lowest of:**

(a) The amount of the total **gain** which is already **exempt under the PPR provisions**
(b) The gain accruing during the letting period (the **letting part of the gain**)
(c) **£40,000** (maximum)

Letting relief cannot convert a gain into an allowable loss.

If a lodger lives as a member of the owner's family, sharing their living accommodation and eating with them, the **whole** property is regarded as the owner's main residence.

Question   Letting relief (1)

Mr Ovett purchased a house in Truro on 5 October 1995 and sold it on 5 April 2010 making a gain of £290,000.

On 5 January 1997 he had been sent to work in Edinburgh, and he did not return to his own house until 6 July 2006. The property was let out during his absence, and he lived in a flat provided for him by his employer. What is the gain?

	£
Gain before PPR exemption	290,000
Less PPR exemption (working)	
£290,000 × 144/174	(240,000)
	50,000

Less letting exemption: Lowest of:

(a)   gain exempt under PPR rules: £240,000

(b)   gain attributable to letting: £290,000 × $\dfrac{30}{174}$ = £50,000

(c)   £40,000 (maximum)   (40,000)

Gain   10,000

Working

Period	Notes	Total ownership months	Exempt months	Chargeable months
5.10.95 – 4.1.97	Actual occupation	15	15	0
5.1.97 – 4.1.01	4 years absence working in the UK	48	48	0
5.1.01 – 4.1.04	3 year of absence for any reason	36	36	0
5.1.04 – 5.7.06	Absent – let	30	0	30
6.7.06 – 5.4.10	Occupied (includes last 36 months)	45	45	0
		174	144	30

Question   Letting relief (2)

Miss Coe purchased a house on 31 March 1995 for £90,000. She sold it on 31 August 2009 for £340,000. In 1998 the house was redecorated and Miss Coe began to live on the top floor renting out the balance of the house (constituting 60% of the total house) to tenants between 1 January 1999 and 31 December 2008. On 2 January 2009 Miss Coe put the whole house on the market but continued to live only on the top floor until the house was sold. What is the chargeable gain?

Answer

	£
Proceeds	340,000
Less: cost	(90,000)
Gain before PPR exemption	250,000
Less PPR exemption (working)	
£250,000 × $\dfrac{117.8}{173}$	(170,231)
	79,769

Less letting exemption: Lowest of:

(a)   gain exempt under PPR rules: £170,231

(b)   gain attributable to letting: £250,000 × $\dfrac{55.2}{173}$ = £79,769

(c)   £40,000 (maximum)   (40,000)

Gain   39,769

Working

Period	Notes	Total ownership months	Exempt months	Chargeable months
1.4.95 – 31.12.98	100% of house occupied	45	45	0
1.1.99 – 31.8.06	40% of house occupied	92	36.8	
	60% of house let			55.2
1.9.06 – 31.8.09	Last 36 months treated as 100% of house occupied	36	36	0
		173	117.8	55.2

Note. The gain on the 40% of the house always occupied by Miss Coe is fully covered by PPR relief. The other 60% of the house has not always been occupied by Miss Coe and thus any gain on this part of the house is taxable where it relates to periods of time when Miss Coe was not actually (or deemed to be) living in it.

As a further point if Miss Coe had reoccupied the lower floors (60% part) of the house prior to the sale then 3 years worth of the non-occupation period between 1.1.99 and 31.8.06 could have been treated as deemed occupation under the special '3 years absence for any reason' rule.

Chapter Roundup

- Gains on most wasting chattels are exempt and losses are not allowable.

- When a non-wasting chattel is sold for less than £6,000, any gain is exempt. There is marginal relief for gains where sale proceeds exceed £6,000.

- A loss on the sale of a non-wasting chattel is restricted where proceeds are less than £6,000.

- The CGT rules are modified for assets eligible for capital allowances.

- When a wasting asset is disposed of its cost must be depreciated over its estimated useful life.

- There is an exemption for gains on principal private residences, but the exemption may be restricted because of periods of non-occupation or because of business use.

Quick Quiz

1   How are gains on non-wasting chattels sold for more than £6,000 restricted?

2   How are losses on non-wasting chattels sold for less than £6,000 restricted?

3   For what periods may an individual be deemed to occupy his principal private residence?

4   The maximum letting exemption is

   A   £30,000
   B   £40,000
   C   £60,000
   D   £80,000

Answers to Quick Quiz

1   Gain restricted to 5/3 × (gross proceeds – £6,000)

2   Allowable loss restricted by deeming proceeds to be £6,000

3   Periods of deemed occupation are:

- last 36 months of ownership, and

- any period of absence up to three years, and

- any period during which the owner was required by his employment to work abroad, and

- any period up to four years during which the owner was required to live elsewhere due to his work (employed or self employed) or that he could not occupy his private residence.

4   B. £40,000.

Now try the questions below from the Exam Question Bank

Number	Level	Marks	Time
Q21	Examination	10	18 mins

15

Business reliefs

Topic list	Syllabus reference
1 Entrepreneurs' relief	D6(a)
2 The replacement of business assets (rollover relief)	D6(b)
3 Gift relief (holdover relief)	D6(c)
4 Incorporation relief	D6(d)

Introduction

Having discussed the general rules for capital gains we now turn our attention to specific reliefs for businesses.

Entrepreneurs' relief is a very important relief. It applies on the sale of a business and certain trading company shares. It has the effect of reducing the rate of tax payable from 18% to 10% on all or part of the chargeable gains arising in such disposals.

Another important relief is rollover relief, which enables a gain on the disposal of a business asset to be rolled over if a new asset is purchased for business use. This enables the payment of tax to be deferred until the business has actually retained the proceeds of sale uninvested so that it can meet the liability. This is the only relief that is available to both individuals and companies.

Next we consider the relief for gifts of business assets. This generous relief allows an entrepreneur to give away his business during his lifetime and pass any gains to the donee.

The final relief, incorporation relief, enables an individual to transfer his sole trade or partnership business into a company without crystallising a tax charge. The gain is deferred until the eventual disposal of the shares in the company.

In the next chapter we will cover the computation of capital gains on the disposal of shares.

Study guide

		Intellectual level
D6	The use of exemptions and reliefs in deferring and minimising tax liabilities arising on the disposal of capital assets	
(a)	Explain and apply entrepreneurs' relief as it applies to individuals.	2
(b)	Explain and apply rollover relief as it applies to individuals and companies.	2
(c)	Explain and apply holdover relief for the gift of business assets.	2
(d)	Explain and apply the incorporation relief that is available upon the transfer of a business to a company.	2

Exam guide

Capital gains form at least 20% of your exam, and may be found in the context of corporation tax or CGT. Rollover relief may be met in either context, and as it is an extremely important relief for all businesses it is likely to be examined. If you are required to compute a gain on a business asset look out for the purchase of a new asset, but carefully check the date and cost of the acquisition. Do not be caught out by the purchase of an investment property.

The relief for gifts of assets is only available to individuals, and effectively passes the gain to the donee. Entrepreneurs' relief is only available to individuals. It was introduced for 2008/09 and so is highly topical. Incorporation relief is again only available to individuals. Note that it can be disclaimed. It is unlikely that these reliefs would form a whole question.

1 Entrepreneurs' relief

FAST FORWARD

Entrepreneurs' relief applies on the disposal of a business and certain trading company shares. It reduces the rate of CGT from 18% to 10%.

1.1 How the relief works

Entrepreneurs' relief is available to reduce the gains on a material disposal of business assets. Relief is given by reducing the eligible gains by $^4/_9$. This leaves $^5/_9$ × gains chargeable, which gives an effective rate (if no annual exemption is available) of 10% ($^5/_9$ × 18% = 10%).

Where there is a material disposal of business assets which results in both gains and losses, losses are netted off against gains before entrepreneurs' relief is applied. Losses on assets not qualifying for entrepreneurs' relief and the annual exemption are deducted after the application of entrepreneurs' relief.

1.2 Example

Simon sells his business, all the assets of which qualify for entrepreneurs' relief, in September 2009. The gains arising are £200,000. He has no other chargeable disposals in the year.

The CGT payable on his disposal is:

	£
Gains	200,000
Less: reduction in gains $^4/_9$ × £200,000	(88,889)
Gains remaining in charge	111,111
Less: annual exemption	(10,100)
Taxable gains	101,011
CGT @ 18%	18,182

Note that if the annual exemption had not been available, the CGT payable would have been £111,111 × 18% = £20,000 ie an effective rate of 10%.

1.3 Lifetime limit

There is a limit of £1 million of gains on which entrepreneurs' relief can be claimed. This is a lifetime amount starting **from 6 April 2008.**

Question   Limit on entrepreneurs' relief

Maureen sells her shareholding which qualifies for entrepreneurs' relief, in January 2010, realising a gain of £900,000. She has already used her annual exemption for 2009/10. Maureen had already made a claim for entrepreneurs' relief in 2008/09 in respect of gains totalling £300,000.

Calculate the CGT payable by Maureen on her disposal in 2009/10.

Answer

	£
Gains	900,000
Less: reduction in gains	
£(1,000,000 (max) − 300,000) = £700,000 × ⁴/₉	(311,111)
Taxable gain	588,889
CGT @ 18%	106,000

Using the effective rate of tax on the gain, the CGT payable is:

	£
£700,000 × 10%	70,000
£200,000 × 18%	36,000
CGT payable	106,000

1.4 Conditions

Entrepreneurs' relief is available where there is a **material disposal of business assets**.

A **material disposal of business assets** is:

- a disposal of the **whole or part of a business** which has been **owned by the individual** throughout the period of **one year** ending with the date of the disposal
- a disposal of **one or more assets in use for the purposes of a business at** the time at which the business **ceases to be carried on** provided that:
  - the business was owned by the individual throughout **the period of one year** ending with the date on which the business ceases to be carried on; **and**
  - the date of cessation is within **three years** ending with the date of the disposal.
- a disposal of **shares or securities of a company where** the company is the individual's **personal company;** the company is either a **trading company** or **holding company of a trading group;** the individual is an **officer or employee** of the company (or a group company) and these conditions are met either:
  - throughout the period of **one year** ending with the date of the disposal; **or**
  - throughout the period of **one year** ending with the date on which the company (or group) **ceases to be a trading company (or trading group)** and that date is within the period of **three years** ending with the date of the disposal.

For the first category to apply, there has be a **disposal of the whole or part of the business as a going concern**, not just a disposal of individual assets. A business includes one carried on as a partnership of which the individual is a partner. The business must be a **trade, profession or vocation** conducted on a **commercial basis with a view to the realisation of profits**.

For both the first and second category, relief is only available on **relevant business assets**. These are assets **used for the purposes of the business** and **cannot include shares and securities** or **assets held as investments**.

In relation to the third category, a **personal company** in relation to an individual is one where:

- the individual holds **at least 5% of the ordinary share capital**; and
- the individual can exercise **at least 5% of the voting rights in the company** by virtue of that holding of shares.

Question

Material disposal of business assets

Robbie started in business as a manufacturer of widgets in July 2001. He acquired a freehold workshop for £80,000 in May 2002. He used the workshop in his business. In August 2006, Robbie invested £40,000 of his business profits in shares in an investment company. He bought a machine for use in his business in January 2009 at a cost of £30,000.

In November 2009, Robbie sold his business to a larger competitor. The sale proceeds were apportioned to capital assets as follows:

	£
Goodwill	50,000
Workshop	125,000
Shares	80,500
Machine	32,000

Calculate Robbie's CGT payable on the disposal, assuming that he does not have any other chargeable assets.

Answer

	£	£
Proceeds of goodwill	50,000	
Less: cost	(nil)	50,000
Proceeds of workshop	125,000	
Less: cost	(80,000)	45,000
Proceeds of machine (N1)	32,000	
Less: cost	(30,000)	2,000
Gains qualifying for entrepreneurs' relief		97,000
Less: reduction is gains $^4/_9 \times £97,000$		(43,111)
Gains remaining in charge		53,889
Proceeds of shares (N2)	80,500	
Less: cost	(40,000)	40,500
Chargeable gains		94,389
Less: annual exemption		(10,100)
Taxable gains		84,289
CGT @ 18%		15,172

Notes

1. The gain on the machine is eligible for entrepreneurs' relief even though it has not been owned for one year. The condition is that the individual has owned the business for one year.
2. The gain on the shares is not eligible for entrepreneurs' relief because it is not a relevant business asset.

1.5 Claim

An individual must claim entrepreneurs' relief: it is not automatic. The claim deadline is the first anniversary of 31 January following the end of the tax year of disposal. For a 2009/10 disposal, the taxpayer must claim by 31 January 2012.

2 The replacement of business assets (rollover relief)

FAST FORWARD

Rollover relief is available to all businesses that reinvest in qualifying assets in the period commencing one year before and ending 36 months after the disposal concerned.

2.1 Conditions

A gain may be 'rolled over' (deferred) where the proceeds received on the disposal of a business asset are spent on a replacement business asset. This is **rollover relief**. A claim cannot specify that only part of a gain is to be rolled over.

All the following conditions must be met.

(a) **The old asset sold and the new asset bought are both used only in the trade** or trades carried on **by the person claiming rollover relief**. Where part of a building is in non-trade use for all or a substantial part of the period of ownership, the building (and the land on which it stands) is treated as two separate assets, the trade part (qualifying) and the non-trade part (non-qualifying). This split cannot be made for other assets.

(b) **The old asset and the new asset both fall within one** (but not necessarily the same one) **of the following classes.**

    (i)   Land and buildings (including parts of buildings) occupied as well as used only for the purpose of the trade

    (ii)   Fixed (that is, immovable) plant and machinery

    (iii) Goodwill.

(c) **Reinvestment of the proceeds received on the disposal of the old asset takes place in a period beginning one year before and ending three years after the date of the disposal.**

(d) **The new asset is brought into use in the trade on its acquisition** (not necessarily immediately, but not after any significant and unnecessary delay).

The new asset can be used in a different trade from the old asset.

A claim for relief must be made within four years of the end of the tax year in which the disposal of the old asset is made.

2.2 Operation of relief

FAST FORWARD

A rolled over gain is deducted from the base cost of the replacement asset acquired.

Deferral is obtained by deducting the chargeable gain from the cost of the new asset. For full relief, the whole of the proceeds must be reinvested. Where only part is reinvested, a gain equal to the amount not reinvested or the full gain, if lower, will be chargeable to tax immediately.

The new asset will have a base cost for chargeable gains purposes of its purchase price less the gain rolled over.

Question   Rollover relief

A freehold factory was purchased by Zoë for business use in August 2001. It was sold in December 2009 for £70,000, giving rise to a gain of £17,950. A replacement factory was purchased in June 2010 for £60,000. Compute the base cost of the replacement factory, taking into account any possible rollover of the gain from the disposal in December 2009.

Answer

	£
Gain	17,950
Less: rollover relief (balancing figure)	(7,950)
Chargeable gain: amount not reinvested £(70,000 – 60,000)	10,000
Cost of new factory	60,000
Less rolled over gain	(7,950)
Base cost of new factory	52,050

2.3 Non-business use

Where the old asset has not been used in the trade for a fraction of its period of ownership, the amount of the gain that can be rolled over is reduced by the same fraction. When considering proceeds not reinvested the restriction on rollover relief is based on the proportion of proceeds relating to the part of the asset used in the trade or the proportion relating to the period of trade use.

Exam focus point

Look out for both the old and the new asset having some non-business use. You must compare the proceeds of the business use proportion with the amount reinvested in the business use portion of the new asset.

Question   Assets with non-business use

John bought a factory for £150,000 on 11 November 2004, for use in his business. From 11 November 2005, he let the factory out for a period of two years. He then used the factory for his own business again, until he sold it on 10 May 2009 for £225,000. On 13 December 2009, he purchased another factory for use in his business. This second factory cost £100,000.

Calculate the chargeable gain on the sale of the first factory and the base cost of the second factory.

Gain on first factory

	Non business £	Business £
Proceeds of sale (24:30) (W1)	100,000	125,000
Less: cost (24:30)	(66,667)	(83,333)
Gain	33,333	41,667
Less: rollover relief		(16,667)
Chargeable gain (W2)	33,333	25,000

Base cost of second factory

	£
Cost	100,000
Less gain rolled over	(16,667)
Base cost c/f	83,333

Workings

1   *Use of factory*

Total ownership period:

11.11.04 – 10.05.09 = 54 months

Attributable to non business use:

11.11.05 – 10.11.07 = 24 months

Attributable to business use (balance: 54m – 24m) = 30 months

2   *Proceeds not reinvested*

	£
Proceeds of business element	125,000
Less: cost of new factory	(100,000)
Not reinvested	25,000

2.4 Depreciating assets

FAST FORWARD

When the replacement asset is a depreciating asset, the gain on the old asset is 'frozen' rather than rolled over.

Where the replacement asset is a depreciating asset, the gain is not rolled over by reducing the cost of the replacement asset. Rather it is deferred until it crystallises on the earliest of:

(a)   The disposal of the replacement asset.

(b)   The date the replacement asset ceases to be used in the trade (but the gain does not crystallise on the taxpayer's death).

(c)   Ten years after the acquisition of the replacement asset (maximum).

Key term

An asset is a **depreciating asset** if it is, or within the next ten years will become, a wasting asset. Thus, any asset with an expected life of 60 years or less is covered by this definition. Plant and machinery is always treated as depreciating.

Question

Norma bought a freehold shop for use in her business in June 2008 for £125,000. She sold it for £140,000 on 1 August 2009. On 10 July 2009, Norma bought some fixed plant and machinery to use in her business, costing £150,000. She then sells the plant and machinery for £167,000 on 19 November 2011. Show Norma's CGT position.

Answer

Gain deferred

	£
Proceeds of shop	140,000
Less cost	(125,000)
Gain	15,000

This gain is deferred in relation to the purchase of the plant and machinery.

Sale of plant and machinery

	£
Proceeds	167,000
Less cost	(150,000)
Gain	17,000

Total gain chargeable on sale (gain on plant and machinery plus deferred gain)
£(15,000 + 17,000) = £32,000

Where a gain on disposal is deferred against a replacement depreciating asset it is possible to transfer the deferred gain to a non-depreciating asset provided the non-depreciating asset is bought before the deferred gain has crystallised.

3 Gift relief (holdover relief)

> **FAST FORWARD**
>
> Gift relief can be claimed on gifts of business assets.

3.1 The relief

If an individual gives away a qualifying asset, the transferor and the transferee can jointly claim within four years of the end of the tax year of the transfer, that the transferor's gain be reduced to nil. The transferee is then deemed to acquire the asset for market value at the date of transfer less the transferor's deferred gain.

If a disposal involves actual consideration rather than being an outright gift, but is still not a bargain made at arm's length (so that the proceeds are deemed to be the market value of the asset), this is known as a sale at undervalue. **Any excess of actual consideration over actual cost) is chargeable immediately and only the balance of the gain is deferred**. The amount chargeable immediately is limited to the full gain.

Exam focus point

> The asset need only be a business asset in the hands of the donor. It is immaterial if the donee does not use it for business purposes.

3.2 Qualifying assets

Gift relief can be claimed on gifts or sales at undervalue on transfers of **business assets**. The definition of a business asset for gift relief is **not** the same as for entrepreneurs' relief.

Business assets are:

(a)   **Assets used in a trade, profession or vocation** carried on:

    (1)   by the donor

    (2)   by the donor's personal company (ie one where the individual holds at least 5% of the voting rights).

If the asset was used for the purposes of the trade, profession or vocation for only part of its period of ownership, the gain to be held over is the gain otherwise eligible × period of such use/total period of ownership.

If the asset was a building or structure only partly used for trade, professional or vocational purposes, only the **part of the gain attributable to the part so used is eligible for gift relief**.

(b)   **Shares and securities in trading companies**

    (1)   the shares or securities are **not listed on a recognised stock exchange** (but they may be on the AIM); or

    (2)   if the donor is an individual, the company concerned is his **personal company** (defined as above);

If the company has chargeable non-business assets at the time of the gift, and (2) applied at any time in the last 12 months, **the gain to be held over is:**

Exam formula

$$\text{Gain} \times \frac{\text{the value of the chargeable business assets (CBA)}}{\text{the value of the chargeable assets (CA)}}$$

Question

Gift relief

On 6 December 2009 Angelo sold to his son Michael a freehold shop valued at £200,000 for £50,000, and claimed gift relief. Angelo had originally purchased the shop from which he had run his business for £30,000. Michael continued to run a business from the shop premises but decided to sell the shop in May 2011 for £195,000. Compute any chargeable gains arising. Assume the rules of CGT in 2009/10 continue to apply in May 2011.

Answer

(a)   *Angelo's CGT position (2009/10)*

	£
Proceeds (market value)	200,000
Less cost	(30,000)
Gain	170,000
Less gain deferred	(150,000)
Chargeable gain £(50,000 – 30,000)	20,000

(b)   *Michael's CGT position (2011/12)*

	£
Proceeds	195,000
Less cost £(200,000 – 150,000)	(50,000)
Gain	145,000

Morris gifts shares in his personal company to his son Minor realising a gain of £100,000. The company balance sheet at the date of the gift shows:

	£
Freehold factory and offices	150,000
Leasehold warehouse	80,000
Investments	120,000
Other net assets	200,000
	550,000

You are required to show the gain qualifying for hold-over relief and the chargeable gain.

Answer

Gain qualifying for hold-over relief:

$$£100,000 \times \frac{\text{Chargeable business assets (CBA)}}{\text{Chargeable assets (CA)}} = £100,000 \times \frac{150+80}{150+80+120}$$

$$= £100,000 \times \frac{230}{350}$$

$$= £65,714$$

The gain which is not held-over is £100,000 − £65,714 = £34,286

4 Incorporation relief

FAST FORWARD

A gain arising on the incorporation of a business is automatically deferred into the base cost of the shares acquired by incorporation relief. However, an individual can elect for the relief not to apply.

If a person transfers his business to a company this is a disposal of the business assets for CGT purposes and he realises net chargeable gains (chargeable gains less allowable losses) on those assets. It is, however, clearly undesirable to discourage individuals from incorporating their businesses and so relief is available.

The relief (incorporation relief) is automatic (so no claim need be made). All, or some, of the gains are held over if all the following conditions are met.

(a) The **business is transferred as a going concern**
(b) **All its assets** (other than cash) **are transferred**
(c) **The consideration is wholly or partly in shares**.

Exam formula

> **The amount held over is found by applying the fraction:**
>
> $$\text{Gain} \times \frac{\text{Value of shares received from the company}}{\text{Total value of consideration from the company}}$$

This amount is then deducted from the base cost of the shares received. The company is deemed to acquire assets transferred at their market values.

An individual can elect not to receive incorporation relief. He might do this, for example, in order to claim entrepreneurs' relief instead.

Question

Mr P transferred his business to a company in May 2009, realising a gain of £24,000 on the only business asset transferred (a factory). The consideration comprised cash of £15,000 and shares at a market value of £75,000.

(a)   What is the chargeable gain on the transfer?

(b)   What is the base cost of the shares for any future disposal?

Answer

(a)

		£
Gain		24,000
Less held over $\dfrac{75,000}{15,000 + 75,000} \times £24,000$		(20,000)
Gain		4,000

(b)

	£
Market value	75,000
Less gain held over	(20,000)
Base cost of shares	55,000

Chapter Roundup

- Entrepreneurs' relief applies on the disposal of a business and certain funding company shares. It reduces the rate of CGT from 18% to 10%.

- Rollover relief is available to all businesses that reinvest in qualifying assets in the period commencing one year before and ending 36 months after the disposal concerned.

- A rolled over gain is deducted from the base cost of the replacement asset acquired.

- When the replacement asset is a depreciating asset, the gain on the old asset is 'frozen' rather than rolled over.

- Gift relief can be claimed on gifts of business assets.

- A gain arising on the incorporation of a business is automatically deferred into the base cost of the shares acquired by incorporation relief. However, an individual can elect for the relief not to apply.

Quick Quiz

1   Patrick has been running a trading business for five years. In 2009/10 he sold the business to Andrew realising gains of £75,000. Patrick has already used his annual exemption for 2009/10. He had not made any previous claim for entrepreneurs' relief. What is Patrick's CGT liability?

2   Alice sells a factory for £500,000 realising a gain of £100,000. She acquires a factory two months later for £480,000. How much rollover relief is available?

    A   £20,000

    B   £60,000

    C   £80,000

    D   £100,000

3   What deferral relief is available when a business asset is replaced with a depreciating business asset?

4   Which disposals of shares qualify for gift relief?

5   List the conditions for deferring gains on the incorporation of a business.

1

	£
Gains	75,000
Less reduction in gains $4/9 \times £75,000$	(33,333)
Taxable gains	41,667
CGT @ 18% (ie £75,000 × 10%)	7,500

2   C. Amount not reinvested £(500,000 − 480,000) = £20,000. Rollover relief £(100,000 − 20,000) = £80,000.

3   Gain is frozen on acquisition of depreciating asset until earlier of: disposal of that asset; asset no longer used in trade; 10 years after acquisition of replacement asset.

4   Shares which qualify for gift relief are those in trading companies

- which are not listed on a recognised stock exchange, or
- which are in the individual's personal company ie the individual holds at least 5% of the voting rights

5   The conditions for incorporation relief are:

- the business is transferred as a going concern
- all of its assets (other than cash) are transferred
- the consideration is wholly or partly in shares

Now try the question below from the Exam Question Bank

Number	Level	Marks	Time
Q22	Examination	14	25 mins
Q23	Introductory	5	9 mins
Q24	Introductory	7	13 mins
Q42	Examination	25	45 mins

Question 42 has been analysed to give you guidance on how to answer exam questions.

Shares and securities

Topic list	Syllabus reference
1 Valuing quoted shares	D4(a)
2 The matching rules for individuals	D4(b)
3 The share pool	D4(c)
4 Bonus and rights issues	D4(d)
5 Reorganisations and takeovers	D4(d)
6 Gilts and qualifying corporate bonds	D4(e)

Introduction

We have now covered most aspects of the capital gains computation apart from shares and securities.

Shares and securities need special rules because an individual may hold several shares or securities in the same company, bought at different times for different prices but otherwise identical. We need to identify the shares which are disposed to compute the gain or loss.

We also discuss bonus and rights issues, takeovers and reorganisations.

In the next chapter we will conclude our study of personal taxation by considering administration.

Study guide

		Intellectual level
D4	**Gains and losses on the disposal of shares and securities**	
(a)	Calculate the value of quoted shares where they are disposed of by way of a gift.	2
(b)	Explain and apply the identification rules as they apply to individuals and to companies, including the same day, nine day, and thirty day matching rules.	2
(c)	Explain the pooling provisions.	2
(d)	Explain the treatment of bonus issues, rights issues, takeovers and reorganisations.	2
(e)	Explain the exemption available for gilt-edged securities and qualifying corporate bonds.	1

Exam guide

Shares and securities are likely to form at least part of a question on capital gains. You must learn the identification rules as they are crucial in calculating the gain correctly. The identification rules for companies are covered later in this Text.

Takeovers and reorganisations are important; remember to apportion the cost across the new holding.

1 Valuing quoted shares

FAST FORWARD

> Quoted shares are valued at the lower of the 'quarter-up' value and the average of the highest and lowest marked bargains.

Quoted shares and securities are valued using prices in The Stock Exchange Daily Official List, taking the lower of:

- the 'quarter-up' value: lower quoted price + $\frac{1}{4}$ × (higher quoted price – lower quoted price)
- the average of the highest and lowest marked bargains (ignoring bargains marked at special prices)

Question
CGT value of shares

Shares in A plc are quoted at 100-110p. The highest and lowest marked bargains were 99p and 110p. What would be the market value for CGT purposes?

Answer

The value will be the lower of:

(a) $100 + \frac{1}{4} \times (110 - 100) = 102.5$;

(b) $\frac{110 + 99}{2} = 104.5$.

The market value for CGT purposes will therefore be 102.5p per share.

2 The matching rules for individuals

FAST FORWARD

> There are special rules for matching shares sold with shares purchased. Disposals are matched first with shares acquired on the same day, then within the following 30 days and finally with the share pool.

Quoted and unquoted shares and securities present special problems when attempting to compute gains or losses on disposal. For instance, suppose that an individual buys some quoted shares in X plc as follows.

Date	Number of shares	Cost
		£
5 May 1983	100	150
17 June 2009	100	375

On 15 June 2009, he sells 120 of the shares for £1,450. To determine the chargeable gain, we need to be able to work out which shares out of the two original holdings were actually sold.

We therefore need **matching rules**. These **allow us to decide which shares have been sold and so work out what the allowable cost on disposal should be.**

At any one time, we will only be concerned with shares or securities of the same class in the same company. If an individual owns both ordinary shares and preference shares in X plc, we will deal with the two classes of share entirely separately, because they are distinguishable.

Below 'shares' refers to both shares and securities.

For individuals, share disposals are matched with acquisitions in the following order.

(a) **Same day acquisitions**.

(b) **Acquisitions within the following 30 days** (known as the 'bed and breakfast rule') if more than one on a 'first in, first out' (FIFO) basis.

(c) **Any shares in the share pool** (see below).

The 'bed and breakfast' rule stops shares being sold to crystallise a capital gain or loss, usually to use the annual exemption, and then being repurchased a day or so later. Without the rule a gain or loss would arise on the sale, since it would be 'matched' to the original acquisition.

Exam focus point

Learn the 'matching rules' because a crucial first step to getting a shares question right is to correctly match the shares sold to the original shares purchased.

3 The share pool

3.1 Composition of pool

We treat any other shares acquired as a 'pool' which grows as new shares are acquired and shrinks as they are sold.

In making computations which use the share pool, we must keep track of:

(a) The **number** of shares
(b) The **cost** of the shares

3.2 Disposals from the share pool

In the case of a disposal the cost attributable to the shares disposed of are deducted from the amounts within the share pool. The proportion of the cost to take out of the pool should be computed using the A/(A + B) fraction that is used for any other part disposal. However, we are not usually given the value of the remaining shares (B in the fraction). We just use numbers of shares.

Question

In August 2005 Oliver acquired 4,000 shares in Twist plc at a cost of £10,000. Oliver sold 3,000 shares on 10 July 2009 for £17,000. Compute the gain and the value of the share pool following the disposal.

Answer

The gain is computed as follows:

	£
Proceeds	17,000
Less cost (working)	(7,500)
Gain	9,500

Working – share pool

	No of shares	Cost £
Acquisition – August 2005	4,000	10,000
Disposal – July 2009	(3,000)	
Cost $\dfrac{3,000}{4,000} \times £10,000$		(7,500)
	1,000	2,500

Question

Anita acquired shares in Kent Ltd as follows:

1 July 1995	1,000 shares for £2,000
11 April 2000	2,500 shares for £7,500
17 May 2009	400 shares for £1,680
10 June 2009	500 shares for £2,000

Anita sold 4,000 shares for £16,400 on 17 May 2009.

Calculate Anita's net gain on sale.

Answer

First match the disposal with the acquisition on the same day:

	£
Proceeds $\dfrac{400}{4,000} \times £16,400$	1,640
Less: cost	(1,680)
Loss	(40)

Next match the disposal with the acquisition in the next thirty days:

	£
Proceeds $\dfrac{500}{4,000} \times £16,400$	2,050
Less: cost	(2,000)
Gain	50

Finally, match the disposal with the shares in the share pool:

	£
Proceeds $\frac{3,100}{4,000} \times £16,400$	12,710
Less: cost (working)	(8,414)
Gain	4,296
Net gain £(50 + 4,296 – 40)	4,306

Working

	No. of shares	Cost £
1.7.95 Acquisition	1,000	2,000
11.4.00 Acquisition	2,500	7,500
	3,500	9,500
17.5.09 Disposal	(3,100)	(8,414)
c/f	400	1,086

4 Bonus and rights issues

Bonus shares are shares acquired at no cost. Rights issue shares are acquired for payment.

4.1 Bonus issues

Bonus shares are shares issued by a company in proportion to each shareholder's existing holding. For example, a shareholder may have 1,000 shares. If the company makes a 2 shares for each 1 share held bonus issue (called a '2 for 1 bonus issue'), the shareholder will receive 2 bonus shares for each 1 share held. So the shareholder will end up with 1,000 original shares and 2,000 bonus shares making 3,000 shares in total.

When a company issues bonus shares all that happens is that the size of the original holding is increased. Since bonus shares are issued at no cost there is no need to adjust the original cost.

4.2 Rights issues

In a rights issue the company offers shareholders rights issue shares in proportion to their existing shareholdings.

The difference between a bonus issue and a rights issue is that in a rights issue the new shares are paid for by the shareholder and this results in an adjustment to the original cost.

Question | Rights issue

Simon had the following transactions in S Ltd.

1.10.96	Bought 10,000 shares for £15,000
1.2.09	Took up rights issue 1 for 2 at £2.75 per share
14.10.09	Sold 2,000 shares for £6,000

Compute the gain arising in October 2009.

Share pool

	Number	Cost
		£
1.10.96 Acquisition	10,000	15,000
1.2.09 Rights issue	5,000	13,750
	15,000	28,750
14.10.09 Sale	(2,000)	(3,833)
c/f	13,000	24,917

Gain

	£
Proceeds	6,000
Less cost	(3,833)
Gain	2,167

5 Reorganisations and takeovers

 FAST FORWARD

The costs of the original holding are allocated to the new holdings pro rata to their values on a takeover or reorganisation.

5.1 Reorganisations

A reorganisation takes place where new shares or a mixture of new shares and debentures are issued in exchange for the original shareholdings. The new shares take the place of the old shares. The problem is how to apportion the original cost between the different types of capital issued on the reorganisation.

If the new shares and securities are quoted, then the cost is apportioned by reference to the market values of the new types of capital on the first day of quotation after the reorganisation.

Question   **Reorganisations**

An original quoted shareholding of 3,000 shares is held in a share pool with a cost of £13,250.

In 2009 there is a reorganisation whereby each ordinary share is exchanged for two 'A' ordinary shares (quoted at £2 each) and one preference share (quoted at £1 each). Show how the original cost will be apportioned.

Answer

Share pool

	New holding	MV	Cost
		£	£
Ords 2 new shares	6,000	12,000	10,600 (W)
Prefs 1 new shares	3,000	3,000	2,650 (W)
Total		15,000	13,250

Working

$^{12}/_{15} \times £13,250$ = cost of ordinary shares

$^{3}/_{15} \times £13,250$ = cost of preference shares

5.2 Takeovers

A chargeable gain does not arise on a 'paper for paper' takeover. The cost of the original holding is passed on to the new holding which takes the place of the original holding. **If part of the takeover consideration is cash then a gain must be computed**: the normal part disposal rules will apply.

The takeover rules apply where the company issuing the new shares ends up with **more than 25%** of the ordinary share capital of the old company or the majority of the voting power in the old company, or the company issuing the new shares makes a general offer to shareholders in the other company which is initially made subject to a condition which, if satisfied, would give the first company control of the second company.

The exchange must take place for bona fide commercial reasons and does not have as its main purpose, or one of its main purposes, the avoidance of CGT or corporation tax.

Question	Takeover

Mr Le Bon held 20,000 £1 shares in Duran plc out of a total number of issued shares of one million. They were bought in 2002 for £2 each. In 2009 the board of Duran plc agreed to a takeover bid by Spandau plc under which shareholders in Duran plc received three ordinary Spandau plc shares plus one preference share for every four shares held in Duran plc. Immediately following the takeover, the ordinary shares in Spandau plc were quoted at £5 each and the preferences shares at 90p. Show the base costs of the ordinary shares and the preference shares.

Answer

The total value due to Mr Le Bon on the takeover is as follows.

		£
Ordinary	20,000 × 3/4 × £5	75,000
Preference	20,000 × 1/4 × 90p	4,500
		79,500

The base costs are therefore:

	£
Ordinary shares: 75,000/79,500 × 20,000 × £2	37,736
Preference shares: 4,500/79,500 × 20,000 × £2	2,264
	40,000

6 Gilts and qualifying corporate bonds

Gilts and Qualifying Corporate bonds held by individuals are exempt from CGT. You should never waste time computing gains and losses on them.

Key term

Gilts are UK Government securities issued by HM Treasury as shown on the Treasury list. You may assume that the list includes all issues of Treasury Loan, Treasury Stock, Exchequer Loan, Exchequer Stock and War Loan.

Disposals of gilt edged securities (gilts) and qualifying corporate bonds by individuals are exempt from CGT.

A **qualifying corporate bond (QCB)** is a security (whether or not secured on assets) which:

(a) represents a **'normal commercial loan'**. This excludes any bonds which are convertible into shares (although bonds convertible into other bonds which would be QCBs are not excluded), or which carry the right to excessive interest or interest which depends on the results of the issuer's business;

(b) is **expressed in sterling** and for which no provision is made for conversion into or redemption in another currency;

(c) was **acquired** by the person now disposing of it **after 13 March 1984**; and

(d) does not have a redemption value which depends on a published index of share prices on a stock exchange.

Permanent interest bearing shares issued by building societies which meet condition (b) above are also QCBs.

Chapter Roundup

- Quoted shares are valued at the lower of the 'quarter-up' value and the average of the highest and lowest marked bargains.

- There are special rules for matching shares sold with shares purchased. Disposals are matched first with acquisitions on the same day, then within the following 30 days and finally with the share pool.

- Bonus shares are shares acquired at no cost. Rights issue shares are acquired for payment.

- The costs of the original holding are allocated to the new holdings pro rata to their values on a takeover or reorganisation.

- Gilts and Qualifying Corporate bonds held by individuals are exempt from CGT. You should never waste time computing gains and losses on them.

1   In what order are acquisitions of shares matched with disposals for individuals?

2   In July 1995 an individual acquired 1,000 shares. He acquired 1,000 more shares on each of 15 January 2005 and 15 January 2010 in X plc. He sells 2,500 shares on 10 January 2010. How are the shares matched on sale?

3   Sharon acquired 10,000 share in Z plc in 1986. She takes up a 1 for 2 rights offer in May 2009. How many shares does Sharon have in her share pool after the takeover?

4   What is a qualifying corporate bond?

Answers to Quick Quiz

1   The matching of shares sold is in the following order.

    (a)   Same day acquisitions.
    (b)   Acquisitions within the following 30 days.
    (c)   Shares in the shares pool.

2   January 2010 1,000 shares (following 30 days)
    Share pool 1,500 shares

3   10,000 + 5,000 = 15,000 shares

4   A qualifying corporate bond is a security which:

    •   represents a normal commercial loan
    •   is expressed in sterling
    •   was acquired after 13 March 1984
    •   is not redeemable in relation to share prices on a stock exchange

Now try the questions below from the Exam Question Bank

Number	Level	Marks	Time
Q25	Examination	10	18 mins

Tax administration for individuals

17

Self assessment and payment of tax by individuals

Topic list	Syllabus reference
1 The self assessment system	G1(a)
2 Tax returns and keeping records	G2(a), (e)
3 Self-assessment and claims	G2(a)
4 Payments of income tax and capital gains tax	G2(b), (c)
5 Revenue powers	G3(a), (b)
6 Penalties	G4(a), (b)
7 Appeals	G4(b)

Introduction

In the earlier chapters we have learned how to calculate an individual's liability to income tax, capital gains tax and national insurance.

In this chapter we see how individuals (including partners) must 'self assess' their liability to income tax, capital gains tax and Class 4 NICs.

In the remaining chapters we will consider the remaining taxes within the syllabus: corporation tax and VAT.

Study guide

		Intellectual level
G1	**The systems for self-assessment and the making of returns**	
(a)	Explain and apply the features of the self assessment system as it applies to individuals.	2
G2	**The time limits for the submission of information, claims and payment of tax, including payments on account**	
(a)	Recognise the time limits that apply to the filing of returns and the making of claims.	2
(b)	Recognise the due dates for the payment of tax under the self-assessment system.	2
(c)	Compute payments on account and balancing payments/repayments for individuals.	2
(e)	List the information and records that taxpayers need to retain for tax purposes.	1
G3	**The procedures relating to enquiries, appeals and disputes**	
(a)	Explain the circumstances in which HM Revenue & Customs can enquire into a self assessment tax return.	2
(b)	Explain the procedures for dealing with appeals and disputes.	1
G4	**Penalties for non-compliance**	
(a)	Calculate interest on overdue tax.	2
(b)	State the penalties that can be charged.	2

Exam guide

Question 1 of the exam will always be on income tax and question 3 on CGT. Either of these could include a part on the self assessment system, be it the filing of a return, the payment of tax or the opening of an enquiry by HMRC, or it could be included in questions 4 or 5. Your knowledge should include the penalties used to enforce the self assessment system.

1 The self assessment system

This section relates to your PER requirement:
19   Evaluate and compute taxes payable

1.1 Introduction

The self assessment system relies upon the taxpayer completing and filing a tax return and paying the tax due. The system is enforced by a system of penalties for failure to comply within the set time limits, and by interest for late payment of tax.

Many taxpayers have very simple affairs: receiving a salary under deduction of tax through PAYE, with a small amount of investment income which can be dealt with through the PAYE code. These individuals will not normally have to complete a tax return. Self-employed taxpayers, company directors and individuals with complicated affairs will have to.

Once a taxpayer is within the self assessment system he will be required to complete and file a return every year unless HMRC recognise that his affairs have become sufficiently straightforward for no return to be required.

Conversely, individuals whose affairs become more complicated so that they are likely to owe tax must notify HMRC that they should be brought within the self assessment system.

1.2 Notification of liability to income tax and CGT

FAST FORWARD

Individuals who do not receive a tax return must notify their chargeability to income tax or CGT.

Individuals who are chargeable to income tax or CGT for any tax year and who have not received a notice to file a return are required to give notice of chargeability to an Officer of the Revenue and Customs within six months from the end of the year ie by 5 October 2010 for 2009/10.

A person who has no chargeable gains and who is not liable to higher rate tax does not have to give notice of chargeability if all his income:

(a)   Is taken into account under PAYE
(b)   Is from a source of income not subject to tax under a self-assessment
(c)   Has had (or is treated as having had) income tax deducted at source, or
(d)   Is UK dividends.

A penalty may be imposed for late notification (see later in this Chapter).

2 Tax returns and keeping records

FAST FORWARD

Tax returns must usually be filed by 31 October (paper) or 31 January (electronic) following the end of the tax year.

2.1 Tax returns

The tax return comprises a basic six-page return form**, together with supplementary pages for particular sources of income.** Taxpayers are sent a return and a number of supplementary pages depending on their known sources of income, together with a Tax Return Guide and various notes relating to the supplementary pages. Taxpayers with new sources of income may have to ask for further supplementary pages. Taxpayers with simple tax returns may be asked to complete a short four- page tax return. If a return for the previous year was filed electronically the taxpayer may be sent a notice to file a return, rather than the official HMRC form.

Partnerships must file a separate return which includes a Partnership Statement showing the firm's profits, losses, proceeds from the sale of assets, tax suffered, tax credits, charges on income and the division of all these amounts between partners.

A partnership return must include a declaration of the name and tax reference of each partner, as well as the usual declaration that the return is correct and complete to the best of the signatory's knowledge. Each partner must then include his share of partnership profits on his personal tax return.

2.2 Time limit for submission of tax returns

Key term

The **latest filing date** for a personal tax return for a tax year (Year 1) is:

*   **31 October** in the next tax year (Year 2), for a **non-electronic return** (eg a paper return).
*   **31 January** in Year 2, for an **electronic return** (eg made via the internet).

There are **two exceptions to this general rule**.

The **first exception applies if the notice to file a tax return is issued by HMRC to the taxpayer after 31 July in Year 2, but on or before 31 October in Year 2**. In this case, the **latest filing date is**:

*   **the end of 3 months following the notice, for a non-electronic return.**
*   **31 January in Year 2, for an electronic return**.

The second exception applies **if the notice to file the tax return is issued to the taxpayer after 31 October in Year 2**. In this case, **the latest filing date is the end of 3 months following the notice.**

Advise each of the following clients of the latest filing date for her personal tax return for 2009/10 if the return is:

(a)   non-electronic; or
(b)   electronic.

Norma	Notice to file tax return issued by HMRC on 6 April 2010
Melanie	Notice to file tax return issued by HMRC on 10 August 2010
Olga	Notice to file tax return issued by HMRC on 12 December 2010

Answer

	Non-electronic	*Electronic*
Norma	31 October 2010	31 January 2011
Melanie	9 November 2010	31 January 2011
Olga	11 March 2011	11 March 2011

A partnership return may be filed as a non-electronic return or an electronic return. **The general rule and the exceptions to the general rule for personal returns apply also to partnership returns**.

2.3 Keeping records

All taxpayers must retain all records required to enable them to make and deliver a correct tax return.

Records must be retained until the later of:

(a)   (i)   **5 years after the 31 January following the tax year where the taxpayer is in business** (as a sole trader or partner or letting property). Note that this applies to all of the records, not only the business records, or

         (ii)   **1 year after the 31 January following the tax year otherwise, or**

(b)   Provided notice to deliver a return is given before the date in (a):

         (i)   **The time after which enquiries by HMRC into the return can no longer be commenced**, or
         (ii)   **The date any such enquiries have been completed.**

HMRC can specify a shorter time limit for keeping records where the records are bulky and the information they contain can be provided in another way.

Where a person receives a notice to deliver a tax return after the normal record keeping period has expired, he must keep all records in his possession at that time until no enquiries can be raised in respect of the return or until such enquiries have been completed.

Taxpayers can keep 'information', rather than 'records', but must show that they have prepared a complete and correct tax return. The information must also be able to be provided in a legible form on request. Records can be kept in electronic format.

HMRC can inspect 'in-year' records, i e *before* a return is submitted, if they believe it is reasonably required to check a tax position.

3 Self-assessment and claims

FAST FORWARD

If a paper return is filed the taxpayer can ask HMRC to compute the tax due. Electronic returns have tax calculated automatically.

3.1 Self-assessment

Key term

A self-assessment is a calculation of the amount of taxable income and gains after deducting reliefs and allowances, a calculation of income tax and CGT payable after taking into account tax deducted at source and tax credits on dividends.

If the taxpayer is filing a **paper return (other than a Short Tax Return), he may make the tax calculation on his return or ask HMRC to do so on his behalf**.

If the taxpayer wishes HMRC to make the calculation for Year 1, a paper return must be filed:

* **on or before 31 October in Year 2 or**,
* **if the notice to file the tax return is issued after 31 August in Year 2, within 2 months of the notice**.

If the taxpayer is filing an **electronic return, the calculation of tax liability is made automatically when the return is made online**.

3.2 Amending the self-assessment

The taxpayer may amend his return (including the tax calculation) for Year 1 within twelve months after the filing date. For this purpose the filing date means:

* **31 January of Year 2**; or
* **where the notice to file a return was issued after 31 October in Year 2, the last day of the three month period starting with the issue**.

A return may be amended by the taxpayer at a time when an enquiry is in progress into the return. The amendment does not restrict the scope of an enquiry into the return but may be taken into account in that enquiry. If the amendment made during an enquiry is the amount of tax payable, the amendment does not take effect while the enquiry is in progress.

A return may be amended by HMRC to correct any obvious error or omission in the return (such as errors of principle and arithmetical mistakes) or anything else that an officer has reason to believe is incorrect in the light of information available. The correction must be usually be made within nine months after the day on which the return was actually filed. The taxpayer can object to the correction but must do so within 30 days of receiving notice of it.

3.3 Claims

All claims and elections which can be made in a tax return must be made in this manner if a return has been issued. A claim for any relief, allowance or repayment of tax must be quantified at the time it is made.

In general, the time limit for making a claim is 4 years from the end of tax year. Where different time limits apply these have been mentioned throughout this Text.

3.4 Recovery of overpaid tax

If a taxpayer discovers that he has overpaid tax, for example because he has made an error in his tax return, he can make a claim to have the overpaid tax repaid to him. The claim must be made within four years of the end of the tax year to which the overpayment relates.

4 Payment of income tax and capital gains tax

> Two payments on account and a final balancing payment of income tax and Class 4 NICs are due. All capital gains tax is due on 31 January following the end of the tax year.

4.1 Payments on account and final payment

4.1.1 Introduction

The self-assessment system may result in the taxpayer making three payments of income tax and Class 4 NICs.

Date	Payment
31 January in the tax year	1st payment on account
31 July after the tax year	2nd payment on account
31 January after the tax year	Final payment to settle the remaining liability

HMRC issue payslips/demand notes in a credit card type 'Statement of Account' format, but there is no statutory obligation for it to do so and **the onus is on the taxpayer to pay the correct amount of tax on the due date.**

4.1.2 Payments on account

Key term

> **Payments on account** are usually required where the income tax and Class 4 NICs due in the previous year exceeded the amount of income tax deducted at source; this excess is known as **'the relevant amount'**. Income tax deducted at source includes tax suffered, PAYE deductions and tax credits on dividends.

The payments on account are each equal to 50% of the relevant amount for the previous year.

Exam focus point

> Payments on account of CGT are never required.

Question — Payments on account

Sue is a self employed writer who paid tax for 2009/10 as follows:

		£
Total amount of income tax charged		9,200
This included:	Tax deducted on savings income	3,200
She also paid:	Class 4 NIC	1,900
	Class 2 NIC	125
	Capital gains tax	4,800

How much are the payments on account for 2010/11?

	£
Income tax:	
Total income tax charged for 2009/10	9,200
Less tax deducted for 2009/10	(3,200)
	6,000
Class 4 NIC	1,900
'Relevant amount'	7,900
Payments on account for 2010/11:	
31 January 2011 £7,900 × 50%	3,950
31 July 2011 As before	3,950

There is no requirement to make payments on account of capital gains tax nor Class 2 NIC.

Payments on account are not required if the relevant amount falls below a de minimis limit of £1,000. Also, payments on account are not required from taxpayers who paid 80% or more of their tax liability for the previous year through PAYE or other deduction at source arrangements.

4.1.3 Reducing payments on account

Payments on account are normally fixed by reference to the previous year's tax liability but if a taxpayer expects his liability to be lower than this **he may claim to reduce his payments on account to:**

(a) **A stated amount**, or
(b) **Nil**.

The claim must state the reason why he believes his tax liability will be lower, or nil.

If the taxpayer's eventual liability is higher than he estimated he will have reduced the payments on account too far. Although the payments on account will not be adjusted, the taxpayer will suffer an interest charge on late payment.

A penalty of the difference between the reduced payment on account and the correct payment on account may be levied if the reduction was claimed fraudulently or negligently.

4.1.4 Balancing payment

The balance of any income tax and Class 4 NICs together with all CGT due for a year, is normally payable on or before the 31 January following the year.

Question   Payment of tax

Giles made payments on account for 2009/10 of £6,500 each on 31 January 2010 and 31 July 2010, based on his 2008/09 liability. He then calculates his total income tax and Class 4 NIC liability for 2009/10 at £18,000 of which £2,750 was deducted at source. In addition he calculated that his CGT liability for disposals in 2009/10 is £5,120.

What is the final payment due for 2009/10?

Answer

Income tax and Class 4 NIC: £18,000 – £2,750 – £6,500 – £6,500 = £2,250. CGT = £5,120.

Final payment due on 31 January 2011 for 2009/2010 £2,250 + £5,120 = £7,370

In one case the due date for the final payment is later than 31 January following the end of the year. **If a taxpayer has notified chargeability by 5 October but the notice to file a tax return is not issued before 31 October, then the due date for the payment is three months after the issue of the notice.**

Tax charged in an amended self-assessment is usually payable on the later of:

(a) The normal due date, generally 31 January following the end of the tax year, and
(b) The day following 30 days after the making of the revised self-assessment.

Tax charged on a discovery assessment (see below) is due thirty days after the issue of the assessment.

4.2 Surcharges

Surcharges are normally imposed in respect of amounts paid late:

	Paid	Surcharge
(a)	Within 28 days of due date:	none
(b)	More than 28 days but not more than six months after the due date:	5%
(c)	More than six months after the due date:	10%

Surcharges apply to:

(a) Balancing payments of income tax and Class 4 NICs and any CGT under self-assessment or a determination
(b) Tax due on the amendment of a self-assessment
(c) Tax due on a discovery assessment

The surcharge rules do not apply to late payments on account.

No surcharge will be applied where the late paid tax liability has attracted a tax-geared penalty on the failure to notify chargeability to tax, or the failure to submit a return, or on the making of an incorrect return (including a partnership return).

4.3 Interest on late paid tax

Interest is chargeable on late payment of both payments on account and balancing payments. In both cases interest runs from the due date until the day before the actual date of payment.

You will be given the rate of interest to use in the exam.

Interest is charged from 31 January following the tax year (or the normal due date for the balancing payment, in the rare event that this is later), even if this is before the due date for payment on:

(a) Tax payable following an amendment to a self-assessment
(b) Tax payable in a discovery assessment, and
(c) Tax postponed under an appeal, which becomes payable.

Since a determination (see below) is treated as if it were a self-assessment, interest runs from 31 January following the tax year.

If a taxpayer claims to reduce his payments on account and there is still a final payment to be made, interest is normally charged on the payments on account as if each of those payments had been the lower of:

(a) the reduced amount, plus 50% of the final income tax liability; and
(b) the amount which would have been payable had no claim for reduction been made.

Question

Herbert's payments on account for 2009/10 based on his income tax liability for 2008/09 were £4,500 each. However when he submitted his 2008/09 income tax return in January 2010 he made a claim to reduce the payments on account for 2009/10 to £3,500 each. The first payment on account was made on 29 January 2010, and the second on 12 August 2010.

Herbert filed his 2009/10 tax return in December 2010. The return showed that his tax liabilities for 2009/10 (before deducting payments on account) were income tax and Class 4 NIC: £10,000, capital gains tax: £2,500. Herbert paid the balance of tax due of £5,500 on 19 February 2011.

For what periods and in respect of what amounts will Herbert be charged interest?

Answer

Herbert made an excessive claim to reduce his payments on account, and will therefore be charged interest on the reduction. The payments on account should have been £4,500 each based on the original 2008/09 liability (not £5,000 each based on the 2009/10 liability). Interest will be charged as follows:

(a) First payment on account

    (i)   On £3,500 – nil – paid on time

    (ii)   On £1,000 from due date of 31 January 2010 to day before payment, 18 February 2011

(b) Second payment on account

    (i)   On £3,500 from due date of 31 July 2010 to day before payment, 11 August 2010

    (ii)   On £1,000 from due date of 31 July 2010 to day before payment, 18 February 2011

(c) Balancing payment

    (i)   On £3,500 from due date of 31 January 2011 to day before payment, 18 February 2011

Where interest has been charged on late payments on account but the final balancing settlement for the year produces a repayment, all or part of the original interest is repaid.

4.4 Repayment of tax and repayment supplement

Tax is repaid when claimed unless a greater payment of tax is due in the following 30 days, in which case it is set-off against that payment.

Technically, interest (repayment supplement) is paid on overpayments of tax. However, for 2009/10, the rate of repayment supplement is 0%.

5 Revenue powers

5.1 Enquiries into returns

FAST FORWARD

HMRC can enquire into tax returns. Strict procedural rules govern enquiries.

5.1.1 Opening an enquiry

An officer of the Revenue and Customs has a limited period within which to commence enquiries into a return or amendment. **The officer must give written notice of his intention by:**

(a) **The first anniversary of the actual filing date (if the return was delivered on or before the due filing date)**, or

(b) **If the return is filed after the due filing date, the quarter day following the first anniversary of the actual filing date. The quarter days are 31 January, 30 April, 31 July and 31 October.**

If the taxpayer amended the return after the due filing date, the enquiry 'window' extends to the quarter day following the first anniversary of the date the amendment was filed. Where the enquiry was not raised within the limit which would have applied had no amendment been filed, the enquiry is restricted to matters contained in the amendment.

The officer does not have to have, or give, any reason for raising an enquiry. In particular the taxpayer will not be advised whether he has been selected at random for an audit. Enquiries may be full enquiries, or may be limited to 'aspect' enquiries.

5.1.2 During the enquiry

In the course of his enquiries **the officer may require the taxpayer to produce documents, accounts or any other information required. The taxpayer can appeal to the Tribunal.**

During the course of his enquiries an officer may amend a self assessment if it appears that insufficient tax has been charged and an immediate amendment is necessary to prevent a loss to the Crown. This might apply if, for example, there is a possibility that the taxpayer will emigrate.

If a return is under enquiry HMRC may postpone any repayment due as shown in the return until the enquiry is complete. HMRC have discretion to make a provisional repayment but there is no facility to appeal if the repayment is withheld.

At any time during the course of an enquiry, the taxpayer may apply to the Tribunal to require the officer to notify the taxpayer within a specified period that the enquiries are complete, unless the officer can demonstrate that he has reasonable grounds for continuing the enquiry.

5.1.3 Closing an enquiry

An officer must issue a notice that the enquiries are complete, state his conclusions and amend the self-assessment, partnership statement or claim accordingly.

If the taxpayer is not satisfied with the officer's amendment he may, within 30 days, appeal to the Tribunal.

Once an enquiry is complete the officer cannot make further enquiries. HMRC may, in limited circumstances, raise a discovery assessment if they believe that there has been a loss of tax (see below).

5.2 Determinations

If notice has been served on a taxpayer to submit a return but the return is not submitted by the due filing date, an officer of HMRC may make a determination of the amounts liable to income tax and CGT and of the tax due. Such a determination must be made to the best of the officer's information and belief, and is then treated as if it were a self-assessment. This enables the officer to seek payment of tax, including payments on account for the following year and to charge interest.

A determination must be made within four year following the end of the relevant tax year.

5.3 Discovery assessments

If an officer of HMRC discovers that profits have been omitted from assessment, that any assessment has become insufficient, or that any relief given is, or has become excessive, an assessment may be raised to recover the tax lost.

If the tax lost results from an error in the taxpayer's return but the return was made in accordance with prevailing practice at the time, no discovery assessment may be made.

A discovery assessment may only be raised where a return has been made if:

(a)   There has been **careless or deliberate understatement** by the taxpayer or his agent, or

(b)   At the time that enquiries into the return were completed, or could no longer be made, the officer **did not have information** to make him aware of the loss of tax.

Information is treated as available to an officer if it is contained in the taxpayer's return or claim for the year or either of the two preceding years, or it has been provided as a result of an enquiry covering those years, or it has been specifically provided.

The time limit for raising a discovery assessment is four years from the end of the tax year but this is extended to 6 years if there has been careless understatement and 20 years if there has been deliberate understatement. The taxpayer may appeal against a discovery assessment within 30 days of issue.

5.4 Information and inspection powers

FAST FORWARD

> HMRC have powers to request documents from taxpayers and third parties. HMRC also has powers to inspect business premises.

5.4.1 Information powers

HMRC has one set of information and inspection powers covering income tax, capital gains tax, corporation tax, VAT and PAYE to ensure taxpayers comply with their obligations, pay the right amount of tax at the right time and claim the correct reliefs and allowances.

HMRC usually informally requests information and documents from taxpayers in connection with their tax affairs. If, however, a taxpayer does not co-operate fully, **HMRC can use its statutory powers to request information and documents** from taxpayers and third parties via a written 'information notice'. HMRC can request both statutory records and supplementary information, such as appointment diaries, notes of board meetings, correspondence and contracts.

HMRC can only issue a taxpayer notice if the information and documents requested are 'reasonably required' for the purpose of checking the taxpayer's tax position. A taxpayer notice may be issued either with or without the approval of the Tribunal.

An information notice issued to a third party must be issued with the agreement of the taxpayer or the approval of the Tribunal, unless the information relates only to the taxpayer's statutory VAT records. The taxpayer to whom the notice relates must receive a summary of the reasons for the third party notice unless the Tribunal believes it would prejudice the assessment or collection of tax.

Tax advisers and auditors cannot be asked to provide information connected with their functions. For example, a tax adviser does not have to provide access to his working papers used in the preparation of the taxpayer's return. In addition, HMRC cannot ask a tax adviser to provide communications between himself and either the taxpayer or his other advisers. This 'professional privilege' does not apply in certain situations, for example, to explanatory material provided to a client in relation to a document already supplied to HMRC.

The taxpayer or third party must provide the information or document requested by the information notice within such period as is reasonably specified within the notice.

The recipient of an information notice has a right of appeal against an information notice unless the Tribunal has approved the issue of the notice.

5.4.2 Inspection powers

An authorised officer of HMRC can enter the business premises of a taxpayer whose liability is being checked and inspect the premises and the business assets and business documents that are on the premises. The power does not extend to any part of the premises used solely as a dwelling. If an information notice has been issued, the documents required in that notice can be inspected at the same time. **The inspection must be reasonably required for the purposes of checking the taxpayer's tax position.**

HMRC will usually agree a time for the inspection with the taxpayer. However, **an authorised HMRC officer can carry out the inspection at 'any reasonable time'** if either:

(a) **The taxpayer receives at least seven days' written notice**, or
(b) **The inspection is carried out by, or with the approval of, an authorised HMRC officer.**

There is no right of appeal against an inspection notice.

6 Penalties

6.1 Penalties for errors

FAST FORWARD

There is a common penalty regime for errors in tax returns, including income tax, NICs, corporation tax and VAT. Penalties range from 30% to 100% of the Potential Lost Revenue. Penalties may be reduced.

A common penalty regime for errors in tax returns for income tax, national insurance contributions, corporation tax and value added tax.

A penalty may be imposed where **a taxpayer makes an inaccurate return** if he has:

- been **careless** because he has not taken reasonable care in making the return or discovers the error later but does not take reasonable steps to inform HMRC; or

- made a **deliberate error** but **does not make arrangements to conceal it**; or

- made a **deliberate error** and **has attempted to conceal it** eg by submitting false evidence in support of an inaccurate figure.

Note that **an error which is made where the taxpayer has taken reasonable care** in making the return and which he **does not discover later, does not result in a penalty**.

In order for a penalty to be charged, the **inaccurate return must result in**:

- **an understatement of the taxpayer's tax liability**; or
- **a false or increased loss for the taxpayer**; or
- **a false or increased repayment of tax to the taxpayer**.

If a return contains more than one error, a penalty can be charged for each error.

The rules also extend to **errors in claims for allowances and reliefs** and in **accounts submitted in relation to a tax liability**.

Penalties for error also apply where **HMRC has issued an assessment estimating a person's liability** where:

- a **return has been issued to that person and has not been returned**, or
- the taxpayer was **required to deliver a return to HMRC but has not delivered it**.

The taxpayer will be charged a penalty where

- the **assessment understates the taxpayer's liability** to income tax, capital gains tax, corporation tax or VAT, and

- **the taxpayer fails to take reasonable steps within 30 days of the date of the assessment** to tell HMRC that there is an under-assessment.

The amount of **the penalty for error is based on the Potential Lost Revenue (PLR)** to HMRC as a result of the error. For example, if there is an understatement of tax, this understatement will be the PLR.

The maximum amount of the penalty for error depends on the type of error:

Type of error	Maximum penalty payable
Careless	30% of PLR
Deliberate not concealed	70% of PLR
Deliberate and concealed	100% of PLR

Question

Alex is a sole trader. He files his tax return for 2009/10 on 10 January 2011. The return shows his trading income to be £60,000. In fact, due to carelessness, his trading income should have been stated to be £68,000.

State the maximum penalty that could be charged by HMRC on Alex for his error.

Answer

The Potential Lost Revenue as a result of Alex's error is:

£(68,000 – 60,000) = £8,000 x [40% (income tax) + 1% (NICs)]   £3,280

Alex's error is careless so the maximum penalty for error is:

£3,280 x 30%   £984

A penalty for error may be reduced if the taxpayer tells HMRC about the error – this is called a disclosure. The reduction depends on the circumstances of the disclosure and the help that the taxpayer gives to HMRC in relation to the disclosure.

An unprompted disclosure is one made at a time when the taxpayer has no reason to believe HMRC has discovered, or is about to discover, the error. Otherwise, the disclosure will be a prompted disclosure. The minimum penalties that can be imposed are as follows:

Type of error	Unprompted	Prompted
Careless	0% of PLR	15% of PLR
Deliberate not concealed	20% of PLR	35% of PLR
Deliberate and concealed	30% of PLR	50% of PLR

Question

Sue is a sole trader. She files her tax return for 2008/09 on 31 January 2010. The return shows a loss for the year of £(80,000). In fact, Sue has deliberately increased this loss by £(12,000) and has submitted false figures in support of her claim. HMRC initiate a review into Sue's return and in reply Sue then makes a disclosure of the error. Sue is a higher rate taxpayer due to her substantial investment income and she has made a claim to set the loss against general income in 2008/09.

State the maximum and minimum penalties that could be charged by HMRC on Sue for her error.

Answer

The potential lost revenue as a result of Sue's error is:
£12,000 x 40%   £4,800

Sue's error is deliberate and concealed so the maximum penalty for error is:
£4,800 x 100%   £4,800

Sue has made a prompted disclosure so the minimum penalty for error is:
£4,800 x 50%   £2,400

The help that the taxpayer gives to HMRC relates to when, how and to what extent the taxpayer:

- **tells HMRC about the error,** making full disclosure and explaining how the error was made;
- **gives reasonable help** to HMRC to enable it **to quantify the error**; and
- **allows access to business and other records** and other relevant documents.

A taxpayer can appeal to the First-tier Tribunal against :

- the **penalty being charged**;
- the **amount of the penalty**.

6.2 Penalties for late notification of chargeability

FAST FORWARD A common penalty regime also applies to late notification of chargeability.

A common penalty regime also applies to certain taxes for failures to notify chargeability to, or liability to register for, tax that result in a loss of tax. The taxes affected include income tax, NICs, PAYE, CGT, corporation tax and VAT. Penalties are behaviour related, increasing for more serious failures, and are based on the 'potential lost revenue'.

The minimum and maximum penalties as percentages of PLR are as follows:

Behaviour	Maximum penalty	Minimum penalty with unprompted disclosure		Minimum penalty with prompted disclosure	
Deliberate and concealed	100%	30%		50%	
Deliberate but not concealed	70%	20%		35%	
		>12m	<12m	>12m	<12m
Careless	30%	10%	0%	20%	10%

Note that there is no zero penalty for reasonable care (as there is for penalties for errors on returns – see above), although the penalty may be reduced to 0% if the failure is rectified within 12 months through unprompted disclosure. The penalties may also be reduced at HMRC's discretion in 'special circumstances'. However, inability to pay the penalty is not a 'special circumstance'.

The same penalties apply for failure to notify HMRC of a new taxable activity.

Where the taxpayer's failure is not classed as deliberate, there is no penalty if he can show he has a 'reasonable excuse'. Reasonable excuse does not include having insufficient money to pay the penalty. Taxpayers have a right of appeal against penalty decisions to the First-tier Tribunal.

6.3 Penalties for late filing

The maximum penalties for delivering a tax return after the filing due date are:

(a) **Return up to 6 months late:**   £100
(b) **Return more than 6 months but not more than 12 months late:**   £200
(c) **Return more than 12 months late:**   £200 + 100% of the tax liability

In addition, the First-tier Tribunal can direct that a maximum penalty of £60 per day be imposed where failure to deliver a tax return continues after notice of the direction has been given to the taxpayer. In this case the additional £100 penalty, imposed under (b) if the return is more than six months late, is not charged.

The fixed penalties of £100/£200 can be set aside by the First-tier Tribunal if they are satisfied that the taxpayer had a reasonable excuse for not delivering the return. If the tax liability shown on the return is less than the fixed penalties, the fixed penalty is reduced to the amount of the tax liability. The tax geared penalty is mitigable by HMRC or the First Tier Tribunal.

A taxpayer only has a reasonable excuse for a late filing if a default occurred because of a factor outside his control. This might be non-receipt of the return by the taxpayer, an industrial dispute in the post office after the return was posted, serious illness of the taxpayer or a close relative, or destruction of records through fire and flood. Illness etc is only accepted as a reasonable excuse if the taxpayer was taking timeous steps to complete the return, and if the return is filed as soon as possible after the illness etc.

6.4 Penalties for failure to keep records

The maximum (mitigable) penalty for each failure to keep and retain records is £3,000 per tax year/accounting period.

7 Appeals

FAST FORWARD

Disputes between taxpayers and HMRC can be dealt with by an HMRC internal review or by a Tribunal hearing.

7.1 Internal reviews

For direct taxes, appeals must first be made to HMRC, which will assign a 'caseworker'.

For indirect taxes, appeals must be sent directly to the Tribunal, although the taxpayer can continue to correspond with his caseworker where, for example, there is new information.

At this stage the taxpayer may be offered, or may ask for, an **'internal review'**, which will be made by an objective HMRC review officer not previously connected with the case. This is a less costly and more effective way to resolve disputes informally, without the need for a Tribunal hearing. An appeal to Tribunal cannot be made until any review has ended.

The taxpayer must either accept the review offer, or notify an appeal to the Tribunal within 30 days of being offered the review, otherwise the appeal will be treated as settled.

HMRC must usually carry out the review within 45 days, or any longer time as agreed with the taxpayer. The review officer may decide to uphold, vary or withdraw decisions.

After the review conclusion is notified, **the taxpayer has 30 days to appeal to the Tribunal.**

7.2 Tribunal hearings

If there is no internal review, or the taxpayer is unhappy with the result of an internal review, the case may be heard by the Tribunal. The person wishing to make an appeal (the appellant) must send a notice of appeal to the Tribunal. The Tribunal must then give notice of the appeal to the respondent (normally HMRC).

The Tribunal is made up of two 'tiers':

(a)   **A First-tier Tribunal and**
(b)   **An Upper Tribunal.**

The case will be allocated to one of four **case 'tracks'**:

(a)   **Complex cases**, which the Tribunal considers will require lengthy or complex evidence or a lengthy hearing, or involve a complex or important principle or issue, or involves a large amount of money. Such cases will usually be heard by the Upper Tribunal,

(b)   **Standard cases, heard by the First Tier Tribunal**, which have detailed case management and are subject to a more formal procedure than basic cases,

(c)   **Basic cases, also heard by the First Tier Tribunal**, which will usually be disposed of after a hearing, with minimal exchange of documents before the hearing, and

(d)   **Paper cases, dealt with by the First Tier Tribunal**, which applies to straightforward matters such as fixed filing penalties and will usually be dealt with in writing, without a hearing.

A decision of the First-tier Tribunal may be appealed to the Upper Tribunal.

Decisions of the Upper Tribunal are binding on the Tribunals and any affected public authorities. A decision of the Upper Tribunal may be appealed to the Court of Appeal.

Chapter Roundup

- Individuals who do not receive a tax return must notify their chargeability to income tax or CGT.

- Tax returns must usually be filed by 31 October (paper) or 31 January (electronic) following the end of the tax year.

- If a paper return is filed the taxpayer can ask HMRC to compute the tax due. Electronic returns have tax calculated automatically.

- Two payments on account and a final balancing payment of income tax and Class 4 NICs are due. All capital gains tax is due on 31 January following the end of the tax year.

- HMRC can enquire into tax returns. Strict procedural rules govern enquiries.

- HMRC have powers to request documents from taxpayers and third parties. HMRC also has powers to inspect business premises.

- There is a common penalty regime for errors in tax returns, including income tax, NICs, corporation tax and VAT. Penalties range from 30% to 100% of the Potential Lost Revenue. Penalties may be reduced.

- A common penalty regime also applies to late notification of chargeability.

- Disputes between taxpayers and HMRC can be dealt with by an HMRC internal review or by a Tribunal hearing.

1   A taxpayer who has not received a tax return must give notice of his chargeability to capital gains tax due in 2009/10 by_____. Fill in the blank.

2   By when must a taxpayer normally file a paper tax return for 2009/10?

    A   31 October 2010
    B   31 December 2010
    C   31 January 2011
    D   5 April 2011

3   What are the normal payment dates for income tax?

4   What surcharges are due in respect of income tax payments on account that are paid two months after the due date?

5   What is the maximum penalty for failure to keep records?

6   Which body hears tax appeals?

Answers to Quick Quiz

1   A taxpayer who has not received a tax return must give notice to his chargeability to capital gains tax due in 2009/10 by 5 October 2010.

2   A. 31 October 2010.

3   Two payments on account of income tax are due on 31 January in the tax year and on 31 July following. A final balancing payment is due on 31 January following the tax year.

4   None. Surcharges do not apply to late payment of payments on account.

5   £3,000

6   The Tax Tribunal which consists of the First-tier Tribunal and the Upper Tribunal.

Now try the question below from the Exam Question Bank

Number	Level	Marks	Time
Q26	Introductory	8	15 mins
Q27	Examination	25	45 mins

Corporation tax

Computing profits chargeable to corporation tax

Topic list	Syllabus reference
1 The scope of corporation tax	C1(a)-(c)
2 Profits chargeable to corporation tax	C2(k)
3 Trading income	C2(a)-(c)
4 Property business income	C2(d)
5 Loan relationships (interest income)	C2(e)
6 Miscellaneous income	C2(k)
7 Gift aid donations	C2(f)
8 Long periods of account	C2(k)

Introduction

Now that we have completed our study of personal tax we turn our attention to corporation tax, ie the tax that a company must pay on its profits.

First we consider the scope of corporation tax and we see that a company must pay tax for an 'accounting period' which may be different from its period of account.

We then learn how to calculate the profits chargeable to corporation tax. This involves calculating income from different sources, such as trading income, interest and property income, adding capital gains and deducting gift aid donations. You have learnt the general rules for calculating income in your earlier studies, but here we see where there are special rules for companies.

In the next chapter you will learn how to compute the corporation tax liability on those profits.

Study guide

		Intellectual level
C1	**The scope of corporation tax**	
(a)	Define the terms 'period of account', 'accounting period', and 'financial year'.	1
(b)	Recognise when an accounting period starts and when an accounting period finishes.	1
(c)	Explain how the residence of a company is determined.	2
C2	**Profits chargeable to corporation tax**	
(a)	Recognise the expenditure that is allowable in calculating the tax-adjusted trading profit.	2
(b)	Explain how relief can be obtained for pre-trading expenditure.	1
(c)	Compute capital allowances (as for income tax).	2
(d)	Compute property business profits.	2
(e)	Explain the treatment of interest paid and received under the loan relationship rules.	1
(f)	Explain the treatment of gift aid donations.	2
(k)	Compute profits chargeable to corporation tax.	2

Exam guide

Question 2 in the exam will focus on corporation tax. Corporation tax may also feature in other questions (apart from question 1 on income tax). When dealing with a corporation tax question you must first be able to identify the accounting period(s) involved; watch out for long periods of account. You must also be able to calculate the profits chargeable to corporation tax; learn the standard layout so that you can easily slot in figures from your workings.

1 The scope of corporation tax

FAST FORWARD 》

Companies pay corporation tax on their profits chargeable to corporation tax (PCTCT).

1.1 Companies

Companies must pay corporation tax on their **profits chargeable to corporation tax** for each **accounting period.** We look at the meaning of these terms below.

Key term

A 'company' is any corporate body (limited or unlimited) or unincorporated association, eg sports club.

1.2 Accounting periods

FAST FORWARD 》

An accounting period cannot exceed 12 months in length so a long period of account must be split into two accounting periods. The first accounting period is always twelve months in length.

Corporation tax is chargeable in respect of accounting periods. It is important to understand the difference between an accounting period and a period of account.

Key term

> A **period of account** is any period for which a company prepares accounts; usually this will be 12 months in length but it may be longer or shorter than this.

Key term

> An **accounting period** is the period for which corporation tax is charged and cannot exceed 12 months. Special rules determine when an accounting period starts and ends.

An accounting period starts when a company starts to trade, or otherwise becomes liable to corporation tax, or immediately after the previous accounting period finishes. An accounting period finishes on the earliest of:

- 12 months after its start
- the end of the company's period of account
- the commencement of the company's winding up
- the company's ceasing to be resident in the UK
- the company's ceasing to be liable to corporation tax

If a company has a period of account exceeding 12 months (a long period), it is split into two accounting periods: the first 12 months and the remainder. For example, if a company prepares accounts for the sixteen months to 30 April 2009, the two accounting periods for which the company will pay corporation tax will be the twelve months to 31 December 2008 and the four months to 30 April 2009.

1.3 Financial year

FAST FORWARD

> Tax rates are set for financial years.

The rates of corporation tax are fixed for financial years.

Key term

> **A financial year runs from 1 April to the following 31 March and is identified by the calendar year in which it begins.** For example, the year ended 31 March 2010 is the Financial year 2009 (FY 2009). This should not be confused with a tax year, which runs from 6 April to the following 5 April.

1.4 Residence of companies

FAST FORWARD

> A company is UK resident if it is incorporated in the UK or if it is incorporated abroad and its central management and control are exercised in the UK.

A company incorporated in the UK is resident in the UK. A company incorporated abroad is resident in the UK if its central management and control are exercised here. Central management and control are usually treated as exercised where the board of directors meet.

Question   Residence of a company

Supraville SARL is a company incorporated in France. It has its head office in London where the board of directors meet monthly. It trades throughout the European Union.

Is Supraville SARL resident in the UK?

Answer

Yes.

The central management and control of Supraville SARL is in London (ie the UK) where the board of directors meet.

2 Profits chargeable to corporation tax

PCTCT comprises the company's income and chargeable gains, less gift aid donations. It does not include dividends received from other UK resident companies.

This section relates to your PER requirement:
19   Evaluate and compute taxes payable

2.1 Proforma computation

Income includes trading income, property income, income from-non trading loan relationships (interest) and miscellaneous income.

A company may have both income and gains. As a general rule income arises from receipts which are expected to recur regularly (such as the profits from a trade) whereas chargeable gains arise on the sale of capital assets which have been owned for several years (such as the sale of a factory used in the trade).

A company pays corporation tax on its profits chargeable to corporation tax (PCTCT). A company may receive income from various sources. All income received must be classified according to the nature of the income as different computational rules apply to different types of income. The main types of income for a company are:

- Profits of a trade
- Profits of a property business
- Investment income
- Miscellaneous income

A company is also chargeable to corporation tax on its chargeable gains. The computation of chargeable gains for a company is dealt with later in this Text. At the moment, you will be given a figure for chargeable gains in order to compute profits chargeable to corporation tax.

A company's profits chargeable to corporation tax are arrived at by aggregating its various sources of income and its chargeable gains and then deducting gift aid donations. Here is a pro forma computation.

	£
Trading profits	X
Investment income	X
Foreign income	X
Miscellaneous income	X
Property business profits	X
Chargeable gains	X
Total profits	X
Less gift aid donations	(X)
Profits chargeable to corporation tax (PCTCT) for an accounting period	X

Exam focus point

It would be of great help in the exam if you could learn the above proforma. When answering a corporation tax question you could immediately reproduce the proforma and insert the appropriate numbers as you are given the information in the question.

Dividends received from UK resident companies are usually exempt and so not included in the profits chargeable to corporation tax. Dividends received from non-UK resident companies are dealt with later in this Study Text.

Exam focus point

The examiner has stated that dividends from UK resident companies which are taxable in the hands of the recipient company are not examinable.

3 Trading income

3.1 Adjustment of profits

> The adjustment of profits computation for companies broadly follows that for computing business profits subject to income tax. There are, however, some minor differences.

The trading income of companies is derived from the net profit figure in the accounts, just as for individuals, adjusted as follows.

	£	£
Net profit per accounts		X
Add expenditure not allowed for taxation purposes		X
		X
Less: income not taxable as trading income	X	
expenditure not charged in the accounts but allowable for the purposes of taxation	X	
capital allowances	X	
		(X)
Trading income		X

Exam focus point

> An examination question requiring adjustment to profit will direct you to start the adjustment with the net profit per accounts of £XXXX and deal with all the items listed indicating with a zero (0) any items which do not require adjustment. Marks will not be given for relevant items unless this approach is used. Therefore students who attempt to rewrite the profit and loss account will be penalised.

The adjustment of profits computation for companies broadly follows that for computing business profits subject to income tax. There are, however, some minor differences. There is no disallowance for 'private use' for companies; instead the director or employee will be taxed on the benefit received.

Gift aid donations are added back in the calculation of adjusted profit. They are treated instead as a deduction from total profits.

Investment income including rents is deducted from net profit in arriving at trading income but brought in again further down in the computation (see below).

Exam focus point

> When adjusting profits as supplied in a profit and loss account confusion can arise as regards whether figures are net or gross. Properly drawn up company accounts should normally include all income gross. However, some examination questions include items 'net'. Read the question carefully.

3.2 Pre-trading expenditure

Pre-trading expenditure incurred by the company within the 7 years before trade commences is treated as an allowable expense incurred on the first day of trading provided it would have been allowable had the company been trading when the expense was actually incurred.

3.3 Capital allowances

The calculation of capital allowances follows income tax principles.

For companies, however, there is never any reduction of allowances to take account of any private use of an asset. The director or employee suffers a taxable benefit instead. As shown above capital allowances must be deducted in arriving at taxable trading income.

A company's accounting period can never exceed 12 months. If the period of account is longer than 12 months it is **divided into two**; one for the first 12 months and one for the balance. **The capital allowances computation must be carried out for each period separately**.

The calculation of trading income should be undertaken as a first step to the calculation of profits chargeable to corporation tax. However, it is important to realise that these are two distinct aspects when calculating a company's liability to corporation tax and you should not attempt to present them in one calculation.

4 Property business income

Rental income is deducted in arriving at trading income but brought in again further down in the computation as property business income.

The calculation of property business income follows income tax principles.

The income tax rules for property businesses were set out earlier in this Text. In summary all UK rental activities are treated as a single source of income calculated in the same way as trading income.

However there are certain differences for companies:

(a)   **Property business losses** are:

- **first set off against non-property business income and gains of the company for the current period**; and any excess is

- **carried forward for set off against future income (of all descriptions)**.

(b)   **Interest paid by a company on a loan to buy or improve property is not a property business expense**. The **loan relationship rules apply** instead (see below).

5 Loan relationships (interest income)

5.1 General principle

If a company borrows or lends money, including issuing or investing in debentures or buying gilts, it has a loan relationship. This can be a creditor relationship (where the company lends or invests money) **or a debtor relationship** (where the company borrows money or issues securities).

5.2 Treatment of trading loan relationships

If the company is a party to a **loan relationship for trade purposes, any debits – ie interest paid or other debt costs – charged through its accounts are allowed as a trading expense** and are therefore deductible in computing trading income.

Similarly **if any credits – ie interest income or other debt returns – arise on a trading loan these are treated as a trading receipt and are taxable as trading income.** This is not likely to arise unless the trade is one of money lending.

5.3 Treatment of non-trading loan relationships

If a loan relationship is not one to which the company is a party for trade purposes any debits or credits must be pooled. A net credit on the pool is chargeable as interest income.

Interest charged on underpaid tax is allowable and interest received on overpaid tax is assessable under the rules for non-trading loan relationships.

You will not be expected to deal with net deficits (ie losses) on non-trading loan relationships in your exam.

5.4 Accounting methods

Debits and credits must be brought into account using the UK generally accepted accounting practice (GAAP) or using the International Accounting Standards (IAS). This will usually be the **accruals basis**.

5.5 Incidental costs of loan finance

Under the loan relationship rules expenses ('debits') are allowed if incurred directly:

(a)   to bring a loan relationship into existence
(b)   entering into or giving effect to any related transactions
(c)   making payment under a loan relationship or related transactions or
(d)   taking steps to ensure the receipt of payments under the loan relationship or related transaction.

A related transaction means 'any disposal or acquisition (in whole or in part) of rights or liabilities under the relationship, including any arising from a security issue in relation to the money debt in question'.

The above categories of incidental costs are also allowable even if the company does not enter into the loan relationship (ie abortive costs). Costs directly incurred in varying the terms of a loan relationship are also allowed.

5.6 Other matters

It is not only the interest costs of borrowing that are allowable or taxable. The capital costs are treated similarly. Thus if a company issues a loan at a discount and repays it eventually at par, the capital cost is usually allowed on redemption (if the accruals basis is adopted).

6 Miscellaneous income

Patent royalties received which do not relate to the trade are taxed as miscellaneous income. Patent royalties which relate to the trade are included in trading income normally on an accruals basis.

7 Gift aid donations

FAST FORWARD   Gift aid donations are paid gross by a company and deducted when computing PCTCT.

Gift aid donations are deductible in computing PCTCT.

Almost all donations of money to charity can be made under the **gift aid scheme** whether they are one off donations or are regular donations. **Gift aid donations are paid gross**.

Donations to local charities which are incurred wholly and exclusively for the purposes of a trade are deducted in the calculation of the tax adjusted trading profits.

8 Long periods of account

FAST FORWARD ⟩⟩ Long periods of account are split into two accounting periods: the first 12 months and the remainder.

As we saw above, **if a company has a long period of account exceeding 12 months, it is split into two accounting periods: the first 12 months and the remainder.**

Where the period of account differs from the corporation tax accounting periods, profits are **allocated to the relevant periods** as follows:

- **Trading income** before capital allowances is apportioned on a **time basis**.
- **Capital allowances** and balancing charges are **calculated for each accounting period.**
- **Other income is allocated to the period to which it relates** (eg rents to the period when accrued). Miscellaneous income, however, is apportioned on a time basis.
- **Chargeable gains and losses** are allocated to the **period in which they are realised.**
- **Gift aid donations** are deducted in the accounting **period in which they are paid.**

Question	Long period of account

Xenon Ltd makes up an 18 month set of accounts to 30 September 2010 with the following results.

	£
Trading profits	180,000
Property income	
18 months @ £500 accruing per month	9,000
Capital gain (1 August 2010 disposal)	250,000
Less: Gift aid donation (paid 31 March 2010)	(50,000)
	389,000

What are the profits chargeable to corporation tax for each of the accounting periods based on the above accounts?

Answer

The 18 month period of account is divided into:

Year ending 31 March 2010
6 months to 30 September 2010

Results are allocated:

	Y/e 31.3.10 £	6m to 30.9.10 £
Trading profits 12:6	120,000	60,000
Property Income		
12 × £500	6,000	
6 × £500		3,000
Capital gain (1.8.10)		250,000
Less: Gift aid donation (31.3.10)	(50,000)	
PCTCT (profits chargeable to corporation tax)	76,000	313,000

Chapter Roundup

- Companies pay corporation tax on their profits chargeable to corporation tax (PCTCT).

- An accounting period cannot exceed 12 months in length so a long period of account must be split into two accounting periods. The first accounting period is always twelve months in length.

- Tax rates are set for financial years.

- A company is UK resident if it is incorporated in the UK or if it is incorporated abroad and its central management and control are exercised in the UK.

- PCTCT comprises the company's income and chargeable gains, less gift aid donations. It does not include dividends received from other UK resident companies.

- Income includes trading income, property income, income from-non trading loan relationships (interest) and miscellaneous income.

- The adjustment of profits computation for companies broadly follows that for computing business profits subject to income tax. There are, however, some minor differences.

- Gift aid donations are paid gross by a company and deducted when computing PCTCT.

- Long periods of account are split into two accounting periods: the first 12 months and the remainder.

Quick Quiz

1   When does an accounting period end?

2   What is the difference between a period of account and an accounting period?

3   Should interest paid on a trading loan be adjusted in the trading income computation?

4   How are trading profits (before capital allowances) of a long period of account divided between accounting periods?

    A   On a receipts basis
    B   On an accruals basis
    C   On a time basis
    D   On any basis the company chooses

Answers to Quick Quiz

1   An accounting period ends on the earliest of:

   (a)   12 months after its start
   (b)   the end of the company's period of account
   (c)   the commencement of the company's winding up
   (d)   the company ceasing to be resident in the UK
   (e)   the company ceasing to be liable to corporation tax

2   A period of account is the period for which a company prepares accounts. An accounting period is the period for which corporation tax is charged. If a company prepares annual accounts the two will coincide.

3   Interest paid on a trading loan should not be adjusted in the trading income computation as it is an allowable expense, computed on the accruals basis.

4   C. Trading income (before capital allowances) is apportioned on a time basis.

Now try the question below from the Exam Question Bank

Number	Level	Marks	Time
Q28	Introductory	10	18 mins

19

Computing the corporation tax liability

Topic list	Syllabus reference
1 Charge to corporation tax	C3(a)-(c)
2 Associated companies	C3(a), C4(a)

Introduction

In the previous chapter you learnt how to identify a company's accounting period and how to compute the profits chargeable to corporation tax for that accounting period.

In this chapter you will learn how to compute the corporation tax liability on those profits.

In the next chapter we will deal with chargeable gains for companies.

Study guide

		Intellectual level
C3	**The comprehensive computation of corporation tax liability**	
(a)	Compute the corporation tax liability and apply marginal relief.	2
(b)	Explain the implications of receiving franked investment income.	2
(c)	Explain how exemptions and reliefs can defer or minimise corporation tax liabilities.	2
C4	**The effect of a group corporate structure for corporation tax purposes**	
(a)	Define an associated company and recognise the effect of being an associated company for corporation tax purposes.	2

Exam guide

Question 2 of the exam will always be on corporation tax, and corporation tax may also be part of questions 3, 4 or 5. Computing the corporation tax is usually an integral part of at least one question, and you must be sure that you understand the rules for marginal relief. Note in particular the consequences of short accounting periods and of having associated companies. It will be crucial for you to know the marginal rate of corporation tax for a company when you are dealing with loss relief and group relief later in your studies.

1 Charge to corporation tax

This section relates to your PER requirement:
19   Evaluate and compute taxes payable

1.1 'Profits'

FAST FORWARD

A company pays corporation tax on its profits chargeable to corporation tax (PCTCT). 'Profits' is PCTCT plus franked investment income (FII).

Although we tax PCTCT another figure needs to be calculated ('profits') to determine the rate of corporation tax to use to tax PCTCT.

'Profits' means profits chargeable to corporation tax plus the grossed-up amount of dividends received from UK and non-UK companies. The exception to this rule is any dividends received from a company which is a 51% or more subsidiary of the receiving company or from a company of which the recipient company is a 51% or more subsidiary of the paying company: these dividends are completely ignored for corporation tax purposes.

The grossed-up amount of dividends is the dividend received multiplied by 100/90. You may see the grossed up amount of dividend received referred to as **franked investment income (FII)**.

Exam focus point

Be careful to charge corporation tax on PCTCT, not on profits.

1.2 The full rate

The rates of corporation tax are fixed for financial years. The full rate of corporation tax is 28% for FY 2009 and FY 2008 (FY 2007 30%), and applies to companies with 'profits' of £1,500,000 or more. A company with PCTCT of, say, £2 million, will pay £560,000 corporation tax.

1.3 The small companies' rate (SCR)

Companies may be taxed at the small companies' rate (SCR) or obtain marginal relief, depending on their 'profits'.

The SCR of corporation tax of 21% for FY 2009 and FY 2008 (FY 2007 20%) applies to the profits chargeable to corporation tax of UK resident companies whose 'profits' are not more than £300,000.

Question
The small companies' rate

B Ltd had the following results for the year ended 31 March 2010.

	£
Trading profits	42,000
Dividend received 1 May 2009	9,000

Compute the corporation tax payable.

Answer

	£
Trading profits	42,000
Dividend plus tax credit £9,000 × 100/90	10,000
'Profits' (less than £300,000 limit)	52,000
Corporation tax payable	
£42,000 × 21%	£8,820

1.4 Marginal relief

Small companies' marginal relief applies where the 'profits' of an accounting period of a UK resident company are over £300,000 but under £1,500,000.

We first calculate the corporation tax at the full rate and then deduct:

$(M - P) \times I/P \times$ marginal relief fraction

where M = upper limit (currently £1,500,000)
     P = 'profits' (see above)
     I = PCTCT

The marginal relief fraction is 7/400 for FY 2009 and FY 2008 (FY 2007 1/40).

This information is given in the rates and allowances section of the exam paper.

Question
Small companies' marginal relief

Lenox Ltd has the following results for the year ended 31 March 2010.

	£
PCTCT	296,000
Dividend received 1 December 2009	12,600

Calculate the corporation tax liability.

		£
PCTCT		296,000
Dividend plus tax credit £12,600 × 100/90		14,000
'Profits'		310,000

'Profits' are above £300,000 but below £1,500,000, so marginal relief applies.

	£
Corporation tax on PCTCT £296,000 × 28%	82,880
Less small companies' marginal relief	
£(1,500,000 – 310,000) × 296,000/310,000 × 7/400	(19,885)
	62,995

FAST FORWARD

> The marginal rate of corporation tax between the small companies' limits is 29.75% (FYs 2009). The marginal tax rate is an effective rate; it is never actually used in working out corporation tax.

In exam questions you often need to be aware that there is a **marginal rate of 29.75%** which applies to any PCTCT that lies in between the small companies' limits.

This is calculated as follows:

	£				£
Upper limit	1,500,000	@	28%		420,000
Lower limit	(300,000)	@	21%		(63,000)
Difference	1,200,000				357,000

$$\frac{357,000}{1,200,000} = 29.75\%$$

Effectively the band of profits (here £1,200,000) falling between the upper and lower limits are taxed at a rate of 29.75%

1.5 Example: effective marginal rate of tax

A Ltd has PCTCT of £350,000 for the year ended 31 March 2010. Its corporation tax liability is

	£
£350,000 × 28%	98,000
Less small companies' marginal relief	
£(1,500,000 – 350,000) × $^7/_{400}$	(20,125)
	77,875

This is the same as calculating tax at 21% × £300,000 + 29.75% × £50,000 = £63,000 + £14,875 = £77,875.

Consequently tax is charged at an effective rate of 29.75% on PCTCT that exceeds the small companies' lower limit.

Note that although there is an effective corporation tax charge of 29.75%, this rate of tax is never used in actually calculating corporation tax. The rate is just an effective marginal rate that you must be aware of. It will be particularly important when considering loss relief and group relief (see later in this Text).

The marginal rate of corporation tax for FY 2007 was 32.5%.

1.6 Accounting period in more than one Financial Year

An accounting period **may fall within more than one Financial Year. If the rates and limits for corporation tax are the same in both Financial Years, tax can be computed for the accounting period as if it fell within one Financial Yea**r.

However, **if the rates and/or limits for corporation tax are different in the Financial Years, PCTCT and 'profits' are time apportioned between the Financial Years**. This will be the case where a company is a small company (or marginal relief company) with an accounting period partly in FY 2007 and partly in FY 2008. **It is also necessary to adjust the upper and lower limits**.

1.7 Example: accounting period in more than one Financial Year

Wentworth Ltd makes up its accounts to 31 December each year. For the year to 31 December 2008, it has PCTCT of £174,000. It receives a dividend of £5,400 on 1 December 2008.

The corporation tax payable by Wentworth Ltd is calculated as follows.

	£
PCTCT	174,000
Dividend plus tax credit £5,400 × 100/90	6,000
'Profits'	180,000

	FY 2007 3 months to 31.3.08 £	FY 2008 9 months to 31.12.08 £
PCTCT (3:9)	43,500	130,500
'Profits' (3:9)	45,000	135,000
Lower limit:		
£300,000 × 3/12	75,000	
£300,000 × 9/12		225,000
Small companies rate applies in both FYs		
FY 2007 £43,500 × 20%	8,700	
FY 2008 £130,500 × 21%		27,405
Total corporation tax payable £(8,700 + 27,405)		£36,105

Question — Accounting period in more than one financial year

Elliot Ltd has the following results for the year to 30 September 2008.

	£
PCTCT	360,000
Dividend received 15 July 2008	8,100

Calculate the corporation tax payable by Elliot Ltd.

Answer

	£
PCTCT	360,000
Add: FII £8,100 × 100/90	9,000
'Profits'	369,000

	FY 2007 6 months to 31.3.08 £	FY 2008 6 months 30.9.08 £
PCTCT (6:6)	180,000	180,000
'Profits' (6:6)	184,500	184,500
Lower limit:		
£300,000 × 6/12	150,000	150,000
Upper limit:		
£1,500,000 × 6/12	750,000	750,000

Marginal relief applies in both FYs

FY 2007		
£180,000 × 30%	54,000	
Less: marginal relief £(750,000 − 184,500) × $\frac{180,000}{184,500}$ × 1/40	(13,793)	
	40,207	
FY 2008		
£180,000 × 28%		50,400
Less: marginal relief £(750,000 − 184,500) × $\frac{180,000}{184,500}$ × 7/400		(9,655)
		40,745
Total corporation tax payable £(40,207 + 40,745)		£80,952

1.8 Short accounting periods

 FAST FORWARD

The upper and lower limits which are used to be determine tax rates are pro-rated on a time basis if an accounting period lasts for less than 12 months.

Question
Short accounting period

Ink Ltd prepared accounts for the six months to 31 March 2010. Profits chargeable to corporation tax for the period were £200,000. No dividends were received. Calculate the corporation tax payable for the period.

Answer

Upper limit £1,500,000 × 6/12 = £750,000

Lower limit £300,000 × 6/12 = £150,000

As 'profits' fall between the limits small companies' marginal relief applies.

	£
Corporation tax (FY 09)	
£200,000 × 28%	56,000
Less small companies' marginal relief	
7/400 × (£750,000 − £200,000)	(9,625)
Corporation tax	46,375

1.9 Long periods of account

Remember that an accounting period cannot be more than 12 months long. If the period of account exceeds 12 months it must be split into two accounting periods, the first of 12 months and the second of the balance.

If you have to deal with a long period of account remember to pro-rate the upper and lower limits on a time basis for the second (short) accounting period.

Question

Long period of account

Xenon Ltd (in the previous chapter) made up an 18 month set of accounts to 30 September 2010.

The 18 month period of account is divided into:

Year ending 31 March 2010
6 months to 30 September 2010

Results were allocated:

	Y/e 31.3.10 £	6m to 30.9.10 £
Trading profits 12:6	120,000	60,000
Property income	6,000	3,000
Capital gain (1.8.10)		250,000
Less: Gift aid donation (31.3.10)	(50,000)	
PCTCT	76,000	313,000

Assuming Xenon Ltd received FII of £27,000 on 31 August 2010 calculate the corporation tax payable for each accounting period. Assume the rates of corporation tax for FY 2009 apply in FY 2010.

Answer

	Y/e 31.3.10 £	6m to 30.9.10 £
PCTCT	76,000	313,000
FII	0	27,000
Profits	76,000	340,000
Small companies lower limit	300,000	150,000
Small companies upper limit	1,500,000	750,000
	Small company	Marginal relief
CT payable		
£76,000 × 21%	15,960	
£313,000 × 28%		87,640
Less marginal relief £(750,000 − 340,000) × 313,000/340,000 × 7/400		(6,605)
		81,035
Total corporation tax payable £(15,960 + 81,035)		96,995

2 Associated companies

FAST FORWARD

> The upper and lower limits which are used to determine tax rates are divided by the total number of associated companies. Broadly, associated companies are worldwide trading companies under common control.

2.1 What is an associated company?

Key term

> The expression **'associated companies'** in tax has no connection with financial accounting. For tax purposes a company is associated with another company if either controls the other or if both are under the control of the same person or persons (individuals, partnerships or companies). Whether such a company is UK resident or not is irrelevant. Control is given by holding over 50% of the share capital or the voting power or being entitled to over 50% of the distributable income or of the net assets in a winding up.

2.2 Effects of associated companies

If a company has one or more 'associated companies', then the profit limits for small companies rate purposes are divided by the number of associated companies + 1 (for the company itself).

Companies which have only been associated for part of an accounting period are deemed to have been associated for the whole period for the purpose of determining the profit limits.

2.3 Exception

An associated company is ignored for these purposes if it has not carried on any trade or business at any time in the accounting period (or the part of the period during which it was associated) ie it is 'dormant'.

Question
Associated companies

For the year to 31 March 2010 a company with two other associated companies had PCTCT of £200,000 and no dividends paid or received. Compute the corporation tax payable.

Answer

(a)   Reduction in the lower limit for SCR

Divide by number of associated companies + 1 = 3

£300,000 ÷ 3 = £100,000

(b)   Reduction in the upper limit for SCR

£1,500,000 ÷ 3 = £500,000

(c)   'Profits' = £200,000

As 'profits' fall between the lower and upper limits for SCR purposes, the full rate less small companies' marginal relief applies:

(d)   Corporation tax

	£
£200,000 × 28%	56,000
Less marginal relief £(500,000 − 200,000) × 7/400	(5,250)
Corporation tax	50,750

2.4 Associated companies and short accounting periods

If a company has associated companies and also a short accounting period, first reduce the upper and lower limits for the associated companies and then prorate them for the short accounting period.

2.5 Example: small company limits

Alpha plc, a company with one subsidiary, prepares accounts for the 9 months to 31 December 2010.

The small companies limit will be multiplied by ½ as there is one associated company, and by 9/12 as the accounting period is only 9 months long.

The small companies lower limit will be £300,000 × ½ × 9/12 = £112,500

The small companies upper limit will be £1,500,000 × ½ × 9/12 = £562,500

Chapter Roundup

- A company pays corporation tax on its profits chargeable to corporation tax (PCTCT). 'Profits' is PCTCT plus franked investment income (FII).

- Companies may be taxed at the small companies' rate (SCR) or obtain marginal relief, depending on their 'profits'.

- The marginal rate of corporation tax between the small companies' limits is 29.75% (FY 2009). The marginal tax rate is an effective rate; it is never actually used in working out corporation tax.

- The upper and lower limits which are used to be determine tax rates are pro-rated on a time basis if an accounting period lasts for less than 12 months.

- The upper and lower limits which are used to determine tax rates are divided by the total number of associated companies. Broadly, associated companies are worldwide trading companies under common control.

Quick Quiz

1   Companies are entitled to the small companies' rate of corporation tax if they have profits of up to £_____. Fill in the blank.

2   What is the marginal relief formula?

3   What is an associated company?

4   What effect do associated companies have on the corporation tax computation?

1   Companies are entitled to the small companies' rate of corporation tax if they have profits of up to £300,000.

2    $(M - P) \times I/P \times$ marginal relief fraction

where:

M = upper limit
P = 'profits'
I = PCTCT

3   A company is associated with another company if either controls the other or if both are under the control of the same person or persons (individuals, partnerships or companies).

4   If a company has associated companies the small companies lower and upper limits are divided by the number of associated companies + 1.

Now try the question below from the Exam Question Bank

Number	Level	Marks	Time
Q29	Examination	15	27 mins
Q30	Examination	10	18 mins

Chargeable gains for companies

Topic list	Syllabus reference
1 Corporation tax on chargeable gains	C2(k)
2 Indexation allowance	D2(b)
3 Disposal of shares by companies	D4(b)–(d)
4 Relief for replacement of business assets (rollover relief)	D6(b)

Introduction

We studied chargeable gains for individuals earlier in this Text. In this chapter, we will consider the treatment of chargeable gains for companies.

Companies pay corporation tax on their chargeable gains, rather than capital gains tax. The computation of gains for companies is slightly more complicated than for individuals because companies are entitled to indexation allowance.

We also consider the matching rules for companies which dispose of shares in other companies. Again, these rules are slightly more complicated than for individuals.

Finally, we look at how the relief for replacement of business assets applies to companies.

In the next chapters we will deal with losses, groups and overseas matters.

Study guide

			Intellectual level
C2	**Profits chargeable to corporation tax**		
(k)	Compute profits chargeable to corporation tax		2
D2	**The basic principles of computing gains and losses**		
(b)	Calculate the indexation allowance available to companies		2
D4	**Gains and losses on the disposal of shares and securities**		
(b)	Explain and apply the identification rules as they apply to companies including the same day and nine-day matching rules		2
(c)	Explain the pooling provisions		2
(d)	Explain the treatment of bonus issues, rights issues, takeovers and reorganisations		2
D6	**The uses of exemptions and reliefs in deferring and minimising tax liabilities arising on the disposal of capital assets**		
(b)	Explain and apply rollover relief as it applies to companies		2

Exam guide

Question 3 of the exam will always be a 20 mark question on capital gains. This may be a question about the gains of a company so it is important that you can deal with the aspects covered in this chapter. There may also be an element of gains in Question 2.

1 Corporation tax on chargeable gains

FAST FORWARD

Chargeable gains for companies are computed in broadly the same way as for individuals, but indexation allowance applies and there is no annual exemption.

Companies do not pay capital gains tax. Instead their chargeable gains are included in the profits chargeable to corporation tax. A company's capital gains or allowable losses are computed in a similar way to individuals but with a few major differences:

- There is relief for inflation called the indexation allowance
- **No annual exemption** is available
- Different matching rules for shares apply if the shareholder is a company.

2 Indexation allowance

FAST FORWARD

The indexation allowance gives relief for the inflation element of a gain.

The purpose of having an indexation allowance is to remove the inflation element of a gain from taxation.

Companies are entitled to indexation allowance from the date of acquisition until the date of disposal of an asset. It is based on the movement in the Retail Price Index (RPI) between those two dates.

For example, if J Ltd bought a painting on 2 January 1987 and sold it on 19 November 2009 the indexation allowance is available from January 1987 until November 2009.

> The indexation factor is:
>
> $$\frac{\text{RPI for month of disposal} - \text{RPI for month of acquisition}}{\text{RPI for month of acquisition}}$$
>
> The calculation is expressed as a decimal and is rounded to three decimal places.

Indexation allowance is available on the allowable cost of the asset from the **date of acquisition** (including incidental costs of acquisition). It is also available on **enhancement expenditure from the month in which such expenditure becomes due and payable**. **Indexation allowance is not available on the costs of disposal.**

Question
The indexation allowance

An asset is acquired by a company on 15 February 1983 (RPI = 83.0) at a cost of £5,000. Enhancement expenditure of £2,000 is incurred on 10 April 1984 (RPI = 88.6). The asset is sold for £25,500 on 20 December 2009 (RPI = 207.2). Incidental costs of sale are £500. Calculate the chargeable gain arising.

Answer

The indexation allowance is available until December 2009 and is computed as follows.

	£
$\dfrac{207.2 - 83.0}{83.0} = 1.496 \times £5,000$	7,480
$\dfrac{207.2 - 88.6}{88.6} = 1.339 \times £2,000$	2,678
	10,158

The computation of the chargeable gain is as follows.

	£
Proceeds	25,500
Less incidental costs of sale	(500)
Net proceeds	25,000
Less allowable costs £(5,000 + 2,000)	(7,000)
Unindexed gain	18,000
Less indexation allowance (see above)	(10,158)
Indexed gain	7,842

Indexation allowance cannot create or increase an allowable loss. If there is a gain before the indexation allowance, the allowance can reduce that gain to zero but no further. If there is a loss before the indexation allowance, there is no indexation allowance.

If the indexation allowance calculation gives a negative figure, treat the indexation as nil: do not add to the unindexed gain.

3 Disposal of shares by companies

FAST FORWARD
> There are special rules for matching shares sold by a company with shares purchased. Disposals are matched with acquisitions on the same day, the previous nine days and the FA 1985 share pool.

3.1 The matching rules

We have discussed the share matching rules for individuals earlier in this Text. We also need special rules for companies.

For companies the matching of shares sold is in the following order.

(a)   Shares acquired on the **same day**
(b)   Shares acquired in the **previous nine days**, if more than one acquisition on a "first in, first out" (FIFO) basis
(c)   Shares from the **FA 1985 pool**

The composition of the FA 1985 pool in relation to companies which are shareholders is explained below.

Exam focus point
> Learn the 'matching rules' because a crucial first step to getting a shares question right is to correctly match the shares sold to the original shares purchased.

3.2 Example: share matching rules for companies

Nor Ltd acquired the following shares in Last plc:

Date of acquisition	No of shares
9.11.02	15,000
15.12.04	15,000
11.7.09	5,000
15.7.09	5,000

Nor Ltd disposed of 20,000 of the shares on 15 July 2009.

We match the shares as follows:

(a)   Acquisition on same day: 5,000 shares acquired 15 July 2009.
(b)   Acquisitions in previous 9 days: 5,000 shares acquired 11 July 2009.
(c)   FA 1985 share pool: 10,000 shares out of 30,000 shares in FA 1985 share pool (9.11.02 and 15.12.04).

3.3 The FA 1985 share pool

Exam focus point
> The examiner has stated that a detailed question will not be set on the pooling provisions. However, work through the examples below as you are expected to understand how the pool works.

The FA 1985 pool comprises the following shares of the same class in the same company.

*   **Shares held by a company on 1 April 1985 and acquired by that company on or after 1 April 1982.**
*   **Shares acquired by that company on or after 1 April 1985.**

We must keep track of:

(a)   the **number** of shares
(b)   the **cost** of the shares ignoring indexation
(c)   the **indexed cost** of the shares

The first step in constructing the FA 1985 share pool is to calculate the value of the pool at 1 April 1985 by indexing the cost of each acquisition before that date up to April 1985.

3.4 Example: the FA 1985 pool

Oliver Ltd bought 1,000 shares in Judith plc for £2,750 in August 1984 and another 1,000 for £3,250 in December 1984. RPIs are August 1984 = 89.9, December 1984 = 90.9 and April 1985 = 94.8. The FA 1985 pool at 1 April 1985 is as follows.

	No of shares	Cost £	Indexed cost £
August 1984 (a)	1,000	2,750	2,750
December 1984 (b)	1,000	3,250	3,250
	2,000	6,000	6,000

Indexation allowance

$$\frac{94.8 - 89.9}{89.9} = 0.055 \times £2,750 \qquad\qquad 151$$

$$\frac{94.8 - 90.9}{90.9} = 0.043 \times £3,250 \qquad\qquad 140$$

Indexed cost of the pool at 1 April 1985   6,291

Disposals and acquisitions of shares which affect the indexed value of the FA 1985 pool are termed **'operative events'. Prior to reflecting each such operative event within the FA 1985 share pool, a further indexation allowance (an 'indexed rise') must be computed up to the date of the operative event concerned from the date of the last such operative event** (or from the later of the first acquisition and April 1985 if the operative event in question is the first one).

Indexation calculations within the FA 1985 pool (after its April 1985 value has been calculated) **are not rounded to three decimal places**. This is because rounding errors would accumulate and have a serious effect after several operative events.

If there are several operative events between 1 April 1985 and the date of a disposal, the indexation procedure described above will have to be performed several times over.

Question   Value of FA 1985 pool

Following on from the above example, assume that Oliver Ltd acquired 2,000 more shares on 10 July 1986 at a cost of £4,000. Recalculate the value of the FA 1985 pool on 10 July 1986 following the acquisition. Assume the RPI in July 1986 = 97.5.

Answer

	No of shares	Cost £	Indexed cost £
Value at 1.4.85 b/f	2,000	6,000	6,291
Indexed rise $\dfrac{97.5 - 94.8}{94.8} \times £6,291$			179
	2,000	6,000	6,470
Acquisition	2,000	4,000	4,000
Value at 10.7.86	4,000	10,000	10,470

In the case of a disposal, following the calculation of the indexed rise to the date of disposal, the cost and the indexed cost attributable to the shares disposed of are deducted from the amounts within the FA 1985 pool. The proportions of the cost and indexed cost to take out of the pool should be computed by using the proportion of cost that the shares disposed of bear to the total number of shares held.

The indexation allowance is the indexed cost taken out of the pool minus the cost taken out. As usual, the indexation allowance cannot create or increase a loss.

Continuing the above exercise, suppose that Oliver Ltd sold 3,000 shares on 10 July 2009 for £22,000. Compute the gain, and the value of the FA 1985 pool following the disposal. Assume RPI July 2009 = 209.3

Answer

	No of shares	Cost £	Indexed cost £
Value at 10.7.86	4,000	10,000	10,470
Indexed rise			
$\dfrac{209.3 - 97.5}{97.5} \times £10,470$			12,006
	4,000	10,000	22,476
Disposal	(3,000)		
Cost and indexed cost $\dfrac{3,000}{4,000} \times £10,000$ and £22,476		(7,500)	(16,857)
Value at 10.7.09	1,000	2,500	5,619

The gain is computed as follows:

	£
Proceeds	22,000
Less cost	(7,500)
Unindexed gain	14,500
Less indexation allowance £(16,857 − 7,500)	(9,357)
Indexed gain	5,143

3.5 Bonus and rights issues

When **bonus issue shares are issued**, all that happens is that **the size of the original holding is increased**. Since **bonus issue shares are issued at no cost** there is **no need to adjust the original cost** and there is **no operative event for the FA 1985 pool** (so no indexation allowance needs to be calculated).

When **rights issue shares are issued**, the **size of the original holding is increased** in the same way as for a bonus issue. So if the original shareholding was part of the FA 1985 pool, the rights issue shares are added to that pool. This might be important for the matching rules if a shareholding containing the rights issue shares is sold shortly after the rights issue.

However, in the case of a rights issue, the **new shares are paid for and this results in an adjustment to the original cost**. For the purpose of **calculating the indexation allowance, expenditure on a rights issue is taken as being incurred on the date of the issue** and not the date of the original holding.

3.6 Example: bonus and rights issue

S Ltd bought 10,000 shares in T plc in May 2000 (RPI = 170.7) at a cost of £45,000.

There was a 2 for 1 bonus issue in October 2002.

There was a 1 for 3 rights issue in June 2006 (RPI = 198.5) at a cost of £4 per share. S Ltd took up all of its rights entitlement.

S Ltd sold 20,000 shares in T plc for £120,000 in January 2010 (RPI = 206.8).

FA 1985 share pool

		No. of shares	Cost £	Indexed cost £
5.00	Acquisition	10,000	45,000	45,000
10.02	Bonus 2:1	20,000		
		30,000		
6.06	Indexed rise			
	$\dfrac{198.5-170.7}{170.7} \times £45,000$			7,329
	Rights 1:3	10,000	40,000	40,000
		40,000	95,000	92,329
1.10	Index rise			
	$\dfrac{206.8-198.5}{198.5} \times £92,329$			3,861
				96,190
	Disposal	(20,000)	(47,500)	(48,095)
c/f		20,000	47,500	48,095

The gain is:

	£
Proceeds	120,000
Less: cost	(47,500)
Unindexed gain	72,500
Less: indexation allowance £(48,095 – 47,500)	(595)
Indexed gain	71,905

3.7 Reorganisations and takeovers

The rules on reorganisation and takeovers apply in a similar way for company shareholders as they do for individuals.

In the case of a **reorganisation, the new shares or securities take the place of the original shares. The original cost and the indexed cost of the original shares is apportioned between the different types of capital issued on the reorganisation.**

Where there is a takeover of shares which qualifies for the 'paper for paper' treatment, the cost and indexed cost of the original holding is passed onto the new holding which take the place of the original holding.

Question

Takeover

J Ltd acquired 20,000 shares in G Ltd in August 1990 (RPI = 128.1) at a cost of £40,000. It acquired a further 5,000 shares in December 2006 (RPI = 202.7) at a cost of £30,000.

In March 2010, G Ltd was taken over by K plc and J Ltd received one ordinary share and two preference shares in K plc for each one share held in G Ltd. Immediately following the takeover, the ordinary shares in K plc were worth £4 per share and the preference shares in K plc were worth £1 per share.

Show the cost and indexed cost of the ordinary shares and the preference shares.

G Ltd FA 1985 share pool

		No. of shares	Cost £	Indexed cost £
8.90	Acquisition	20,000	40,000	40,000
12.06	Indexed rise			
	$\dfrac{202.7 - 128.1}{128.1} \times £40,000$			23,294
	Acquisition	5,000	30,000	30,000
Pool at takeover		25,000	70,000	93,294

Note that the takeover is not a operative event because the pool of cost is not increased or decreased and so it is not necessary to calculate an indexed rise.

Apportionment of cost/indexed cost to K plc shares

	No. of shares	MV £	Cost £	Indexed cost £
Ords × 1	25,000	100,000	46,667	62,196
Prefs × 2	50,000	50,000	23,333	31,098
Totals		150,000	70,000	93,294

On a disposal of shares in K plc, indexation allowance will be calculated from December 2006.

4 Relief for replacement of business assets (rollover relief)

FAST FORWARD

Rollover relief for replacement of business assets is available to companies to defer gains arising on the disposal of business assets.

4.1 Conditions for relief

As for individuals, **a gain may be rollover by a company where the proceeds on the disposal of a business asset are spent on a replacement business asset under rollover relief**.

The conditions for the relief to apply to company disposals are:

(a) **The old assets sold and the new asset bought are both used only in the trade of the company** (apportionment into business and non-business parts available for buildings).

(b) **The old asset and the new asset both fall within one** (but not necessarily the same one) **of the following classes**.

    (i) **Land and buildings** (including parts of buildings) occupied as well as used only for the purposes of the trade

    (ii) **Fixed plant and machinery**

(c) **Reinvestment of the proceeds received on the disposal of the old asset takes place in a period beginning one year before and ending three years after the date of the disposal.**

(d) **The new asset is brought into use in the trade on its acquisition.**

Note that goodwill is not a qualifying asset for the purposes of corporation tax.

A claim for relief must be made within four years of the end of the accounting period in which the disposal of the old asset is made.

4.2 Operation of relief

Deferral is obtained by deducting the indexed gain from the cost of the new asset. For full relief, the whole of the proceeds must be reinvested. If only part is reinvested, a gain equal to the amount not invested, or the full gain, if lower, will be chargeable to tax immediately.

The new asset will have a base cost for chargeable gains purposes of its purchase price less the gain rollover over.

Question	Rollover relief

D Ltd acquired a factory in April 2000 (RPI = 170.1) at a cost of £120,000. It used the factory in its trade throughout the period of its ownership.

In August 2009 (RPI = 208.8), D Ltd sold the factory for £210,000. In November 2009, it acquired another factory at a cost of £180,000.

Calculate the gain chargeable on the sale of the first factory and the base cost of the second factory.

Answer

Chargeable gain on sale of first factory

	£
Proceeds	210,000
Less: cost	(120,000)
Unindexed gain	90,000
$\dfrac{208.8 - 170.1}{170.1} = 0.228 \times £120{,}000$	(27,360)
Indexed gain	62,640
Less: rollover relief (balancing figure)	(32,640)
Chargeable gain: amount not reinvested £(210,000 – 180,000)	30,000

Base cost of second factory

	£
Cost of second factory	180,000
Less: rolled over gain	(32,640)
Base cost	147,360

4.3 Depreciating assets

The relief for investment into depreciating assets works in the same way for companies as it does for individuals.

The indexed gain is calculated on the old asset and is deferred until the gain crystallises on the earliest of:

(a)   The disposal of the replacement asset
(b)   The date the replacement asset ceases to be used in the trade
(c)   Ten years after the acquisition of the replacement asset.

Chapter Roundup

- Chargeable gains for companies are computed in broadly the same way as for individuals, but indexation allowance applies and there is no annual exemption.

- The indexation allowance gives relief for the inflation element of a gain.

- There are special rules for matching shares sold by a company with shares purchased. Disposals are matched with acquisitions on the same day, the previous nine days and the FA 1985 share pool.

- Rollover relief for replacement of business assets is available to companies to defer gains arising on the disposal of business assets.

Quick Quiz

1 A company is entitled to an annual exemption against its chargeable gains. TRUE/FALSE?

2 Indexation allowance runs from the date of _____ to date of _____. Fill in the blanks.

3 What are the share matching rules for company shareholders?

4 H Ltd sells a warehouse for £400,000. The warehouse cost £220,000 and the indexation allowance available is £40,000. The company acquires another warehouse ten months later for £375,000. What is the amount of rollover relief?

Answers to Quick Quiz

1 FALSE. A company is not entitled to an annual exemption against its chargeable gains.

2 Indexation allowance runs from the date of acquisition to date of disposal.

3 The matching rules for shares disposed of by a company shareholder are:

   (a) Shares acquired on the same day
   (b) Shares acquired in the previous nine days
   (c) Shares from the FA 1985 pool

4 The gain on the sale of first warehouse is:

	£
Proceeds	400,000
Less: cost	(220,000)
Unindexed gain	180,000
Less: indexation allowance	(40,000)
Indexed gain	140,000
Less: rollover relief (balancing figure)	(115,000)
Chargeable gain: amount not reinvested £(400,000 – 375,000)	25,000

Now try the questions below from the Exam Question Bank

Number	Level	Marks	Time
Q31	Introductory	5	9 mins
Q32	Examination	15	27 mins

Losses

Topic list	Syllabus reference
1 Trading losses	C2
2 Carry forward trade loss relief	C2(g)
3 Trade loss relief against total profits	C2(h)
4 Choosing loss reliefs and other planning points	C2(i)
5 Other losses	C2(j), D2(c)

Introduction

In the previous two chapters we have seen how a company calculates its profits chargeable to corporation tax and the corporation tax payable.

We now look at how a company may obtain relief for losses. An important factor in deciding what relief to claim is the **marginal rate** of tax, which may be 21%, 28% or 29.75% as seen earlier.

In the next chapter we will look at groups, and in particular how losses can be relieved by group relief.

Study guide

		Intellectual level
C2	**Profits chargeable to corporation tax**	
(g)	Understand how trading losses can be carried forward.	2
(h)	Understand how trading losses can be claimed against income of the current or previous accounting periods.	2
(i)	Recognise the factors that will influence the choice of loss relief claim.	2
(j)	Explain how relief for a property business loss is given.	1

Exam guide

Losses could form part of question 2 on corporation tax in the exam, they may also be included in questions 3, 4 or 5, or they may not be examined at all. If they do appear, they may be a significant part of the question. Dealing with losses involves a methodical approach: first establish what loss is available for relief, second identify the different reliefs available, and third evaluate the options. Do check the question for specific instructions; you may be told that loss relief should be taken as early as possible.

1 Trading losses

FAST FORWARD

Trading losses may be relieved against current total profits, against total profits of earlier periods or against future trading income.

In summary, the following reliefs are available for trading losses incurred by a company.

(a)   **Set-off against current profits**
(b)   **Carry back against earlier profits**
(c)   **Carry forward against future trading profits**

Reliefs (a) and (b) must be claimed, and are given in the order shown. Relief (c) is given automatically for any loss for which the other reliefs are not claimed.

2 Carry forward trade loss relief

FAST FORWARD

Trading losses carried forward can only be set against future trading profits arising from the same trade.

A company must set off a trading loss which is carried forward against income from the same trade in future accounting periods (unless it has been otherwise relieved see below). **Relief is against the first available profits.**

Question   Carry forward trade loss relief

A Ltd has the following results for the three years to 31 March 2010.

	Year ended		
	31.3.08	*31.3.09*	*31.3.10*
	£	£	£
Trading profit/(loss)	(8,550)	3,000	6,000
Property income	0	1,000	1,000
Gift aid donation	300	1,400	1,700

Calculate the profits chargeable to corporation tax for all three years showing any losses available to carry forward at 1 April 2010.

	Year ended		
	31.3.08	*31.3.09*	*31.3.10*
	£	£	£
Trading profits	0	3,000	6,000
Less: carry forward loss relief		(3,000)	(5,550)
	0	0	450
Property income	0	1,000	1,000
Less: Gift aid donation	0	(1,000)	(1,450)
PCTCT	0	0	0
Unrelieved gift aid donation	300	400	250

Note that the trading loss carried forward is set only against the trading profit in future years. It cannot be set against the property income.

The gift aid donations that become unrelieved remain unrelieved as they cannot be carried forward.

Loss memorandum

	£
Loss for y/e 31.3.08	8,550
Less used y/e 31.3.09	(3,000)
Loss carried forward at 1.4.09	5,550
Less used y/e 31.3.10	(5,550)
Loss carried forward at 1.4.10	0

3 Trade loss relief against total profits

> Loss relief against total profits is given before gift aid donations. Gift aid donations may be unrelieved.

3.1 Current year relief

A company may claim to set a trading loss incurred in an accounting period against total profits before deducting gift aid donations of the same accounting period.

3.2 Carry back relief

> Loss relief against total profits may be given against current period profits and against profits of the previous 12 months. For accounting periods ending between 24 November 2008 and 23 November 2010, this is extended to 36 months, subject to maximum relief of £50,000 outside the usual 12 month carryback period.

Such a loss may then be carried back and set against total profits before deducting gift aid donations of an accounting period falling wholly or partly within the 12 months of the start of the period in which the loss was incurred.

For accounting periods ending between 24 November 2008 and 23 November 2010, the carryback period is extended to 36 months, subject to maximum relief of £50,000 outside the usual 12 month carryback period.

In the tax rates and allowances given to you in the examination, the following information will be given:

Extended loss relief is capped at a maximum of £50,000. For limited companies it applies to loss making accounting periods ending between 24 November 2008 and 23 November 2010.

FAST FORARD

A claim for current period loss relief can be made without a claim for carryback. However, if a loss is to be carried back a claim for current period relief must have been made first.

Any possible loss relief claim for the period of the loss must be made before any excess loss can be carried back to a previous period. Any carryback is to more recent periods before earlier periods. Relief for earlier losses is given before relief for later losses.

Any loss remaining unrelieved after any loss relief claims against total profits is carried forward to set against future profits of the same trade.

Question
Loss relief against total profits

Helix Ltd has the following results.

	Year ended 30.9.06	30.9.07	30.9.08	30.9.09
	£	£	£	£
Trading profit/(loss)	22,500	30,500	20,000	(85,000)
Bank interest	500	500	500	500
Chargeable gains	0	0	0	4,000
Gift Aid donation	250	250	250	250

Show the PCTCT for all the years affected assuming that loss relief against total profits is claimed.

Answer

The loss of the year to 30 September 2009 is relieved against current year profits and against profits of the previous 36 months.

	Year ended 30.9.06	30.9.07	30.9.08	30.9.09
	£	£	£	£
Trading profit	22,500	30,500	20,000	0
Investment income	500	500	500	500
Chargeable gains	0	0	0	4,000
	23,000	31,000	20,500	4,500
Less current period loss relief	0	0	0	(4,500)
	23,000	31,000	20,500	0
Less carry back loss relief	(19,000)	(31,000)	(20,500)	0
	4,000	0	0	0
Less gift aid donation	(250)	0	0	0
PCTCT	3,750	0	0	0
Unrelieved gift aid donation		250	250	250

Loss memorandum	£
Loss incurred in y/e 30.9.09	85,000
Less used: y/e 30.9.09	(4,500)
y/e 30.9.08	(20,500)
y/e 30.9.07	(31,000)
y/e 30.9.06 (max)	(19,000)
Loss available to carry forward	10,000

The maximum loss carried back to year ending 30.9.06 is £(50,000 – 31,000) = £19,000.

If a period falls partly outside the 12 (or 36) months, loss relief is limited to the proportion of the period's profits (before gift aid donations) equal to the proportion of the period which falls within the 12 (or 36) months.

Question

Tallis Ltd started trading on 1 April 2006 and had the following results for the five accounting periods to 31 July 2009.

	Y/e 30.4.06 £	Y/e 30.4.07 £	3 months to 31.7.07 £	Y/e 31.7.08 £	Y/e 31.7.09 £
Trading profit (loss)	20,000	4,000	12,000	15,000	(60,000)
Building society interest	1,000	1,000	400	1,000	1,800
Gift aid donations	600	600	500	0	0

Show the profits chargeable to corporation tax for all years. Assume loss relief is claimed against total profits where possible.

Answer

	Y/e 30.4.06 £	Y/e 30.4.07 £	3 months to 31.7.07 £	Y/e 31.7.08 £	Y/e 31.7.09 £
Trading profit	20,000	4,000	12,000	15,000	0
Interest income	1,000	1,000	400	1,000	1,800
	21,000	5,000	12,400	16,000	1,800
Less current period loss relief					(1,800)
	21,000	5,000	12,400	16,000	0
Less carry back loss relief	(15,750)	(5,000)	(12,400)	(16,000)	
	5,250	0	0	0	0
Less gift aid donations	(600)				0
PCTCT	4,650	0	0	0	0
Unrelieved gift aid donations	0	600	500	0	0

Loss memorandum	£
Loss incurred in y/e 31.7.09	60,000
Less used y/e 31.7.09	(1,800)
Less used y/e 31.7.08	(16,000)
Less used 3 months to 31.7.07	(12,400)
Less used y/e 30.4.07	(5,000)
Less used y/e 30.4.06 9/12 × £21,000	(15,750)
C/f	9,050

Notes

1   The loss can be carried back to set against profits of the previous **36 months**. This means profits in the y/e 30.4.06 must be time apportioned by multiplying by 9/12.

2   The £50,000 maximum does not apply because the loss relieved beyond the 12 month carryback period is £(12,400 + 5,000 + £15,750) = £33,150.

3   Losses remaining after the loss relief claims against total profits are carried forward to set against future trading profits.

If the loss making period is a short period of account, the £50,000 limit is restricted. For example, if the loss making period is 9 months in length, the maximum carryback relief will be £(50,000 x 9/12) = £37,500.

3.3 Claims

A claim for relief against current or prior period profits must be made within four years of the end of the accounting period in which the loss arose. Any claim must be for the *whole* loss (to the extent that profits are available to relieve it). The loss can however be reduced by not claiming full capital allowances, so that higher capital allowances are given (on higher tax written down values) in future years.

3.4 Interaction with losses brought forward

A trading loss carried back is relieved after any trading losses brought forward have been offset.

Question	Losses carried forward and back

Chile Ltd has the following results.

	Year ended		
	30.9.08	30.9.09	30.9.10
	£	£	£
Trading profit/(loss)	21,000	(20,000)	40,000
Bank interest	1,000	1,500	500
Chargeable gains	0	2,000	0
Gift Aid donations	500	500	500

Chile Ltd had a trading loss of £16,000 carried forward at 1 October 2007.

Show the PCTCT for all the years affected assuming that loss relief against total profits is claimed.

Answer

The loss of the year to 30.9.09 is relieved against current year profits and against profits of the previous twelve months. The trading loss brought forward at 1 October 2007 is relieved in the year ended 30 September 2008 before the loss brought back.

	Year ended		
	30.9.08	30.9.09	30.9.10
	£	£	£
Trading profit	21,000	0	40,000
Less carry forward loss relief	(16,000)	0	(10,500)
	5,000	0	29,500
Investment income	1,000	1,500	500
Chargeable gains	0	2,000	0
	6,000	3,500	30,000
Less current period loss relief	0	(3,500)	0
	6,000	0	30,000
Less carry back loss relief	(6,000)	0	0
	0	0	30,000
Less gift aid donation	0	0	(500)
PCTCT	0	0	29,500
Unrelieved gift aid donations	500	500	

Loss memorandum	£
Loss brought forward at 1 October 2007	16,000
Less used y/e 30.9.08	(16,000)
	0

	£
Loss incurred in y/e 30.9.09	20,000
Less used: y/e 30.9.09	(3,500)
y/e 30.9.08	(6,000)
	10,500
Less used: y/e 30.9.10	(10,500)
C/f	Nil

3.5 Terminal trade loss relief

FAST FORWARD

Trading losses in the last 12 months of trading can be carried back and set against profits of the previous 36 months without limit.

For trading losses incurred in the twelve months up to the cessation of trade the carry back period is extended from twelve months to three years, later years first. There is no maximum loss relief.

Question — Terminal losses

Brazil Ltd had the following results for the accounting periods up to the cessation of trade on 30 September 2009.

	Y/e 30.9.06 £	Y/e 30.9.07 £	Y/e 30.9.08 £	Y/e 30.9.09 £
Trading profits	60,000	40,000	15,000	(180,000)
Gains	0	10,000	0	6,000
Rental income	12,000	12,000	12,000	12,000

You are required to show how the losses are relieved assuming the maximum use is made of loss relief against total profits.

Answer

	Y/e 30.9.06 £	Y/e 30.9.07 £	Y/e 30.9.08 £	Y/e 30.9.09 £
Trading profits	60,000	40,000	15,000	0
Rental income	12,000	12,000	12,000	12,000
Gains	0	10,000	0	6,000
	72,000	62,000	27,000	18,000
Less current period loss relief Y/e 30.9.09				(18,000)
				0
Less carry back loss relief	(72,000)	(62,000)	(27,000)	
PCTCT	0	0	0	0

Loss memorandum

	£
Loss in y/e 30.9.09	180,000
Less used y/e 30.9.09	(18,000)
Loss of y/e 30.9.09 available for 36 months carry back	162,000
Less used y/e 30.9.08	(27,000)
	135,000
Less used y/e 30.9.07	(62,000)
	73,000
Less used y/e 30.9.06	(72,000)
Loss remaining unrelieved	1,000

4 Choosing loss reliefs and other planning points

> **FAST FORWARD**
>
> When selecting a loss relief, first consider the rate at which relief is obtained and, secondly, the timing of the relief.

> ⚠️ **PER alert**
>
> This section relates to your PER requirement:
> 20   Assist with tax planning

4.1 Making the choice

Several alternative loss reliefs may be available. In making a choice consider:

- **The rate at which relief will be obtained:**
  - 28% at the full rate (FY 2009 and 2008); 30% for FY 2007
  - 21% at the small companies' rate (FY 2009 and FY 2008); 20% for FY 2007
  - 29.75% if the small companies' marginal relief applies (FY 2009 and FY 2008); 32.5%; for FY 2007

  We previously outlined how the 29.75% marginal rate is calculated. Remember it is just a marginal rate of tax; it is never actually used in computing a company's corporation tax.

- **How quickly relief will be obtained**: loss relief against total profits is quicker than carry forward loss relief.

- **The extent to which relief for gift aid donations might be lost.**

Exam focus point

> When choosing between loss relief claims **always** consider the rate of tax 'saved' by the loss first.
>
> If in the current period the loss 'saves' 21% tax but if carried forward saves 28% tax then a carry forward is the better choice (even though the timing of loss relief is later).
>
> If the tax saved now is 28% and in the future is the same (28%) **then** consider timing (in this example a current claim is better timing wise).
>
> So, first – rate of tax saved, second – timing.

M Ltd has had the following results.

| | Year ended 31 March | | | |
	2007	2008	2009	2010
	£	£	£	£
Trading profit/(loss)	2,000	(1,000,000)	200,000	138,000
Chargeable gains	35,000	750,000	0	0
Gift aid donations paid	30,000	20,000	20,000	20,000

Recommend appropriate loss relief claims, and compute the corporation tax for all years based on your recommendations. Assume that future years' profits will be similar to those of the year ended 31 March 2010 and the rates of corporation tax in FY 2009 apply in later years. The small companies rate of corporation tax in FY06 was 20%.

Answer

A loss relief against total profits claim for the year ended 31 March 2008 will save tax partly in the small companies' marginal relief band and partly at the small companies rate. It will waste the gift aid donation of £20,000.

PCTCT in the previous year is £7,000 (£35,000 + £2,000 – £30,000) and falls in the small companies' band. Carry back would waste gift aid donations of £30,000 and would use £37,000 of loss to save tax on £7,000.

If no current period loss relief claim is made, £200,000 of the loss will save tax at the small companies' rate in the year ended 31 March 2009, with £20,000 of gift aid donations being wasted. The remaining £800,000 of the loss, would be carried forward to the year ended 31 March 2010 and later years to save tax at the small companies' rate.

To conclude a loss relief claim against total income should be made for the year of the loss but not in the previous year. £20,000 of gift aid donations would be wasted in the current year, but much of the loss would save tax at the small companies' marginal corporation tax rate and relief would be obtained quickly.

The final computations are as follows.

| | Year ended 31 March | | | |
	2007	2008	2009	2010
	£	£	£	£
Trading income	2,000	0	200,000	138,000
Less carry forward loss relief	0	0	(200,000)	(50,000)
	2,000	0	0	88,000
Chargeable gains	35,000	750,000	0	0
	37,000	750,000	0	88,000
Less current period loss relief	0	(750,000)	0	0
	37,000	0	0	88,000
Less gift aid donations	(30,000)	0	0	(20,000)
Profits chargeable to corporation tax	7,000	0	0	68,000

| | Year ended 31 March | | | |
	2007	2008	2009	2010
	£	£	£	£
CT at 20%/21%	1,400	0	0	14,280
Unrelieved gift aid donations	0	20,000	20,000	0

4.2 Other tax planning points

A company must normally claim capital allowances on its tax return. A company with losses should consider claiming less than the maximum amount of capital allowances available. This will result in a higher tax written down value to carry forward and therefore higher capital allowances in future years.

Reducing capital allowances in the current period reduces the loss available for relief against total profits. As this relief, if claimed, must be claimed for all of a loss available, a reduced capital allowance claim could be advantageous where all of a loss would be relieved at a lower tax rate in the current (or previous) period than the effective rate of relief for capital allowances will be in future periods.

5 Other losses

5.1 Capital losses

FAST FORWARD

> Capital losses can only be set against capital gains in the same or future accounting periods.

Capital losses can only be set against capital gains in the same or future accounting periods, never against income. Capital losses must be set against the first available gains and cannot be carried back.

5.2 Property business losses

FAST FORWARD

> Property business losses are set off first against non-property business income and gains for the current period and then carried forward against future income.

Property business losses are first set off against non-property business income and gains of the company for the current period. Any excess is then:

(a) Carried forward against future income (of all descriptions), or
(b) Available for surrender as group relief (see later in this Text).

Chapter Roundup

- Trading losses may be relieved against current total profits, against total profits of earlier periods or against future trading income.

- Trading losses carried forward can only be set against future trading profits arising from the same trade.

- Loss relief against total profits is given before gift aid donations. Gift aid donations remain unrelieved.

- Loss relief against total profits may be given against current period profits and against profits of the previous 12 months. For accounting periods ending between 24 November 2008 and 23 November 2010, this is extended to 36 months, subject to maximum relief of £50,000 outside the usual 12 month carryback period.

- A claim for current period loss relief can be made without a claim for carryback. However, if a loss is to be carried back, a claim for current period relief must have been made first.

- Trading losses in the last 12 months of trading can be carried back and set against profits of the previous 36 months without limit.

- When selecting a loss relief, first consider the rate at which relief is obtained and, secondly, the timing of the relief.

- Capital losses can only be set against capital gains in the same or future accounting periods.

- Property business losses are set off first against non-property business income and gains for the current period and then carried forward against future income.

1   Against what profits may trading losses carried forward be set?

    A   Against all trading profits
    B   Against total profits
    C   Against profits from the same trade
    D   Against trading profits and gains

2   To what extent may losses be carried back?

3   Why might a company make a reduced capital allowances claim?

Answers to Quick Quiz

1   C. Against profits from the same trade.

2   A loss may be carried back and set against total profits (before deducting gift aid donations) of the prior 12 months (36 months for accounting periods ending between 24 November 2008 and 23 November 2010 limited to £50,000 outside the usual 12 month carryback period). A loss arising on the final 12 months of trading can be carried back to set against profits arising in the previous 36 months without limit. The loss carried back is the trading loss left unrelieved after a claim against total profits (before deducting gift aid donations) of the loss making AP has been made.

3   Reducing capital allowances in the current AP reduces the loss available for relief against total profits. Such a loss relief claim demands that all of the available loss is utilised. Reducing capital allowances reduces the size of the available loss.

Now try the question below from the Exam Question Bank

Number	Level	Marks	Time
Q33	Examination	15	27 mins

Groups

Topic list	Syllabus reference
1 Types of group	C4(a)
2 Group relief	C4(b), C5
3 Capital gains group	C4(c), C5

Introduction

In the previous chapters in this section we have covered corporation tax on single companies, including the reliefs for losses.

In this chapter we consider the extent to which tax law recognises group relationships between companies. Companies in a group are still separate entities with their own tax liabilities, but tax law recognises the close relationship between group companies. They can, if they meet certain conditions, share their losses and also pass assets between each other without chargeable gains.

In the next chapter we consider overseas aspects of corporation tax.

Study guide

		Intellectual level
C4	**The effect of a group corporate structure for corporation tax purposes**	
(b)	Define a 75% group, and recognise the reliefs that are available to members of such a group.	2
(c)	Define a 75% capital gains group, and recognise the reliefs that are available to members of such a group.	2
C5	**The use of exemptions and reliefs in deferring and minimising corporation tax liabilities**	

Exam guide

Groups will only feature in your examination as part of question 2, which will always be on corporation tax. Your first step in dealing with any group question must be to establish the relationship between the companies and identify what group or groups exist. You may find it helpful to draw a diagram. You must be aware that 75% groups and capital gains groups do not always coincide. The next steps will be to identify the amounts eligible for relief and to work out your strategy for maximising tax relief. Always look out for companies receiving marginal relief; they will have the highest marginal tax rate of 29.75%.

1 Types of group

A group exists for taxation purposes where one company is a subsidiary of another. The percentage shareholding involved determines the taxation consequences of the fact that there is a group.

The three examinable types of relationship for tax purposes are:

- **Associated companies** (see earlier in this text)
- **75% subsidiaries**
- **Groups for chargeable gains purposes** (capital gains groups)

2 Group relief

FAST FORWARD

Within a 75% group, current period trading losses, excess property business losses and excess gift aid donations can be surrendered between UK companies. Profits and losses of corresponding accounting periods must be matched up. Group relief is available where the existence of a group is established through companies resident anywhere in the world.

2.1 Group relief provisions

The group relief provisions enable companies within a 75% group to transfer trading losses to other companies within the group, in order to set these against taxable profits and reduce the group's overall corporation tax liability.

2.2 Definition of a 75% group

Key term

For one company to be a **75% subsidiary** of another, the holding company must have:

- At least 75% of the ordinary share capital of the subsidiary
- A right to at least 75% of the distributable income of the subsidiary, and
- A right to at least 75% of the net assets of the subsidiary were it to be wound up.

Two companies are members of a 75% group where one is a 75% subsidiary of the other, or both are 75% subsidiaries of a third company.

Two companies are in a 75% group only if there is a 75% effective interest. Thus an 80% subsidiary (T) of an 80% subsidiary (S) is not in a 75% group with the holding company (H), because the effective interest is only 80% × 80% = 64%. However, S and T are in a 75% group and can claim group relief from each other. S *cannot* claim group relief from T and pass it on to H; it can only claim group relief for its own use.

A 75% group may include non-UK resident companies. **However, losses may generally only be surrendered between UK resident companies**.

Exam focus point

Relief for trading losses incurred by an overseas subsidiary is not examinable in your paper.

Illustration of a 75% group:

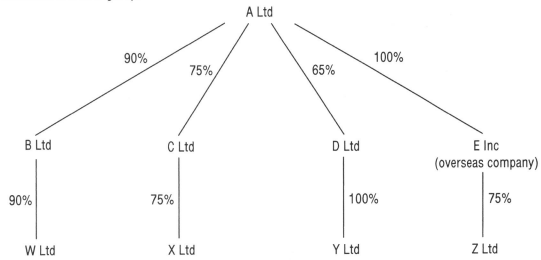

The companies in the 75% group are:

A Ltd
B Ltd
W Ltd (81% effective holding by A)
C Ltd
E Inc
Z Ltd (75% effective holding by A)

In addition C Ltd and X Ltd and also D Ltd and Y Ltd form their own separate mini-75% groups.

Note that a 75% group may also be called a 'group relief' group.

2.3 The relief

A surrendering company can surrender any amount of its loss but a claimant company can only claim an amount up to its available profits. The best option is normally to surrender losses to set against profits of the company suffering the highest marginal rate of tax.

2.3.1 Transfer of loss

A company which has made a loss (the surrendering company) may transfer its loss to another member of the 75% group (the claimant company).

2.3.2 The claimant company

A **claimant company** is assumed to use its own current year losses or losses brought forward in working out the profits against which it may claim group relief, even if it does not in fact claim relief for current losses against total profits.

Furthermore, **group relief is against profits after all other reliefs for the current period or brought forward from earlier periods** including gift aid donations.

Group relief is given before relief for any amounts carried back from later periods.

2.3.3 The surrendering company

A surrendering company may group relieve a loss before setting it against its own profits for the period of the loss, and may specify any amount to be surrendered.

This is **important** for **tax planning as it enables the surrendering company to leave profits in its own computation to be charged to corporation tax at the small companies' rate**, while surrendering its losses to other companies to cover profits which would otherwise fall into the marginal relief band or be taxed at the full rate. Remember that profits in the small companies' marginal relief band are taxed at the marginal rate of 29.75%.

Question	Group relief of losses

In a group relief group of four companies, the results for the year ended 31 March 2010 are as follows.

	Profit/(loss) £
A Ltd	52,000
B Ltd	212,500
C Ltd	1,000,000
D Ltd	(400,000)

How should the loss be allocated to save as much tax as possible? How much tax is saved?

Answer

The upper and lower limits for small companies' marginal relief are £1,500,000/4 = £375,000 and £300,000/4 = £75,000 respectively.

	A Ltd £	B Ltd £	C Ltd £
Profits before group relief	52,000	212,500	1,000,000
Less group relief (note)	0	(137,500)	(262,500)
PCTCT	52,000	75,000	737,500
Tax saved			
£137,500 × 29.75%		40,906	
£262,500 × 28%			73,500

Total £(40,906 + 73,500) = £114,406

Note. We wish to save the most tax possible for the group.

Since A Ltd is in the small companies' band any loss given to it will save tax at the small companies rate of 21%.

B Ltd is in the marginal relief for small companies' rate band. Therefore, any loss given to B saves the effective marginal rate of 29.75% until the profits fall to £75,000 (the small companies' lower limit). After this only 21% is saved.

C Ltd is in the full rate band of 28% until profits fall to £375,000 (the small companies' upper limit).

So to conclude it is best to give B Ltd £137,500 of loss and save 29.75% tax on the profits in the marginal rellef band. The balance of the loss is then given to C Ltd to save 28% tax.

2.4 Losses eligible for relief

A company may surrender to other group companies trading losses, excess property income losses and excess gift aid donations. Gift aid donations can only be group relieved to the extent that they exceed profits before taking account of any losses of the current period or brought forward or back from other accounting periods. Excess gift aid donations must be surrendered before excess property income losses.

Only current period losses are available for group relief.

Capital losses cannot be group relieved. However, see later in this chapter for details of how a group may net off its gains and losses.

2.5 Corresponding accounting periods

Surrendered losses must be set against profits of a corresponding accounting period. If the accounting periods of a surrendering company and a claimant company are not the same this means that both the profits and losses must be apportioned so that only the results of the period of overlap may be set off. Apportionment is on a time basis. However, in the period when a company joins or leaves a group, an alternative method may be used if the result given by time-apportionment would be unjust or unreasonable.

Question	Corresponding accounting periods
	£
S Ltd incurs a trading loss for the year to 30 September 2009	(150,000)
H Ltd makes taxable profits:	
for the year to 31 December 2008	200,000
for the year to 31 December 2009	100,000
What group relief can H Ltd claim from S Ltd?	

Answer	
H Ltd can claim group relief as follows.	
	£
For the year ended 31 December 2008 profits of the corresponding accounting period (1.10.08 – 31.12.08) are £200,000 × 3/12	50,000
Losses of the corresponding accounting period are £150,000 × 3/12	37,500
A claim for £37,500 of group relief may be made against H Ltd's profits	
For the year ended 31 December 2009 profits of the corresponding accounting period (1.1.09 – 30.9.09) are £100,000 × 9/12	75,000
Losses of the corresponding accounting period are £150,000 × 9/12	112,500
A claim for £75,000 of group relief may be made against H Ltd's profits	

If a claimant company claims relief for losses surrendered by more than one company, the total relief that may be claimed for a period that overlaps is limited to the proportion of the claimant's profits attributable to that period. Similarly, if a company surrenders losses to more than one claimant, the total losses that may be surrendered in a period that overlaps is limited to the proportion of the surrendering company's losses attributable to that period.

2.6 Claims

A claim for group relief is normally made on the claimant company's tax return. It is ineffective unless a notice of consent is also given by the surrendering company.

Groupwide claims/surrenders can be made as one person can act for two or more companies at once.

Any payment by the claimant company for group relief, up to the amount of the loss surrendered, is ignored for all corporation tax purposes.

2.7 Tax planning for group relief

This section outlines some tax planning points to bear in mind when dealing with a group.

Group relief should first be given in this order:

1st   To companies in the small companies marginal relief band paying **29.75%** tax (FY 2009) (but only **sufficient loss to bring profits down to the SCR limit**)

2nd   To companies paying the full rate of tax at **28%** (FY 2009)

3rd   To companies paying SCR at **21%** (FY 2009)

Similarly, a company should make a claim to use a loss itself rather than surrender the loss to other group companies if the claim against its own profits would lead to a tax saving at a higher rate.

Companies with profits may benefit by reducing their claims for capital allowances in a particular year. This may leave sufficient profits to take advantage of group relief which may only be available for the current year. The amount on which writing-down allowances can be claimed in later years is increased accordingly.

3 Capital gains group

FAST FORWARD

A capital gains group consists of the top company plus companies in which the top company has a 50% effective interest, provided there is a 75% holding at each level. Within a capital gains group, assets are transferred at no gain and no loss.

3.1 Definition

Companies are in a capital gains group if:

(a)   At each level, there is a 75% holding, and
(b)   The top company has an effective interest of over 50% in the group companies.

If A holds 75% of B, B holds 75% of C and C holds 75% of D, then A, B and C are in such a group, but D is outside the group because A's interest in D is only 75% × 75% × 75% = 42.1875%. Furthermore, D is not in a group with C, because the group must include the top company (A).

The definition of a capital gains group is wider than a that of a 75% group as only a effective 50% interest is needed compared to a 75% interest. However a company can only be in one capital gains group although it may be a member of more than one 75% group.

Illustration of a capital gains group:

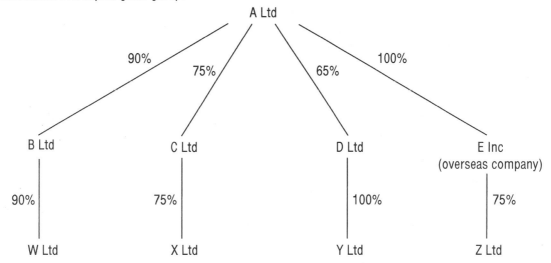

The companies in a group for capital gains purposes are:

A Ltd
B Ltd
W Ltd
C Ltd
X Ltd (75% subsidiary of 75% subsidiary, effective interest over 50%)
E Inc
Z Ltd

There is a separate capital gains group of D Ltd and Y Ltd.

3.2 Intra-group transfers

Companies in a capital gains group make intra-group transfers of chargeable assets without a chargeable gain or an allowable loss arising. No election is needed, as this relief is compulsory. The assets are deemed to be transferred at such a price as will give the transferor no gain and no loss.

3.3 Matching group gains and losses

Gains and losses can be matched within a group. This can be done by electing that all or part of any gain or loss is treated as transferred between group companies.

This section relates to your PER requirement:
20   Assist with tax planning

Two members of a capital gains group can elect to transfer a chargeable gain or allowable loss, or any part of a gain or loss, between them. This election must be made within two years of the end of the accounting period in which the gain or loss accrues in the company which is making the transfer.

From a tax planning point of view, elections(s) should be made to match gains and losses and ensure that net taxable gains arise in the company subject to the lowest rate of corporation tax.

Question

D plc group has had the following results for the year ended 30 June 2010.

	D plc £	A Ltd £	B Ltd £	C Ltd £
Trading profit	400,000	46,000	20,000	220,000
Interest income	10,000	11,000	12,000	14,000
Chargeable gains/ (allowable losses)	18,000	(5,000)	6,000	(2,000)

Reliefs are always claimed as early as possible.

Required

Compute the PCTCT for all companies and show all amounts to be carried forward at 30 June 2010. Assume that the rates of corporation tax for FY 2009 also apply in FY 2010.

Answer

Year ended 30.6.10

	D plc £	A Ltd £	B Ltd £	C Ltd £
Trading profit	400,000	46,000	20,000	220,000
Interest income	10,000	11,000	12,000	14,000
Income before gains	410,000	57,000	32,000	234,000

There are 4 companies in the group.

Upper limit   1,500,000/4 = £375,000
Lower limit   300,000/4 = £75,000

D plc is paying CT at 28%.

A Ltd and B Ltd are paying CT at 21%.

C Ltd is paying CT at a marginal rate of 29.75%.

Since the election can be used to transfer all or part of any of the gains, the simplest way to achieve the optimum result is to identify where the resultant net gains should be taxed:

A Ltd up to the lower limit capacity = £75,000 − £57,000 = £18,000 of gains

B Ltd up to the lower limit capacity = £75,000 − £32,000 = £43,000 of gains

One way of achieving this would be to:

(a)   elect that D plc's gain is transferred to A Ltd offsetting A Ltd's loss, and
(b)   elect that C plc's loss is transferred to B Ltd offsetting B Ltd's gain.

The PCTCT becomes:

	D plc £	A Ltd £	B Ltd £	C Ltd £
Income before gains	410,000	57,000	32,000	234,000
Capital Gain				
(18,000 − 5,000)/(6,000 − 2,000)		13,000	4,000	
Income before gains	410,000	70,000	36,000	234,000

Note that there are other alternatives: all the gains and losses could have been transferred to A Ltd, so that the total net gains of £17,000 resulted in A Ltd having a PCTCT of £74,000.

3.4 Rollover relief

Rollover relief is available in a capital gains group.

If a member of a capital gains group disposes of an asset eligible for capital gains rollover relief it may treat all of the group companies as a single unit for the purpose of claiming such relief. Acquisitions by other group members within the qualifying period of one year before the disposal to three years afterwards may therefore **be matched with the disposal**. However, both the disposing company and the acquiring company must make the claim. If an asset is transferred at no gain and no loss between group members, that transfer does not count as the acquisition of an asset for rollover or holdover relief purpose.

Exam focus point

Try to remember the following summary – it will be of great help in the exam.

Parent Co **controls** over 50% of subsidiary

- associated companies for upper and lower limits

Parent Co **owns** 75% or more of subsidiary

- surrender trading losses, property business losses, excess gift aid donations to companies with some PCTCT for same time period

Parent Co **owns** 75% or more of subsidiary and subsidiary owns 75% or more of its subsidiaries

- transfer assets between companies automatically at no gain/no loss
- capital gains and losses can be matched between group member companies
- all companies treated as one for rollover relief purposes.

Chapter Roundup

- Within a 75% group, current period trading losses, excess property business losses and excess gift aid donations can be surrendered between UK companies. Profits and losses of corresponding accounting periods must be matched up. Group relief is available where the existence of a group is established through companies resident anywhere in the world.

- A surrendering company can surrender any amount of its loss but a claimant company can only claim an amount up to its available profits. The best option is normally to surrender losses to set against profits of the company suffering the highest marginal rate of tax.

- A capital gains group consists of the top company plus companies in which the top company has a 50% effective interest, provided there is a 75% holding at each level. Within a capital gains group, assets are transferred at no gain and no loss.

- Gains and losses can be matched within a group. This can be done by electing that all or part of any gain or loss is treated as transferred between group companies.

- Rollover relief is available in a capital gains group.

Quick Quiz

1   List the types of losses which may be group relieved.

2   When may assets be transferred intra-group at no gain and no loss?

3   How can capital gains and losses within a group be matched with each other?

Answers to Quick Quiz

1   Trading losses, excess property business losses and excess gift aid donations.

2   No gain no loss asset transfers are mandatory between companies in a capital gains group.

3   Two members of a gains group can elect that all or part of a gain or loss is transferred between them within two years of the end of the accounting period in which the gain or loss accrued. This election allows the group to match its gains and losses in one company.

Now try the questions below from the Exam Question Bank

Number	Level	Marks	Time
Q34	Examination	15	27 mins
Q35	Examination	15	27 mins

23

Overseas matters for companies

Topic list	Syllabus reference
1 Branch or subsidiary abroad	C4(d)
2 Double taxation relief (DTR)	C4(e)
3 Transfer pricing	C4(f)

Introduction

In the previous chapter we considered group relationships. We now turn our attention to UK companies trading abroad. We see how relief may be given for overseas taxes suffered and how the transfer pricing legislation applies.

We will conclude our corporation tax studies in the next chapter by considering the administration of corporation tax.

Study guide

		Intellectual level
C4	The effect of a group corporate structure for corporation tax purposes	
(d)	Compare the UK tax treatment of an overseas branch to an overseas subsidiary.	2
(e)	Calculate double taxation relief for withholding tax and underlying tax.	2
(f)	Explain the basic principles of the transfer pricing rules.	2

Exam guide

Overseas aspects of corporation tax will only be tested in question 2, ie as part of a larger question. Questions dealing with DTR need a methodical approach: first calculate the taxable foreign income and the amount of foreign tax available for relief, next compute the UK corporation tax payable, allocating it between UK income and foreign income, and finally apply DTR, which will be the lower of the foreign tax paid and the UK corporation tax payable. The transfer pricing rules are designed to stop profits being shifted abroad; the concept is straightforward – the UK profits must be increased by the shifted profits.

1 Branch or subsidiary abroad

> **FAST FORWARD**
>
> A UK resident company intending to do business abroad must choose between an overseas branch and an overseas subsidiary. A branch may be useful if losses are expected in the early years. If a subsidiary is chosen, the rules on trading at artificial prices must be considered.

1.1 Taxation of foreign income and gains

A UK resident company is subject to corporation tax on its worldwide profits. It is also (unlike a non-resident company) entitled to the small companies' rate of tax and to marginal relief.

If a UK resident company makes investments abroad or has a foreign branch, it will be liable to corporation tax on the income made, the taxable amount being the gross amount, ie before the deduction of any foreign taxes.

A UK resident company may receive dividends from an overseas subsidiary. All dividends received by a UK resident company from a non-UK resident company are exempt from corporation tax for the purposes of the F6 examination. However, such dividends may still affect the calculation of corporation tax. This is because franked investment income includes all dividends received by a company (other than group income), whether received from a UK company or a foreign company.

1.2 Taxation of foreign branches and foreign subsidiaries

An overseas branch of a UK company is effectively an extension of the UK trade, and 100% of the branch profits are assessed to UK corporation tax. Whether or not profits are remitted to the UK is irrelevant.

Question	Overseas branch

T Ltd is a UK company with an overseas branch. The results of T Ltd for the year ended 31 March 2010 are as follows:

	Total	UK	Branch
	£	£	£
Tax adjusted profit	1,000,000	800,000	200,000

The overseas branch is subject to tax overseas at the rate of 25%. Calculate the UK tax liability.

The corporation tax liability of T Ltd for the year ended 31 March 2010 is as follows.

	£
UK trading profit	800,000
Overseas trading profit	200,000
Trading profit/ PCTCT	1,000,000
Corporation tax at 28%	280,000
Marginal relief 7/400 (1,500,000 – 1,000,000)	(8,750)
	271,250
Double taxation relief (see below)	(50,000)
	221,250

(1) Double taxation relief is calculated as £50,000 (200,000 at 25%) being the amount of overseas tax paid.

(2) This is lower than the UK corporation tax on the branch profits of £54,250 (271,250 × 200,000/1,000,000). The UK corporation tax rate is 27.125%.

Note. Double tax relief is covered in more detail in Section 2.

It is important to appreciate the difference between operating overseas through a branch and operating overseas through a subsidiary.

(1) Relief is usually available in the UK for trading losses if incurred by an overseas branch but usually no UK relief is available for trading losses incurred by an overseas subsidiary.

(2) UK capital allowances will be available in respect of plant and machinery purchased by an overseas branch.

(3) An overseas subsidiary will be an associated company, and so the small companies lower and upper limits will be reduced. This may increase the rate of UK corporation tax.

2 Double taxation relief (DTR)

A company may be subject to overseas taxes as well as to UK corporation tax on the same profits. Double taxation relief is available in respect of the foreign tax suffered.

2.1 Types of DTR

In the UK, relief for foreign tax suffered by a company is available in three ways:

(a) **Treaty relief**

Under a treaty entered into between the UK and the overseas country, a treaty may exempt certain profits from taxation in one of the countries involved, thus completely avoiding double taxation. More usually treaties provide for credit to be given for tax suffered in one of the countries against the tax liability in the other.

(b) **Unilateral credit relief**

Where no treaty relief is available, unilateral relief may be available in the UK giving credit for the foreign tax against the UK tax.

(c) **Unilateral expense relief**

Not examined in your syllabus.

2.2 Credit relief

Double tax relief (DTR) is the lower of:
* the UK tax on a source of income
* the overseas tax on that income source.

Relief is available for overseas tax suffered on branch profits and investment income, up to the amount of the UK corporation tax (at the company's average rate) attributable to that income. The gross income including the overseas tax is included within the UK profits chargeable to corporation tax.

2.3 Withholding tax

Overseas tax may be deducted from foreign income arising to the UK company, for example on the profits of a foreign branch. This tax is called withholding tax.

Question
Unilateral credit relief

AS plc has UK trading income of £2,000,000 and received £80,000 from a foreign branch for the year to 31 March 2010. The foreign income was paid subject to 20% withholding tax. Show that the foreign income is £100,000 and compute the corporation tax payable.

Answer

	Total £	UK £	Overseas £
Trading income	2,000,000	2,000,000	
Foreign income (W)	100,000		100,000
PCTCT	2,100,000	2,000,000	100,000
Corporation tax at 28%	588,000	560,000	28,000
Less DTR: lower of:			
(a) overseas tax: £20,000; or			
(b) UK tax on overseas income: £28,000	(20,000)		(20,000)
	568,000	560,000	8,000

Working: Foreign income

£80,000 × 100/(100 – 20) = £100,000.

2.4 Allocation of losses and gift aid donations

Gift aid donations and losses should initially be set against UK income. They should subsequently be set against the overseas income source that suffers the lowest rate of overseas tax.

One further factor affects the computation of UK tax on overseas income against which credit for overseas tax may be claimed. This is the allocation of gift aid donations and losses relieved against total profits.

A company may allocate its gift aid donations and losses relieved against total profits in whatever manner it likes for the purpose of computing double taxation relief. It should set the maximum amount against any UK profits, thereby maximising the corporation tax attributable to the foreign profits and hence maximising the double taxation relief available.

If a company has several sources of overseas profits, then gift aid donations and losses should be allocated first to UK profits, and then to overseas sources which have suffered the **lowest** rates of overseas taxation.

Losses relieved by carry forward must in any case be set against the first available profits of the trade which gave rise to the loss.

A company with a choice of loss reliefs should consider the effect of its choice on double taxation relief. For example, a claim against total profits might lead to there being no UK tax liability, or a very small liability, so that foreign tax would go unrelieved. Carry forward loss relief might avoid this problem and still leave very little UK tax to pay for the period of the loss.

Question
Allocation of gift aid

Kairo plc is a UK resident company with five UK resident subsidiaries and two overseas branches, one in Atlantis and one in Utopia. The company produced the following results for the year to 31 March 2010.

	£
UK trading profits	10,000
Profits from overseas branch in Atlantis (before overseas tax of £8,000)	40,000
Profits from overseas branch in Utopia (before overseas tax of £110,000)	250,000
Gift aid donations	(15,000)

Compute the UK corporation tax liability.

Answer

KAIRO PLC – CORPORATION TAX – YEAR TO 31 MARCH 2010

	Total £	UK £	Atlantis £	Utopia £
Income	300,000	10,000	40,000	250,000
Less Gift aid donations (W)	(15,000)	(10,000)	(5,000)	
Taxable profits	285,000	Nil	35,000	250,000
Corporation tax @ 28% (N)	79,800	–	9,800	70,000
Less DTR (W)	(78,000)	–	(8,000)	(70,000)
Corporation tax	1,800	–	1,800	–

Note

The full rate of corporation tax applies, since the upper limit for profits (£1,500,000 ÷ 6 = £250,000) is exceeded.

Working
The DTR is the lower of:

Atlantis: UK tax £9,800;
            Overseas tax £8,000 (Rate of overseas tax = 20%), ie £8,000

Utopia: UK tax £70,000;
            Overseas tax £110,000 (Rate of overseas tax = 44%), ie £70,000

Note. The Atlantis branch profits suffer the lower rate of overseas tax so the gift aid donations remaining after offset against the UK income are allocated against the Atlantis branch income in preference to the Utopia branch income.

3 Transfer pricing

The transfer pricing legislation restricts the freedom of a company to buy and sell goods at whatever price it wishes between associated persons. A profit on such a transfer must be computed as though the transfer had been made at an arm's length price. The transfer pricing legislation does not apply to transactions between two UK resident persons unless they are large enterprises.

Companies under common control could structure their transactions in such a way that they can shift profit (or losses) from one company to another.

For example consider a company which wishes to sell goods valued at £20,000 to an independent third party.

In this case all the profit on the sale arises to the selling company. Alternatively the sale could be rearranged:

In this case £4,000 of the profit has been diverted to the subsidiary.

This technique could be used to direct profits to a company which will pay less tax on those profits.

This is a 'tax advantage' and there is **anti avoidance legislation** which **requires the profit to be computed as if the transactions had been carried out at arm's length and not at the prices actually used.**

The transfer pricing rules apply to transactions between two persons if either:

(a)   one person directly or indirectly participates in the management, control or capital of the other; or
(b)   a third party directly or indirectly participates in the management, control or capital of both.

Exam focus point

> You will only be expected to deal with situations where profits are being shifted to an overseas company in your exam.

Companies must self-assess their liability to tax under the transfer pricing rules and pay any corporation tax due. A statutory procedure exists for advance pricing arrangements (APAs) whereby a company can agree in advance that its transfer pricing policy is acceptable to HMRC – ie not requiring a self-assessment adjustment. The APA facility is voluntary but companies may feel the need to use the facility as it provides necessary advance confirmation that their approach to transfer pricing in their self-assessment is acceptable.

Chapter Roundup

- A UK resident company intending to do business abroad must choose between an overseas branch and an overseas subsidiary. A branch may be useful if losses are expected in the early years. If a subsidiary is chosen, the rules on trading at artificial prices must be considered.

- Double tax relief is the lower of:
  - the UK tax on a source of income
  - the overseas tax on that income source.

- Gift aid donations and losses should initially be set against UK income. They should subsequently be set against the overseas income source that suffers the lowest rate of overseas tax.

- The transfer pricing legislation restricts the freedom of a company to buy and sell goods at whatever price it wishes between associated persons. A profit on such a transfer must be computed as though the transfer had been made at an arm's length price. The transfer pricing legislation does not apply to transactions between UK resident persons unless they are large enterprises.

Quick Quiz

1   A UK company is planning to set up a new operation in Australia that will initially be loss making. It should set up as a branch of the UK company rather than as a subsidiary. TRUE/FALSE?

2   How best should gift aid donations be allocated in computing credit relief for foreign tax?

   A   Against UK profits first
   B   Against profits generally
   C   Against overseas profits first
   D   Against UK and overseas profits in proportion

3   What measures are included in tax legislation against the use of artificial transfer prices?

Answers to Quick Quiz

1   True. If losses are expected to arise then a branch operation is best since relief is usually available for losses of a foreign branch.

2   A. Gift aid donations should be set firstly against any UK profits, then against overseas income sources suffering the lowest rates of overseas taxation before those suffering at higher rates.

3   Although a company may buy and sell goods at any price it wishes, the transfer pricing anti-avoidance legislation requires profit to be computed as if the transactions had been carried out at arm's length, in certain circumstances.

Now try the question below from the Exam Question Bank

Number	Level	Marks	Time
Q36	Examination	10	18 mins

Self assessment and payment of tax by companies

Topic list	Syllabus reference
1 Corporation tax self assessment	G1(b)
2 Returns, records and claims	G2(a), (e)
3 Enquiries and assessments	G3(a), (b)
4 Payment of corporation tax and interest	G2(b), (d), G4(a)
5 Penalties	G4(b)

Introduction

We now complete our corporation tax studies by looking at the self assessment system for corporation tax, under which companies must file returns and pay the tax due.

In the following chapters we will turn our attention to VAT, which applies to both incorporated and unincorporated businesses.

Study guide

		Intellectual level
G1	**The systems for self-assessment and the making of returns**	
(b)	Explain and apply the features of the self assessment system as it applies to companies.	2
G2	**The time limits for the submission of information, claims and payment of tax, including payments on account**	
(a)	Recognise the time limits that apply to the filing of returns and the making of claims.	2
(b)	Recognise the due dates for the payment of tax under the self-assessment system.	2
(d)	Explain how large companies are required to account for corporation tax on a quarterly basis.	2
(e)	List the information and records that taxpayers need to retain for tax purposes.	1
G3	**The procedures relating to enquiries, appeals and disputes**	
(a)	Explain the circumstances in which HM Revenue & Customs can enquire into a self assessment tax return.	2
(b)	Explain the procedures for dealing with appeals and disputes.	1
G4	**Penalties for non-compliance**	
(a)	Calculate interest on overdue tax.	2
(b)	State the penalties that can be charged.	2

Exam guide

Although question 2 of the exam will always be on corporation tax it will not necessarily include any of the administrative procedures of the self assessment system. They could, however, feature in either question 4 or 5. It is unlikely, but not impossible, that you will be tested on the administrative rules for companies and individuals in the same paper.

1 Corporation tax self assessment

FAST FORWARD

A company that does not receive a notice requiring a return to be filed must, if it is chargeable to tax, notify HMRC within twelve months of the end of the accounting period.

1.1 Introduction

This section relates to your PER requirement:
19   Evaluate and compute taxes payable

The self assessment system relies upon the company completing and filing a tax return and paying the tax due. The system is enforced by a system of penalties for failure to comply within the set time limits, and by interest for late payment of tax.

Dormant companies and companies which have not yet started to trade may not be required to complete tax returns. Such companies have a duty to notify HMRC when they should be brought within the self assessment system.

1.2 Notification of first accounting period

A company must notify HMRC of the beginning of its first accounting period (ie usually when it starts to trade) and the beginning of any subsequent period that does not immediately follow the end of a previous accounting period. The notice must be in the prescribed form and submitted within three months of the relevant date.

1.3 Notification of chargeability

A company that does not receive a notice requiring a return to be filed must, if it is chargeable to tax, **notify HMRC within twelve months of the end of the accounting period**.

2 Returns, records and claims

FAST FORWARD

A company must, in general, file a CT600 tax return within twelve months of the end of an accounting period.

2.1 Returns

A company's tax return (CT600 version 2) must include a self assessment of any tax payable.

An obligation to file a return arises only when the company receives a notice requiring a return. A return is required for each accounting period ending during or at the end of the period specified in the notice requiring a return. A company also has to file a return for certain other periods which are not accounting periods (eg for a period when the company is dormant).

A notice to file a return may also require other information, accounts and reports. For a UK resident company the requirement to deliver accounts normally extends only to the accounts required under the Companies Act.

A return is due on or before the filing date. This is normally the later of:

(a)   **12 months after the end of the period to which the return relates**;
(b)   **three months from the date on which the notice requiring the return was made**.

The relevant period of account is that in which the accounting period to which the return relates ends.

2.2 Amending a return

A company may amend a return within twelve months of the filing date.

HMRC may amend a return to correct obvious errors, or anything else that an officer has reason to believe is incorrect in the light of information available, within nine months of the day the return was filed, or if the correction is to an amended return, within nine months of the filing of an amendment. The company may amend its return so as to reject the correction. If the time limit for amendments has expired, the company may reject the correction by giving notice within three months.

2.3 Records

Companies must keep records until the latest of:

(a)   **six years from the end of the accounting period**;
(b)   the date any enquiries are completed;
(c)   the date after which enquiries may not be commenced.

All business records and accounts, including contracts and receipts, must be kept or information showing that the company has prepared a complete and correct tax return.

If a return is demanded more than six years after the end of the accounting period, any records or information which the company still has must be kept until the later of the end of any enquiry and the expiry of the right to start an enquiry.

2.4 Claims

Wherever possible claims must be made on a tax return or on an amendment to it and must be quantified at the time the return is made.

If a company believes that it has paid excessive tax, for example as a result of an error in its tax return, a claim may be made within four years from the end of the accounting period. An appeal against a decision on such a claim must be made within 30 days. A claim may not be made if the return was made in accordance with a generally accepted practice which prevailed at the time.

Other claims must be made by four years after the end of the accounting period, unless a different time limit is specified.

If HMRC amend a self assessment or issue a discovery assessment then the company has a further period to make, vary or withdraw a claim (unless the claim is irrevocable) even if this is outside the normal time limit. The period is one year from the end of the accounting period in which the amendment or assessment was made, or one year from the end of the accounting period in which the enquiry was closed if the amendment is the result of an enquiry. The relief is limited where there has been fraudulent or negligent conduct by the company or its agent.

3 Enquiries and assessments

FAST FORWARD   HMRC can enquire into returns.

3.1 Enquiries

3.1.1 Opening an enquiry

A return or an amendment need not be accepted at face value by HMRC. **They may enquire into it, provided that they first give written notice that they are going to enquire.** The notice must be given by a year after the later of:

(a)   Where the return is filed by the due filing date, the due filing date (most group companies) or the actual filing date (other companies)

(b)   Where the return is filed late, the 31 January, 30 April, 31 July or 31 October next following the actual date of delivery of the return or amendment.

Only one enquiry may be made in respect of any one return or amendment.

3.1.2 During an enquiry

If a notice of an enquiry has been given, HMRC may demand that the company **produce documents** for inspection and copying. However, documents relating to an appeal need not be produced and the company may appeal against a notice requiring documents to be produced.

HMRC may amend a self assessment at any time during an enquiry if they believe there might otherwise be a loss of tax. The company may appeal against such an amendment within 30 days. The company may itself make amendments during an enquiry under the normal rules for amendments. No effect will be given to such amendments during the enquiry but they may be taken into account in the enquiry.

3.1.3 Closing an enquiry

An enquiry ends when HMRC give notice that it has been completed and notify what they believe to be the correct amount of tax payable. Before that time, the company may ask the Tribunal to order HMRC to notify the completion of its enquiry by a specified date. Such a direction will be given unless HMRC can demonstrate that they have reasonable grounds for continuing the enquiry.

Enquiries relating to a company are closed by the issuing of a closure notice in the same way as for income tax enquiries.

3.2 Determinations

If a return is not delivered by the filing date, HMRC may issue a determination of the tax payable within the four years from the filing date. This is treated as a self assessment and there is no appeal against it. However, it is automatically replaced by any self assessment made by the company by the later of four years from the filing date and 12 months from the determination.

3.3 Discovery assessments

If HMRC believe that not enough tax has been assessed for an accounting period they can make a discovery assessment to collect the extra tax. However, when a tax return has been delivered this power is limited as outlined below.

No discovery assessment can be made on account of an error or mistake as to the basis on which the tax liability ought to be computed, if the basis generally prevailing at the time when the return was made was applied.

A discovery assessment can only be made if either:

(a)   the loss of tax is due to **deliberate or careless understatement** by the company or by someone acting on its behalf; or

(b)   **HMRC could not reasonably be expected to have been aware of the loss of tax, given the information so far supplied to them,** when their right to start an enquiry expired or when they notified the company that an enquiry had finished. The information supplied must be sufficiently detailed to draw HMRC's attention to contentious matters such as the use of a valuation or estimate.

The time limit for raising a discovery assessment is four years from the end of the accounting period but this is extended to 6 years if there has been careless understatement and 20 years if there has been deliberate understatement. The company may appeal against a discovery assessment within 30 days of issue.

4 Payment of corporation tax and interest

FAST FORWARD

In general, corporation tax is due nine months and one day after the end of an accounting period but large companies must pay their corporation tax in four quarterly instalments.

4.1 Payment dates – small and medium companies

Corporation tax is due for payment by small and medium sized companies **nine months and one day after the end of the accounting period**. For example, if a company has an accounting period ending on 31 December 2009, the corporation tax for the period is payable on 1 October 2010.

4.2 Payment dates – large companies

Large companies must pay their corporation tax in instalments. **Broadly, a large company is any company that pays corporation tax at the full rate.**

Instalments are due on the 14th day of the month, starting in the seventh month. Provided that the accounting period is twelve months long subsequent instalments are due in the tenth month during the accounting period and in the first and fourth months after the end of the accounting period.

If an accounting period is less than twelve months long subsequent instalments are due at three monthly intervals but with the final payment being due in the fourth month of the next accounting period.

4.3 Example: quarterly instalments

X Ltd is a large company with a 31 December accounting year end. Instalments of corporation tax will be due to be paid by X Ltd on:

*   14 July and 14 October in the accounting period;
*   14 January and 14 April after the accounting period ends

Thus for the year ended 31 December 2009 instalment payments are due on 14 July 2009, 14 October 2009, 14 January 2010 and 14 April 2010.

4.4 Calculating the instalments

Instalments are based on the estimated corporation tax liability for the current period (not the previous period). **A company is required to estimate its corporation tax liability before the end of the accounting period, and must revise its estimate each quarter.** It is extremely important for companies to forecast their tax liabilities accurately. Large companies whose directors are poor at estimating may find their companies incurring significant interest charges.

The amount of each instalment is computed by:

(a)   **working out 3 × CT/n** where CT is the amount of the estimated corporation tax liability payable in instalments for the period and n is the number of months in the period

(b)   **allocating the smaller of that amount and the total estimated corporation tax liability to the first instalment**

(c)   **repeating the process for later instalments until the amount allocated is equal to the corporation tax liability**.

If the company has an accounting period of 12 months, there will be four instalments and each instalment will be 25% of the estimated amount due.

The position is slightly more complicated if the company has an accounting period of less than 12 months, as is shown in the following question.

Question
Short accounting period

A large company has a CT liability of £880,000 for the eight month period to 30 September 2009. Accounts had previously always been prepared to 31 January. Show when the CT liability is due for payment.

Answer

£880,000 must be paid in instalments.

The amount of each instalment is $3 \times \dfrac{£880,000}{8} = £330,000$

The due dates are:

	£
14 August 2009	330,000
14 November 2009	330,000
14 January 2010	220,000 (balance)

Companies can have instalments repaid if they later conclude the instalments ought not to have been paid.

4.5 Exceptions

A company is not required to pay instalments in the first year that it is 'large', unless its profits exceed £10 million. The £10 million limit is reduced proportionately if there are associated companies. For this purpose only, a company will be regarded as an associated company where it was an associated company at the **start** of an accounting period. (This differs from the normal approach in CT where being an associated company for any part of the AP affects the thresholds of both companies for the whole of the AP).

Any company whose liability does not exceed £10,000 need not pay by instalments.

4.6 Interest on late or overpaid tax

Interest runs from the due date on over/underpaid instalments. The position is looked at cumulatively after the due date for each instalment. HMRC calculate the interest position after the company submits its corporation tax return.

Small and medium companies are charged interest if they pay their corporation tax after the due date, and will receive interest if they overpay their tax or pay it early.

Interest paid/received on late payments or over payments of corporation tax is dealt with as investment income as interest paid/received on a non-trading loan relationship. However, at the moment, the rate of interest on overpaid tax is 0%.

5 Penalties

FAST FORWARD Penalties may be levied for failure to notify the first accounting period, failure to notify chargeability, the late filing of returns, failure to keep records, failure to produce documents during an enquiry and errors in returns.

5.1 Notification of first accounting period

Failure to notify the first accounting period will mean a **maximum penalty of £3,000.**

5.2 Notification of chargeability

The common penalty regime for late notification of chargeability discussed earlier in this Text applies for corporation tax.

5.3 Late filing penalties

There is a £100 penalty for a failure to submit a return on time, rising to £200 if the delay exceeds three months. These penalties become £500 and £1,000 respectively when a return was late (or never submitted) for each of the preceding two accounting periods.

An additional tax geared penalty is applied if a return is more than six months late. The penalty is 10% of the tax unpaid six months after the return was due if the total delay is up to 12 months, and 20% of that tax if the return is over 12 months late.

There is a tax geared penalty for a fraudulent or negligent return and for failing to correct an innocent error without unreasonable delay. The maximum penalty is equal to the tax that would have been lost had the return been accepted as correct. HMRC can mitigate this penalty. If a company is liable to more than one tax geared penalty, the total penalty is limited to the maximum single penalty that could be charged.

5.4 Failure to keep records

Failure to keep records can lead to a **penalty of up to £3,000** for each accounting period affected. However, this penalty does not apply when the only records which have not been kept are ones which could only have been needed for the purposes of claims, elections or notices not included in the return.

5.5 Failure to produce documents during an enquiry

If HMRC demand documents, but the company does not produce them, there is a **penalty of £50**. There is also a **daily penalty**, which applies for each day from the day after the imposition of the £50 penalty until the documents are produced. The daily penalty may be imposed by HMRC, in which case it is £30. If, however, HMRC ask the Tribunal to impose the penalty, it is £150.

5.6 Errors in returns

The **common penalty regime for making errors in tax returns** discussed earlier in this Text applies for corporation tax.

Chapter Roundup

- A company that does not receive a notice requiring a return to be filed must, if it is chargeable to tax, notify HMRC within twelve months of the end of the accounting period.

- A company must, in general, file a CT600 tax return within twelve months of the end of an accounting period.

- HMRC can enquire into returns.

- In general, corporation tax is due nine months and one day after the end of an accounting period, but large companies must pay their corporation tax in four quarterly instalments.

- Penalties may be levied for failure to notify the first accounting period, failure to notify chargeability, the late filing of returns, failure to keep records, failure to produce documents during an enquiry and errors in returns.

1   What are the fixed penalties for failure to deliver a corporation tax return on time?

2   When must HMRC give notice to a non-group company that it is going to start an enquiry if the return was filed by the due filing date?

3   _____ companies must pay quarterly instalments of their corporation tax liability. Fill in the blank.

4   State the due dates for the payment of quarterly instalments of corporation tax for a 12 month accounting period.

5   What is the penalty if a company fails to keep records?

   A   £1,000
   B   £2,000
   C   £3,000
   D   £4,000

Answers to Quick Quiz

1   There is a £100 penalty for failure to submit a return on time rising to £200 if the delay exceeds three months. These penalties increase to £500 and £1,000 respectively when a return was late for each of the preceding two accounting periods.

2   Notice must be given by one year after the actual filing date.

3   'Large' companies, ie companies that pay corporation tax at the full rate.

4   14th day of:

    (a)   7th month in AP
    (b)   10th month in AP
    (c)   1st month after AP ends
    (d)   4th month after AP ends

5   C. £3,000 for each accounting period affected.

Now try the questions below from the Exam Question Bank

Number	Level	Marks	Time
Q37	Introductory	5	9 mins
Q41	Examination	30	54 mins

Q41 has been analysed to give you guidance on how to answer exam questions.

Value added tax

25

An introduction to VAT

Topic list	Syllabus reference
1 The scope of VAT	F1(a)
2 Zero-rated and exempt supplies	F1(b)
3 Registration	F2(a), (b)
4 Deregistration	F2(d)
5 Pre-registration input tax	F2(c)
6 Accounting for and administering VAT	F3(a)
7 The tax point	F3(b)
8 The valuation of supplies	F3(d)
9 The deduction of input tax	F3(e)
10 Relief for impairment losses (bad debts)	F3(f)

Introduction

The final topic in our studies is value added tax (VAT). We cover VAT in this and the next chapter.

VAT is a tax on turnover rather than on profits. As the name suggests, it is charged on the value added. The VAT is collected bit by bit along the chain of manufacturer, wholesaler, retailer, until it finally hits the consumer who does not add value, but uses up the goods.

In this chapter we look at the scope of VAT and then consider when a business must, or may, be registered for VAT. We also look at administration and accounting. VAT is a tax with simple computations but many detailed rules to ensure its enforcement. You may find it easier to absorb the detail if you ask yourself, in relation to each rule, exactly how it helps to enforce the tax.

Next we look at the rules regarding the deduction of input tax.

In the following chapter we will conclude our study of VAT and the F6 syllabus.

Study guide

		Intellectual level
F1	**The scope of value added tax (VAT)**	
(a)	Describe the scope of VAT.	2
(b)	List the principal zero-rated and exempt supplies.	1
F2	**The VAT registration requirements**	
(a)	Recognise the circumstances in which a person must register for VAT.	2
(b)	Explain the advantages of voluntary VAT registration.	2
(c)	Explain the circumstances in which preregistration input VAT can be recovered.	2
(d)	Explain how and when a person can deregister for VAT.	1
F3	**The computation of VAT liabilities**	
(a)	Explain how VAT is accounted for and administered.	2
(b)	Recognise the tax point when goods or services are supplied.	2
(d)	Explain and apply the principles regarding the valuation of supplies.	2
(e)	Recognise the circumstances in which input VAT is non-deductible.	2
(f)	Compute the relief that is available for impairment losses on trade debts.	2

Exam guide

There will always be at least 10% of the marks in the exam on VAT. Although this will usually be in question 1 or 2 there may be a separate question on VAT. The registration requirements are often examined; make sure that you know the difference between the historical test and the future test, and the dates by which HMRC must be notified and registration takes effect. Do not overlook pre-registration input VAT. You may be required to calculate the VAT due for a return period; watch out for non deductible input tax and check the dates if there are impairment losses.

1 The scope of VAT

FAST FORWARD

> VAT is charged on turnover at each stage in a production process, but in such a way that the burden is borne by the final consumer.

1.1 The nature of VAT

VAT is a tax on turnover, not on profits. The basic principle is that the VAT should be borne by the final consumer. Registered traders may deduct the tax which they suffer on supplies to them (input tax) from the tax which they charge to their customers (output tax) at the time this is paid to HMRC. Thus, at each stage of the manufacturing or service process, the net VAT paid is on the value added at that stage.

1.2 Example: the VAT charge

A forester sells wood to a furniture maker for £100 plus VAT. The furniture maker uses this wood to make a table and sells the table to a shop for £150 plus VAT. The shop then sells the table to the final consumer for £300 plus VAT of 17.5%. VAT will be accounted for to HMRC as follows.

	Cost £	Input tax 17.5% £	Net sale price £	Output tax 17.5% £	Payable to HMRC £
Forester	0	0	100	17.50	17.50
Furniture maker	100	17.50	150	26.25	8.75
Shop	150	26.25	300	52.50	26.25
					52.50

Because the traders involved account to HMRC for VAT charged less VAT suffered, their profits for income tax or corporation tax purposes are based on sales and purchases net of VAT.

1.3 Taxable supplies

FAST FORWARD

> VAT is chargeable on taxable supplies made by a taxable person in the course or furtherance of any business carried on by him. Supplies may be of goods or services.

Key term

A **taxable supply** is a supply of goods or services made in the UK, other than an exempt supply.

A taxable supply is either standard-rated or zero-rated. The standard rate is usually 17.5%, although from 1 December 2008 until 31 December 2009, the standard rate has been reduced to 15%. It will revert to 17.5% on 1 January 2010.

The following information will be available in the tax rates and allowances given in the examination:

Standard rate	Up to 31 December 2009	15.0%
Standard rate	From 1 January 2010	17.5%

Exam focus point

You must be prepared to deal with both standard rates in your exam and so you need to look carefully at the information you are given in the question to decide which rate is applicable. However, **the examiner has stated that a question will not be set involving a VAT period that spans 31 December 2009**. This means that you will only have to deal with one of the VAT standard rates in a VAT period.

Certain supplies, which fall within the classification of standard rate supplies, are charged at a reduced rate of 5%. An example is the supply of domestic fuel.

Zero-rated supplies are taxable at 0%. A taxable supplier whose outputs are zero-rated but whose inputs are standard-rated will obtain repayments of the VAT paid on purchases.

An exempt supply is not chargeable to VAT. A person making exempt supplies is unable to recover VAT on inputs. The exempt supplier thus has to shoulder the burden of VAT. Of course, he may increase his prices to pass on the charge, but he cannot issue a VAT invoice which would enable a taxable customer to obtain a credit for VAT, since no VAT is chargeable on his supplies.

1.4 Example: standard-rated, zero-rated and exempt supplies

Here are figures for three traders, the first with standard-rated outputs, the second with zero-rated outputs and the third with exempt outputs. All their inputs are standard-rated. The standard rate is 17.5%.

	Standard-rated £	Zero-rated £	Exempt £
Inputs	20,000	20,000	20,000
VAT	3,500	3,500	3,500
	23,500	23,500	23,500
Outputs	30,000	30,000	30,000
VAT	5,250	0	0
	35,250	30,000	30,000
Pay/(reclaim)	1,750	(3,500)	0
Net profit	10,000	10,000	6,500

VAT legislation lists zero-rated, reduced rate and exempt supplies. There is no list of standard-rated supplies.

We look at the main categories of zero-rated and exempt supplies later in this chapter.

1.5 Supplies of goods

Goods are supplied if exclusive ownership of the goods passes to another person.

The following are treated as supplies of goods.

- The supply of any form of power, heat, refrigeration or ventilation, or of water
- The grant, assignment or surrender of a major interest (the freehold or a lease for over 21 years) in land
- Taking goods permanently out of the business for the non-business use of a taxable person or for other private purposes including the supply of goods by an employer to an employee for his private use
- Transfers under an agreement contemplating a transfer of ownership, such as a hire purchase agreement

Gifts of goods are normally treated as sales at cost (so VAT is due). **However, business gifts are not supplies of goods if**:

(a) **The total cost of gifts made to the same person does not exceed £50 in any 12 month period**. If the £50 limit is exceeded, output tax will be due in full on the total of gifts made. Once the limit has been exceeded a new £50 limit and new 12 month period begins.

(b) **The gift is a sample**. However, if two or more identical samples are given to the same person, all but one of them are treated as supplies.

1.6 Supplies of services

Apart from a few specific exceptions, **any supply which is not a supply of goods and which is done for a consideration is a supply of services**. A consideration is any form of payment in money or in kind, including anything which is itself a supply.

A supply of services also takes place if:

- Goods are lent to someone for use outside the business
- Goods are hired to someone
- Services bought for business purposes are used for private purposes

The European Court of Justice has ruled that restaurants supply services rather than goods.

1.7 Taxable persons

The term 'person' includes **individuals, partnerships** (which are treated as single entities, ignoring the individual partners) and **companies. If a person is in business making taxable supplies, then the value of these supplies is called the taxable turnover. If a person's taxable turnover exceeds certain limits then he is a taxable person and should be registered for VAT** (see later in this Text).

2 Zero-rated and exempt supplies

FAST FORWARD

Some supplies are taxable (either standard-rated, reduced-rated or zero-rated). Others are exempt.

2.1 Types of supply

We have seen that a trader may make standard rated, reduced-rated, zero-rated or exempt supplies.

If a trader makes a supply we need to categorise that supply for VAT as follows:

Step 1   Consider the zero-rated list to see if it is zero-rated. If not:

Step 2   Consider the exempt list to see if it is exempt. If not:

Step 3   Consider the reduced rate list to see if the reduced rate of VAT applies. If not:

Step 4   The supply is standard rated.

Exam focus point

In the exam students will not be expected to categorise all the zero-rated and exempt supplies. The main supplies in each group are highlighted below.

2.2 Zero-rated supplies

The following are items on the **zero-rated list**.

(a)   Human and animal food
(b)   Sewerage services and water
(c)   Printed matter used for reading (eg books, newspapers)
(d)   Construction work on new homes or the sale of the freehold of new homes by builders
(e)   Transport of goods and passengers
(f)   Drugs and medicines on prescription or provided in private hospitals
(g)   Clothing and footwear for young children and certain protective clothing eg motor cyclists' crash helmets

2.3 Exempt supplies

The following are items on the **exempt** list.

(a)   Financial services
(b)   Insurance
(c)   Postal services provided by the Post Office
(d)   Betting and gaming
(e)   Certain education and vocational training
(f)   Health services
(g)   Burial and cremation services
(h)   Sale of freeholds of buildings (other than commercial buildings less than 3 years old) and leaseholds of land and buildings.

2.4 Exceptions to the general rule

The zero-rated, exempt and reduced rate lists outline general categories of goods or services which are either zero-rated or exempt or charged at a rate of 5%. However, the VAT legislation then goes into great detail to outline exceptions to the general rule.

For example the zero-rated list states human food is zero-rated. However, the legislation then states that food supplied in the course of catering (eg restaurant meals, hot takeaways) is not zero-rated. Luxury items of food (eg crisps, peanuts, chocolate covered biscuits) are also not zero-rated.

In the exempt list we are told that financial services are exempt. However the legislation then goes on to state that credit management and processing services are not exempt. Investment advice is also not exempt.

Land and buildings is a complex topic. Broadly, sales of new homes are zero-rated, sales of new commercial buildings are standard rated and most other transactions are exempt.

Thus great care must be taken when categorising goods or services as zero-rated, exempt or standard-rated. It is not as straightforward as it may first appear.

3 Registration

FAST FORWARD

A trader becomes liable to register for VAT if the value of taxable supplies in any period up to 12 months exceeds £68,000 or if there are reasonable grounds for believing that the value of the taxable supplies will exceed £68,000 in the next 30 days. A trader may also register voluntarily.

3.1 Compulsory registration

3.1.1 Historical test

At the end of every month a trader must calculate his cumulative turnover of taxable supplies for the previous 12 months to date. **The trader becomes liable to register for VAT if the value of his cumulative taxable supplies** (excluding VAT) **exceeds £68,000** (from 1 May 2009 onwards). The person is required to notify HMRC within 30 days of the end of the month in which the £68,000 limit is exceeded. HMRC will then register the person with effect from the end of the month following the month in which the £68,000 was exceeded, or from an earlier date if they and the trader agree.

Registration under this rule is not required if HMRC are satisfied that the value of the trader's taxable supplies (excluding VAT) in the year then starting will not exceed £66,000 (from 1 May 2009 onwards).

Question   **VAT registration**

Fred started to trade cutlery on 1 January 2009. Sales (excluding VAT) were £6,225 a month for the first nine months and £7,700 a month thereafter. From what date should Fred be registered for VAT?

Answer

	£
Sales to 31 October 2009	63,725
Sales to 30 November 2009	71,425 (exceeds £68,000)

Fred must notify his liability to register by 30 December 2009 (not 31 December) and will be registered from 1 January 2010 or from an agreed earlier date.

3.1.2 Future test

A person is also liable to register at any time if there are reasonable grounds for believing that his taxable supplies (excluding VAT) in the following 30 days will exceed £68,000. Only taxable turnover of that 30 day period is considered **not** cumulative turnover. HMRC must be notified by the end of the 30 day period and registration will be with effect from the beginning of that period.

Exam focus point

Be sure you know the difference between the historic and future tests.

Question		Future test

Constant Ltd started to trade on 1 February 2009 with sales of goods as follows

	VAT status	£ per month
Goods A	standard rated	5,000
Goods B	zero rated	2,000

On 1 June 2009 Constant Ltd signed a contract to provide £40,000 of Goods A and £30,000 of Goods B to Unicorn plc by 25 June 2009. This is in addition to normal sales.

From which date should Constant Ltd be registered for VAT?

Answer

Goods A and B are taxable supplies.

Cumulative turnover at end of May 2009 is £28,000.

Cumulative turnover at end of June 2009 is £105,000.

But on 1 June 2009 the company signed a contract and hence 'knew' that within the next 30 days it would supply £77,000 of taxable supplies – this meets the future test conditions. Therefore the company needs to notify HMRC of their need to register within 30 days of 1 June 2009, ie by 30 June 2009.

HMRC will then register the company from 1 June 2009.

The historic test is met at the end of June 2009 (this would require notification by 30 July 2009 and registration by 1 August 2009).

However when a trader satisfies both tests HMRC will use the test that gives the earlier registration date.

In this case the future test gives the earliest date, 1 June 2009.

3.1.3 Other registration issues

When determining the value of a person's taxable supplies for the purposes of registration, supplies of goods and services that are *capital assets* of the business are to be disregarded, except for non zero-rated taxable supplies of interests in land.

When a person is liable to register in respect of a past period, it is his responsibility to pay VAT. If he is unable to collect it from those to whom he made taxable supplies, the VAT burden will fall on him. A person must start keeping VAT records and charging VAT to customers as soon as it is known that he is required to register. However, VAT should not be shown separately on any invoices until the registration number is known. The invoice should show the VAT inclusive price and customers should be informed that VAT invoices will be forwarded once the registration number is known. Formal VAT invoices should then be sent to such customers within 30 days of receiving the registration number.

Notification of liability to register must be made on form VAT 1. Simply writing to, or telephoning, a local VAT office is not enough. On registration the VAT office will send the trader a certificate of registration. This shows the VAT registration number, the date of registration, the end of the first VAT period and the length of the VAT periods.

If a trader makes a supply before becoming liable to register, but gets paid after registration, VAT is not due on that supply.

3.2 Voluntary registration

A person may decide to become registered even though his taxable turnover falls below the registration limit. Unless a person is registered he cannot recover the input tax he pays on purchases.

Voluntary registration is advantageous where a person wishes to recover input tax on purchases. For example, consider a trader who has one input during the year which cost £1,000 plus £175 VAT at 17.5%; he works on the input which becomes his sole output for the year and he decides to make a profit of £1,000.

(a)   If he is not registered he will charge £2,175 and his customer will obtain no relief for any VAT.

(b)   If he is registered he will charge £2,000 plus VAT of £350. His customer will have input tax of £350 which he will be able to recover if he, too, is registered.

If the customer is a non-taxable person he will prefer (a) as the cost to him is £2,175. If he is taxable he will prefer (b) as the net cost is £2,000. Thus, a decision whether or not to register voluntarily may depend upon the status of customers. It may also depend on the status of the outputs and the image of the business the trader wishes to project (registration may give the impression of a substantial business). The administrative burden of registration should also be considered.

4 Deregistration

FAST FORWARD

A trader may deregister voluntarily if he expects the value of his taxable supplies in the following one year period will not exceed £66,000. Alternatively, a trader who no longer makes taxable supplies may be compulsorily deregistered.

4.1 Voluntary deregistration

A person is eligible for voluntary deregistration if HMRC are satisfied that the value of his taxable supplies (net of VAT and excluding supplies of capital assets) **in the following one year period will not exceed £66,000 (from 1 May 2009).** However, voluntary deregistration will not be allowed if the reason for the expected fall in value of taxable supplies is the cessation of taxable supplies or the suspension of taxable supplies for a period of 30 days or more in that following year.

HMRC will cancel a person's registration from the date the request is made or from an agreed later date.

4.2 Compulsory deregistration

A trader may be compulsorily deregistered if HMRC are satisfied that he is no longer making nor intending to make taxable supplies. Failure to notify a requirement to deregister within 30 days may lead to a penalty. Compulsory deregistration may also lead to HMRC reclaiming input tax which has been wrongly recovered by the trader since the date on which he should have deregistered.

4.3 The consequences of deregistration

FAST FORWARD

VAT is chargeable on all goods and services on hand at the date of deregistration.

On deregistration, VAT is chargeable on all stocks and capital assets in a business on which input tax was claimed, since the registered trader is in effect making a taxable supply to himself as a newly unregistered trader. If the VAT chargeable does not exceed £1,000, it need not be paid.

4.4 Transfer of a going concern

> The transfer of a business as a going concern is outside the scope of VAT.

There is no VAT charge if a business (or a separately viable part of it) **is sold as a going concern to another taxable person** (or a person who immediately becomes a taxable person as a result of the transfer). Such a sale is **outside the scope of VAT**.

If a transfer of a going concern (TOGC) is from a VAT registered trader to a new owner who is not VAT registered then it is possible to apply to transfer the registration number of the previous owner to the new owner. This would also transfer to the new owner the responsibility for the past VAT history of the old business. So, if the previous owner had committed any VAT misdemeanours the liability for those would transfer to the new owner of the business. As a result of this it may not be wise to apply to transfer the VAT registration number between old and new owners unless of course, it is a situation where there is a very close connection between the two.

If the VAT registration number is not transferred then the new owners do not have any responsibility for the VAT affairs of the previous owner of the business. This is probably a safer way to structure the transfer of a business.

5 Pre-registration input tax

5.1 Introduction

VAT incurred before registration can be treated as input tax and recovered from HMRC subject to certain conditions.

5.2 Pre-registration goods

If the claim is for input tax suffered on goods purchased prior to registration then the following conditions must be satisfied.

(a)   The goods were acquired for the purpose of the business which either was carried on or was to be carried on by him at the time of supply.

(b)   The goods have not been supplied onwards or consumed before the date of registration (although they may have been used to make other goods which are still held).

(c)   The VAT must have been incurred in the four years prior to the effective date of registration.

5.3 Pre-registration services

If the claim is for input tax suffered on the supply of services prior to registration then the following conditions must be satisfied.

(a)   The services were supplied for the purposes of a business which either was carried on or was to be carried on by him at the time of supply.

(b)   The services were supplied within the six months prior to the date of registration.

Input tax attributable to supplies made before registration is not deductible even if the input tax concerned is treated as having been incurred after registration.

6 Accounting for and administering VAT

6.1 Administration

FAST FORWARD

VAT is administered by HMRC. Appeals are heard by the Tax Tribunal

6.1.1 Introduction

The administration of VAT is dealt with by HM Revenue and Customs (HMRC).

Local offices are responsible for the local administration of VAT and for providing advice to registered persons whose principal place of business is in their area. They are controlled by regional collectors.

Completed VAT returns should be sent to the VAT Central Unit at Southend, not to a local office.

From time to time a registered person will be visited by staff from a local office (a control visit) to ensure that the law is understood and is being applied properly. If a trader disagrees with any decision as to the application of VAT given by HMRC he can ask his local office to reconsider the decision. It is not necessary to appeal formally while a case is being reviewed in this way. Where an appeal can be settled by agreement, a written settlement has the same force as a decision by the Revenue and Customs Prosecution Office.

6.1.2 Assessments

HMRC may issue assessments of VAT due to the best of their judgement if they believe that a trader has failed to make returns or if they believe those returns to be incorrect or incomplete. The time limit for making assessments is normally three years after the end of a VAT period, but this is extended to 20 years in the case of fraud, dishonest conduct, certain registration irregularities and the unauthorised issue of VAT invoices.

HMRC sometimes write to traders, setting out their calculations, before issuing assessments. The traders can then query the calculations.

6.1.3 Appeals

A trader may appeal to the Tax Tribunal in the same way as an appeal may be made for income tax and corporation tax (see earlier in this Study Text). VAT returns and payments shown thereon must have been made before an appeal can be heard.

6.2 VAT periods

FAST FORWARD

VAT is accounted for on regular returns. Extensive records must be kept.

The VAT period (also known as the tax period) is the period covered by a VAT return. It is usually three calendar months. The return shows the total input and output tax for the tax period and must be **submitted, along with any VAT due, within one month of the end of the period. Businesses which pay VAT electronically automatically receive a seven-day extension to this time limit.**

HMRC allocate VAT periods according to the class of trade carried on (ending in June, September, December and March; July, October, January and April; or August, November, February and May), to spread the flow of VAT returns evenly over the year. When applying for registration a trader can ask for VAT periods which fit in with his own accounting year. It is also possible to have VAT periods to cover accounting systems not based on calendar months.

A registered person whose input tax will regularly exceed his output tax can elect for a one month VAT period, but will have to balance the inconvenience of making 12 returns a year against the advantage of obtaining more rapid repayments of VAT.

Certain small businesses may submit an annual VAT return.

6.3 Substantial traders

If a trader does not make monthly returns, and the total VAT liability over 12 months to the end of a VAT period exceeds £2,000,000, he must make payments on account of each quarter's VAT liability during the quarter. Payments are due a month before the end of the quarter and at the end of the quarter, with the final payment due at the usual time, a month after the end of the quarter. An electronic payment system must be used, not a cheque through the post.

For a trader who exceeds the £2,000,000 limit in the 12 months to 30 September, 31 October or 30 November, the amount of each of the two payments on account is 1/24 of the total VAT liability of those 12 months. The obligation to pay on account starts with the first VAT period starting *after* 31 March.

6.4 Refunds of VAT

There is a four year time limit on the right to reclaim overpaid VAT. This time limit does not apply to input tax which a business could not have reclaimed earlier because the supplier only recently invoiced the VAT, even though it related to a purchase made some time ago. Nor does it apply to overpaid VAT penalties.

If a taxpayer has overpaid VAT and has overclaimed input tax by reason of the same mistake, HMRC can set off any tax, penalty, interest or surcharge due to them against any repayment due to the taxpayer and repay only the net amount. In such cases the normal four year time limit for recovering VAT, penalties, interest, etc by assessment does not apply.

HMRC can refuse to make any repayment which would unjustly enrich the claimant. They can also refuse a repayment of VAT where all or part of the tax has, for practical purposes, been borne by a person other than the taxpayer (eg by a customer of the taxpayer) except to the extent that the taxpayer can show loss or damage to any of his businesses as a result of mistaken assumptions about VAT.

7 The tax point

FAST FORWARD

The tax point is the deemed date of supply. The basic tax point is the date on which goods are removed or made available to the customer, or the date on which services are completed. If a VAT invoice is issued or payment is received before the basic tax point, the earlier of these dates becomes the tax point. If the earlier date rule does not apply, and the VAT invoice is issued within 14 days of the basic tax point, the invoice date becomes the actual tax point.

7.1 The basic tax point

The tax point of each supply is the deemed date of supply. The basic tax point is the date on which the goods are removed or made available to the customer, or the date on which services are completed.

The tax point determines the VAT period in which output tax must be accounted for and credit for input tax will be allowed. The tax point also determines which rate applies if the rate of VAT or a VAT category changes (for example when a supply ceases to be zero-rated and becomes standard-rated).

7.2 The actual tax point

If a VAT invoice is issued or payment is received before the basic tax point, the earlier of these dates automatically becomes the tax point. If the earlier date rule does not apply and if the VAT invoice is issued within 14 days after the basic tax point, the invoice date becomes the tax point (although the trader can elect to use the basic tax point for all his supplies if he wishes). This 14 day period may be extended to accommodate, for example, monthly invoicing; the tax point is then the VAT invoice date or the end of the month, whichever is applied consistently.

Julia sells a sculpture to the value of £1,000 net of VAT. She receives a payment on account of £250 plus VAT on 25 March 2010. The sculpture is delivered on 28 April 2010. Julia's VAT returns are made up to calendar quarters. She issues an invoice on 4 May 2010.

Outline the tax point(s) and amount(s) due.

Answer

A separate tax point arises in respect of the £250 deposit and the £750 balance payable.

Julia should account for VAT as follows.

(a) *Deposit*

25 March 2010: tax at 17.5% × £250 = £43.75. This is accounted for in her VAT return to 31 March 2010. The charge arises on 25 March 2010 because payment is received before the basic tax point (which is 28 April 2010 – date of delivery).

(b) *Balance*

4 May 2010: tax at 17.5% × £750 = £131.25. This is accounted for on the VAT return to 30 June 2010. The charge arises on 4 May because the invoice was issued within 14 days of the basic tax point of 28 April 2010 (delivery date).

7.3 Miscellaneous points

Goods supplied on sale or return are treated as supplied on the earlier of adoption by the customer or 12 months after despatch.

Continuous supplies of services paid for periodically normally have tax points on the earlier of the receipt of each payment and the issue of each VAT invoice, unless one invoice covering several payments is issued in advance for up to a year. The tax point is then the earlier of each due date or date of actual payment. However, for connected businesses the tax point will be created periodically, in most cases based on 12 month periods.

8 The valuation of supplies

FAST FORWARD

In order to ascertain the amount of VAT on a supply, the supply must be valued. If a discount is offered for prompt payment, VAT is chargeable on the net amount even if the discount is not taken up.

8.1 Value of supply

The value of a supply is the VAT-exclusive price on which VAT is charged. The consideration for a supply is the amount paid in money or money's worth.

Thus with a standard rate of 17.5%:

Value + VAT = consideration
£100 + £17.50 = £117.50

The VAT proportion of the consideration is known as the 'VAT fraction'. It is

$$\frac{\text{rate of tax}}{100 + \text{rate of tax}} = \frac{17.5}{100 + 17.5} = \frac{7}{47}$$

With a standard rate of 15%:

Value + VAT = consideration
£100 + £15 = £115

and the VAT fraction is

$$\frac{\text{rate of tax}}{100 + \text{rate of tax}} = \frac{15}{100 + 15} = \frac{3}{23}$$

Provided the consideration for a bargain made at arm's length is paid in money, the value for VAT purposes is the VAT exclusive price charged by the trader. If it is paid in something other than money, as in a barter of some goods or services for others, it must be valued and VAT will be due on the value.

If the price of goods is effectively reduced with money off coupons, the value of the supply is the amount actually received by the taxpayer.

8.2 Discounts

Where a discount is offered for prompt payment, VAT is chargeable on the net amount, regardless of whether the discount is taken up.

When goods are sold to staff at a discount, VAT is only due on the discounted price.

8.3 Miscellaneous

For goods supplied under a hire purchase agreement VAT is chargeable on the cash selling price at the start of the contract.

When goods are permanently taken from a business for non-business purposes VAT must be accounted for on their market value. Where business goods are put to a private or non-business use, the value of the resulting supply of services is the cost to the taxable person of providing the services. If services bought for business purposes are used for non-business purposes (without charge), then VAT must be accounted for on their cost, but the VAT to be accounted for is not allowed to exceed the input tax deductible on the purchase of the services.

9 The deduction of input tax

9.1 Input tax recovery

FAST FORWARD

Not all input VAT is deductible, eg VAT on most motor cars.

For input tax to be deductible, the payer must be a taxable person, with the supply being to him in the course of his business. In addition a VAT invoice must be held (except for payments of up to £25 including VAT which are for telephone calls or car park fees or which are made through cash operated machines).

Input tax recovery can be denied to any business that does not hold a valid VAT invoice and cannot provide alternative evidence to prove the supply took place.

9.2 Capital items

The distinction between capital and revenue which is important in other areas of tax **does not apply to VAT**. Thus a manufacturer buying plant subject to VAT will be able to obtain a credit for all the VAT immediately. The plant must of course be used to make taxable supplies, and if it is only partly so used only part of the VAT can be reclaimed. Conversely, if plant is sold secondhand then VAT should be charged on the sale and is output tax in the normal way.

9.3 Non-deductible input tax

Exam focus point

In the F6 exam students are not required to know actual cases where VAT decisions were made. They are included below for your information only.

The following input tax is not deductible even for a taxable person with taxable outputs.

(a) **VAT on motor cars** not used wholly for business purposes. VAT on cars is never reclaimable unless the car is acquired new for resale or is acquired for use in or leasing to a taxi business, a self-drive car hire business or a driving school (see further below).

(b) **VAT on business entertaining** where the cost of the entertaining is not a tax deductible trading expense. If the items bought are used partly for such entertaining and partly for other purposes, the proportion of the VAT relating to the entertainment is non-deductible.

In *Ernst & Young v CCE* the Tribunal held that staff entertaining was wholly for business purposes and a full input tax recovery was allowed. HMRC accept this decision in respect of staff entertainment but maintain that following the case *KPMG v CCE* input tax on entertaining guests at a staff party is non-deductible.

(c) **VAT on expenses incurred on domestic accommodation for directors.**

(d) **VAT on non-business items passed through the business accounts.** However, when goods are bought partly for business use, the purchaser may:

(i) Deduct all the input tax, and account for output tax in respect of the private use, or
(ii) Deduct only the business proportion of the input tax.

Where services are bought partly for business use, only method (ii) may be used. If services are initially bought for business use but the use then changes, a fair proportion of the input tax (relating to the private use) is reclaimed by HMRC by making the trader account for output tax.

(e) **VAT which does not relate to the** making of supplies by the buyer in the course of a **business**.

9.4 Irrecoverable VAT

Where all (as with many cars) or some (as for partial business use) of the input tax on a purchase is not deductible, the **non-deductible VAT is included in the cost for income tax, corporation tax, capital allowance or capital gains purposes. Deductible VAT is omitted from costs, so that only net amounts are included in accounts. Similarly, sales** (and proceeds in chargeable gains computations) **are shown net of VAT**, because the VAT is paid over to HMRC.

9.5 Motoring expenses

9.5.1 Cars

The VAT incurred on the purchase of a car not used wholly for business purposes is not recoverable (except as mentioned above). If accessories are fitted after the original purchase and a separate invoice is raised then the VAT on the accessories can be treated as input tax so long as the accessories are for business use.

If a car is used wholly for business purposes (including leasing, so long as the charges are at the open market rate), the input tax is recoverable but the buyer must account for VAT when he sells the car. **If a car is leased, the lessor recovered the input tax when the car was purchased and the lessee makes some private use of the car** (for example private use by employees), **the lessee can only recover 50% of the input tax on the lease charges. A hiring of five days or less is assumed to be for wholly business use.**

If a car is used for business purposes then any VAT charged on repair and maintenance costs can be treated as input tax. No apportionment has to be made for private use.

9.5.2 Fuel for business use

The VAT incurred on fuel used for business purposes is fully deductible as input tax. If the fuel is bought by employees who are reimbursed for the actual cost or by a mileage allowance, the employer may deduct the input tax provided he **holds a VAT invoice (or invoices) showing sufficient VAT to cover the input tax claim being made**. Normally there will not be an invoice showing the exact amount of input VAT reclaimed because some of the fuel may have been used by employees for private purposes and only business use is reimbursed (or a mileage allowance is used). It is sufficient to hold invoice(s) showing an amount of input tax on fuel at least equal to the input tax being recovered by the business.

9.5.3 Fuel for private use

FAST FORWARD

If fuel is supplied for private purposes all input VAT incurred on the fuel is allowed but the business must account for output VAT using a set of scale charges.

When fuel is supplied for an individual's private use at less than the cost of that fuel to the business, all input tax incurred on the fuel is allowed, but the business must account for output tax using set scale charges per VAT return period, based on the CO_2 emissions of the car. As for income tax, the CO_2 emissions are rounded down to the nearest 5%. The scale figures will be stated in the exam if required. However, take care to note whether the examiner has given you the VAT inclusive or the VAT exclusive scale figure.

The output tax is the VAT inclusive scale charge × 7/47 or 3/23 as appropriate or the VAT exclusive scale charge × 17.5% or 15% as appropriate.

If the employee has to pay the full cost of fuel (or more than its cost) to the employer, the employer must account for VAT on the amount paid, rather than on the scale charge.

Question
Fuel scale charge

Iain is an employee of ABC Ltd. He has the use of a car with CO_2 emissions of 176 g/km for one month and a car with CO_2 emissions of 208 g/km for two months during the quarter ended 31 March 2010.

ABC Ltd pay all the petrol costs in respect of both cars without requiring Iain to make any reimbursement in respect of private fuel. Total petrol costs for the quarter amount to £300 (including VAT).

What is the VAT effect of the above on ABC Ltd?

VAT scale rates (VAT inclusive) for 3 month periods

CO_2 emissions	£
175	289
205	365

Answer

Value for the quarter:

	£
Car 1	
£289 × 1/3 =	96.33
Car 2	
£365 × 2/3 =	243.33
	339.66
Output tax:	
7/47 × £339.66	£50.59
Input tax	
7/47 × £300	£44.68

---

10 Relief for impairment losses (bad debts)

FAST FORWARD

Relief for VAT on impairment losses (bad debts) is available if the debt is over six months old (measured from when the payment is due) and has been written off in the trader's accounts.

Where a supplier of goods or services has accounted for VAT on the supply and the customer does not pay, the supplier may claim a refund of VAT on the amount unpaid. **Relief is available for VAT on impairment losses (bad debts) if the debt is over six months old (measured from when payment is due) and has been written off in the creditor's accounts.** Where payments on account have been received, they are attributed to debts in chronological order. If the debtor later pays all or part of the amount owed, a corresponding part of the VAT repaid must be paid back to HMRC.

Impairment loss relief claims must be made within three years of the time the debt became eligible for relief. The creditor must have a copy of the VAT invoice, and records to show that the VAT in question has been accounted for and that the debt has been written off. The VAT is reclaimed on the creditor's VAT return.

A business which has claimed input tax on a supply, but which has not paid the supplier of the goods or services within six months of date of supply (or the date on which the payment is due, if later), must repay the input tax, irrespective of whether the supplier has made a claim for bad debt relief. The input tax will be repaid by making an adjustment to the input tax on the VAT return for the accounting period in which the end of the six months falls.

Exam focus point

Watch out for the six month rule when claiming relief for impairment losses.

Chapter Roundup

- VAT is charged on turnover at each stage in a production process, but in such a way that the burden is borne by the final consumer.

- VAT is chargeable on taxable supplies made by a taxable person in the course or furtherance of any business carried on by him. Supplies may be of goods or services.

- Some supplies are taxable (either standard-rated, reduced-rated or zero-rated). Others are exempt.

- A trader becomes liable to register for VAT if the value of taxable supplies in any period up to 12 months exceeds £68,000 or if there are reasonable grounds for believing that the value of the taxable supplies will exceed £68,000 in the next 30 days. A trader may also register voluntarily.

- A trader may deregister voluntarily if he expects the value of his taxable supplies in the following one year period will not exceed £66,000. Alternatively, a trader who no longer makes taxable supplies may be compulsorily deregistered.

- VAT is chargeable on all goods and services on hand at the date of deregistration.

- The transfer of a business as a going concern is outside the scope of VAT.

- VAT is administered by HMRC. The Tax Tribunal hears appeals.

- VAT is accounted for on regular returns. Extensive records must be kept.

- The tax point is the deemed date of supply. The basic tax point is the date on which goods are removed or made available to the customer, or the date on which services are completed. If a VAT invoice is issued or payment is received before the basic tax point, the earlier of these dates becomes the tax point. If the earlier date rule does not apply, and the VAT invoice is issued within 14 days of the basic tax point, the invoice date becomes the actual tax point.

- In order to ascertain the amount of VAT on a supply, the supply must be valued. If a discount is offered for prompt payment, VAT is chargeable on the net amount even if the discount is not taken up.

- Not all input VAT is deductible, eg VAT on most motor cars.

- If fuel is supplied for private purposes all input VAT incurred on the fuel is allowed but the business must account for output VAT using a set of scale charges.

- Relief for VAT on impairment losses (bad debts) is available if the debt is over six months old (measured from when the payment is due) and has been written off in the trader's accounts.

Quick Quiz

1   On what transactions will VAT be charged?

2   What is a taxable person?

3   When may a person choose to be deregistered?

4   What is the time limit in respect of claiming pre-registration input tax on goods?

5   On what amount is VAT charged if a discount is offered for prompt payment?

6   What input tax is never deductible?

7   What relief is available for bad debts?

Answers to Quick Quiz

1   VAT is charged on taxable supplies of goods and services made in the UK by a taxable person in the course or furtherance of any business carried on by him.

2   Any 'person' whose taxable turnover exceeds the registration limit. The term 'person' includes individuals, partnerships and companies.

3   A person is eligible for voluntary deregistration if HMRC are satisfied that the value of his taxable supplies in the following year will not exceed £66,000.

4   The VAT must have been incurred in the three years prior to the effective date of registration.

5   VAT is chargeable on the net price, regardless of whether the discount is taken up.

6   VAT on:

   - motor cars
   - business entertaining
   - expenses incurred on domestic accommodation for directors
   - non-business items passed through the accounts
   - items which do not relate to making business supplies

7   Where a supplier has accounted for VAT on a supply and the customer fails to pay, then the supplier may claim a refund of the VAT accounted for to HMRC but never actually collected from the customer.

Now try the question below from the Exam Question Bank

Number	Level	Marks	Time
Q38	Examination	10	18 mins

26

Further aspects of VAT

Topic list	Syllabus reference
1 VAT invoices and records	F3(c)
2 Penalties	F3(g)
3 Special schemes	F4(a)-(c)

Introduction

In the previous chapter we looked at the scope of VAT and when businesses must, or may, register for VAT.

In this chapter we consider the contents of a valid VAT invoice and the main penalties used to enforce the VAT system.

Finally we look at the three special schemes which are intended to reduce the administrative burden for small businesses.

This chapter concludes our study of UK taxation and the F6 syllabus.

Study guide

		Intellectual level
F3	**The computation of VAT liabilities**	
(c)	List the information that must be given on a VAT invoice.	1
(g)	Explain the circumstances in which the default surcharge, a serious misdeclaration penalty, and default interest will be applied.	1
F4	**The effect of special schemes**	
(a)	Describe the cash accounting scheme, and recognise when it will be advantageous to use the scheme.	2
(b)	Describe the annual accounting scheme, and recognise when it will be advantageous to use the scheme.	2
(c)	Describe the flat rate scheme, and recognise when it will be advantageous to use the scheme.	2

Exam guide

There will always be at least 10% of the marks in the exam on VAT. Although this may be in question 1 or 2 there may be a separate question on VAT. Penalties are an important topic as they are used to enforce the VAT system, but the special schemes are designed to make life simpler for small businesses. The flat rate scheme may also lead to a small extra profit for the business, depending on the flat rate percentage and the level of inputs.

1 VAT invoices and records

1.1 VAT invoices

> **FAST FORWARD**
>
> A taxable person making a taxable supply to another registered person must supply a VAT invoice within 30 days.

A taxable person making a taxable supply to another person registered for VAT must supply a VAT invoice within 30 days of the time of supply, and must keep a copy. The invoice must show:

(a) The supplier's name, address and registration number
(b) The date of issue, the tax point and an invoice number
(c) The name and address of the customer
(d) A description of the goods or services supplied, giving for each description the quantity, the unit price, the rate of VAT and the VAT exclusive amount
(e) The rate of any cash discount
(f) The total invoice price excluding VAT (with separate totals for zero-rated and exempt supplies)
(g) Each VAT rate applicable and the total amount of VAT

If an invoice is issued, and a change in price then alters the VAT due, a credit note or debit note to adjust the VAT must be issued.

Credit notes must give the reason for the credit (such as 'returned goods'), and the number and date of the original VAT invoice. If a credit note makes no VAT adjustment, it should state this.

A less detailed VAT invoice may be issued by a retailer where the invoice is for a total including VAT of up to £250. Such an invoice must show:

(a)   The supplier's name, address and registration number
(b)   The date of the supply
(c)   A description of the goods or services supplied
(d)   The rate of VAT chargeable
(e)   The total amount chargeable including VAT

Zero-rated and exempt supplies must not be included in less detailed invoices.

VAT invoices are not required for payments of up to £25 including VAT which are for telephone calls or car park fees or are made through cash operated machines. In such cases, input tax can be claimed without a VAT invoice.

1.2 Records

FAST FORWARD

Every VAT registered trader must keep records for six years.

Every VAT registered trader must keep records for six years, although HMRC may sometimes grant permission for their earlier destruction. They may be kept on paper, on microfilm or microfiche or on computer. However, there must be adequate facilities for HMRC to inspect records.

All records must be kept up to date and in a way which allows:

•   The calculation of VAT due
•   Officers of HMRC to check the figures on VAT returns

The following records are needed.

•   Copies of VAT invoices, credit notes and debit notes issued

•   A summary of supplies made

•   VAT invoices, credit notes and debit notes received

•   A summary of supplies received

•   A VAT account

•   Order and delivery notes, correspondence, appointment books, job books, purchases and sales books, cash books, account books, records of takings (such as till rolls), bank paying-in slips, bank statements and annual accounts

•   Records of zero-rated and exempt supplies, gifts or loans of goods, taxable self-supplies and any goods taken for non-business use

2 Penalties

2.1 The default surcharge

FAST FORWARD

A default occurs when a trader either submits his VAT return late, or submits the return on time but pays the VAT late. A default surcharge is applied if there is a default during a default surcharge period.

A default occurs when a trader either submits his VAT return late, or submits the return on time but pays the VAT late. If a trader defaults, HMRC will serve a surcharge liability notice on the trader. The notice specifies a surcharge period running from the date of the notice to the anniversary of the end of the period for which the trader is in default.

If a further default occurs in respect of a return period ending during the specified surcharge period, the original surcharge period will be extended to the anniversary of the end of the period to which the new default relates. In addition, if the default involves the late payment of VAT (as opposed to simply a late return) **a surcharge is levied.**

The surcharge depends on the number of defaults involving late payment of VAT which have occurred in respect of periods ending in the surcharge period, as follows.

Default involving late payment of VAT in the surcharge period	Surcharge as a percentage of the VAT outstanding at the due date
First	2%
Second	5%
Third	10%
Fourth or more	15%

Surcharges at the 2% and 5% rates are not normally demanded unless the amount due would be at least £400 but for surcharges calculated using the 10% or 15% rates there is a minimum amount of £30 payable.

A trader must submit one year's returns on time and pay the VAT shown on them on time in order to break out of the surcharge liability period and the escalation of surcharge percentages.

Question
Default surcharge

Peter Popper has an annual turnover of around £300,000. His VAT return for the quarter to 31.12.08 is late. He then submits returns for the quarters to 30.9.09 and 31.3.10 late as well as making late payment of the tax due of £12,000 and £500 respectively.

Peter's VAT return to 31.3.11 is also late and the VAT due of £1,100 is also paid late. All other VAT returns and VAT payments are made on time. Outline Peter Popper's exposure to default surcharge.

Answer

A surcharge liability notice will be issued after the late filing on the 31.12.08 return outlining a surcharge period extending to 31.12.09.

The late 30.9.09 return is in the surcharge period so the period is extended to 30.9.10. The late VAT payment triggers a 2% penalty. 2% × £12,000 = £240. Since £240 is less than the £400 de minimis limit it is not collected by HMRC.

The late 31.3.10 return is in the surcharge period so the period is now extended to 31.3.11. The late payment triggers a 5% penalty. 5% × £500 = £25. Since £25 is less than the £400 de minimis limit it is not collected by HMRC.

The late 31.03.11 return is in the surcharge period. The period is extended to 31.03.12. The late payment triggers a 10% penalty 10% × £1,100 = £110. This is collected by HMRC since the £400 de minimis does not apply to penalties calculated at the 10% (and 15%) rate.

Peter will have to submit all four quarterly VAT returns to 31.3.12 on time and pay the VAT on time to 'escape' the default surcharge regime.

A default will be ignored for all default surcharge purposes if the trader can show that the return or payment was sent at such a time, and in such a manner, that it was reasonable to expect that HMRC would receive it by the due date. Posting the return and payment first class the day before the due date is generally accepted as meeting this requirement. A default will also be ignored if the trader can demonstrate a reasonable excuse for the late submission or payment.

The application of the default surcharge regime to small businesses is modified. **A small business is one with a turnover below £150,000.** When a small business is late submitting a VAT return or paying VAT it will receive a letter from HMRC offering help. No penalty will be charged. If a further default occurs within 12 months a surcharge liability notice will be issued.

2.2 Penalties for errors

There is a common penalty regime for errors in tax returns, including VAT. Errors in a VAT return up to certain amounts may be corrected in the next return.

2.2.1 Common penalty regime

The common penalty regime for making errors in tax returns discussed earlier in this Text applies for value added tax..

2.2.2 Errors corrected in next return

Errors on a VAT return not exceeding the greater of:

- **£10,000** (net under-declaration minus over-declaration); or
- **1% x net VAT turnover for return period** (maximum £50,000);

may be **corrected on the next return**.

Other errors should be notified to HMRC in writing eg by letter.

In both cases, a penalty for error may be imposed. Correction of an error on a later return is not, of itself, an unprompted disclosure of the error and fuller disclosure is required for the penalty to be reduced.

2.3 Interest on unpaid VAT

Interest (not deductible in computing taxable profits) **is charged on VAT which is the subject of an assessment** (where returns were not made or were incorrect), **or which could have been the subject of an assessment but was paid before the assessment was raised. It runs from the reckonable date until the date of payment.** This interest is sometimes called 'default interest'.

The reckonable date is when the VAT should have been paid (one month from the end of the return period), or in the case of VAT repayments, seven days from the issue of the repayment order. However, where VAT is charged by an assessment, interest does not run from more than three years before the date of the assessment; where the VAT was paid before an assessment was raised, interest does not run for more than three years before the date of payment.

In practice, interest is only charged when there would otherwise be a loss to the Exchequer. It is not, for example, charged when a company failed to charge VAT but if it had done so another company would have been able to recover the VAT.

3 Special schemes

Special schemes include the cash accounting scheme, the annual accounting scheme and the optional flat rate scheme. These schemes can make VAT accounting easier and ease cash flow for certain types of trader.

3.1 The cash accounting scheme

The cash accounting scheme enables businesses to account for VAT on the basis of cash paid and received. That is, the date of payment or receipt determines the return in which the transaction is dealt with. This means that the cash accounting scheme gives automatic impairment loss relief (bad debt relief) because VAT is not due on a supply until payment has been received.

The scheme can only be used by a trader whose annual taxable turnover (exclusive of VAT) does not exceed £1,350,000. A trader can join the scheme only if all returns and VAT payments are up to date (or arrangements have been made to pay outstanding VAT by instalments).

If the value of taxable supplies exceeds £1,600,000 in the 12 months to the end of a VAT period a trader must leave the cash accounting scheme immediately.

Businesses which leave the scheme (either voluntarily or because they have breached the £1,600,000 limit) can account for any outstanding VAT due under the scheme on a cash basis for a further six months.

3.2 The annual accounting scheme

The annual accounting scheme is only available to traders who regularly pay VAT to HMRC, not to traders who normally receive repayments. It is available for traders whose taxable turnover (exclusive of VAT) for the 12 months starting on their application to join the scheme is not expected to exceed £1,350,000.

Under the annual accounting scheme traders file annual VAT returns but throughout the year they must make payments on account of their VAT liability by direct debit. The year for which each return is made may end at the end of any calendar month. Unless HMRC agree otherwise, the trader must pay 90% of the previous year's net VAT liability during the year by means of nine monthly payments commencing at the end of the fourth month of the year. The balance of the year's VAT is then paid with the annual return. There is an option for businesses to pay three larger interim instalments.

Late payment of instalments is not a default for the purposes of the default surcharge.

An annual VAT return must be submitted to HMRC along with any balancing payment due within two months of the end of the year.

It is not possible to use the annual accounting scheme if input tax exceeded output tax in the year prior to application. In addition, all returns must have been made up to date.

If the expected value of a trader's taxable supplies exceeds £1,600,000, notice must be given to HMRC within 30 days and he may then be required to leave the scheme. If the £1,600,000 limit is in fact exceeded, the trader must leave the scheme.

If a trader fails to make the regular payments required by the scheme or the final payment for a year, or has not paid all VAT shown on returns made before joining the scheme, he may be expelled from the scheme. HMRC can also prevent a trader using the scheme 'if they consider it necessary to do so for the protection of the revenue'.

Advantages of annual accounting:

- Only one VAT return each year so fewer occasions to trigger a default surcharge
- Ability to manage cash flow more accurately
- Avoids need for quarterly calculations for input tax recovery

Disadvantages of annual accounting:

- Need to monitor future taxable supplies to ensure turnover limit not exceeded
- Timing of payments have less correlation to turnover (and hence cash received) by business
- Payments based on previous year's turnover may not reflect current year turnover which may be a problem if the scale of activities has reduced

3.3 Flat rate scheme

The optional flat rate scheme enables businesses to calculate VAT due simply by applying a flat rate percentage to their turnover.

Under the scheme, businesses calculate VAT by applying a fixed percentage to their tax inclusive turnover, ie the total turnover, including all reduced rate, zero-rated and exempt income.

The percentage depends upon the trade sector into which a business falls. It ranges from 2% for retailing food, confectionery or newspapers to 13% for legal services (12% while the standard rate is 15%). The percentage for accountancy and book-keeping is 13% (11.5% while the standard rate is 15%).

A 1% reduction off the flat rate % can be made by businesses in their first year of VAT registration.

The flat rate percentage will be given to you in your examination.

Businesses using the scheme must issue VAT invoices to their VAT registered customers but they do not have to record all the details of the invoices issued or purchase invoices received to calculate the VAT due. Invoices issued will show VAT at the normal rate rather than the flat rate.

To join the flat rate scheme businesses must have a tax exclusive annual taxable turnover of up to £150,000.

A business must leave the flat rat scheme if the total value of its tax inclusive supplies in the year (excluding sales of capital assets) is more than £225,000.

3.4 Example: flat rate scheme

An accountant undertakes work for individuals and for business clients. In a VAT year, the business client work amounts to £35,000 and the accountant will issue VAT invoices totalling £41,125 (£35,000 plus VAT at 17.5%). Turnover from work for individuals totals £18,000, including VAT. Total gross sales are therefore £59,125. The flat rate percentage for an accountancy businesses is 13%. Assume that the standard rate of VAT is 17.5% throughout the VAT year.

VAT due to HMRC will be 13% × £59,125 = £7,686.25

Under the normal VAT rules the output tax due would be:

	£
£35,000 × 17.5%	6,125.00
£18,000 × 7/47	2,680.85
	8,805.85

Whether the accountant is better off under the scheme depends on the amount of input tax incurred as this would be offset, under normal rules, from output tax due.

Chapter Roundup

- A taxable person making a taxable supply to another registered person must supply a VAT invoice within 30 days.

- Every VAT registered trader must keep records for six years.

- A default occurs when a trader either submits his VAT return late, or submits the return on time but pays the VAT late. A default surcharge is applied if there is a default during a default surcharge period.

- There is a common penalty regime for errors in tax returns, including VAT. Errors in a VAT return up to certain amounts may be corrected in the next return.

- Special schemes include the cash accounting scheme, the annual accounting scheme and the optional flat rate scheme. These schemes can make VAT accounting easier and ease cash flow for certain types of trader.

Quick Quiz

1   How long must a VAT trader keep records?

2   What is a default?

3   Dylan makes an error in his VAT for the quarter ending 31 March 2010 which results in a net under-declaration of £5,000. His net VAT turnover for the period is £150,000. How can Dylan correct the error?

4   How does the cash accounting scheme operate?

5   The turnover limits for the annual accounting scheme are not exceeding £_____m to join the scheme and once turnover exceeds £_____m the trade must leave the scheme. Fill in the blanks.

6   What is the optional flat rate scheme?

Answers to Quick Quiz

1   A VAT trader must keep records for 6 years.

2   A default occurs when a trader either submits his VAT return late or submits the return on time but pays the VAT late.

3   Dylan can correct the error in his VAT return for the quarter ending 30 June 2010. This is because the error is less than £10,000 and also less than 1% of his net VAT turnover for the return period.

4   The cash accounting scheme operates by a trader accounting for VAT on the basis of cash paid and received (rather than invoices). The date of payment or receipt determines the return in which the transaction is dealt with. The scheme gives automatic impairment loss relief because VAT on a supply is not due until payment is received.

5   The turnover limits for the annual accounting scheme are not exceeding £1.35 m to join the scheme and once turnover exceeds £1.6 m the trade must leave the scheme

6   The optional flat rate scheme enables businesses to calculate VAT simply by applying a percentage to their tax-inclusive turnover. Under the scheme, businesses calculate VAT due by applying a flat rate percentage to their tax inclusive turnover, ie the total turnover generated, including all reduced-rate, zero-rated and exempt income. The percentage depends upon the trade sector in which a business falls.

Now try the questions below from the Exam Question Bank

Number	Level	Marks	Time
Q39	Examination	10	18 mins
Q40	Examination	10	18 mins

Exam question and answer bank

1 Mary and Luke

22 mins

(a) Mary (aged 25) has partnership trading income of £14,500. She also receives building society interest of £6,400 (net), dividends of £1,800 (net), and pays interest of £2,500 each year on a loan to purchase an interest in the partnership.

Required

Calculate how much cash Mary will have available to spend in 2009/10. Ignore national insurance.

(7 marks)

(b) Luke is aged 78. In 2009/10, he has pension income of £20,100 and receives bank interest of £4,000.

Required

Calculate Luke's tax liability for 2009/10.

(5 marks)

(Total = 12 marks)

2 Jane and Chris

13 mins

Jane and Chris Bradbury, both in their 30s, had been married for only two years when Chris was killed in a car accident on 6 October 2009.

Jane and Chris had worked for the same company each earning £13,500 gross per annum. PAYE of £100 per month was deducted.

The couple's other income received in the year to 6 April 2010 was as follows:

	£
Jane	
Building society interest	800
Chris	
Building society interest	2,000

Required

Calculate the couple's tax payable or repayable for 2009/10.

(7 marks)

3 Mr and Mrs Lowrie

27 mins

John Lowrie and Helen Lowrie who are both in their thirties are a married couple. Mr and Mrs Lowrie received the following income in 2009/10.

	Mr Lowrie £	Mrs Lowrie £
Salary (gross)	43,540	20,000
PAYE tax deducted	7,400	2,600
Dividends (amount received)	1,090	2,538
Bank deposit interest (amount received)	600	76
Building society interest (amount received)	592	420

Required

Compute the tax payable by Mr Lowrie and by Mrs Lowrie for 2009/10.

(15 marks)

4 Employment and self-employment

27 mins

Discuss the factors to be taken into consideration when deciding whether a person is employed or self-employed for the purposes of income tax.

(15 marks)

5 Azure plc

27 mins

The following items have been provided by a UK company, Azure plc, to employees earning more than £8,500 a year.

(a) A loan of £16,000 at 1% a year to Mr Andrews on 6 October 2009 which has been used to improve his private residence.

(b) A £1,000 interest free loan to Mrs Preece on 6 April 2009 which was used to finance her daughter's wedding.

(c) The loan of a TV and video system to Mr Charles from 6 June 2009, the asset having cost the company £800 in 2005 and having had a market value of £500 in June 2009.

(d) A long service award in December 2009 to Mrs Davies, the company secretary, comprising a gold wrist watch costing £400. Mrs Davies has been employed by the company since December 1984.

(e) The loan of a petrol engined BMW motor car to Mr Edgar from 6 April 2009. The company had acquired the car new on 1 August 2005 with a list price of £23,000 and its market value in April 2009 was estimated to be £15,000. The car emits CO_2 of 134g/km. The company pays all running costs, including fuel.

(f) The exclusive private use of a company flat in central London, by Mr Ford, the managing director. The company acquired the flat in February 2007 for £100,000 and Mr Ford has used it since that date. The flat is fully furnished at a cost of £5,000 and the council tax paid by the company amounted to £500. The annual value is £900. The running costs of the flat amounting to £1,200 for 2009/10 were paid directly by Mr Ford.

(g) Removal expenses of £9,500 to Miss Jackson in September 2009 who moved from Plymouth to Liverpool to take up a new position in the Liverpool office in July 2009.

(h) The provision of two mobile phones to Mr Long on 6 April 2009 both of which were available for private use as well as business use. Azure Ltd paid £500 in respect of each of the mobile phones of which HMRC have agreed that 70% related to business use.

Required

State in detail how each of the above items would be treated for 2009/10, computing the amount of any taxable benefit.
(15 marks)

6 Gary and George

13 mins

(a) Gary had employment income of £55,000 for 2009/10. He paid £4,000 into his personal pension scheme.

Required

Calculate Gary's income tax payable.
(2 marks)

(b) What would your answer in part (a) be if Gary paid £65,000 (gross) into his personal pension scheme?

(2 marks)

(c) George has regularly made substantial contributions to his personal pension scheme and wishes to put £270,000 (gross) into his personal pension scheme in 2009/10. His employment income will be £320,000 in 2009/10.

Required

Outline the tax implications of this investment.
(3 marks)

(Total = 7 marks)

7 Mr Lee

27 mins

You have received the following e-mail from a client, Mr Lee:

'I have just started a new job and thought that I ought to start making some pension provision now that I am in my mid-30s. My initial salary is £100,000 a year, but I am hoping that, with bonuses, it may increase in the next few years.

My employer operates a pension scheme and I have been given a booklet about it. The booklet says that the scheme is a 'money purchase' scheme. If I join the scheme, my employer will make contributions to the scheme in addition to the amount that I pay into it.

Could you answer the following questions:

(1) Do I have to join my employer's pension scheme or can I make other pension arrangements? What is a 'money purchase' scheme?

(2) If I join my employer's pension scheme, how much can I contribute to the scheme and how much can my employer contribute? The booklet refers to an annual limit and a lifetime limit. How do these work?

(3) I have heard that there is tax relief on my contributions to a pension scheme. How does that work if I join my employer's pension scheme?

Required

Draft an e-mail in response. You are not required to consider the tax restrictions on contributions made by individuals with high incomes. **(15 marks)**

8 Rafe

27 mins

On 1 May 2009, Rafe started to invest in rented properties. He bought three houses in the first three months, as follows.

House 1

Rafe bought house 1 for £62,000 on 1 May 2009. It needed a new roof, and Rafe paid £5,000 for the work to be done in May. He then let it unfurnished for £600 a month from 1 June to 30 November 2009. The first tenant then left, and the house was empty throughout December 2009. On 1 January 2010, a new tenant moved in. The house was again let unfurnished. The rent was £6,000 a year, payable annually in advance.

Rafe paid water rates of £320 for the period from 1 May 2009 to 5 April 2010 and a buildings insurance premium of £480 for the period from 1 June 2009 to 31 May 2010.

House 2

Rafe bought house 2 for £84,000 on 1 June 2009. He immediately bought furniture for £4,300, and let the house fully furnished for £5,000 a year from 1 August 2009. The rent was payable quarterly in arrears. Rafe paid water rates of £240 for the period from 1 June 2009 to 5 April 2010. He claimed the wear and tear allowance for furniture.

House 3

Rafe bought house 3 for £45,000 on 1 July 2009. He spent £1,200 on routine redecoration and £2,300 on furniture in July, and let the house fully furnished from 1 August 2009 for £7,800 a year, payable annually in advance. Rafe paid water rates of £360 for the period from 1 July 2009 to 5 April 2010, a buildings insurance premium of £440 for the period from 1 July 2009 to 30 June 2010 and a contents insurance premium of £180 for the period from 1 August 2009 to 31 July 2010. He claimed the wear and tear allowance for furniture.

During 2009/10 Rafe also rented out one furnished room of his main residence. He received £4,600 and incurred allowable expenses of £875.

Required

Compute Rafe's property business income for 2009/10. **(15 marks)**

9 A Trader

27 mins

A Trader's profit and loss account for the year to 31 March 2010 was as follows.

	£		£
General expenses	73,611	Gross trading profit	246,250
Repairs and renewals	15,000	Impairment losses recovered	
Legal and accountancy charges	1,200	(previously written off)	373
Subscriptions and donations	7,000	Profit on sale of office	5,265
Impairment losses (trade)	500	Building society interest	1,900
Salaries and wages	30,000		
Travel	8,000		
Depreciation	15,000		
Rent and rates	1,500		
Net profit	101,977		
	253,788		253,788

Notes

(1) *General expenses include the following.*

	£
Entertaining staff	1,000
Entertaining suppliers	600

(2) *Repairs and renewals include the following.*

	£
Redecorating existing premises	300
Renovations to new premises to remedy wear and tear of previous owner (the premises were usable before these renovations)	500

(3) *Legal and accountancy charges are made up as follows.*

	£
Debt collection service	200
Staff service agreements	50
Tax consultant's fees for special advice	30
45 year lease on new premises	100
Audit and accountancy	820
	1,200

(4) *Subscriptions and donations include the following.*

	£
Donations under the gift aid scheme	5,200
Donation to a political party	500
Sports facilities for staff	500
Contribution to a local enterprise agency	200

(5) Travel expenses included A Trader's motoring expenses of £2,000. 25% of his use of his car was for private purposes.

(6) Capital allowances amounted to £2,200.

Required

Compute A Trader's taxable trading profits for the accounting period to 31 March 2010. You should start with the net profit of £101,977 and you should indicate by the use of zero (0) any items which do not require adjustment. **(15 marks)**

10 Tom Hardy

27 mins

Tom Hardy makes accounts to 30 June. Despite substantial investment in new equipment, business has been indifferent and he will cease trading on 31 December 2013. His last accounts will be prepared for the six months to 31 December 2013.

The tax written down value of fixed assets at 1 July 2009 was as follows.

	£
Main pool	32,000
Short life asset (acquired 1.5.09)	4,400

Additions and disposals have been as follows.

		£
20.9.09	Plant cost	52,000
15.7.10	Car for own use cost	13,400
14.7.12	Plant sold for	340
10.5.13	Short life asset sold for	2,900

Private use of the car was agreed at 20% for all years. The car emits CO_2 of 125g/km.

At the end of 2013, the plant will be worth £24,000 and the car £10,600.

Required

Calculate the capital allowances for the periods from 1 July 2009 to 31 December 2013, assuming FY09 rates and allowances continue to apply in the future. **(15 marks)**

11 Saruman

18 mins

Saruman is the sole proprietor of a small engineering business. He prepares accounts annually to 5 April and has been in business since 6 April 2002.

(a)   Main pool brought forward on 6 April 2009   £52,000

Tax written down value of motor car for Saruman's use on 6 April 2009   £600

Private use of this car has been agreed with HMRC at 25%.

The following events occurred during the year ended 5 April 2010.

Disposals:	20 April 2009	–	Plant £12,000 (original cost £10,000)
	21 May 2009	–	Motor car for Saruman's own use £920 (original cost £1,896)
	20 June 2009	–	Plant £800 (original cost £3,000)
Additions:	21 May 2009	–	New car for Saruman's use £19,000 CO_2 emissions 170 g/km
	1 October 2009	–	Car for use by sales representative £4,800 CO_2 emissions 120 g/km

(b)   A new small factory was bought from a builder for a total cost of £40,000, including land £10,000 and office accommodation £3,000. The factory was brought into use in the trade immediately.

Required

Calculate Saruman's capital allowances for the year ended 5 April 2010. **(10 marks)**

12 Mr Cobbler

27 mins

Mr Cobbler starts a business as a sole trader on 1 January 2010.

His business plan shows that his monthly profits are likely to be as follows.

January 2010 to June 2010 (inclusive)	£800	a month
July 2010 to December 2010 (inclusive)	£1,200	a month
Thereafter	£2,000	a month

Mr Cobbler is considering two alternative accounting dates, 31 March and 30 April, in each case commencing with a period ending in 2010.

Required

Show the taxable trading profits which will arise for each of the first four tax years under each of the two alternative accounting dates, and recommend an accounting date. **(15 marks)**

13 Miss Farrington

27 mins

Miss Farrington started to trade as a baker on 1 January 2010 and made up her first accounts to 30 April 2011. Adjusted profits before capital allowances are as follows.

	£
Period to 30 April 2011	84,256
Year to 30 April 2012	25,497

Miss Farrington incurred the following expenditure on plant and machinery.

Date	Item	£
4.1.10	General plant	22,280
1.3.10	Second-hand oven acquired from Miss Farrington's father	11,200
25.3.10	Delivery van	11,800
15.4.10	General plant	21,000
15.5.10	Car for Miss Farrington	6,600
30.1.12	General plant	10,000
30.4.12	Mixer	1,200

In addition Miss Farrington brought into the business on 1 January 2010 a desk and other office furniture. The agreed value was £1,500.

The agreed private use of the car is 35%. The car has CO_2 emissions of 123g/km.

Required

Calculate the taxable profits for the first four tax years and the overlap profits carried forward. Assume that the capital allowances rules and rates applicable in 2009/10 apply in later years apart from the temporary FYA. **(15 marks)**

14 Langland

27 mins

Langland started to trade on 1 February 2005 and decided to retire on 31 October 2010. His accounts show the following profits as adjusted for income tax purposes.

	£
P/e 30 April 2006	12,000
Y/e 30 April 2007	6,000
Y/e 30 April 2008	8,000
Y/e 30 April 2009	10,000
Y/e 30 April 2010	6,000
P/e 31 October 2010	4,000

Required

Calculate the trading assessments for all tax years in question. **(15 marks)**

15 Morgan   27 mins

Morgan started to trade on 6 April 2005. His business has the following results.

Year ending 5 April		£
2006	Profit	6,000
2007	Profit	8,000
2008	Profit	10,000
2009	Profit	14,000
2010 (projected)	Loss	(32,000)

It is expected that the business will show healthy profits thereafter. In addition to his business Morgan has gross savings income of £6,000 a year.

Required

(a)   Outline how Morgan could obtain relief for his loss.   **(10 marks)**

(b)   Prepare a statement showing the best way for the loss to be relieved. Assume that the personal allowance and the rates of income tax applicable in 2009/10 apply in all years.   **(5 marks)**

(Total = 15 marks)

16 Adam, Bert and Charlie   27 mins

Adam, Bert and Charlie started in partnership as secondhand car dealers on 6 April 2006, sharing profits in the ratio 2:2:1, after charging annual salaries of £15,000, £12,000 and £10,000 respectively.

On 5 July 2007 Adam retired and Bert and Charlie continue, taking the same salaries as before, but dividing the balance of the profits in the ratio 3:2.

On 6 May 2009 Donald is admitted as a partner on the terms that he received a salary of £18,000 a year, that the salaries of Bert and Charlie should be increased to £18,000 a year each and that of the balance of the profits, Donald should take one tenth, Bert six tenths and Charlie three tenths.

The trade profits of the partnership as adjusted for tax purposes are as follows.

Year ending 5 April	Profits £
2007	102,000
2008	208,000
2009	126,000
2010	180,000

Required

Show the taxable trade profits for each partner for 2006/07 to 2009/10 inclusive.   **(15 marks)**

17 Partnerships

27 mins

(a) *Required*

Briefly explain the basis by which partners are assessed in respect of their share of a partnership's taxable trading profit. **(3 marks)**

(b) Anne and Betty have been in partnership since 1 January 2003 sharing profits equally. On 30 June 2009 Betty resigned as a partner, and was replaced on 1 July 2009 by Chloe. Profit continued to be shared equally. The partnership's taxable trading profits are as follows:

	£
Year ended 31 December 2009	60,000
Year ended 31 December 2010	72,000

As at 6 April 2009 Anne and Betty each have unrelieved overlap profits of £3,000.

Required

Calculate the taxable trading profits of Anne, Betty and Chloe for 2009/10. **(6 marks)**

(c) Daniel and Edward have been in partnership since 6 April 2001, making up accounts to 5 April. On 31 December 2009 Edward resigned as a partner, and was replaced on 1 January 2009 by Frank. For 2009/10 the partnership made a trading loss of £40,000, and this has been allocated between the partners as follows.

	£
Daniel	20,000
Edward	15,000
Frank	5,000

Each of the partners has investment income. None of them have any capital gains.

Required

State the possible ways in which Daniel, Edward and Frank can relieve their trading losses for 2009/10. **(6 marks)**

(Total = 15 marks)

18 Denise

18 mins

Denise started business on 6 April 2009 as a designer dressmaker. Her trading profits in her first year of trading were £115,000.

Required

(a) Outline briefly what payments Denise could make into a personal pension scheme and the tax relief such payments would receive. You are not required to consider the restriction on pension contributions for individuals with income of £150,000 but you should outline the restrictions of the annual allowance and the lifetime allowance. **(7 marks)**

(b) Show the Class 2 and Class 4 contributions payable by Denise in 2009/10. **(3 marks)**

Assume 2009/10 tax rates and allowances apply throughout.

(Total = 10 marks)

19 Sasha Shah

27 mins

Sasha Shah is a computer programmer. Until 5 April 2009 she was employed by Net Computers plc, but since then has worked independently from home. Sasha's income for the year ended 5 April 2010 is £60,000. All of this relates to work done for Net Computers plc. Her expenditure for the year ended 5 April 2010 is as follows:

(1)   The business proportion of light, heat and telephone for Sasha's home is £800.

(2)   Computer equipment was purchased on 6 April 2009 for £4,000.

(3)   A motor car was purchased on 6 April 2009 for £10,000 with CO_2 of 150g/km. Motor expenses for the year ended 5 April 2010 amount to £3,500, of which 40% relate to journeys between home and the premises of Net Computers plc. The other 60% relate to private mileage.

Required

(a)   List eight factors that will indicate that a worker should be treated as an employee rather than as self-employed.   **(4 marks)**

(b)   (i)   Calculate the amount of taxable trading profits if Sasha is treated as self-employed during 2009/10.

        (ii)   Calculate the amount of Sasha's taxable earnings if she is treated as an employee during 2009/10.   **(7 marks)**

(c)   (i)   Calculate Sasha's liability to Class 2 and Class 4 NIC if she is treated as self-employed during 2009/10.

        (ii)   Calculate Sasha's liability to Class 1 NIC if she is treated as an employee during 2009/10.   **(4 marks)**

(Total = 15 marks)

20 Peter Robinson

13 mins

Peter Robinson made the following disposals of assets during the tax year 2009/10.

30 April 2009

Investment property for £150,000 less costs of disposal £1,280. Acquired for £79,500.

27 June 2009

Part of a plot of land. The proceeds of sale were £35,000. The costs of disposal were £700. The original cost of the land was £54,000. The remainder of the land is worth £70,000.

1 September 2009

A vase which was destroyed. It cost £12,000. Compensation of £20,000 was received on 30 September 2009. Peter bought a new vase as a replacement for £17,000 on 21 December 2009.

Required

Calculate Peter's capital gains tax payable for the year 2009/10.   **(7 marks)**

21 John Harley

18 mins

(a) John Harley purchased a property in England on 1 August 1987 for £40,000 and lived in it until 31 May 1988 when he moved overseas to take up an offer of employment. He returned to the UK on 1 August 1992 and took employment in Scotland until 31 October 1998. During these periods he lived in rented accommodation. On 1 November 1998 he moved back into his own house until he moved out permanently on 30 June 2001. The house was then put up for sale and was finally sold on 30 November 2009 for £120,000. At all times when John was not in the house it remained empty.

Required

Prepare a schedule of periods of exemption and non-exemption, together with the reasons where applicable. **(5 marks)**

(b) Elsie Phillips made the following disposals of assets during the tax year 2009/10.

2 June 2009

An oil painting for £5,000 (net of £400 commission). She had purchased this at a cost of £11,500.

1 February 2010

A crystal chandelier for £7,500. She had purchased this for £4,000.

Required

Calculate Elsie's chargeable gains or allowable losses on these two transactions. **(5 marks)**

(Total = 10 marks)

22 The White family

25 mins

(a) Mr White is a sole trader. He bought a factory for use in his trade on 10 July 2005 for £150,000.

On 1 December 2009, Mr White gave the factory to his son, Gary. The market value of the factory at that time was £260,000.

Required

Show the chargeable gains (if any) for Mr White for 2009/10 assuming that any claims to defer gains are made. **(3 marks)**

(b) Gary sells the factory to a developer on 1 March 2010 for £320,000.

Required

Compute the chargeable gain on the sale for Gary. **(2 marks)**

(c) Mrs White is also a sole trader. She acquired a freehold shop for use in the business in May 2003 for £40,000 and sold it in August 2009 for £80,000.

Mrs White is considering buying a new shop. She has located two possible shops. One is a small freehold shop which would cost £72,000. The other is a larger leasehold shop with a lease of 55 years. The cost of the lease would be £90,000.

Required

Explain the tax consequences of acquiring each of the shops. **(9 marks)**

(Total = 14 marks)

23 Alice
9 mins

Alice decided to incorporate her sole trader business on 9 January 2010. She started this business in 1992. All of the business assets were transferred to the new company. The consideration consisted of 200,000 £1 ordinary shares valued at £200,000 and £100,000 in cash. The transfer of the business assets resulted in total gains of £120,000.

Required

Calculate the gain arising on the transfer before any claim for entrepreneurs' relief and the base cost of the shares for the future.

(5 marks)

24 Kai
13 mins

Kai started in business as a sole trader in August 2004. He acquired a freehold shop for £80,000 and a warehouse for £150,000.

Kai sold his business as a going concern to Jibran in December 2009 and received £50,000 for goodwill, £90,000 for the shop and £130,000 for the warehouse.

Other than those listed above, Kai had never undertaken any transactions which were relevant for capital gains purposes.

Required

Compute the capital gains tax payable by Kai on his disposal. **(7 marks)**

25 Melissa
18 mins

Melissa bought shares in Fisher plc as follows:

12 July 2001	6,000 shares for £21,000
14 December 2006	2,000 shares for £6,500
11 July 2009	4,000 shares for £16,000

She sold 10,000 shares for £42,000 on 2 July 2009.

Required
Compute Melissa's gain on sale. **(10 marks)**

26 Tim
15 mins

Tim is a medical consultant. His total tax liability for 2008/09 was £16,800. Of this £7,200 was paid under the PAYE system, £800 was withheld at source from bank interest and £200 was suffered on dividends received during the year.

Tim's total tax liability for 2009/10 was £22,000. £7,100 of this was paid under PAYE system, £900 was withheld at source from bank interest and there was a £250 tax credit on dividends.

Tim did not make any claim in respect of his payments on account for 2009/10. HM Revenue and Customs issued a 2009/10 tax return to Tim on 5 May 2010.

Required

State what payments Tim was required to make in respect of his 2009/10 tax liability and the due dates for the payment of these amounts. **(8 marks)**

27 Lai Chan   45 mins

Until 31 December 2009 Lai Chan was employed by Put-it-Right plc as a management consultant. The following information relates to the period of employment from 6 April to 31 December 2009.

(1)   Lai was paid a gross salary of £3,250 per month.

(2)   She contributed 6% of her gross salary into Put-it-right plc's registered occupational pension scheme. The company contributed a further 6%.

(3)   Put-it-Right plc provided Lai with a motor car with a list price of £26,400. The motor car's CO_2 emissions were 185g/km. Lai paid Put-it-Right plc £130 per month for the use of the motor car.

Put-it-Right plc paid for the petrol in respect of all the mileage done by Lai during 2009/10. She paid the company £30 per month towards the cost of her private petrol.

The motor car was returned to Put-it-Right plc on 31 December 2009.

(4)   Put-it-Right plc provided Lai with an interest free loan of £30,000 on 1 January 2006. She repaid £20,000 of the loan on 30 June 2009 with the balance of £10,000 being repaid on 31 December 2009.

On 1 January 2010 Lai commenced in self-employment running a music recording studio. The following information relates to the period of self-employment from 1 January to 5 April 2010.

(1)   The trading profit for the period 1 January to 5 April 2010 is £32,000. This figure is *before* taking account of capital allowances.

(2)   Lai purchased the following assets:

1 January 2010	Recording equipment	£10,000
15 January 2010	Motor car CO_2 emissions 175g/km	£18,800
20 February 2010	Motor car CO_2 emissions 145g/km	£10,400
4 March 2010	Mixing desk	£4,000

The motor car purchased on 15 January 2010 is used by Lai, and 40% of the mileage is for private purposes. The motor car purchased on 20 February 2010 is used by an employee, and 10% of the mileage is for private purposes.

The mixing desk purchased on 4 March 2010 is to be treated as a short-life asset.

(3)   Since becoming self-employed Lai has paid £400 (net) per month into a personal pension scheme. Payments are made on the 20th of each month.

Required

(a)   Calculate Lai's income tax liability for 2009/10.   **(20 marks)**

(b)   Briefly explain how Lai's income tax liability for 2009/10 will be paid to the HM Revenue and Customs.   **(5 marks)**

(Total = 25 marks)

28 P Ltd
18 mins

P Ltd starts to let out property on 1 July 2009. The company has the following transactions.

(a) On 1 July 2009, it lets an office block which it has owned for several years. The tenant is required to pay an initial premium of £20,000 for a 30 year lease, and then to pay annual rent of £4,000, quarterly in advance. The office is let unfurnished.

(b) On 1 October 2009 it buys a badly dilapidated office block for £37,000. During October, it spends £8,000 on making the office block useable. It lets it for £600 a month from 1 November 2009, but the tenant leaves on 31 January 2010. A new tenant moves in on 1 March 2010, paying £2,100 a quarter in arrears. Water rates are £390 a year, payable by P Ltd. P Ltd also pays buildings insurance of £440 for the period from 1 October 2009 to 31 August 2010. P Ltd financed the purchase (but not the repairs) with a bank loan at 7% interest. This office is also let unfurnished.

Required

Compute P Ltd's property business income for the year to 31 March 2010. **(10 marks)**

29 Tree Ltd
27 mins

(a) Tree Ltd, a company with no associated companies, had the following results for the twelve months to 31 March 2010:

	£
Trading profits	180,000
Chargeable gain	105,000
Gift aid donation	27,000
Bank interest	36,000
Dividend received	29,700

The bank interest accrued evenly over the period.

Required

Compute the corporation tax liability in respect of the profits arising in the twelve months to 31 March 2010. **(7 marks)**

(b) Dealers plc had profits chargeable to corporation tax of £420,000 for its six month accounting period ended 31 March 2010. No dividends were received by the company during the year.

Required

Compute Dealers plc's corporation tax liability for the period. **(3 marks)**

(c) Springer Ltd had profits chargeable to corporation tax of £600,000 in the year to 31 December 2008. It received a dividend of £27,000 on 1 September 2008.

Required

Calculate Springer Ltd's corporation tax liability for the year. **(5 marks)**

(Total = 15 marks)

30 Righteous plc

18 mins

Righteous plc used to make its accounts up to 31 December. A decision has been made to change its year end to 31 May. The following information relates to the period of account from 1 January 2008 to 31 May 2009.

	£
Trading profits	500,000
Bank interest receivable	
30.6.08	15,000
31.12.08	6,000
31.5.09	2,500
Capital gain on property sold on	
1 May 2009	5,000
Gift Aid donations paid	
28.2.08	15,000
31.8.08	15,000
28.2.09	40,000

No capital allowances are claimed.

Required

Calculate the corporation tax liability.

(10 marks)

31 E Ltd

9 mins

E Ltd disposed of assets as follows.

(a) On 1 January 2009 it sold a car which had been used by a company director at a loss of £10,700.
(b) On 28 February 2009 it sold some shares at a loss of £16,400.
(c) On 1 May 2009 it sold some shares and realised a gain of £17,700.
(d) On 1 October 2009 it sold some shares at a loss of £6,000.
(e) On 1 December 2009 it sold a picture to a collector for £50,000, making a gain of £3,000.

Required

What loss, if any, is available to be carried forward at the end of its year ended 31 March 2010? **(5 marks)**

32 Hardup Ltd

27 mins

Hardup Ltd made the following disposals in the year ended 31 March 2010.

(a) On 31 May 2009 it sold an office block for £120,000. The company had bought the offices for £65,000 on 1 July 1992. The company had invested £100,000 in another office block on 1 May 2008.

(b) On 18 June 2009 it sold a plot of land for £69,000. It had bought it for £20,000 on 1 April 1985 and had spent £4,000 on defending its title to the land in July 1989.

(c) On 25 June 2009 the company exchanged contracts for the sale of a workshop for £173,000. Completion took place on 24 July 2009. It had bought the workshop for £65,000 on 16 October 1987.

Required

Compute Hardup Ltd's chargeable gains for the year end 31 March 2010.

(15 marks)

Assume retail prices index

May 2009 = 210.3	July 1992 = 138.8
June 2009 = 209.8	July 1989 = 115.5
July 2009 = 209.3	October 1987 = 102.9
	April 1985 = 94.78

33 Ferraro Ltd

27 mins

Ferraro Ltd has the following results.

	y/e 31.12.05 £	y/e 31.12.06 £	y/e 31.12.07 £	9m to 30.9.08 £	y/e 30.9.09 £
Trading profit (loss)	10,600	34,480	6,200	4,320	(100,000)
Bank deposit interest accrued	100	200	80	240	260
Rents receivable	1,300	1,200	1,420	1,440	1,600
Capital gain				12,680	
Allowable capital loss		(5,000)			(9,423)
Gift aid donation paid (gross)	1,000	1,000	0	1,000	1,500

Required

Compute all profits chargeable to corporation tax, claiming loss reliefs as early as possible. State any amounts carried forward as at 30 September 2009. **(15 marks)**

34 P Ltd

27 mins

P Ltd owns the following holdings in ordinary shares in other companies, which are all UK resident.

Q Ltd   83%
R Ltd   77%
S Ltd   67%
M Ltd   80%
T Ltd   70%

In each case, the conditions for claiming group relief, where appropriate, are satisfied.

The following are the results of the above companies for the year ended 31 March 2010.

	M Ltd £	P Ltd £	Q Ltd £	R Ltd £	S Ltd £	T Ltd £
Income						
Trading profit	20,000	0	64,000	260,000	0	70,000
Trading loss	0	226,000	0	0	8,000	0
Property business income	0	6,000	4,000	0	0	0
Gift aid donation paid	4,000	4,500	2,000	5,000	0	0

Required

(a) Compute the corporation tax payable for the above accounting period by each of the above companies, assuming group relief is claimed, where appropriate, in the most efficient manner.

(b) Advise the board of P Ltd of the advantages of increasing its holding in S Ltd, a company likely to sustain trading losses for the next two years before becoming profitable. P Ltd itself is likely only to break even in the next few years.

(15 marks)

35 Apple Ltd

27 mins

Apple Ltd owns 100% of the ordinary share capital of Banana Ltd and Cherry Ltd. The results of each company for the year ended 31 March 2010 are as follows:

	Apple Ltd £	Banana Ltd £	Cherry Ltd £
Tax adjusted trading profit/(loss)	(125,000)	650,000	130,000
Capital gain/(loss)	188,000	(8,000)	–

Apple Ltd's capital gain arose from the sale of a freehold warehouse on 15 April 2009 for £418,000. Cherry Ltd purchased a freehold office building for £290,000 on 10 January 2010.

Required

(a) Explain the group relationship that must exist in order that group relief can be claimed. **(3 marks)**

(b) Explain how group relief should be allocated between the respective claimant companies in order to maximise the potential benefit obtained from the relief. **(4 marks)**

(c) Assuming that reliefs are claimed in the most favourable manner, calculate the corporation tax liabilities of Apple Ltd, Banana Ltd and Cherry Ltd for the year ended 31 March 2010. **(8 marks)**

(Total = 15 marks)

36 M Ltd

18 mins

M Ltd is a UK resident company which owns controlling interests in four other UK resident companies and has three overseas branches.

In the year to 31 March 2010 the branches had the following results:

Branch	After tax profits	Foreign tax paid
	£	£
A	170,000	30,000
B	150,000	50,000
C	120,000	67,500

M Ltd had experienced a prolonged period of poor trading and, as a result of losses brought forward from earlier years, its chargeable trading profits for the year ended 31 March 2010 are only £20,000.

During the year, a gift aid donation of £75,000 had been paid to charity and this had been added back in arriving at the adjusted taxable trading profits.

Required

Compute the corporation tax payable by M Ltd in respect of the year ended 31 March 2010. Your answer should show clearly your treatment of the gift aid payment and of the foreign taxes suffered. You should explain why you are dealing with items in a particular way and you should use a columnar layout.

(10 marks)

37 Hogg Ltd
9 mins

(a)   Hogg Ltd prepares accounts for the year to 31 March 2010. Its profits chargeable to corporation tax for the year will be £1,750,000. The company has always paid corporation tax at the full rate.

Required

State the amounts and due dates for the payment of corporation tax by Hogg Ltd in respect of the year to 31 March 2010.   **(3 marks)**

(b)   State the due date for submission of Hogg Ltd's corporation tax return assuming a notice to file the return is issued on:

(i)   12 April 2010

(ii)   12 February 2011   **(2 marks)**

(Total = 5 marks)

38 Newcomer Ltd and Au Revoir Ltd
18 mins

(a)   Newcomer Ltd commenced trading on 1 October 2009. Its forecast sales are as follows.

		£
2009	October	11,500
	November	15,200
	December	22,400
2010	January	19,300
	February	15,700
	March	1,200

The company's sales are all standard rated, and the above figures are exclusive of VAT.

Required

Explain when Newcomer Ltd will be required to compulsorily register for VAT.   **(6 marks)**

(b)   Au Revoir Ltd has been registered for VAT since 1996, and its sales are all standard rated. The company has recently seen a downturn in its business activities, and sales for the years ended 31 October 2009 and 2010 are forecast to be £64,000 and £60,500 respectively. Both of these figures are exclusive of VAT.

Required

Explain why Au Revoir Ltd will be permitted to voluntarily deregister for VAT, and from what date deregistration will be effective.   **(4 marks)**

(Total = 10 marks)

39 Justin

18 mins

Justin has the following transactions in the quarter ended 31 March 2010. All amounts exclude any VAT unless otherwise stated.

	£
Purchases (all standard rated)	
Furniture for resale	275,000
Computer for use in the business	2,400
Restaurant bills: entertaining customers	1,900
Petrol for cars owned by Justin and used only by his employees	2,800
Sales	
Furniture (standard rated)	490,000
Books on interior design (zero rated)	2,400

Only one employee's car has petrol for private motoring provided by Justin (the appropriate fuel scale charge is £428 inclusive of VAT).

Required

Calculate the amount of VAT which Justin must pay to HM Revenue and Customs for the quarter.

(10 marks)

40 Ongoing Ltd

18 mins

Ongoing Ltd is registered for VAT, and its sales and purchases are all standard rated. The following information relates to the company's VAT return for the quarter ended 30 September 2009:

(1)   Standard rated sales amounted to £120,000. Ongoing Ltd offers its customers a 5% discount for prompt payment, and this discount is taken by half of the customers.

(2)   Standard rated purchases and expenses amounted to £35,640. This figure includes £480 for entertaining customers.

(3)   On 15 September 2009 the company wrote off impairment losses (bad debts) of £2,100 and £840 in respect of invoices due for payment on 10 February and 5 May 2009 respectively.

(4)   On 30 September 2009 the company purchased a motor car at a cost of £16,450 for the use of a salesperson, and machinery at a cost of £21,150. Both these figures are inclusive of VAT. The motor car is used for both business and private mileage.

Unless stated otherwise, all of the above figures are exclusive of VAT. Ongoing Ltd does not operate the cash accounting scheme.

Required

Calculate the amount of VAT payable by Ongoing Ltd for the quarter ended 30 September 2009.

(10 marks)

41 Industrial Ltd

54 mins

Industrial Ltd is a UK resident company that manufactures furniture. The company's results for the year ended 31 March 2010 are summarised as follows:

	£
Trading profit (as adjusted for taxation but before taking account of capital allowances)	1,710,000
Income from property (note 1)	110,400
Bank interest received (note 2)	12,500
Loan interest received (note 3)	36,000
Profit on disposal of quoted shares (note 4)	90,622
Donation to charity (note 5)	(1,500)

Note 1 – Income from property

Since 1 January 2010 Industrial Ltd has leased an office building that is surplus to requirements. On that date the company received a premium of £80,000 for the grant of a ten-year lease, and the annual rent of £30,400 which is payable in advance.

Note 2 – Bank interest received

The bank interest was received on 31 March 2010. The bank deposits are held for non-trading purposes. There were no accruals of bank interest at the beginning or end of the year.

Note 3 – Loan interest received

The loan interest was received on 31 March 2010. The loan was made for non-trading purposes to another UK company. There were no accruals of loan interest at the beginning or end of the year.

Note 4 – Profit on disposal of quoted shares

The profit on disposal of quoted shares is in respect of a shareholding that was sold on 15 January 2010 for £224,203. The shareholding was purchased on 1 April 2004 for £135,800. The indexation allowance from April 2004 to January 2010 is £15,481.

At 1 April 2009 Industrial Ltd had unused capital losses brought forward of £10,800.

Note 5 – Donation to charity

The donation to charity was the amount paid under the gift aid scheme.

Note 6 – Industrial building

Industrial Ltd has a new factory constructed at a cost of £600,000 that was brought into use on 30 September 2009.

	£
Land	130,000
Levelling the land	13,800
Architects fees	36,450
Heating system	12,800
Fire alarm system	7,200
Strengthened concrete floor to support machinery	24,750
General offices	93,750
Factory	281,250
	600,000

Note 7 – Plant and machinery

On 1 April 2009 the tax written down values of plant and machinery were as follows:

	£
Main pool	84,600
Expensive motor car	15,400

The expensive motor car was sold on 31 August 2009 for £19,600.

In addition to any items of plant and machinery included in the cost of the industrial building (see note 6), the following assets were purchased during the year ended 31 March 2010.

		£
15 June 2009	Machinery	3,400
15 August 2009	Motor car (CO_2 emissions 170g/km)	17,200
12 October 2009	Lorry	32,000
10 December 2009	General plant	27,000

Note 8 – Other information

Industrial Ltd has no associated companies. For the year ended 31 March 2009 Industrial Ltd had profits chargeable to corporation tax of £1,650,000.

Required

(a)   Calculate the corporation tax payable by Industrial Ltd for the year ended 31 March 2010.

(25 marks)

(b)   (i)   Explain why Industrial Ltd is required to make quarterly instalment payments in respect of its corporation tax liability for the year ended 31 March 2010.   **(2 marks)**

(ii)   State the relevant due dates for payment of the corporation tax liability.   **(3 marks)**

(Total = 30 marks)

Approaching the answer

You should read through the requirement before working through and annotating the question as we have so that you know what you are looking for.

Industrial Ltd is a UK resident company that manufactures furniture. The company's results for the year

ALL in FY 09

ended 31 March 2010 are summarised as follows:

	£
Trading profit (as adjusted for taxation but before taking account of capital allowances)	1,710,000
Income from property (note 1)	110,400
Bank interest received (note 2)	12,500
Loan interest received (note 3)	36,000
Profit on disposal of quoted shares (note 4)	90,622
Donation to charity (note 5)	(1,500)

Note 1 – Income from property

Since 1 January 2010 Industrial Ltd has leased an office building that is surplus to requirements. On that

date the company received a premium of £80,000 for the grant of a ten-year lease, and the annual rent of

Prorate × 3/12

£30,400 which is payable in advance.

Property income charge on short leases

Note 2 – Bank interest received

The bank interest was received on 31 March 2010. The bank deposits are held for non-trading purposes.

There were no accruals of bank interest at the beginning or end of the year.

Investment income received

Note 3 – Loan interest received

Received gross

The loan interest was received on 31 March 2010. The loan was made for non-trading purposes to another UK company. There were no accruals of loan interest at the beginning or end of the year.

Also investment income

Note 4 – Profit on disposal of quoted shares

The profit on disposal of quoted shares is in respect of a 2% shareholding that was sold on 15 January 2010 for £224,203. The shareholding was purchased on 1 April 2004 for £135,800. The indexation allowance from April 2004 to January 2010 is £28,404.

Set off capital loss b/f against gain

At 1 April 2009 Industrial Ltd had unused capital losses brought forward of £10,800.

Note 5 – Donation to charity

Deduction

The donation to charity was the amount paid under the gift aid scheme.

Note 6 – Industrial building

Industrial Ltd has a new factory constructed at a cost of £600,000 that was brought into use on 30 September 2009.

	£
Land	130,000
Levelling the land	13,800
Architects fees	36,450
Heating system	12,800
Fire alarm system	7,200
Strengthened concrete floor to support machinery	24,750
General offices	93,750
Factory	281,250
	600,000

Not eligible for IBAs

Plant and machinery items

Is it less that 25% total – if so allow for IBAs

Note 7 – Plant and machinery

On 1 April 2009 the tax written down values of plant and machinery were as follows:

	£
Main pool	84,600
Expensive motor car	15,400

The expensive motor car was sold on 31 August 2009 for £19,600

Balancing charge

In addition to any items of plant and machinery included in the cost of the industrial building (see note 6), the following assets were purchased during the year ended 31 March 2010.

AIA available

		£
15 June 2009	Machinery	3,400
15 August 2009	Motor car (CO$_2$ emissions 170g/km)	17,200
12 October 2009	Lorry	32,000
10 December 2009	General plant	27,000

Note 8 – Other information

Industrial Ltd has no associated companies. For the year ended 31 March 2009 Industrial Ltd had profits chargeable to corporation tax of £1,650,000.

> Paid CT at full rate

Required

(a)   Calculate the corporation tax payable by Industrial Ltd for the year ended 31 March 2010.

(25 marks)

(b)   (i)   Explain why Industrial Ltd is required to make quarterly instalment payments in respect of its corporation tax liability for the year ended 31 March 2010. (2 marks)

(ii)   State the relevant due dates for payment of the corporation tax liability. (3 marks)

> Instalment dates

(Total = 30 marks)

42 Carolyn Kraft   45 mins

Carolyn Kraft is aged 34. She is employed as a buyer for a large retail group of companies. She is married to Mike.

In the tax year 2009/10, Carolyn was paid a salary of £36,000 (PAYE £5,900). Carolyn also received bank interest of £8,000 in 2009/10. On 14 November 2009 Carolyn made a one off donation under Gift Aid to Cancer Research UK of £800.

Mike undertakes a business from home. His accounts for the year ended 31 December 2009 show an adjusted profit of £56,500. He is also entitled to capital allowances of £1,600. Mike had owned a freehold shop which he had used in his business. He had acquired the shop on 10 April 2008 for £53,300 and sold it for £85,000 in August 2009. He is considering acquiring another shop to replace this one.

Mike also received dividends of £9,000 in 2009/10 and makes a contribution of £200 each month to his personal pension.

Carolyn bought a flat in August 2007 for £180,000. Carolyn arranged for renovation work to be undertaken, which cost £30,000 in January 2009. Carolyn sold the flat for £250,000 in December 2009. The flat was unoccupied between the date of purchase and the date of sale.

Required

(a)   Calculate both Carolyn and Mike's income tax due for 2009/10 and state when it is due. (11 marks)

(b)   Calculate the amount of national insurance contributions payable by both Carolyn and Mike for 2009/10. (4 marks)

(c)   Calculate Carolyn's and Mike's 2009/10 capital gains tax liability stating the due date. Assume Mike does not acquire another shop. (7 marks)

(d)   Briefly explain the relief available to Mike if he does acquire another shop. (3 marks)

(Total = 25 marks)

Approaching the answer

You should read through the requirement before working through and annotating the question as we have so that you know what you are looking for.

Carolyn Kraft is aged 34. She is `employed` as a buyer for a large retail group of companies. She is married to Mike.

In the tax year 2009/10, Carolyn was paid a salary of £36,000 (PAYE £5,900). Carolyn also received bank interest of £8,000 in 2009/10. On 14 November 2009 Carolyn made a one off `donation` `under Gift Aid` to Cancer Research UK of £800.

> **Extends basic rate band**

Mike undertakes a `business from home`. His accounts for the year ended 31 December 2009 show an adjusted profit of £56,500. He is also entitled to capital allowances of £1,600. Mike had owned a freehold shop which he had used in his business. He had acquired the shop on 10 April 2008 for £53,300 and sold it for £85,000 in August 2009. He is considering `acquiring another shop` to replace this one.

> **Self employment**

> **Looks like rollover relief**

Mike also received dividends of £9,000 in 2009/10 and makes a contribution of £200 each month to his `personal pension`.

> **Extends basic rate band**

Carolyn bought a flat in August 2007 for £180,000. Carolyn arranged for `renovation work` to be undertaken, which cost £30,000 in January 2009. Carolyn `sold the flat` for £250,000 in December 2009. The `flat was unoccupied` between the date of purchase and the date of sale.

> **Enhancement expenditure**

> **CGT**

> **No PPR**

Required

> **Easy marks**

(a)   Calculate both Carolyn and Mike's income tax due for 2009/10 and `state when it is due`. **(11 marks)**

(b)   Calculate the amount of national insurance contributions payable by both Carolyn and Mike for 2009/10. **(4 marks)**

(c)   Calculate Carolyn's and Mike's 2009/10 capital gains tax liability `stating the due date`. Assume Mike does not acquire another shop. **(8 marks)**

> **Easy marks**

(d)   `Briefly` explain the relief available to Mike if he does acquire another shop. **(2 marks)**

(Total = 25 marks)

> **Follow instructions**

Exam question and answer bank **341**

1 Mary and Luke

(a)   *Mary 2009/10*

	Non-savings income £	Savings income £	Dividend income £	Total £
Trading income	14,500			
Building society interest × 100/80		8,000		
Dividends × 100/90			2,000	
Total income	14,500	8,000	2,000	
Less interest paid	(2,500)	0	0	
Net income	12,000	8,000	2,000	22,000
Less personal allowance	(6,475)	0	0	
Taxable income	5,525	8,000	2,000	15,525

	£
Non-savings income	
£5,525 × 20%	1,105
Savings income	
£8,000 × 20%	1,600
Dividend income	
£2,000 × 10%	200
	2,905
Less tax credit on dividend income	(200)
tax suffered on building society interest	(1,600)
Balance of tax still to pay	1,105

	£	£
Profits received		14,500
Building society interest received		6,400
Dividend received		1,800
		22,700
Less interest paid on loan	2,500	
income tax to pay	1,105	
		(3,605)
Available to spend		19,095

(b)   *Luke 2009/10*

	Non-savings income £	Savings income £	Total £
Pension income	20,100		
Bank interest × 100/80		5,000	
Net income	20,100	5,000	25,100
Less: age allowance (W)	(8,540)		
Taxable income	11,560	5,000	16,560

	£
Non-savings income	
£11,560 × 20%	2,312
Savings income	
£5,000 × 20%	1,000
Tax liability	3,312

Working

	£
Net income	25,100
Less income limit	(22,900)
Excess	2,200
Age allowance (75+)	9,640
Less half excess £2,200 × ½	(1,100)
Revised age allowance	8,540

2 Jane and Chris

> **Tutorial note.** Remember that building society interest is received net of 20% tax. This tax credit is repayable (unlike the tax credit attaching to dividends). The personal allowance is <u>not</u> pro-rated.

Jane 2009/10

	Non-savings income £	Savings income £	Total £
Employment income	13,500		
BSI × $^{100}/_{80}$		1,000	
Net income	13,500	1,000	14,500
Less personal allowance	(6,475)	–	
Taxable income	7,025	1,000	8,025

	£
Non-savings income	
£7,025 × 20%	1,405
Savings income	
£1,000 × 20%	200
Tax liability	1,605
Less: tax suffered at source £(100 × 12) + £200	(1,400)
Tax payable	205

Chris 2009/10

	Non-savings income £	Savings income £	Total £
Employment income × 6/12	6,750		
BSI × $^{100}/_{80}$		2,500	
Net income	6,750	2,500	9,250
Less personal allowance	(6,475)	–	
Taxable income	275	2,500	2,775

	£
Non-savings income	
£275 × 20%	55
Savings income	
£(2,440 – 275) = 2,165 × 10%	216
£(2,500 – 2,165) = 335 × 20%	67
Tax liability	338
Less: tax suffered at source £(100 × 6) + £500	(1,100)
Tax repayable	(762)

3 Mr and Mrs Lowrie

> **Tutorial note**. Mr Lowrie's dividend income is above the higher rate threshold, so it is taxed at 32.5%. Mrs Lowrie's dividends, however, fall below this threshold and are consequently taxed at 10%.

	Non-savings income £	Savings income £	Dividend income £	Total £
Mr Lowrie				
Employment income	43,540			
Dividends × 100/90			1,211	
Bank deposit interest × 100/80		750		
Building society interest × 100/80		740		
Net income	43,540	1,490	1,211	46,241
Less personal allowance	(6,475)			
Taxable income	37,065	1,490	1,211	39,766

	£	£
Non savings income		
£37,065 × 20%		7,413
Savings income		
£335 × 20%		67
£1,155 × 40%		462
Dividend income		
£1,211 × 32.5%		394
		8,336
Less: tax credit on dividend	121	
tax suffered on savings income	298	
PAYE	7,400	
		(7,819)
Tax payable		517

	Non-savings income £	Savings income £	Dividend income £	Total £
Mrs Lowrie				
Employment income	20,000			
Dividends × 100/90			2,820	
Bank deposit interest × 100/80		95		
Building society interest × 100/80		525		
Net income	20,000	620	2,820	23,440
Less personal allowance	(6,475)			
Taxable income	13,525	620	2,820	16,965

	£	£
Non-savings income		
£13,525 × 20%		2,705
Savings income		
£620 × 20%		124
Dividend income		
£2,820 × 10%		282
Tax liability		3,111
Less: tax credit on dividends	282	
tax suffered on savings income	124	
PAYE	2,600	
		(3,006)
Tax payable		105

4 Employment and self-employment

Tutorial note. In general, individuals prefer self-employment to employment because NICs are lower and the rules on the deductibility of expenses are less onerous. HM Revenue and Customs will decide any particular case of employment or self-employment by looking at all the relevant facts.

You are unlikely to get a full question with no computation in the exam but do ensure that you are comfortable providing brief written answers.

The factors to consider in deciding whether someone is employed or self-employed for income tax purposes are as follows.

(a) How much control is exercised over the way work is done? The greater the control, the more likely it is that the worker is an employee.

(b) Does the worker provide his own equipment? If so, that would indicate self-employment.

(c) If the worker hires his own helpers, that indicates self-employment.

(d) If the worker can profit by his own sound management, or lose money through errors, that indicates self-employment.

(e) If there is a continuing obligation to provide work for the worker, and an obligation on the worker to do whatever job is offered next, that indicates employment.

(f) If the worker accepts work from any independent sources, that indicates self-employment.

(g) If the worker can work whenever he chooses, that indicates self-employment.

These tests are summed up in the general rule that there is employment when there is a contract **of** service, and self-employment when is a contract **for** services.

5 Azure plc

> **Tutorial note**. The calculation of benefits is particularly important for exam purposes. Ensure that you pro-rate the benefits if they are not available for the entire year.

(a) A taxable benefit must be computed for Mr Andrews. The benefit will equal the difference between the interest which would have arisen at the official rate and the actual interest paid. The benefit for 2009/10 is therefore £16,000 × (4.75 − 1)% × 6/12 months = £300.

(b) The loan to Mrs Preece is less than £5,000, so the taxable benefit is nil.

(c) Mr Charles will have a taxable benefit of the annual value of the TV and video system, which will be computed as 20% of the value of the asset when first provided as a benefit to any employee. If the system had been lent to an employee when it was bought, the benefit for 2009/10 would be £800 × 20% = £160 × 10/12 = £133. If the system was first provided as a benefit in June 2009, the benefit would be £500 × 20% = £100 × 10/12 = £83.

(d) Long service awards of tangible property to employees with at least 20 years service are not taxed provided the cost to the employer does not exceed £50 for each year of service and no similar award has been made to the same person within the previous ten years. In Mrs Davies's case the limit on value would be £50 × 25 = £1,250, so there will be no taxable benefit.

(e) The car benefit and fuel scale benefit will apply to the car provided for Mr Edgar. The car benefit is calculated as price of car × %. The % depends on the CO_2 emissions of the car.

    (i) Because CO_2 emissions are 134g/km the percentage is 15%. The emissions figure is rounded down to the nearest 5 below ie to 130g/km. This is below the 135g/km baseline but more than 120g/km (low emission cars) so the percentage is 15%.

    (ii) The fuel scale benefit will be at £16,900 multiplied by the percentage used in calculating the car benefit, in this case 15%.

    (iii) The charges will not be reduced on a time basis because the car was provided for the whole of 2009/10.

The taxable benefit will therefore be as follows.

	£
Car £23,000 × 15%	3,450
Fuel £16,900 × 15%	2,535
	5,985

(f) Mr Ford will be taxed on the annual value of the flat and of the furniture. The company's payment of his council tax will also be a taxable benefit.

The following rules will apply.

    (i) There will be a basic accommodation benefit equal to the annual value.

    (ii) There will be an additional accommodation benefit equal to the excess of the flat's cost over £75,000, multiplied by the official rate of interest at the start of the tax year.

    (iii) There will be a benefit in respect of the use of the furniture, equal to 20% of its value when first provided as a benefit to any employee.

The taxable benefit will therefore be as follows.

	£
Flat: annual value	900
additional charge £(100,000 − 75,000) × 4.75%	1,187
	2,087
Furniture £5,000 × 20%	1,000
Council tax	500
	3,587

(g)   The first £8,000 of removal expenses payable to Miss Jackson will be an exempt benefit because:

(i)   She does not already live within a reasonable daily travelling distance of her new place of employment, but will do so after moving, and

(ii)   the expenses are incurred or the benefits provided by the end of the tax year following the tax year of the start of employment at the new location.

Miss Jackson will be taxable on the excess removal expenses £(9,500 – 8,000) = £1,500.

(h)   The private use of one mobile phone is an exempt benefit. As more than one mobile phone is provided to Mr Long, the private use of the second phone is a taxable benefit valued using 'cost of provision to the employer' ie £500 x 30% = £150.

6 Gary and George

Tutorial note. Tax relief is available on pension contributions up to the higher of relevant earnings and the basic amount (£3,600). However, tax relief on contributions in excess of the annual allowance are clawed back by the excess contributions charge.

(a)   *Gary 2009/10*

	Non-savings income £
Employment income	55,000
Less personal allowance	(6,475)
Taxable income	48,525

Tax

	£
£37,400 × 20%	7,480
£5,000 (£4,000 × $^{100}/_{80}$) × 20% (extended band)	1,000
£6,125 × 40%	2,450
48,525	10,930

(b)   As Gary's earnings are only £55,000 (gross) for 2009/10 only £55,000 of his contribution of £65,000 would qualify for tax relief.

His income tax liability will be:

	£
£37,400 × 20%	7,480
£11,125 × 20%	2,225
48,525	9,705

(c)   All of George's contribution of £270,000 will qualify for tax relief. He will therefore pay £270,000 × 80% = £216,000 to the scheme. As he is a higher rate taxpayer his basic rate band will be extended by £270,000. However there will be a 40% tax charge on the excess contribution above the annual allowance of £245,000. His income tax liability is as follows:

	Non-savings income £
Employment income	320,000
Less personal allowance	(6,475)
Taxable income	313,525

Tax	£
£37,400 × 20%	7,480
£270,000 × 20%	54,000
£6,125 × 40%	2,450
313,525	63,930
Excess contribution charge £(270,000 – 245,000) × 40%	10,000
Tax liability	73,930

7 Mr Lee

> **Tutorial note.** You are writing an e-mail it is to a client and you should aim to be clear but concise.

To: Mr Lee@red.co.uk
From: An Advisor@taxadvice.co.uk
Date: [   ]
Re: Pension advice

Thank you for your e-mail about pension advice. My answers to your questions are as follows:

(1)   You do not have to join your new employer's pension scheme. Instead you could start a pension with a financial institution such as a bank or insurance company. However, your employer may not want to contribute to private pension arrangements so you need to bear this in mind when considering whether or not to join your employer's scheme.

A money purchase scheme is one where the value of your pension benefits depends on the value of the investments in the pension scheme at the date that you set aside ('vest') funds to produce those benefits. This is distinct from a defined benefits scheme where the benefits are defined from the outset. If you decide to use private pension arrangements, these are also likely to be money purchase arrangements.

(2)   You can contribute an amount up to your earnings into the pension scheme and obtain tax-relief on those contributions. You can also make any amount of further contributions, for example out of capital, but these will not obtain initial tax relief. However, since there is no income tax or capital gains tax payable by a pension fund, it may still be beneficial for such extra contributions to be made into this tax-exempt fund.

In addition, your employer can make any amount of contributions provided that the tax authorities are happy that such contributions are not excessive and so not for the purposes of the employer's trade.

The annual allowance which limits the inputs that can be put into the pension fund. For 2009/10, this limit is £245,000. The amounts that you contribute **and** obtain tax relief on, plus any contributions made by your employer, will count towards the annual allowance. If those contributions exceed the annual allowance, there will be a tax charge at 40% on the excess which is payable by you. This might be relevant in later years when your earnings may be above the annual allowance limit.

The lifetime allowance limit is the maximum value of the pension fund that you are allowed to build up to provide pension benefits without incurring adverse tax consequences. The lifetime allowance is £1,750,000 in 2009/10. This limit is tested against the value of your pension fund when you vest pension benefits. If your fund exceeds the lifetime allowance at that time, there will be a tax charge of 55% on funds vested to provide a lump sum and 25% on funds vested to provide a pension income. Although there are no adverse tax consequences if your pension fund exceeds the lifetime allowance other than at the time that pension benefits are vested, it would be wise to keep an eye on how your fund is growing so that you can adjust your contributions accordingly so as to keep within the lifetime allowance.

(3)   Your employer will deduct your pension contributions gross from your pay before applying PAYE. This means that tax relief is given automatically at your highest rate of tax and no adjustment is needed in your tax return. As an example, if you contribute £1,000 to your pension and that amount of income would have been taxed at 40%, your pay will be reduced by £1,000 but the amount of tax that would be deducted from your pay would be reduced by £400, so that the net amount of the contribution payable by you would be £600.

The above is only an outline of the basics of pension provision as this is very complex area, so I suggest that we meet once you have decided how you wish to proceed.

AN Advisor

8 Rafe

> **Tutorial note.** Remember to accrue the rents receivable and expenses payable for the tax year. Where you disallow an expenses, such as the new roof, note this in your computation to show that you have considered it.

	£	£
Rent		
House 1: first letting £600 × 6		3,600
House 1: second letting £6,000 × 3/12		1,500
House 2: £5,000 × 8/12		3,333
House 3: £7,800 × 8/12		5,200
		13,633
Expenses		
House 1: new roof, disallowable because capital	0	
House 1: water rates	320	
House 1: buildings insurance £480 × 10/12	400	
House 2: water rates	240	
House 2: wear and tear £(3,333 – 240) × 10%	309	
House 3: redecoration	1,200	
House 3: water rates	360	
House 3: buildings insurance £440 × 9/12	330	
House 3: contents insurance £180 × 8/12	120	
House 3: wear and tear £(5,200 – 360) × 10%	484	
		(3,763)
Income from houses		9,870
Rent a room (*Working*)		350
Total property business income		10,220

Working

Rafe should claim rent a room relief in respect of the letting of the furnished room in his main residence, since this is more beneficial than the normal basis of assessment (£4,600 – £875 = £3,725). This means that Rafe will be taxed on an additional £350 (£4,600 – £4,250) of property business income.

9 A Trader

> **Tutorial note**. You are extremely likely to be required to adjust accounts profit in your exam to arrive at your taxable trading profits. The best way to familiarise yourself with the adjustments required is to practise plenty of questions like this.

	£	£
Net profit per accounts		101,977
Add: general expenses: entertaining suppliers	600	
repairs and renewals	0	
legal and accountancy: tax consultancy	30	
legal and accountancy: lease on new premises	100	
subscription and donations: gift aid donation	5,200	
subscription and donations: political donation	500	
Impairment losses	0	
salaries and wages	0	
travel: private travel expenses 25% × £2,000	500	
rent and rates	0	
depreciation	15,000	
		21,930
c/f		123,907
b/f		123,907
Less: profit on sale of office	5,265	
impairment losses recovered	0	
capital allowances	2,200	
building society interest	1,900	
		(9,365)
Taxable trading profit		114,542

10 Tom Hardy

> **Tutorial note.** The key to being able to deal with a capital allowances computation correctly is to get the layout right. Once you have done this, the figures should fall into place.

	AIA/FYA £	Main Pool £	Private Use car (80%) £	Short life asset £	Allowances £
1.7.09 – 30.6.10					
Brought forward		32,000		4,400	
Addition qualifying for AIA and FYA					
Plant	52,000				
AIA	(50,000)				50,000
	2,000				
FYA @ 40%	(800)				800
WDA @ 20%		(6,400)		(880)	7,280
Balance to pool	(1,200)	1,200			
Carried forward		26,800		3,520	
Allowances					58,080
1.7.10 – 30.6.11					
Addition (not AIA)			13,400		
WDA @ 20%		(5,360)	(2,680) × 80%	(704)	8,208
Carried forward		21,440	10,400	2,816	
Allowances					8,208
1.7.11 – 30.6.12					
WDA @ 20%		(4,288)	(2,080) × 80%	(563)	6,515
Carried forward		17,152	8,320	2,253	
Allowances					6,515
1.7.12 – 30.6.13					
Disposals		(340)		(2,900)	
		16,812		(647)	
Balancing charge				647	(647)
WDA @ 20%		(3,362)	(1,664) × 80%		4,693
Carried forward		13,450	6,656		
Allowances					4,046
1.7.13 – 31.12.13					
Disposals		(24,000)	(10,600)		
		(10,550)	(3,944)		
Balancing charges		10,550	3,944 × 80%		(13,705)

> **Tutorial note.** The capital allowances are restricted as a result of the private use of an asset by the proprietor.

11 Saruman

Capital allowances computation for year ended 5 April 2010

Plant and machinery

	Main Pool £	Saruman's car (75%) £		Allowances/ (charges) £
TWDV b/f	52,000	600		
Addition (no AIA or FYA on car)	4,800			
Disposals (10,000 + 800)	(10,800)	(920)		
	46,000			
Balancing charge		(320)	× 75%	(240)
Private use car		19,000		
WDA 20%	(9,200)			9,200
WDA 10%		(1,900)	× 75%	1,425
TWDV c/f	36,800	17,100		
Allowances				10,385

Industrial building

Cost excluding land (office accommodation included as less than 25% of qualifying cost)	£30,000
WDA @ 2%	£600

Total capital allowances are £10,385 + £600 = £10,985

12 Mr Cobbler

TAXABLE PROFITS FOR THE FOUR YEARS 2009/10 TO 2012/13

The accounts profits will be as follows.

		Accounting date	
Period ending in	Working	31 March £	30 April £
2010	3 × £800	2,400	
	4 × £800		3,200
2011	3 × £800 + 6 × £1,200 + 3 × £2,000	15,600	
	2 × £800 + 6 × £1,200 + 4 × £2,000		16,800
2012	12 × £2,000	24,000	24,000
2013	12 × £2,000	24,000	24,000

The taxable profits will be as follows.

		Accounting date	
		31 March	30 April
		£	£
2009/10	Actual basis	2,400	
	£3,200 × 3/4		2,400
2010/11	Year to 31.3.11	15,600	
	First 12 months		
	£3,200 + £16,800 × 8/12		14,400
2011/12	Year to 31.3.12	24,000	
	Year to 30.4.11		16,800
2012/13	Year to 31.3.13	24,000	
	Year to 30.4.12		24,000
		66,000	57,600

30 April is the better choice of accounting date as it will give a considerable cash flow advantage.

13 Miss Farrington

> **Tutorial note**. In a question like this, work out the capital allowances for each period of account before you think about allocating profits to tax years.
>
> Writing down allowances and the annual investment allowance are time apportioned in a long period of account.

We must first work out the capital allowances.

	AIA/FYA £	Main Pool £	Private use Car (65%) £	Allowances £
1.1.10 – 30.4.11				
Additions qualifying for AIA/FYA				
Desk and office furniture (1.1.10)	1,500			
General plant (4.1.10)	22,280			
Secondhand oven (1.3.10)	11,200			
Delivery van (25.3.10)	11,800			
General plant (15.4.10)	21,000			
	67,780			
AIA £50,000 × 16/12	(66,667)			66,667
	1,113			
FYA @ 40%	(445)			445
Addition not qualifying for AIA/FYA				
Car (15.5.10)			6,600	
WDA @ 20% × 16/12			(1,760) × 65%	1,144
Transfer to pool	668	668		
Carried forward		668	4,840	
Allowances				68,256

	AIA/FYA £	Main Pool £	Private use Car (65%) £	Allowances £
1.5.11 – 30.4.12				
Brought forward		668	4,840	
Additions qualifying for AIA				
General plant (30.1.12)	10,000			
Mixer (30.4.12)	1,200			
	11,200			
AIA	(11,200)			11,200
WDA small pool		(668)		668
WDA @ 20%			(968) × 65%	629
Carried forward		0	3,872	
Allowances				12,497

Profits are as follows.

Period	Profit £	Capital allowances £	Adjusted profit £
1.1.10 – 30.4.11	84,256	68,256	16,000
1.5.11 – 30.4.12	25,497	12,497	13,000

The taxable profits are as follows.

Year	Basis period	Working	Taxable profit £
2009/10	1.1.10 – 5.4.10	£16,000 × 3/16	3,000
2010/11	6.4.10 – 5.4.11	£16,000 × 12/16	12,000
2011/12	1.5.10 – 30.4.11	£16,000 × 12/16	12,000
2012/13	1.5.11 – 30.4.12		13,000

The overlap profits are the profits from 1 May 2010 to 5 April 2011: £16,000 × 11/16 = £11,000.

14 Langland

> **Tutorial note**. Work out the tax years which the trading covers, then allocate the profits to the relevant years. Don't forget overlap profits. A good check is to add up the profits throughout the life of the business: the result should be the same as the total of the profits assessed in each tax year.

		£
2004/05	1.2.05 – 5.4.05	1,600
	$(12,000 \times \frac{2}{15})$	
2005/6	6.4.05 – 5.4.06	9,600
	$(12,000 \times \frac{12}{15})$	
2006/07	12m to 30.4.06	9,600
	$(12,000 \times \frac{12}{15})$	
2007/08	Y/e 30.4.07	6,000
2008/09	Y/e 30.4.08	8,000
2009/10	Y/e 30.4.09	10,000

			£
2010/11	Y/e 30.4.10		6,000
	P/e 31.10.10		4,000
			10,000

Less: Overlap profits
1.5.05 to 5.4.06

$$\left(\frac{11}{15} \times 12,000\right)$$

	(8,800)
	1,200

15 Morgan

> **Tutorial note**. In a losses question take care to consider all available reliefs. When deciding on the best relief you must consider the rate of tax saved, the wasting of the personal allowance and the timing of the relief. In this case, since the rate of tax is assumed to be the same in all years, the key factors are ensuring that the personal allowance is not waste the personal allowance and obtaining loss relief as quickly as possible.

(a)   Loss relief could be claimed:

(i)   against general income of the year of loss (2009/10) only, ie the savings income of £6,000, then carrying the balance of £(32,000 – 6,000) = £26,000 forward and setting it against the first available future profits of the trade;

(ii)   against general income of the preceding year (2008/09) only, ie the trading income of £14,000 plus savings income of £6,000, giving a total of £20,000, then carrying the balance of £(32,000 – 20,000) = £12,000 forward and setting it against the first available future profits of the trade;

(iii)   against general income of both the year of the loss (2009/10) of £6,000 and the preceding year (2008/09) of £20,000, giving a total of £26,000, then carrying the balance of £(32,000 – 26,000) = £6,000 forward and setting it against the first available future profits of the trade;

(iv)   against general income of the year of the loss (2009/10) of £6,000, then against trading income of the preceding year (2008/09) of £14,000, then against trading income of the second preceding year (2007/08) of £10,000, then the balance of £(32,000 – 6,000 – 14,000 – 10,000) = £2,000 against trading income of the third preceding year (2006/07);

(v)   against general income of both the year of the loss (2009/10) of £6,000 and the preceding year (2008/09) of £20,000, giving a total of £26,000, then the balance of £(32,000 – 26,000) = £6,000 against trading income of the second preceding year (2007/08).

(vi)   carry forward whole loss against first available profits of the trade.

(b)   *The best claim*

The best way to obtain relief would be for Morgan to use loss relief against general income in 2009/10 and then carry back against trading income in 2008/09, 2007/08 and 2006/07. This would preserve the use of the personal allowance in 2008/09 and obtain tax relief as quickly as possible for 2007/08 and 2006/07. The tax computations would then be as follows.

	2006/07	*2007/08*	*2008/09*	*2009/10*
	£	£	£	£
Trading income	8,000	10,000	14,000	0
Less: loss relief against trading income	(2,000)	(10,000)	(14,000)	0
	6,000	0	0	0
Savings income	6,000	6,000	6,000	6,000
	12,000	6,000	6,000	6,000
Less loss relief against general income	0	0	0	(6,000)
Net income	12,000	6,000	6,000	0
Less personal allowance	(6,475)	(6,475)	(6,475)	(6,475)
Taxable income	5,525	0	0	0

> **Tutorial note**. Because of Morgan's choice of accounting date, no overlap profits arose on commencement.

16 Adam, Bert and Charlie

	Total £	A £	B £	C £	D £
Year ending 5 April 2007					
Salaries	37,000	15,000	12,000	10,000	
PSR (balance)	65,000	26,000	26,000	13,000	
Total	102,000	41,000	38,000	23,000	
Year ending 5 April 2008					
6 April to 5 July					
Salaries	9,250	3,750	3,000	2,500	
PSR (balance)	42,750	17,100	17,100	8,550	
Total	52,000	20,850	20,100	11,050	
6 July to 5 April					
Salaries	16,500		9,000	7,500	
PSR (balance)	139,500		83,700	55,800	
Total	156,000		92,700	63,300	
Totals for the year	208,000	20,850	112,800	74,350	
Year ending 5 April 2009					
Salaries	22,000		12,000	10,000	
PSR (balance)	104,000		62,400	41,600	
Total	126,000		74,400	51,600	
Year ending 5 April 2010					
6 April to 5 May					
Salaries	1,833		1,000	833	
Balance	13,167		7,900	5,267	
Total	15,000		8,900	6,100	
6 May to 5 April					
Salaries	49,500		16,500	16,500	16,500
Balance	115,500		69,300	34,650	11,550
Total	165,000		85,800	51,150	28,050
Totals for the year	180,000		94,700	57,250	28,050

Taxable trade profits are as follows.

	A £	B £	C £	D £
Year				
2006/07	41,000	38,000	23,000	
2007/08	20,850	112,800	74,350	
2008/09		74,400	51,600	
2009/10		94,700	57,250	28,050

17 Partnerships

> **Tutorial note.** This is a comprehensive question as it asks you to explain how partners are taxed, followed by a computation including joining and retiring partners, and finishes with a discussion of losses.
>
> Overlap profits are relieved either on a change of accounting date or on a cessation. Each partner obtains relief for their own overlap profits and their own losses.

(a)   Each partner is taxed like a sole trader who runs a business which starts when he joins the partnership, finishes when he leaves the partnership, has the same periods of account as the partnership, and makes profits or losses equal to the partner's share of the partnership profits or losses.

(b)

	Total £	Anne £	Betty £	Chloe £
1.1.09 – 31.12.09				
January to June	30,000	15,000	15,000	
July to December	30,000	15,000	–	15,000
Totals	60,000	30,000	15,000	15,000
1.1.10 – 31.12.10	72,000	36,000	–	36,000

Trading profit assessments 2009/10

	Anne £	Betty £	Chloe £
Profits y/e 31.12.09	30,000		
Profits 1.1.09 – 30.6.09		15,000	
Profits 1.7.09 – 31.12.09			15,000
Profits 1.1.10 – 5.4.10			
3/12 × £36,000			9,000
	30,000	15,000	24,000
Less overlap relief for Betty on cessation		(3,000)	
Profits assessable 2009/10	30,000	12,000	24,000

(c)   (i)   *Daniel*

Daniel can use his £20,000 loss:

- against general income of 2009/10 and/or of 2008/09 and then against trading income of 2008/09 (if no claim against general income made for that year), 2007/08 and 2006/07
- against future trading profits

(ii)   *Edward*

Edward can use his £15,000 loss:

- against general income of 2009/10 and/or of 2008/09 and then against trading income of 2008/09 (if no claim against general income made for that year), 2007/08 and 2006/07

- if there is a terminal loss in the last 12 months of trading, against trading profits of the tax year of cessation and the three preceding years, later years first

(iii)   *Frank*

Frank can use his loss of £5,000:

- against general income of 2009/10 and/or 2008/09
- against general income of 2005/06, 2006/07 and 2008/09
- against future trading profits

18 Denise

(a)   Denise can contribute an amount up to her earnings into a personal pension scheme and obtain tax relief on those contributions ie up to £115,000 for 2009/10. She can also make any amount of further contributions, for example out of capital, but these will not obtain initial tax relief. However, since there is no income tax or capital gains tax payable by a pension fund, it may still be beneficial for such extra contributions to be made into this tax exempt fund.

However, there are two limits that Denise needs to be aware of. First, there is an annual allowance which limits the inputs that can be put into the pension fund. For 2009/10, this limit is £245,000. The amounts that Denise contributes and obtains tax relief on, will count towards the annual allowance. If those contributions exceed the annual allowance, there will be a tax charge at 40% on the excess which is payable by Denise. This might be relevant in later years when Denise's earnings may be above the annual allowance limit.

The second limit is the lifetime allowance limit. This is the maximum value of the pension fund that Denise is allowed to build up to provide pension benefits without incurring adverse tax consequences. The lifetime allowance is £1,750,000 in 2009/10. This limit is tested against the value of her pension fund at the date she sets aside (vests) the fund to provide these benefits. If her fund exceeds the lifetime allowance at that time, there will be a tax charge of 55% on funds vested to provide a lump sum and 25% on funds vested to provide a pension income.

Personal pension contributions are entitled to tax relief at source. The pension payments made will be treated as being net of basic rate tax at 20%. As she is a higher rate tax payer, she will then need to claim higher rate tax relief of 20% through her tax return. Thus for a gross contribution of £1,000, Denise would pay £800 to the pension provider and then she would claim an additional £200 through her tax return.

(b)

	£
Class 2 NICs	
£2.40 × 52	125

	£
Class 4 NICs	
£(43,875 − 5,715) × 8%	3,053
£(115,000 − 43,875) × 1%	711
	3,764

19 Sasha Shah

> **Tutorial notes.**
>
> 1 Strictly, expenses are only deductible in calculating net taxable earnings if they are incurred wholly, necessarily and exclusively in the performance of the duties. In practice, however, HM Revenue and Customs allow an apportionment between private and business use as here.
>
> 2 Capital allowances are available to an employee who provides plant and machinery necessarily for use in the performance of his duties, in the same way as a sole trader.
>
> 3 The use of the car for travel between home and work is ordinary commuting and not business use.
>
> 4 'Earnings' for Class 4 NIC purposes are trading profits. However, earnings for Class 1 NIC purposes are gross earnings before the deductions of any expenses.

(a) Factors that will indicate that a worker should be treated as an employee rather than as self employed are:

    (i) control by employer over employee's work;

    (ii) employee must accept further work if offered (and employer must offer work);

    (iii) employee does not provide own equipment;

    (iv) employee does not hire own helpers;

    (v) employee does not take substantial financial risk;

    (vi) employee does not have responsibility for investment and management of business and cannot benefit from sound management;

    (vii) employee cannot work when he chooses but when an employer tells him to work;

    (viii) described as an employee in any agreement between parties.

(b) (i) *Income assessable as trading profits*

	£	£
Gross income		60,000
Less: business expenses on heating etc	800	
computer – AIA	4,000	
business expenses re car (£3,500 × 40%)	1,400	
WDA @ 20% on business car (CO_2 less than 160g/km) £10,000 × 20% × 40% (business proportion)	800	(7,000)
Assessable as trading profits		53,000

    (ii) *Net taxable earnings*

	£	£
Gross income		60,000
Less: business expenses on heating etc	800	
computer – AIA	4,000	(4,800)
Net taxable earnings		55,200

(c) (i) *Class 2 and Class 4 NIC*

		£
Class 2	£2.40 × 52	125
Class 4	£(43,875 – 5,715) × 8%	3,053
	£(53,000 – 43,875) × 1%	91
Total		3,269

    (ii) *Class 1 NIC (Primary)*

	£
£(43,875 – 5,715) × 11%	4,198
£(60,000 – 43,875) × 1%	161
Total	4,359

20 Peter Robinson

Tutorial note. The first disposal is a basic computation. The second disposal tests the A/(A+B) formula and the third part tests compensation for the destruction of an asset.

Peter Robinson CGT payable 2009/10

Summary of gains

	£
Investment property (W1)	69,220
Land (W2)	16,300
Destroyed asset (W3)	3,000
	88,520
Less: annual exemption	(10,100)
Taxable gains	78,420

CGT payable

	£
£78,420 × 18%	14,116

Workings

1 *Investment property*

	£
Proceeds	150,000
Less cost of disposal	(1,280)
Net proceeds	148,720
Less cost	(79,500)
Gain	69,220

2 *Land*

	£
Proceeds	35,000
Less cost of disposal	(700)
Net proceeds	34,300
Less cost	

$$£54,000 \times \frac{35,000}{35,000 + 70,000}$$

	£
	(18,000)
Gain	16,300

3 *Vase*

	£
Proceeds	20,000
Less cost	(12,000)
Gain	8,000
Gain immediately chargeable	
£(20,000 – 17,000)	3,000

Remainder rolled into base cost of new vase (£8,000 – £3,000 = £5,000)

21 John Harley

> **Tutorial note.** Part (a) is a typical question examining principal private residence relief. You are asked to present your answer as a schedule (ie table) showing periods of exemption and non-exemption with reasons (ie explanation of your application of the rules). To obtain good marks you must comply with these instructions.

(a)   **John Harley – Gain on house**

	Chargeable months	Exempt months
1.8.87 – 31.5.88 – actual residence		10
1.6.88 – 31.7.92 – employed abroad any period		50
1.8.92 – 31.7.96 – up to 4 years work elsewhere		48
1.8.96 – 31.10.98 – up to 3 years any reason		27
1.11.98 – 30.6.01 – actual residence		32
1.7.01 – 30.11.06 – absent	65	
1.12.06 – 30.11.09 – last 3 years ownership for any reason		36
Totals	65	203

(b)   **Elsie Phillips**

   (i)   *Painting*

	£
Proceeds (deemed)	6,000
Less costs of disposal	(400)
Gain	5,600
Less: cost	(11,500)
Loss	(5,900)

   (ii)   *Chandelier*

	£
Proceeds	7,500
Less: cost	(4,000)
Gain	3,500
Cannot exceed £(7,500 – 6,000) × 5/3	2,500

22 The White family

> **Tutorial note.** In an exam question you should watch out for the CGT reliefs. When dealing with rollover relief look out for depreciating assets.

(a)   2009/10

   Gift relief can apply to the gift of the factory because it is an asset used in the trade of the donor. Full relief is available as no payment is made by Gary ie it is an outright gift.

	£
Market value at gift	260,000
Less cost	(150,000)
Gain heldover	110,000

(b)   Gary's gain on sale is:

	£
Proceeds	320,000
Less cost £(260,000 – 110,000)	(150,000)
Gain	170,000

(c)   Mrs White has made a gain of £40,000 (£80,000 – 40,000) on the sale of the shop. If she acquires a replacement shop within 3 years of the sale, she can claim rollover relief.

Freehold Shop

Less than the full proceeds have been reinvested. A gain equal to the amount not reinvested (£80,000 – £72,000 = £8,000) will remain in charge.

The remainder of the gain of £32,000 can be rolled over into the base cost of the freehold shop. The base cost will therefore be £72,000 – £32,000 = £40,000 for the purposes of computing a gain on its disposal.

Leasehold Shop

Full deferral of the gain is available as the whole of the proceeds of sale are reinvested.

The leasehold shop is a depreciating asset as the lease has less than 60 years to run. The gain is not deducted from the base cost of the leasehold shop, but is deferred until the earliest of the disposal of the leasehold shop, ceasing to use it in the business or 10 years from its acquisition. The gain which will come into charge at that date will be £40,000.

If a non depreciating asset is acquired before the gain crystallises it can be rolled over into that new asset.

23 Alice

> **Tutorial note.** Remember that incorporation relief only applies to the extent that shares are received in exchange for the assets transferred to the company.

	£
Gains on incorporation	120,000
Less: incorporation relief $\dfrac{200,000}{200,000 + 100,000} \times £120,000$	(80,000)
Gain before entrepreneurs' relief	40,000
Base cost of shares £(200,000 – 80,000)	£120,000

24 Kai

> **Tutorial note.** Remember that entrepreneurs' relief is given on the net gains (ie gains less losses) on the disposal of a business.

Net gains on disposal of business

	£	£
Proceeds of goodwill	50,000	
Less: cost	(nil)	50,000
Proceeds of shop	90,000	
Less: cost	(80,000)	10,000
Proceeds of warehouse	130,000	
Less: cost	(150,000)	(20,000)
Net gains eligible for entrepreneurs' relief		40,000
Less: entrepreneurs' relief £40,000 × 4/9		(17,778)
Chargeable gains		22,222
Less: annual exemption		(10,100)
Taxable gains		12,122
CGT on £12,122 @ 18%		2,182

25 Melissa

First match the disposal with the acquisition in the next 30 days:

	£	£
Proceeds $\frac{4,000}{10,000} \times £42,000$	16,800	
Less: cost	(16,000)	800

Next match the remaining shares with the share pool:

	£	£
Proceeds $\frac{6,000}{10,000} \times £42,000$	25,200	
Less: cost (W)	(20,625)	4,575
Total gains		5,375

Working

	No. of shares	Cost
12 July 2001 acquisition	6,000	21,000
14 December 2006 acquisition	2,000	6,500
	8,000	27,500
2 July 2009 disposal	(6,000)	(20,625)
c/f	2,000	6,875

26 Tim

Tim's payments on account for 2009/10 were based on the excess of his 2008/09 tax liability over amounts deducted under the PAYE system, amounts deducted at source and tax credits on dividends:

	£
2008/09 tax liability	16,800
Less: PAYE	(7,200)
tax deducted at source	(800)
tax credit on dividends	(200)
Total payments on account for 2009/10	8,600

Two equal payments on account of £4,300 (£8,600/2) were required. The due dates for these payments were 31 January 2010 and 31 July 2010 respectively.

The final payment in respect of Tim's 2009/10 tax liability was due on 31 January 2011 and was calculated as follows:

	£
2009/10 tax liability	22,000
Less: PAYE	(7,100)
tax deducted at source	(900)
tax credit on dividends	(250)
	13,750
Less payments on account	(8,600)
Final payment due 31 January 2011	5,150

27 Lai Chan

Tutorial notes. This is a good example of the type of question that you might find as question 1 of the exam.

1   For capital allowance purposes the AIA and WDA are restricted by the length of the basis period.

2   There is no capital allowance restriction in respect of the private use of an asset by an employee.

3   The basic rate band is extended by the gross amount of personal pension contributions made. Occupational pension contributions are, however, deducted in computing total income.

4   There is no taxable benefit in respect of the company's contribution to the occupational pension scheme.

(a)   *Income tax liability*

	£	Non-savings income £
Gross salary 9 × £3,250	29,250	
Less pension contribution (6%)	(1,755)	
	27,495	
Car benefit (W1)	3,780	
Fuel benefit (W2)	3,169	
Taxable cheap loan (W3)	594	
Employment income		35,038
Trading profit	32,000	
Less Capital allowances (W4)	(13,902)	
Taxable trading profit		18,098
Net income		53,136
Less personal allowance		(6,475)
Taxable income		46,661

Tax

	£
£38,900 × 20% (W5)	7,780
£7,761 (46,661 − 38,900) × 40%	3,104
Tax liability	10,884

Workings

1   *Car benefit*

		£
25% × £26,400 × 9/12 (note)		4,950
Less contribution £130 × 9		(1,170)
		3,780

Note. The % depends on the CO_2 emissions of the car.

CO_2 emissions = 185 g/km

Amount above baseline figure 185 − 135 = 50 g/km

Divide by 5 = 10 g/km

Taxable percentage = 15% + 10% = 25%

The benefit is time apportioned as the car is available for only nine months of the year.

2   *Fuel benefit*

£16,900 × 25% × 9/12 = £3,169

No reduction for partial reimbursement of private fuel cost. The benefit is time apportioned as the car was available for only nine months of the year.

The taxable percentage used in calculating the fuel benefit is the same as the percentage used in calculating the car benefit.

3   *Taxable cheap loan*

Average method

$$4.75\% \times \frac{30,000 + 10,000}{2} \times 9/12 = £712$$

Alternative method (strict method)

		£
£30,000 × 3/12 × 4.75% =		356
£10,000 × 6/12 × 4.75% =		238
		594

Elect for strict method

4

	AIA/FYA £	Main pool £	Private use car (60%) £	Short life asset £	Allowances £
Additions qualifying for AIA/FYA					
1 January 2010	10,000				
AIA £50,000 × 3/12 =					
£12,500	(10,000)				10,000
4 March 2010	4,000				
AIA £(12,500 – 10,000)	(2,500)				2,500
	1,500				
FYA @ 40%	(600)				600
Additions not qualifying for AIA/FYA					
15 January 2010			18,800		
20 February 2010		10,400			
		10,400	18,800		
WDA @ 20% × 3/12		(520)			520
WDA @ 10% × 3/12			(470)		282
			× 60%		
Balance transferred	900			900	
TWDV c/f		9,880	18,330	900	
Allowances					13,902

5   Basic rate band

£37,400 + (£400 × 100/80 × 3) = £38,900

(b)   Up to 31.12.09 PAYE will have been deducted from Lai Chan's salary. It is likely that her PAYE code was adjusted to take account of her benefits. Further tax payable (or tax repayable) will be dealt with under the self-assessment system.

As Lai Chan was employed before starting in business on her own account, she is unlikely to have made any payments on account for 2009/10. Therefore, the tax on her trading profit will be collected in full on 31 January 2011 under the self assessment system.

28 P Ltd

> **Tutorial notes.**
>
> 1 The interest on the loan is dealt with under the loan relationship rules. It is not a property business expense.
>
> 2 Income and expenses are dealt with on the accruals basis when calculating the property business profit.

P LTD: PROPERTY BUSINESS INCOME

	£	£	£
First Property			
Premium £20,000 less [2% × (30 − 1) × £20,000]			8,400
Rent £4,000 × 9/12			3,000
			11,400
Second Property			
Rent £600 × 3		1,800	
Rent £2,100 × 1/3		700	
		2,500	
Less: water rates £390 × 6/12	195		
insurance £440 × 6/11	240		
repairs: capital	0		
		(435)	
			2,065
Property business income			13,465

29 Tree Ltd

> **Tutorial note.** You need to calculate both PCTCT and 'profits'. 'Profits' determine which tax rate applies.

(a) Tree Ltd

	Year to 31.3.10 £
Trading profits	180,000
Chargeable gain	105,000
Investment income	36,000
Less: Gift aid donation	(27,000)
Profits chargeable to corporation tax	294,000
FII: £29,700 × 100/90	33,000
'Profits'	327,000

Marginal relief applies

	£
Year to 31.3.10	
Corporation tax (FY 09)	
£294,000 × 28%	82,320
Less 7/400 (1,500,000 − 327,000) × $\dfrac{294,000}{327,000}$	(18,456)
	63,864

(b) Dealers plc's profits for small companies' rate purposes are £420,000 so tax is payable at the small companies marginal rate.

	6 months to 31.3.10 £
Profits chargeable to corporation tax	420,000
'Profits'	420,000
Upper limit £1,500,000 × 6/12	750,000
Lower limit £300,000 × 6/12	150,000

	£
Corporation tax (FY 09)	
£420,000 × 28%	117,600
Less small companies' marginal relief	
£(750,000 − 420,000) × 7/400	(5,775)
	111,825

(c) Springer Ltd's accounting period to 31 December 2008 falls partly in FY 07 and partly in FY 08. PCTCT and 'profits' are apportioned to each FY.

	£
PCTCT	600,000
FII: £27,000 × 100/90	30,000
'Profits'	630,000

	FY 07 3 months to 31.3.08 £	FY 08 9 months to 31.12.08 £
PCTCT (3:9)	150,000	450,000
'Profits' (3:9)	157,500	472,500
Lower limit:		
£300,000 × $^3/_{12}$ / $^9/_{12}$	75,000	225,000
Upper limit:		
£1,500,000 × $^3/_{12}$ / $^9/_{12}$	375,000	1,125,000
Marginal relief applies in both FYs		
FY 07		
£150,000 × 30%	45,000	
Less: marginal relief		
£(375,000 − 157,500) × $\frac{150,000}{157,500}$ × $^1/_{40}$	(5,179)	
	39,821	
FY 08		
£450,000 × 28%		126,000
Less: marginal relief		
£(1,125,000 − 472,500) × $\frac{450,000}{472,500}$ × $^7/_{400}$		(10,875)
		115,125
Total corporation tax £(39,821+ 115,125)		154,946

30 Righteous plc

> **Tutorial note.** Where a company has a long period of account, it has two accounting periods: first 12 months and then the remainder.

	1.1.08- 31.12.08 (12m) £	1.1.09 - 31.5.09 (5m) £
Trading income (12:5)	352,941	147,059
Investment income (15,000 + 6,000)	21,000	2,500
Chargeable gain	–	5,000
	373,941	154,559
Less: gift aid donations (15,000 + 15,000)	(30,000)	(40,000)
Profits chargeable to CT	343,941	114,559

12 m/e 31.12.08

PCTCT/'profits' £343,941

Marginal relief applies for both FYs

	FY 07 3 months to 31.3.08 £	FY 08 9 months to 31.12.08 £
PCTCT (3:9)	85,985	257,956
Lower limit:		
£300,000 × $\frac{3}{12}$ / $\frac{9}{12}$	75,000	225,000
Upper limit:		
£1,500,000 × $\frac{3}{12}$ / $\frac{9}{12}$	375,000	1,125,000

Marginal relief applies in both FYs

FY 07

£85,985 × 30%	25,795	
Less: £(375,000 – 85,985) × $\frac{1}{40}$	(7,225)	
	18,570	

FY 08

£257,956 × 28%		72,228
Less: £(1,125,000 – 257,956) × $\frac{7}{400}$		(15,173)
		57,055

Total tax due for y.e. 31.12.08 £(18,570 + 57,055) 75,625

5 m/e 31.5.09

'Profits'/PCTCT £114,559

Lower limit:

FY08/FY09 £300,000 × $\frac{5}{12}$ = £125,000

Small companies' rate applies for both years
FY 08 £114,559 × $\frac{3}{5}$ × 21% £14,434
FY 09 £114,559 × $\frac{2}{5}$ × 21% £9,623

31 E Ltd

Motor cars are exempt assets, so the loss brought forward from the year ended 31 March 2009 is £16,400.

The position for the year ended 31 March 2010 is as follows.

	£
Gains	
Shares	17,700
Picture	3,000
	20,700
Less loss on shares	(6,000)
	14,700
Less loss brought forward	(14,700)
Chargeable gains	Nil

The loss carried forward at 31 March 2010 is £(16,400 − 14,700) = £1,700.

32 Hardup Ltd

CAPITAL GAINS COMPUTATION

	£
Office block (W1)	21,525
Plot of land (W2)	17,456
Workshop (W3)	40,465
Chargeable gains	79,446

Workings

1   *The office block*

	£
Proceeds	120,000
Less cost	(65,000)
	55,000
Less indexation allowance $\dfrac{210.3 - 138.8}{138.8}$ (0.515) × £65,000	(33,475)
	21,525

Rollover relief is not available as replacement asset acquired outside the qualifying period.

2   *The plot of land*

	£
Proceeds	69,000
Less cost	(20,000)
expenditure in July 1989	(4,000)
	45,000

Less indexation allowance

$$\frac{209.8 - 94.78}{94.78} \ (1.214) \times £20,000 \qquad\qquad (24,280)$$

$$\frac{209.8 - 115.5}{115.5} \ (0.816) \times £4,000 \qquad\qquad (3,264)$$

	17,456

3   *The workshop*

	£
Proceeds	173,000
Less cost	(65,000)
	108,000

Less indexation allowance $\dfrac{209.8 - 102.9}{102.9} (1.039) \times £65,000$ (67,535)

	40,465

33 Ferraro Ltd

> **Tutorial note**. The pro-forma for loss relief is important. If you learn the proforma you should find that the figures slot into place. Note that the result of a losses claim may be that, as here, gift aid donations become unrelieved.

	Accounting periods				
	12m to	*12m to*	*12m to*	*9m to*	*12m to*
	31.12.05	*31.12.06*	*31.12.07*	*30.9.08*	*30.9.09*
	£	£	£	£	£
Trading profits	10,600	34,480	6,200	4,320	0
Investment income	100	200	80	240	260
Property business income	1,300	1,200	1,420	1,440	1,600
Chargeable gain (12,680 – 5,000)	0	0	0	7,680	0
	12,000	35,880	7,700	13,680	1,860
Less current period loss relief	0	0	0	0	(1,860)
	12,000	35,880	7,700	13,680	0
Less carry back loss relief	(3,000)	(35,880)	(7,700)	(13,680)	(0)
Less Gift Aid donations	(1,000)	(0)	(0)	(0)	(0)
PCTCT	8,000	0	0	0	0
Unrelieved Gift Aid donations		1,000		1,000	1,500

Loss memo	£
Loss of y/e 30.9.09	100,000
Less used y/e 30.9.09	(1,860)
	98,140
Less used 9m/e 30.9.08	(13,680)
	84,460
Less used y/e 31.12.07	(7,700)
	76,760
Less used y/e 31.12.06	(35,880)
	40,880
Less used y/e 31.12.05 3m/12 × £12,000	(3,000)
c/f	37,880

The allowable capital loss of £9,423 during the year ended 30 September 2009 is carried forward against future chargeable gains.

> **Tutorial note**. The loss is carried back to set against profits arising in the previous 36 months. This means that the set off in the y/e 31.12.05 is restricted to 3/12 × £12,000 = £3,000.

34 P Ltd

> **Tutorial note**. You are asked to use group relief in the most efficient manner. This means giving it first to companies in the small companies' marginal relief band, then to companies paying tax at the full rate.
>
> Note that groups will be tested only as part of the longer question in the exam.

(a)   There are six associated companies, so the lower and upper limits for small companies' rate purposes are £50,000 and £250,000 respectively.

S Ltd and T Ltd are outside the P Ltd group for group relief purposes. P Ltd's loss should be surrendered to Q Ltd, to bring its taxable profits down to £50,000, and to R Ltd to bring its taxable profits down to £50,000. The balance of £5,000 should be surrendered to either M Ltd, Q Ltd or R Ltd. In this case M Ltd has been selected. A claim by P Ltd against its own profits would have wasted gift aid, and carrying the loss forward would not obtain relief for several years.

	M Ltd £	P Ltd £	Q Ltd £	R Ltd £	S Ltd £	T Ltd £
Trading profits	20,000	0	64,000	260,000	0	70,000
Property business income	0	6,000	4,000	0	0	0
	20,000	6,000	68,000	260,000	0	70,000
Less Gift aid donation	(4,000)	(4,500)	(2,000)	(5,000)	0	0
	16,000	1,500	66,000	255,000	0	70,000
Less group relief	(5,000)	0	(16,000)	(205,000)	0	0
PCTCT	11,000	1,500	50,000	50,000	0	70,000
Corporation tax:						
at 21%	2,310	315	10,500	10,500	0	
at 28%						19,600
Less small companies						
Marginal relief						
7/400 (£250,000 – 70,000)						(3,150)
MCT payable	2,310	315	10,500	10,500	0	16,450

(b)   If P Ltd were to acquire another 8% of the share capital of S Ltd, bringing the total holding to 75%, S Ltd's losses could be surrendered to P Ltd, Q Ltd, R Ltd or M Ltd.

35 Apple Ltd

> **Tutorial note**. The marginal rate of tax of 29.75% is an effective tax rate only. It is never actually used in working out corporation tax.
>
> Again remember groups will form part of a longer question in the exam.

(a)   Group relief is available within a 75% group. This is one where one company is a 75% subsidiary of another company or both are 75% subsidiaries of a third company. The holding company must have at least 75% of the ordinary share capital of the subsidiary, a right to at least 75% of the distributable income of the subsidiary, and the right to at least 75% of the net assets of the subsidiary were it to be wound up.

Two companies are in a group only if there is a 75% effective interest eg if Company A holds 90% of Company B which holds 90% of Company C, all three companies are in a group because 90% × 90% = 81%.

(b)   Losses should be allocated to the company with the highest marginal rate of tax. This is Cherry Ltd and Apple Ltd to the extent that profits exceed £100,000 since the small companies rate lower limit is £300,000 ÷ 3 = £100,000. Such profits are taxed at the marginal rate of 29.75%. Then, the remainder of the loss should be set against the profits of Banana Ltd which bears tax at 28%. The capital loss cannot be group relieved.

(c)   Rollover relief for part of Apple Ltd's gain can be claimed in respect of the investment by Cherry Ltd. The excess of amount of proceeds over the amount invested remains in charge ie £(418,000 − 290,000) = £128,000.

An election should be made so that the loss by Banana Ltd is transferred to Apple Ltd. Apple Ltd will then be able to offset the loss of £8,000 against the gain of £128,000, leaving £120,000 chargeable.

Apple Ltd should then make a current year loss relief claim to bring its profits down to £100,000.

	Apple Ltd £	Banana Ltd £	Cherry Ltd £
Trading profits	–	650,000	130,000
Net capital gain	120,000	–	–
	120,000	650,000	130,000
Less: loss relief against total profits	(20,000)		
group relief		(75,000)	(30,000)
PCTCT	100,000	575,000	100,000
Tax @ 21%	21,000		21,000
Tax @ 28%		161,000	

Note that the SCR upper limit is £1,500,000 ÷ 3 = £500,000.

36 M Ltd

> **Tutorial note**. In order to maximise the set off of double tax relief, gift aid payments are allocated firstly to UK profits and then to overseas sources of income that have suffered the lowest rate of overseas tax.
>
> There are five associated companies so the full rate of corporation tax applies.
>
> The overseas aspects of corporation tax will only be tested as part of a longer question in the exam.

Year ended 31 March 2010

	Total £	UK £	A £	B £	C £
Trading profits	20,000	20,000			
Foreign income (W1)	587,500	–	200,000	200,000	187,500
	607,500	20,000	200,000	200,000	187,500
Less Gift aid donations	(75,000)	(20,000)	(55,000)	–	–
Profits chargeable to corporation tax	532,500	–	145,000	200,000	187,500
CT @ 28%	149,100	–	40,600	56,000	52,500
Less DTR (W2)	(132,500)	–	(30,000)	(50,000)	(52,500)
Corporation tax	16,600	–	10,600	6,000	–

Workings

1   *Overseas profits*

		Net £	Tax paid £	Gross £
A	`15% tax suffered	170,000	30,000	200,000
B	25% tax suffered	150,000	50,000	200,000
C	36% tax suffered	120,000	67,500	187,500

2   *Double tax relief*

		A £	B £	C £
Lower of				
(i)	UK tax	40,600	56,000	52,500
(ii)	Overseas tax	30,000	50,000	67,500
		£30,000	£50,000	£52,500

37 Hogg Ltd

> **Tutorial note**. 'Large' companies must pay their CT liabilities in quarterly instalments.

(a)   Hogg Ltd's corporation tax liability for the year is £1,750,000 × 28% = £490,000. The due dates for the payment of corporation tax by Hogg Ltd in respect of the year to 31.3.10 are:

	£
14 October 2009 1/4 × £490,000	122,500
14 January 2010 1/4 × £490,000	122,500
14 April 2010 1/4 × £490,000	122,500
14 July 2010 1/4 × £490,000	122,500
Total	490,000

(b)   (i)   31 March 2011 – 12 months after the end of the accounting period.
       (ii) 12 May 2011 – 3 months after the notice to file the return.

38 Newcomer Ltd and Au Revoir Ltd

> **Tutorial note**. This question is a typical question on registration and deregistration. Note the importance of the dates.

(a)   The registration threshold is £68,000 (from 1.5.09) during any consecutive 12 month period.

This is exceeded in January 2010:

		£
2009	October	11,500
	November	15,200
	December	22,400
2010	January	19,300
		68,400

Therefore, Newcomer Ltd must register within 30 days of the end of the month the threshold was exceeded, ie by 2 March 2010.

Newcomer Ltd will be registered from 1 March 2010 or an earlier date agreed between the company and HM Revenue and Customs.

(b)   A person is eligible for voluntary deregistration if HM Revenue and Customs are satisfied that the rate of his taxable supplies (net of VAT) in the following one year period will not exceed £66,000 (from 1.5.09). However, voluntary deregistration will not be allowed if the reasons for the expected fall in value of taxable supplies is the cessation of taxable supplies or the suspension of taxable supplies for a period of 30 days or more in that following year. HM Revenue and Customs will cancel a person's registration from the date the request is made or an agreed later date.

39 Justin

Tutorial note. This question is a very basic VAT computation. Look carefully at the date that the quarter ends and what this tells you about the rate of VAT applicable. Note how the input and output VAT is accounted for in respect of petrol. Note also that the VAT incurred on the entertaining is blocked from recovery.

	£	£
Output VAT		
Furniture: £490,000 × 17.5%	85,750	
Books: £2,400 × 0%	0	
Petrol (VAT scale charge): £428 × 7/47	64	
		85,814
Input VAT		
Furniture: £275,000 × 17.5%	48,125	
Computer: £2,400 × 17.5%	420	
Entertaining: irrecoverable	0	
Petrol: £2,800 × 17.5%	490	
		(49,035)
VAT to account for quarter ending 31 March 2010		36,779

40 Ongoing Ltd

Tutorial notes.

1   Where a discount is offered for prompt payment, VAT is chargeable on the net amount, regardless of whether the discount is taken up.

2   VAT on business entertaining is not recoverable where the cost of the entertaining is not a deductible trading expense.

3   Impairment loss (bad debt) relief is only available for debts over six months old (measured from when the payment is due).

4   VAT incurred on the purchase of a car not used wholly for business purposes is not recoverable.

	£	£
Output tax		
£120,000 × 95% = 114,000 × 15% (note 1)		17,100
Input tax		
£(35,640 – 480) = 35,160 × 15% (note 2)	5,274	
£(2,100 × 95%) = £2,000 × 15% (note 3)	300	
£21,150 × 3/23 (note 4)	2,759	(8,333)
VAT payable for quarter ending 30 September 2009		8,767

Notes

1   VAT is calculated after the deduction of the prompt payment discount.

2   Entertaining is not an expense on which input tax can be recovered.

3   The debt must be 6 months old to claim bad debt relief. The output tax accounted for on the supply was net of the 5% discount for prompt payment even though the discount was obviously not taken up. The same amount of input tax can therefore be recovered under bad debt relief.

4   Input tax on motor cars is blocked.

41 Industrial Ltd

(a)　*Corporation tax payable y/e 31.3.10*

	£	£
Trading profit	1,710,000	
Less: capital allowances		
– on Factory (W1)	(9,000)	
– on Plant and machinery (W2)	(77,400)	
Trading profit		1,623,600
Investment income	12,500	
Loan interest received	36,000	48,500
Property business income (W3)		73,200
Capital gains (W4)		62,122
Total profits		1,807,422
Less: Gift aid donation		(1,500)
PCTCT		1,805,922

Full rate of CT applies

Tax

£1,805,922 × 28% = £505,658

Workings

1　*IBA*

Expenditure eligible for IBAs

	£
Levelling the land	13,800
Architect's fees	36,450
Concrete floor	24,750
Factory	281,250
General offices (less than 25% of total)	93,750
	450,000
IBA @ 2% (building in use on 31.3.11)	£9,000

Watch out for this point

2 Plant and machinery

	AIA/FYA £	Main pool £	Special rate pool £	Expensive car £	Allowances £
TWDVs b/f		84,600		15,400	
Additions qualifying for AIA/FYA					
Heating system	12,800				
Less: AIA	(12,800)		0		12,800
Fire alarm system	7,200				
Computer	3,400				
Lorry	32,000				
General plant	27,000				
	69,600				
Less: AIA (balance)	(37,200)				37,200
	32,400				
FYA @ 40%	(12,960)				12,960
Addition not qualifying for AIA/FYA					
Car			17,200		
Disposal					
Car				(19,600)	
Balancing charge				4,200	(4,200)
WDA @ 10%			(1,720)		1,720
WDA @ 20%		(16,920)			16,920
Transfer to pool	(19,440)	19,440			
TWDVs c/f		87,120	15,480		
Allowances					77,400

Use against special rate pool first

3 Property business profit

	£	£
Premium		
Amount received	80,000	
Less 2% × (10 – 1) × 80,000	(14,400)	
Assessable as property income		65,600
Rental (3/12 × £30,400)		7,600
Property business profit		73,200

Don't forget to add the rental income

4 Capital gain on sale of shares

	£
Proceeds	224,203
Less cost	(135,800)
Unindexed gain	88,403
Less indexation allowance	(15,481)
Indexed gain	72,922
Less loss b/f	(10,800)
Net gains	62,122

No annual exemption for companies

(b) (i) Industrial Ltd is a 'large' company as it pays corporation tax at the full rate and did so in the previous year. Therefore it is required to make quarterly payments on account of corporation tax.

(ii) Industrial Ltd must pay its liability in four equal instalments. These are due on: 14 October 2009; 14 January 2010; 14 April 2010 and 14 July 2010.

42 Carolyn Kraft

Tutorial note. The requirement is already helpfully broken down, so first of all deal with the part you know best to pick up marks early on and boost your confidence. You can really improve your presentation by starting each requirement on a new page. However, do not spend too much time on any one requirement – use the mark allocation as an indication of how much time to spend on each. Finally, do not miss out on the easy marks available for stating payment dates – you could even answer these parts of the relevant requirements first so you don't forget.

(a)   *Income tax calculations 2009/10*

Carolyn

	Non-savings income £	Savings income £
Salary	36,000	
Bank interest £8,000 × 100/80		10,000
Net income	36,000	10,000
Less personal allowance	(6,475)	
Taxable income	29,525	10,000

> **Don't forget to gross up net income**

	£
Tax	
£29,525 × 20%	5,905
£7,875 × 20%	1,575
£1,000 × 20% (W1)	200
£1,125 × 40%	450
Total tax liability	8,130
Less tax credits	
(i) PAYE	(5,900)
(ii) Interest: £10,000 @ 20%	(2,000)
Tax due by 31 January 2011	230

> **Do a working to show the extension of the basic rate band**

> **Always state the due dates – it's a good habit to get into**

Mike

	Non-savings income £	Dividend income £
Trade profit (W2)	54,900	
Dividends £9,000 × 100/90		10,000
Net income	54,900	10,000
Less personal allowance	(6,475)	
Taxable income	48,425	10,000

	£
Tax	
£37,400 × 20%	7,480
£3,000 × 20% (W3)	600
£8,025 × 40%	3,210
£10,000 × 32.5%	3,250
Total tax liability	14,540
Less tax credit on dividends: £10,000 @ 10%	(1,000)
Tax due 31 January 2010	13,540

> **Consider POAs for anyone whose tax is not all collected at source**

Mike also needs to make payments on account as more than 20% of his tax is **not** collected at source:

1st POA: 50% × £13,540 = 6,770

Total due 31 January 2011: 20,310

2nd POA: due 31 July 2011: 6,770

> Make sure you reference your workings clearly

Workings

1   *Carolyn's basic rate band*

    Extend by gross donation: £800 × 100/80 = £1,000

2   *Mike's taxable trading profits*

	£
Adjusted profit	56,500
Less capital allowances	(1,600)
Taxable trade profits	54,900

3   *Mike's basic rate band*

    Extend by gross pension contribution: (£200 × 12) × 100/80 = £3,000

(b)   *National Insurance contributions 2009/10*

(i)   *Carolyn*

Class 1 primary contributions

First   £5,715 @ 0%
        £30,285 @ 11% = £3,331
        £36,000 (below UEL)

(ii)   *Mike*

Class 2

£2.40 × 52 = £125

Class 4

	£
£(43,875 – 5,715) = £36,161 @ 8%	3,053
£(54,900 – 43,875) = £11,025 @ 1%	110
	3,163

(c)   **Capital gains tax**

(i)   *Carolyn*

	£
Proceeds	250,000
Less cost	(180,000)
renovation (enhancement expenditure)	(30,000)
Gain	40,000
Less annual exemption	(10,100)
Taxable gain	29,900

> Don't forget to get the easy marks!

CGT @ 18% due 31 January 2011: £5,382

(ii)   *Mike*

	£
Proceeds	85,000
Less cost	(53,300)
Gain	31,700
Less annual exemption	(10,100)
Taxable gain	21,600

CGT @ 18% due 31 January 2011: £3,888

Be brief. Make
your sentences
snappy. Use
bullet points for
clarity.

(d)   **Available relief**

(i)   Mike can claim 'rollover' relief for reinvestment into replacement business assets.

(ii)   He must invest in the new shop within three years of the disposal of the original shop.

(iii)   If any proceeds are not reinvested they will be chargeable immediately and only the balance of the gain can be deferred.

Tax tables

SUPPLEMENTARY INFORMATION

1.   Calculations and workings need only be made to the nearest £.

2.   All apportionments may be made to the nearest month.

3.   All workings should be shown.

TAX RATES AND ALLOWANCES

The following tax rates and allowances are to be used in answering the questions

Income tax

Basic rate	£1 – £37,400	20%
Higher rate	£37,401 and above	40%

A starting rate of 10% applies to savings income where it falls within the first £2,440 of taxable income.

Personal allowances

	£
Personal allowance	6,475
Personal allowance aged 65 to 74	9,490
Personal allowance aged 75 and over	9,640
Income limit for age-related allowances	22,900

Car benefit percentage

The base level of CO_2 emissions is 135 grams per kilometre. A lower rate of 10% applies to petrol cars with CO_2 emissions of 120 grams per kilometre or less.

Car fuel benefit

The base figure for calculating the car fuel benefit is £16,900.

Authorised mileage allowances: cars

Up to 10,000 miles	40p
Over 10,000 miles	25p

Pension scheme limits

Annual allowance	£245,000

The maximum contribution that can qualify for tax relief without any earnings is £3,600.

Capital allowances

Plant and machinery

Main pool – First Year Allowance	40%
Main pool – Writing Down Allowance	20%
Special rate pool	10%

Motor cars

CO_2 emissions up to 110 grams per kilometre	100%
CO_2 emissions between 111 and 160 grams per kilometre	20%
CO_2 emissions over 160 grams per kilometre	10%

Annual investment allowance	£50,000

Industrial buildings

Writing-down allowance	2%

Corporation tax

Financial year	2007	2008	2009
Small companies rate	20%	21%	21%
Full rate	30%	28%	28%
Lower limit	£300,000	£300,000	£300,000
Upper limit	£1,500,000	£1,500,000	£1,500,000
Marginal relief fraction:	1/40	7/400	7/400

Marginal relief

$(M - P) \times I/P \times$ marginal relief fraction

Extended loss relief

Extended loss relief is capped at a maximum of £50,000. For limited companies it applies to loss making accounting periods ending between 24 November 2008 and 23 November 2010.

Value Added Tax

Registration limit		£68,000
Deregistration limit		£66,000
Standard rate	Up to 31 December 2009	15.0%
Standard rate	From 1 January 2010	17.5%

Capital gains tax

Annual exemption	£10,100
Rate of tax for individuals	18%
Entrepreneurs' relief	
Lifetime limit	£1,000,000
Reducing faction	4/9

National insurance (not contracted-out rates)

		%
Class 1 employee	£1 – £5,715 per year	Nil
	£5,716 – £43,875 per year	11.0
	£43,876 and above per year	1.0
Class 1 employer	£1 – £5,715 per year	Nil
	£5,716 and above per year	12.8
Class 1A		12.8
Class 2	£2.40 per week	
Class 4	£1 – £5,715 per year	Nil
	£5,716 – £43,875 per year	8.0
	£43,876 and above per year	1.0

Rates of Interest

Official rate of interest	4.75%
Rate of interest on underpaid tax	2.5% (assumed)
Rate of interest on overpaid tax	0% (assumed)

Calculations and workings need only be made to the nearest £.

All apportionments may be made to the nearest month.

All workings should be shown.

Index

Review Form & Free Prize Draw – Paper F6 Taxation (UK) FA 2009 (8/09)

All original review forms from the entire BPP range, completed with genuine comments, will be entered into one of two draws on 31 July 2010 and 31 January 2011. The names on the first four forms picked out on each occasion will be sent a cheque for £50.

Name: _____   Address: _____

_____

_____

How have you used this Text?
(Tick one box only)

☐ Home study (book only)

☐ On a course: college _____

☐ With 'correspondence' package

☐ Other _____

Why did you decide to purchase this Text? *(Tick one box only)*

☐ Have used BPP Texts in the past

☐ Recommendation by friend/colleague

☐ Recommendation by a lecturer at college

☐ Saw advertising

☐ Saw information on BPP website

☐ Other _____

During the past six months do you recall seeing/receiving any of the following?
(Tick as many boxes as are relevant)

☐ Our advertisement in *ACCA Student Accountant*

☐ Our advertisement in *Pass*

☐ Our advertisement in *PQ*

☐ Our brochure with a letter through the post

☐ Our website www.bpp.com

Which (if any) aspects of our advertising do you find useful?
(Tick as many boxes as are relevant)

☐ Prices and publication dates of new editions

☐ Information on Text content

☐ Facility to order books off-the-page

☐ None of the above

Which BPP products have you used?

Text	☑	Success CD	☐	Learn Online	☐
Kit	☐	i-Learn	☐	Home Study Package	☐
Passcard	☐	i-Pass	☐	Home Study PLUS	☐

Your ratings, comments and suggestions would be appreciated on the following areas.

	Very useful	Useful	Not useful
Introductory section (Key study steps, personal study)	☐	☐	☐
Chapter introductions	☐	☐	☐
Key terms	☐	☐	☐
Quality of explanations	☐	☐	☐
Exam focus points	☐	☐	☐
Questions and answers in each chapter	☐	☐	☐
Fast forwards and chapter roundups	☐	☐	☐
Quick quizzes	☐	☐	☐
Question Bank	☐	☐	☐
Answer Bank	☐	☐	☐
Index	☐	☐	☐

Overall opinion of this Study Text	Excellent ☐	Good ☐	Adequate ☐	Poor ☐

Do you intend to continue using BPP products?   Yes ☐   No ☐

On the reverse of this page are noted particular areas of the text about which we would welcome your feedback. The BPP author of this edition can be e-mailed at: suedexter@bpp.com

Please return this form to: Nick Weller, ACCA Publishing Manager, BPP Learning Media Ltd, FREEPOST, London, W12 8BR

Review Form & Free Prize Draw (continued)

TELL US WHAT YOU THINK

Please note any further comments and suggestions/errors below

Free Prize Draw Rules

1   Closing date for 31 July 2010 draw is 30 June 2010. Closing date for 31 January 2011 draw is 31 December 2010.

2   Restricted to entries with UK and Eire addresses only. BPP employees, their families and business associates are excluded.

3   No purchase necessary. Entry forms are available upon request from BPP Learning Media. No more than one entry per title, per person. Draw restricted to persons aged 16 and over.

4   Winners will be notified by post and receive their cheques not later than 6 weeks after the relevant draw date.

5   The decision of the promoter in all matters is final and binding. No correspondence will be entered into.